BITTER CROP

Also by Paul Alexander

Machiavelli's Shadow: The Rise and Fall of Karl Rove

The Candidate

Salinger

Death and Disaster:
The Rise of the Warhol Empire and the Race for Andy's Millions

Boulevard of Broken Dreams:
The Life, Times, and Legend of James Dean

Rough Magic

Ariel Ascending: Writings About Sylvia Plath (editor)

BITTER CROP

The Heartache and Triumph of Billie Holiday's Last Year

Paul Alexander

CANONGATE

First published in Great Britain in 2024
by Canongate Books Ltd, 14 High Street, Edinburgh EH1 1TE

canongate.co.uk

First published in the USA in 2024 by Alfred A Knopf, a division of
Penguin Random House LLC, New York

1

Epigraph taken from *Satchmo The Great* by Louis Armstrong, Edward R. Murrow and
Leonard Bernstein. Copyright © 1957, Columbia Records

Grateful acknowledgment is made to the following for permission to reprint
previously published material:
Frank O'Hara, 'The Day Lady Died' from *Lunch Poems*. Copyright © 1964
by Frank O'Hara. Reprinted with the permission of The Permissions Company, LLC
on behalf of City Lights Books, citylights.com

Epigraph taken from 'Sonny's Blues' from *Going to Meet the Man*. Originally published in
Partisan Review. Copyright © 1957 and renewed 1985 by James Baldwin. Reprinted with the
permission of The Permissions Company LLC on behalf of the James Baldwin Estate

A Note to the Reader: As a convention, all quotations in the book resulting from an
author's interview use present tense verbs for attribution; all quotations from
secondary sources use past tense verbs for attribution.

British Library Cataloguing-in-Publication Data
A catalogue record for this book is available on
request from the British Library

ISBN 978 1 83726 241 0

Typeset by North Market Street Graphics, Lancaster, Pennsylvania
Designed by Maria Carella

Printed and bound by CPI Group (UK) Ltd, Croydon CR0 4YY

For Elizabeth Mara Broccolo

What we play is life.

LOUIS ARMSTRONG

And I was yet aware that this was only
a moment, that the world waited outside,
as hungry as a tiger, and that trouble
stretched above us, longer than the sky.

JAMES BALDWIN, "SONNY'S BLUES"

Sing the truth!

BILLIE HOLIDAY

Contents

Bitter Crop

CHAPTER I

The Last Night
at the Flamingo Lounge

Billie Holiday photographed by Jay Maisel during the last year of her life.

May 1959

She had come so far in her life. From hardscrabble beginnings, she had done whatever she had to do to forge a career that over time had taken her to such heights she was sometimes now referred to as a living legend. Yet there was so much more she wanted to accomplish— albums to record, shows to perform, movies to make. Fighting through the anxiety that often seized her before she went onstage, she glanced around her modest dressing room. She had been in better, to be sure, but she had also been in worse. Rows of empty glasses were lined up on the dressing table where she sat; staring into the mirror, she had just applied the final touches to her makeup. For tonight's show, she had chosen to wear a turquoise evening dress; nearby stood a rack on which hung additional stage attire. Relaxing in a chair close by was Mal Waldron, a handsomely attired bearded man in his midthirties who had served as her piano accompanist for the past two years. Classically trained since childhood and a graduate of Queens College with a degree in music composition whose song "Soul Eyes" was made popular by John Coltrane, he was influenced in his style by the minimalism of Thelonious Monk. An accomplished chess player, Waldron was such a chain-smoker he always seemed to be holding between two fingers his trademark thin brown cigarette. She had worked with other pianists—Carl Drinkard, Bobby Tucker, Teddy Wilson—but she felt a special connection with Waldron. When he backed her, he knew exactly how to "fill the space" between lyrics without stepping on a line. No singer interpreted a song the way she did, and Waldron complemented her while never interfering with her pacing or, equally as important, her phrasing, which included her tendency to "bend the note," as she called it.

Beyond appreciating his musical acumen, she considered Waldron a friend; they were good together, on and off the stage. She had not enjoyed this kind of symbiosis with a musician since the years she worked with Lester Young, the tenor saxophonist with whom she had shared a profound bond; his death two months ago had left her heartbroken and bereft. Taking a sip from her scotch-and-water, she could hear the voice of Norm Crosby coming from the main room, where he was performing his stand-up comedy set. She could not count the number of warm-up acts she had sat through over the years. Judging from the laughter and applause Crosby was receiving tonight, it sounded like the audience was capacity-sized and lively. For that, she was grateful. She had endured more than her share of half-filled rooms and dead audiences.

It was May 1959, and Billie Holiday had been performing in nightclubs since the late 1920s, when she broke into the music business by singing in dive bars in Brooklyn and Queens and then in clubs in Harlem like the Hot Cha and Pod's and Jerry's. She had appeared in some of the most venerable venues in the world, from La Scala in Milan to the Savoy Ballroom in Chicago to the Hollywood Bowl in Los Angeles. She was the first African-American woman to headline an all-white orchestra. She was the first African-American woman to sing on the stage of the Metropolitan Opera House. But for more than a decade now, because of a past conviction for narcotics possession, she had been unable to convince authorities in New York City to issue her a Cabaret Identification Card, which a performer was required to have to work in a venue that sold liquor. As a result, she could not gain employment in most of the nightlife establishments in the city where she lived. So her manager, Joe Glaser, was forced to book her out of town in clubs like the one in which she was headlining this week—the Flamingo Lounge, on upper Merrimack Street in Lowell, Massachusetts, a midsized city twenty-six miles northwest of Boston that years ago was a vital industrial center but today was mostly known for being the home of Jack Kerouac, a founder of the Beat Generation whose novel *On the Road* had been published two years ago. A manufacturing hub for decades, Lowell took an economic hit during the Great Depression, when a number of its mills and factories relocated to the South. Billie had played Lowell during that time when she was an "added attraction" with Artie Shaw and His Orchestra at the Commodore Ballroom in April 1938. Now the city fought to remain relevant. Among its vibrant neighborhoods was an entertainment district downtown that was home to clubs like the Flamingo Lounge, which featured a house band that included a trombone player named "Birdcage" and a talented pianist, known only as Madeline, who, according to one regular patron, "always wore a long black cape like she came out of a horror movie." Despite the house band's musicality, the club, to quote a local observer, was "[not] exactly El Morocco. It was a small club, and it booked matching talent. Sometimes, though, it was big talent, big talent on the skids." Whether or not Billie was "on the skids"—she certainly did not think so—she was pleased to have the gig. An audience, after all, was an audience.

Actually, she should not even have been here, since her doctor warned her she was too sick to appear in nightclubs. For a year or more now, she had been deteriorating physically, mostly because she was suffering from—and not adequately treating—cirrhosis of the liver, the result of years of heavy drinking. She had lost weight, perhaps as much as fifty pounds, a good portion of it in recent months. The disquieting weight loss was affecting her general health, a decline that had been publicly documented. In mid-April, Dorothy Kilgallen announced in her widely read national column "Voice of Broadway": "Jazz singer Billie Holiday . . . is suffering from a serious case of cirrhosis of the liver, but is disregarding doctors' advice and resisting hospitalization." Another columnist echoed the story in May: "Billie Holiday has been told to give up liquor or else. The doctors say it will be only a matter of time if she starts boozing it up big."

In fact, Billie had never stopped drinking, as evidenced by the scotch-and-water she was nursing as she waited to go onstage. Not surprisingly, the drinking continued to affect her health, as recently as this week. For the first two nights of the run, when she tried to make it through one of her seven-song sets, she could finish no more than a song or two before she had to leave the stage. Finally, Jimmy Makris, the club's managing director, a hard-boiled businessman who nevertheless had an amiable side to him, approached her in her dressing room. "Listen, Billie," he said, "no hard feelings. I'll pay you what the contract calls for, and you come back another time, when you're feeling better." It was hurtful for him to watch an artist of Billie's eminence struggle but fail to do what had once come so effortlessly to her. He also had to deal with his audiences, who were crestfallen by her inability to finish a show.

Billie was unnerved by the offer; no, she absolutely did *not* want to cut short her engagement. She would do whatever it took to carry on. And she did, too, turning in shows that were as good as any of her recent efforts. It was as if she tapped into some force deep within herself—the very drive that had compelled her to step onstage in the first place all those years ago—that allowed her to do whatever she had to do to perform. She demonstrated that same primal strength tonight when, once Norm Crosby finished his set to resounding applause and Waldron preceded her onstage with the rest of the trio to vamp for her entrance, she took her place in the wings and, hearing her name announced over the house audio system to a sold-out crowd buzzing with anticipation, stepped through the darkness to head toward the spotlight awaiting her at center stage. Her entrance brought a collective hush over the crowd, then gasps, then a thunderous ovation.

A reporter in the room, on hand from the Lowell newspaper, documented what happened: "The fabled Billie Holiday takes slow steps into the spotlight, walking like a dreamer over a carpet of eggshells. Before the microphone, as the celebrated voice lifts and pours, she is alive again, as though all the long, long road leads always and only to this moment in the lights. She stands there, with nothing in her stance of lure and invitation, and immobile as she is, she establishes an instant and private contact." One song ended; another began. "[Her] face is still curiously unlined . . . the forehead high and serene where the hair is pulled tightly back. The oriental lids hood eyes with tears that have welled, but never fall. She wears a dress of shining turquoise silk, cut like a dashing trench coat. The only movement is in the hands that clutch pink Kleenex, that shake slightly down to their black fingernail polish."

Billie proceeded on to "Lover Come Back to Me." As she sang, she moved so little the long gold chain and pendant hanging around her neck barely swayed back and forth on her chest. Once she finished, the room exploded with applause, as it did at the conclusion of each song. At last, for the first and only time during her set, she spoke to the audience, before her final number.

"Now," she said softly, almost offhandedly, "I'd like to do a song I wrote myself." Then she launched into "Lady Sings the Blues."

At the end of the song, she turned and, without saying anything by way of conclusion, without addressing the audience in any way, lowered her head and walked slowly away from the microphone toward the dimly lit wings as the deafening applause rained down on her.

Back in her dressing room, she returned to her seat at the vanity. Pouring herself another scotch-and-water and lighting up a cigarette, she was soon joined by Waldron, who sat back down in his chair. But before she could get on with the rest of her night, Billie had an obligation to keep, an interview Jimmy Makris had arranged for her with a reporter from *The Lowell Sun.* To steel herself for the conversation—she had never taken pleasure in talking to the press even though she was close friends with William Dufty, a reporter for the *New York Post,* and had particularly enjoyed an interview she once gave to Mike Wallace for his show *Night Beat*—she slipped over her shoulders a silver mink stole.

Over the years, one way Billie often dealt with journalists was to tell them tales she invented about her life, since she thoroughly embraced the adage that said the truth should never stand in the way of a good story. Her penchant for enhancement or outright fabrication was a principal reason why future biographers would find the documentation of her life to be such a challenge. Articles and books about her would be riddled with errors in part because she paid so little attention to the facts herself. Both while she was alive and after she died, a recurring predicament encountered by anyone hoping to write about her truthfully was sorting through the stories to determine which part was true and which part was not. The image of Billie Holiday the public came to know was, according to author Russell Banks, "as much our elaboration and refinement of her own calculated disinformation." Or as Frank Harriott, who interviewed her for *PM,* a progressive newspaper, described it: "No one fed the fires of the Holiday myth machine more than Holiday herself." Consequently, for many years, basic facts about her life—the year of her birth, the marital status of her parents, the number of husbands she had—were incorrect because of her fabulistic tendencies. It was easier for her to tell the truth to an audience in a song than to convey accurate facts about her life to a journalist.

The article of clothing Billie added to her outfit tonight as she waited to be interviewed—a silver mink stole—often prompted her to hearken back to the past, to a time when she experienced her first flirtations with music, in her early teenage years. The result of a fleeting affair between Sadie Fagan and Clarence Holiday, Eleanora, as she was known in those days, was living in Baltimore in a neighborhood called Fells Point, or simply "the Point," which was the city's red-light district. At the time, Sadie had taken a "transportation" job as a maid-cook with a family in Cedarhurst on Long Island, and Eleanora was living with Miss Lu, the mother of Sadie's current romantic interest—a ladies' man named Charles "Wee Wee" Hill— who did her best as a custodian considering she was in effect an invalid. With limited supervision, Eleanora soon ingratiated herself with Alice Dean, who, as Billie later wrote, "used to keep a whorehouse on the corner nearest our place—and I used to run errands for her and the girls."

On South Dallas, under the watchful eye of Alice Dean, a glamorous woman proud of her beautiful evening dresses and fur coats, Eleanora was first indoctrinated into the profession of prostitution and, more importantly, because Dean owned a gramophone, the world of popular music. Eleanora would while away the hours in the parlor of Alice Dean's bordello listening to the recordings of Bessie

Smith and Louis Armstrong. She was especially fond of Armstrong's "West End Blues," which was released in the summer of 1928. The record deeply impressed the nascent singer, as she later recalled: "[Armstrong] doesn't say any words, and I thought this is wonderful! And I liked the feeling he got from it. . . . Sometimes the record would make me so sad I'd cry up a storm. Other times the same damn record would make me so happy."

While she spent time at the bordello, Eleanora started "turning tricks as a call girl," as she would write. Mary "Pony" Kane, a family friend, remembered Eleanora during her time at Alice Dean's: "She was a tall girl, shaped pretty nice. She was liked by a whole lot of boys, but she used to call them country boys, they were working fellas, and she would get the money and she wouldn't have no time for them." Alice Dean's son Sleepy recalled that "Eleanora hustled [and the] people she hung around with were hustling people."

Eventually, Eleanora moved on to work at a house at 10 North Bond Street run by Ethel Moore—she "was known as the classy woman in the ghetto," according to journalist Linda Kuehl—in part because Moore allowed Eleanora to entertain the girls and their clients by singing for them. "Ethel used to have a famous goodtime house, and Eleanora took up to her like to an older sister," remembered Johnny Fagan, Eleanora's cousin. "[She] sung in Ethel's house. She worked in it too. She had to make ends meet. She had to survive." Pony Kane recalled Eleanora singing in other venues as well: "They have a place on Caroline Street where a man play the piano. Eleanora pick up a couple bucks there. Sings shows at the Star Theatre too." A neighborhood local called Skinny remembered: "Eleanora tell us where she be and we follow her from club to club. The clubs close up and we take her to goodtime houses." These venues—Ethel Moore's house, other goodtime houses, bars, theaters—were the first establishments in which Eleanora honed her skills as a singer. Even then, even in these early appearances, she was fostering a singing style so unique, so captivating, she found herself developing an ardent following of admirers eager to hear her perform wherever she was allowed to sing.

During this time, as Eleanora started drinking bootleg whiskey and smoking reefer cigarettes, those close to her became concerned she was too young to be living such a fast life. Finally, Miss Lu wrote to Sadie, who sent for Eleanora to come to New York. "After Sadie left," Wee Wee Hill recalled, "Eleanora was alone here maybe two years. She hung in there with Ethel Moore. Ethel was a hustling woman. Finally, Eleanora left Baltimore. I took her to Penn Station. She was glad to go. I imagine she got tired of bumming around." Her departure left a lasting impression on Pony Kane: "I'll never forget when Eleanora leave Baltimore. She have on a white voile dress with a red skinny belt."

While she sat on the train heading for New York, Eleanora left behind Baltimore and all it had come to represent—a dysfunctional home life but also two women who introduced her into the world of nightlife, where she would spend the entirety of a career that would make her a legend. "Her mentors—Alice Dean and Ethel Moore—were madams," Linda Kuehl wrote. "In their houses she began turning tricks, drinking bootleg liquor, smoking reefers, perhaps snorting cocaine, and certainly singing the pop tunes of the day." Indeed, she would use the trappings of that world—the evening gowns and minks, the drugs and alcohol, the music—to create a persona that allowed her to record a body of work that ultimately would stand as art.

The next interlude in her journey came when Eleanora reunited with her mother in New York, and after the pair settled in Harlem, only to endure a brush with the authorities, they moved in October 1929 to Brooklyn, where they rented a small apartment at 7 Glenada Place. It was here that, based on the encouraging response she received at Ethel Moore's and nightspots on the Point, Eleanora decided to resume her pursuit of singing. Tenor saxophonist Kenneth Hollon, who lived nearby, remembered Eleanora's newly inspired attempt at forging a career in music: "I used to take my sax around to her house. And I used to try to play melodies while she sang along with me. An opportunity came where we got a job at a cabaret"— the Gray Dawn, on Jamaica Avenue and South Street in Queens. "And I took [her] with us"—his group was named the Hat Hunter Band—"and once we were going good, I asked [her] if she wanted to join in. 'Yeah,' she said, and she did. At that time, I remember the old-timers used to throw money out on the floor for singers. The tunes she sang that night were 'My Fate Is in Your Hands' by Fats Waller and 'Oh How Am I to Know?' and 'Honeysuckle Rose.' That night she collected over one hundred dollars in tips."

The evening was so successful Eleanora and Hollon performed together in Brooklyn and Queens for the next two years. It was during these years, when she came to view music as a way to make a living, that Eleanora decided she needed a more commercial-sounding stage name. So she chose "Billie" for her first name—after her favorite movie star, Billie Dove, whose pictures included *American Beauty, The Painted Angel,* and *The Black Pirate*—and "Holiday" for her last name—after her father. Early on, she spelled her last name differently—Halliday—to avoid possible confusion with her father, but that minor discrepancy soon disappeared and she became, as she would be known throughout her career although she never changed her name legally, Billie Holiday.

Tonight, as she sat at her vanity in her dressing room, her emergent years in show business seemed far removed from her life now. At the moment, she felt tired from her show and more than slightly exercised by the prospect of reliving episodes from her past, accurately or not, with her scheduled visitor, whom she greeted warmly when she was shown into the room. Her name was Mary Sampas, and she published a daily column in *The Lowell Sun* under the nom de plume Pertinax, an homage to the French author André Géraud, who used the same pseudonym. Women were beginning to break cultural norms—no woman represented this trend more than Billie Holiday—but the public was still unaccustomed to women assuming prominent roles in the newspaper business, which was why Sampas relied on pseudonyms in her career. Previously, she had written a column called "Girl Friday" before moving on to Pertinax. Her husband, Charles, worked at *The Sun* as the executive news editor.

Sampas was an elegant, nattily coiffed woman who had a penchant for stylish dresses and fur hats. She affected a professional yet congenial manner. She was, as one friend recalls, the kind of woman "you just had to hug." She sat in a chair across from Billie, who was polite but standoffish in the early part of their exchange, which was defined by non sequiturs and fits and starts—not what Sampas needed to write an engaging column. As they spoke, however, Billie came to feel that the reporter was there not because she hoped to determine if the long sleeves Billie wore on this unseasonably warm May evening were meant to cover up telltale track marks on her arms but, rather, because she admired her work and respected her as an artist. In time, Billie felt trustful enough to answer her questions.

"Do you consider yourself a jazz singer or a blues singer?" Sampas asked.

"No, I'm just a song stylist," Billie said, taking a puff on her cigarette before sipping her scotch-and-water.

"You know," Sampas said, "I recently saw *New Orleans* on television."

Even though Billie was forced to portray a maid in the motion picture—can you imagine, she plaintively asked friends at the time, Billie Holiday playing *a maid?*—she harbored fondness for *New Orleans* because it afforded her the opportunity to appear on-screen with Louis Armstrong, who had exerted a germinal influence on her singing style when she was learning early lessons. "I made that movie thirteen years ago," Billie said, smiling whimsically, as if she could not fathom where all the years had gone.

"So, what city do you play next?" Sampas inquired.

"Montreal at the first of June," Billie said, glancing over to confirm the date with Waldron, who nodded affirmatively.

Finally, the two women had spoken long enough that Sampas ventured to ask Billie how she was feeling, not as a pleasantry but as a legitimate line of questioning, since news of Billie's health was in the press.

"My doctor wants me to give up singing," Billie said. "He thinks I'm too ill. But what else am I made for?" She let out a brief, impervious laugh. "So as long as I have breath to sing and someone still to listen . . ."

She did not finish the sentence. Instead, she reached for a book on the dressing table. "This is what I'm reading between shows," Billie said, fixing her gaze on Sampas as she held up the book version of *Some Like It Hot*—the picture had been released in late March— with a shot of Marilyn Monroe displayed prominently on the cover. "I have to laugh a little."

After thirty minutes, Sampas wrapped up the interview. And when it was over, when Sampas said good night and departed the dressing room, Billie did what she had done on so many nights in so many other dressing rooms over the years—she got ready for the next show.

In the coming days, when Sampas published the piece in her Pertinax column, Billie knew she was right to trust her. Admiration coursed through the article. Sampas *got* her. "In the style that made her the toast of two continents," Sampas wrote about Billie's stage performance, "she mourns love grown old and cold, and you know a special sorrow. You hear rain fall, and you sense that dark clouds obscure the moon, and you feel a lonely whistle pierce a completer loneliness. All God's children got troubles, and my Mama was right, there's blues in the night."

Following the problematic shows on Monday and Tuesday nights, Billie flourished for the rest of her weeklong run, which lasted from May 11 to 17. She even felt well enough on Sunday to perform an advertised "jam session" at two o'clock in the afternoon. Years later, Waldron recalled the Flamingo Lounge engagement as being "a very big, successful week for Billie." The houses were full; the audiences, enthusiastic. Proof was comments Sampas included in her column that she overheard audience members make after the show she attended—"Unforgettable!" "She breaks my heart!" "I [saw] her ten years ago at the Ebony Club and her voice is as marvelous as ever."

So as Billie traveled back to New York, she anticipated with excitement the dates Joe Glaser had lined up for her: the gig in Canada in early June but first an appearance, along with the Dave Pell Octet, on the weekend of May 29 at Club Jazz Seville, Harry Schiller's nitery on Santa Monica Boulevard in Los Angeles. A press report promised a show featuring Billie's "all-time great renditions of jazz classics, plus some of her sensational new recordings." What kept Billie going was the next gig—and the gig after that. It was her longing to move on to whatever was to come—a show, a recording session, a television appearance—that allowed her to cling to her unwavering sense of hope. As one friend put it, "She had a tremendous drive for survival." Yet in the end the incessant planning for the future was all an illusion that obscured what was occurring in the present. She was in a state of precipitous decline. Even so, there was no way she could have known that the conversation she had with Mary Sampas would mark the last formal interview she gave to a journalist. There was no way she could have known that, after coming so far in her life from the early years in Fells Point to the most celebrated stages in America and abroad, the last night at the Flamingo Lounge would be her final appearance in a nightclub. There was no way she could have known that, as of mid-May in 1959, she had two months left to live.

Or maybe there *was* a way. For months, her doctor had warned her that if she did not take better care of herself—and specifically treat her liver condition—she ran the risk of suffering a potentially fatal health crisis. For months, friends and associates implored her to heed her doctor's advice—to no avail. Her gradual but persistent decline had started a year ago during a time when she was dealing with an amalgam of challenges, from financial problems and romantic complications to struggles with substance abuse and run-ins with authorities, all emblematic of the myriad difficulties that had come to constitute the perennial hardships of her life.

CHAPTER 2

ℒ

A Woman *of the* World

Billie Holiday with Louis Armstrong. Billie often referred to Armstrong as the musician who had the most profound effect on her singing style. Once she broke onto the national scene, the two regularly performed together throughout her career. This photograph was taken in conjunction with the release of New Orleans, *the 1947 motion picture in which they played "sweethearts." "Ump Ump Ump. Now isn't that something?" Armstrong wrote to a friend.*

June 1958

I.

One year earlier, in the first days of summer in 1958, Billie began to exhibit problems with her health. The years of alcohol consumption and drug use were seemingly catching up with her. A condition related to alcohol abuse would not have been unexpected, considering how much and for how long she had been drinking, yet it would not be without irony, since for more than a decade now the press had feverishly reported on her battle with narcotics addiction, announcing in glaring headlines each brush with police, each drug bust, each court appearance. Few public figures had endured such damning coverage carried out by a press often exuberant in its attack. That coverage did not reflect the fact that she had periodically given up drugs, sometimes remaining clean for extended periods of time, by curbing her "drug hunger" with liquor. As her longtime friend Hazel Scott would contend, some people "were fascinated by [Billie's] addiction to narcotics and didn't seem to know that, except for a couple of highly publicized arrests, she handled that problem very, very well until the end of her life." Alcohol, however, was another matter; it was a rare day that passed when Billie did not drink. And now, after nearly three decades of hard living, the undeniable truth was that she was not well. She sensed it, even if she remained unable to acknowledge the severity of her condition. "She didn't complain," one friend later said. "Sometimes her legs would swell when she flew on airplanes. She was moody. [But] I don't think she realized how sick she was."

Despite her health concerns, Billie pushed ahead with work. Two years earlier, Doubleday and Company published *Lady Sings the Blues,* her autobiography, which she coauthored with William Dufty, and currently a prominent Hollywood producer was attempting to turn it into a motion picture. Dorothy Kilgallen, who wrote about Billie often, sometimes on a weekly basis, recently reported that "casting rumors in the Billie Holiday film biography get sillier and sillier. Some months ago, Ava Gardner was sought for the leading role, but apparently she wasn't available—or Miss Holiday wouldn't okay her—and now the producer is trying to get Lana Turner." It was not noted, perhaps because it was unimportant to the powers-that-be who controlled Hollywood at the time, that neither Ava Gardner nor Lana Turner was African American.

In June, Billie enjoyed two major career developments. In the United Kingdom, Barris released *Lady Sings the Blues,* proclaiming the book to be "the pithy, uninhibited autobiography of the great Coloured American blues singer." Typical of its critical reception was a review that appeared in *The Guardian* written by Philip Larkin, who referred to Billie as "the coloured singer Billie Holiday (nee Eleanora Fagan)" and described her book as "an account in tough vernacular of Miss Holiday's life and hard times." Beyond that, Larkin, a poet who had developed a keen love of jazz, believed "all Miss Holiday's admirers will want to read [the book], if only to see how her personality corresponds with her own special brand of bitter-sweet balladry (in spite of the title, she is not a blues-singer). When one reads that she once had to black her face in order to be as dark as the band she was fronting, and that she never got more than a recording fee for making all her finest records, one wonders, really, how the sweetness crept in."

June also brought the release of *Lady in Satin,* Billie's latest album. At this time, Columbia Records ran advertisements for it, and there was extensive review coverage, but Billie had also agreed to make media and concert appearances during which she would sing songs from the album in order to promote it. Her first engagement was on May 10 on *Club Oasis,* an NBC television show hosted by Martha Raye, when she sang "You've Changed," a cut from the album. On the twenty-ninth, she appeared on *Art Ford's Jazz Party,* which was simulcast on AM and FM radio and on WNTA-TV, Channel 13, from studios in Newark, New Jersey. The broadcast aired from 9:00 to 10:30 p.m. and featured Billie performing three songs backed by Mal Waldron along with a house band that included Vinnie Burke on bass and Harry Leon on drums. One of her selections was, once again, "You've Changed." Then, in June, Billie was set to appear in a live concert in Manhattan. It was next in the series of promotional engagements at which, regardless of her health issues that were now becoming harder and harder to ignore, she had agreed to appear over the summer.

2.

The day—June 21, 1958—was like any other Saturday in the summer in New York. Anyone who was able to leave for the season had already left, but many residents, like Billie, had commitments that kept them in the city. That evening, she was scheduled to sing in a midnight jazz show in Greenwich Village, so she was spending her day at home, which, since September, had been an unassuming apartment steps away from Central Park on the Upper West Side. She had lived in grander places in the past—among them a stately house she once owned in St. Albans, Queens, where she counted among her neighbors Count Basie, Ella Fitzgerald, and Fats Waller—but presently she resided at 26 West Eighty-Seventh Street, number 1B, a one-bedroom garden-level apartment in a brownstone building. The name on the doorbell read "Eleanora Fagan" (her maiden name), and it was only after the landlord, Dr. Leon Tshernoff, a physician originally from Palestine, agreed to grant her a three-year lease at a rent of $135 a month that he learned his tenant was Billie Holiday. The hard, sad truth was that her reputation had become so tarnished by the never-ending stream of negative publicity that if the landlord had known the true identity of his prospective renter he might not have allowed her to lease the apartment. He had agreed, however, and once Billie moved in her belongings—the evening gowns she wore in her shows, a few necessary pieces of furniture, her phonograph and record collection, kitchenware with which she indulged her passion for cooking—she had come to love her new home, which she shared with her constant companion, a Chihuahua she adored named Pepe. Her friend Annie Ross recalls: "There was a bedroom, a bath, and a kitchen, but what I remember most is the record player in the living room. She loved to sit in there and listen to music." A large picture window allowed her to gaze out onto a courtyard and garden as she listened to song after song.

For the past three weeks, Billie had lived in the apartment alone, Pepe notwithstanding, because her husband, Louis McKay, who was listed on the lease as a tenant, had abruptly moved to California. Six years older than Billie, McKay first met her in Harlem in the early 1930s when she was sixteen. He later claimed he dated her at that time; if there was a courtship, it was short-lived. They did not see each other again until March 1951, when they met in Detroit, where McKay was living, while Billie was appearing at the Club Juana. By then, Billie was a major jazz artist, and McKay had developed a reputation for being a Mafia "enforcer." Three years earlier, Billie had been released from prison for narcotics possession, after which she struggled to stay clean. She often found herself in need of being protected from drug dealers trying to sell her narcotics. McKay presented himself as a solution to her problem. Within two weeks of their reconnecting in Detroit, he was her manager. Their relationship soon moved beyond the professional as McKay insinuated himself into Billie's life as her love interest.

For the first two or three years, their relationship was largely harmonious, although McKay had a tendency to become violent with her. Eventually, he stopped protecting her from the drug dealers and started to facilitate her heroin supply himself in an effort to guarantee his continued access to her money, which was coming in steadily in the early and mid-1950s. Their relationship was clearly beginning to falter when they were arrested in Philadelphia in 1956—Billie for narcotics possession, McKay on weapons charges—yet they remained together. Then, in 1957, a decision was made for them to marry, in all likelihood because McKay threatened to testify against her at trial if they did not. (A person cannot be compelled to testify against a spouse.) "She had to marry him out of self-defense," William Dufty later told journalist Joel Lobenthal. "She was in his power [after] they were arrested together." There was one obstacle they had to overcome. In 1941, Billie was briefly married to Jimmy Monroe, and she had never bothered to get a divorce. So, in March 1957, Billie and McKay traveled to Juárez, Mexico, where Billie secured a "quickie" divorce on the twenty-seventh and, the following morning, married McKay.

For the rest of 1957 and into 1958, the couple remained together, although McKay routinely traveled for business. But a new level of complication entered into their relationship in the early months of 1958, and Billie began secretly passing documents from her apartment to Earle Warren Zaidins, her attorney, toward whom McKay developed such an extreme jealousy he was convinced Zaidins had a romantic—or at least sexual—interest in Billie. The situation had come to a head on Memorial Day weekend three weeks earlier when McKay discovered documents were missing and Billie confessed to giving them to Zaidins. McKay erupted in rage. He later admitted to assaulting her: "I blew my top. . . . She offered to telephone Zaidins to get back the papers. [Afterwards], I was almost crying. I grabbed the phone from her and threw it. I would guess I didn't care whether it hit her or not. It would be hard to admit that I threw it at her"—and yet, in effect, that was exactly what he admitted he did.

McKay's cruel behavior was nothing new. Friends knew about his brutal treatment of her. Annie Ross would hold strong memories of McKay and the stories Billie told her about him: "He was awful. He did not love her. He was there for the money. He was a pimp. He was a kind of take-over guy. He did not treat her well. He was horrible to her." A telephone call between McKay and Maely Dufty, the wife of William Dufty, in February 1958, around the time Billie was recording *Lady in Satin,* reflected the animus McKay had come to feel for Billie. "I'm through with her," he told Maely. "That bitch is going to see some bad days around here. I put the skids on her tonight. . . . She took the money and used it up. . . . She go

around here and give away all her cunt and everything and don't get
no money for it." When Maely pointed out that these days Billie
rarely left her apartment except to fulfill professional commitments,
McKay retorted, "I know what this woman done." Maely implored
him not to "be crazy," but McKay responded by threatening Billie:
"Holiday's ass in the gutter in the East River somewhere! I'll get
someone to do it! . . . I'll catch her somewhere and whip her all over
the goddam street." Maely noted the obvious: if he caused harm to
Billie, directly or indirectly, he could face legal jeopardy. McKay
remained defiant: "I got enough to finish her off and go downtown
and take a chance on my liberty." Did he intend to kill Billie? "I ain't
talking about killing her. I'm going to do her up so goddam bad
she's going to remember as long as she lives. . . . I hate her. . . . I kept
that woman alive. Kept her away from junkies in the street and in
the corners." The telephone call concluded with McKay declaring it
was time for them to "go ahead and get a divorce and stop fighting."

As for the Memorial Day weekend disturbance, the events as
documented by Zaidins, contained in a legal affidavit, were, perhaps
not surprisingly, more damning than McKay's version: "It was the
Sunday morning of Memorial Day weekend, [and] I received a hysterical telephone call from [Billie]. The subject of the conversation
related to the fact that I should turn back to her all of the business and personal documents and papers given to me by her. . . . I
informed [her] that I would surely accede to her wishes [on] Monday,
when I would be in the office. . . . Within the next hour . . . my doorbell started to ring. I opened the door only to be met with a fainting
Billie Holiday, covered with blood. Immediately I telephoned [my
physician] Dr. Stillerman [and] my wife and I placed her upon our
convertible couch in the living room. [Billie] had nothing with her
except for the clothing on her back. She wore a black diamond mink
coat, underneath which was merely a nightgown. By the time Dr.
Stillerman arrived, [Billie] had regained consciousness [and] it was
disclosed that [Billie] suffered from an open wound on her scalp.
According to [Billie], Louis McKay . . . had forced her to make the
telephone call to me to obtain the return of these papers and that

immediately following the telephone conversation in a fit of rage
[had] picked up the telephone and proceeded to hit her on and about
the head." The incident was reported to the police, but Billie refused
to press charges for assault. Within a day or two, as Billie stayed
away from him, McKay packed his belongings in his car and headed
for Los Angeles. After years of manipulating her, he was leaving now
that he had gotten what he always wanted—a binding legal bond to
Billie Holiday.

To keep her company once McKay was gone, Billie relied on
friends like Alice Vrbsky, a young woman in her midtwenties who
was hired originally to work for Billie only to become more of a
companion. Alice was a fan who first met Billie in July 1957 after
a group concert in the Wollman Memorial Theatre in Central Park
called Jazz Under the Stars, when she sought out Billie to autograph
her program and a record album. ("Thank you for loving me," Billie
wrote on the album cover.) Subsequent visits led to McKay hiring
Alice to serve as an assistant to Billie on a prolonged engagement
in Los Angeles. "Louis paid me once and he never paid me again,"
Vrbsky recalled. "Billie gave me as much as she could. But there was
no real regular salary." Over time, Alice helped out when she was
able, and Billie looked forward to her visits. "Billie liked to cook
Baltimore specials like crab cakes, red beans and rice, and pigs' feet,"
Vrbsky said. "She liked to watch old movies on TV, and sometimes
she'd drag me down to Forty-Second Street and there would be a
double feature. We'd get there at one in the morning and stay all
night." But mostly the two women sat in Billie's living room and
talked. As Billie chain-smoked—"all of her nightgowns had holes
burned in them from cigarettes"—the conversation often turned to
Billie sharing her thoughts on music and singers: "Billie didn't care
for Ethel Waters. She loved Lena Horne. About Ella Fitzgerald, she
said if she were white, she'd be considered the greatest singer in the
world. Billie once said, 'The only white woman I ever heard who
could sing the blues was Kay Starr.' I happened to agree with her.
Billie also told me about going to see Sarah Vaughan at Birdland.
When Vaughan came up to her at the bar and asked her how she

liked the show, Billie said, 'Sassy' "—Vaughan's nickname—" 'you sound like you piss ice water.' "

Despite the unassuming nature of her current circumstances, because of the position to which she had ascended in her profession, because of what she had come to represent in the broader culture, Billie Holiday was a woman of the world. This fact was not universally celebrated. Her critics routinely marginalized her, pointing out that she was untrained as a musician, could neither read nor write music, and enjoyed a grammar-school education that had progressed no further than the fifth grade. Her detractors wanted to portray her as unread, uncouth, and unworthy of her fame. Their goal was to depict her as a drug addict who never rose above the trappings of a troubled and impoverished youth in Baltimore that was defined by an unstable home life, truancy as a child, and prostitution as a teenager, all of which she readily acknowledged in her autobiography. She did so in part because Billie did not view herself as a victim. "What she really felt," a friend later said, "the Rosebud to understanding her, was that her life was a triumph." And it *was* a triumph. Despite the shortcomings of her background, she had become a vital force in the entertainment industry. She traveled extensively, both nationally and internationally, to fulfill engagements. She worked with some of the most prominent members of her generation. She often fraternized with socialites, fellow artists, and titans in the political and show business communities. She enjoyed such success because, like other notable figures of her time—Marlene Dietrich, Greta Garbo, Howard Hughes—she was a persona of her own creation. To the public, through her singing and public appearances, she projected an aura of style and sophistication. She was the personification of dignity and class, which she achieved despite efforts made by her enemies—and sometimes by those who claimed to be her friends—to tarnish the image she crafted for herself. "There was an elegance about her," composer David Amram says. "Compared to some of the rough characters in her life, she somehow was able to rise above that. She knew that she deserved better; she understood how terrific she was. She wasn't an egomaniac or conceited; she just knew her own worth. She carried herself like a lady. It was something she had *become*. She appreciated her value and the beauty of her music."

Still, she was not without her colorful side. During her big-band touring days, she played cards and rolled dice with the boys on the bus. She called everyone "baby," friends and strangers alike, and her favorite word was "motherfucker." Depending on her tone of voice, it was meant either as a term of endearment (as in "Buck Clayton, you motherfucker, come over here and let me see what color your eyes are today," a line she was known to say to her close friend) or as an indication of her contempt (as in "if that evil motherfucker believes in God, I'm thinking it over," she ultimately said of Louis McKay). If provoked, she was proficient at throwing a right hook, and more than one unsuspecting accoster was the recipient of a slug. She was particularly infuriated when someone made a racial slur. "She had antennae that were so highly developed," William Dufty said, "she could hear somebody making a racist remark thirty feet down the bar, and before you knew it, she would have a beer bottle smashed and would be at the guy's throat. The rage came from how she had to live her life—day after day after day, night after night after night. The thing that galled her was being treated like a queen uptown, and then nobody knows you when you come down to the fifties."

Her friend Greer Johnson remembered her intellect: "Billie was extremely bright, as intelligent as anyone I have ever known. She appealed to such an astonishingly broad range of people. I daresay Billie appealed to everyone from the crème de la crème of the so-called intellectuals down to the 'lowest' pusher." Irene Wilson Kitchens recalled her independent personality: "You couldn't dictate to her. She had a mind of her own and a will of her own."

Billie's fondness for cartoons and comic strips was well known, but she read books and kept up with current events by reading newspapers and magazines. And when she leafed through a newspaper, she encountered a world she knew all too well, sometimes on a personal basis. Take the newspaper for this day, June 21, 1958. In the nation section, it was reported that Vice President Richard Nixon was reassuring Republicans on Capitol Hill that they would not be harmed in the upcoming midterm elections by a scandal involving Sherman Adams, an assistant to President Dwight D. Eisenhower. Billie had once appeared with Nixon at a civic rally in Harlem, but, because she was a lifelong Democrat, she much preferred Franklin D. Roosevelt, her favorite president, whom she had met at the White House when she and Hazel Scott were guests at one of the annual fundraisers the president hosted to fight infantile paralysis, with which he was afflicted.

In the international section, there was coverage of Sputnik 3, an unmanned orbiting rocket launched into space by the Soviet Union in May—the ship could be seen in the skies over New England the following morning—a mission that prompted Eisenhower to propose establishing the National Aeronautics and Space Administration, which would be founded in July. No doubt a public fascinated by space was one reason why the nation's current Number 1 single was "The Purple People Eater," a novelty song about space invaders sung by Sheb Wooley. Billie had an aversion to novelty songs, as did other artists like her friend Frank Sinatra, who eventually acquiesced to pressure from his record label to record them ("Mama Will Bark" featured a dog howling in response to his lyrics), while Billie never did.

In the entertainment section, advertisements appeared for *Touch of Evil,* a picture starring Charlton Heston and Janet Leigh and written and directed by Orson Welles. In a complicated romantic life that all too often featured destructive relationships, Billie enjoyed in mid-1942 one of her more pleasurable liaisons with Welles, who had won acclaim for *Citizen Kane* the previous year and was preparing to release *The Magnificent Ambersons.* Welles feted Billie around Los Angeles, from swanky restaurants to Central Avenue jazz clubs to late-night hot spots, while she appeared as a headliner act at Billy Berg's Trouville Club in West Hollywood and lived in a comfortable apartment on Clark Street, where Welles often spent the night. In a departure from other affairs she pursued with a variety of men— and women, for that matter, since two of her most significant relationships were with women—Billie and Welles maintained a cordial involvement that ended on good terms. "I liked him and he liked me, and jazz," Billie wrote. "There wasn't a damn thing or person he wasn't interested in. He wanted to see everything and find out who and why it ticked. I guess that's part of what made him such a great artist."

But of all the stories in the present news cycle, one that resonated with Billie on a visceral level was a report out of Arkansas about events transpiring in Little Rock. In the wake of *Brown v. Board of Education*, the 1954 landmark decision of the United States Supreme Court that ended segregation in public schools, all-white Central High School in Little Rock was integrated by nine African-American students, dubbed the Little Rock Nine, in 1957. Now a U.S. district court judge ruled that the city school board could delay integration for two and a half years—a move seen as a blow to efforts to desegregate public schools nationwide. *The Saturday Evening Post* dated this day featured a sepia-toned cover created by John Falter that summed up the present situation regarding race in certain parts of America. In a bucolic setting stands a quaint mid-twentieth-century brick schoolhouse with a flood of carefree children—all of them white—rushing out the front door on their way to a yellow school bus. Though the image evokes a sentimentality worthy of Norman Rockwell, it captures a world defined by segregation as enshrined by the Jim Crow laws, which some citizens were fighting vehemently to maintain, if not permanently, then at least for as long as possible.

Billie had experienced Jim Crow firsthand. When she toured with Artie Shaw and his band in the late 1930s, she was the first African-American woman to sing with an all-white orchestra and encountered discrimination down south but, most painfully, also in Boston and New York. Jim Crow was one reason why, in 1939, Billie began to sing "Strange Fruit," an anti-lynching protest song disturbing in its graphic imagery and emotional impact. As the song became increasingly controversial, garnering national press coverage and selling a million copies when it was released as a single, Billie made it her own, even though it was written by Abel Meeropol. Her close association with the song drew the ire of Harry Anslinger, the director of the Federal Bureau of Narcotics, who was supported in

his efforts by J. Edgar Hoover, the director of the Federal Bureau of
Investigation. The government feared "Strange Fruit" would foment
discontent within the African-American community and beyond.
Because of this, Billie was warned to stop singing the song. When
she refused, the government launched a vendetta against her, which
resulted in a drug bust in 1947 that landed her in prison in Alderson, West Virginia, for a year-and-a-day sentence. Her release nine
and a half months later (two and a half months early for good behavior) served only to generate a protracted campaign of harassment by
the government that continued for the next decade. Even in recent
months, the surveillance had persisted, prompting Dorothy Kilgallen to report that Billie was "still under observation by Uncle Sam's
boys."

As it turned out, the government was right. "Strange Fruit" was
an early catalyst that contributed to the growing civic consciousness that, especially after the mid-1950s, sparked a movement that
demanded civil rights and equality for African Americans. Before
the Little Rock Nine entered the front doors of Central High School;
before Rosa Parks was jailed in 1955 for refusing to give up her seat
on a bus in Montgomery, Alabama; before a young unknown Baptist preacher named Martin Luther King, Jr., organized the ensuing Montgomery bus boycott, Billie Holiday was singing "Strange
Fruit." By doing so, she made herself an object of derision to audiences resistant to the song's message and a target of the government.
Despite suffering considerable repercussions, Billie never abandoned
the song. Her method of protest was not to make a speech or to join
a march in the streets but to attempt to change public sentiment
through the power of a song.

3.

As the afternoon passed—June 21, a cool, cloudy day in Manhattan,
happened to be the summer solstice—Billie began to contemplate
that evening's engagement. Originally, she was supposed to be in
Europe during June, performing a show at the Royal Festival Hall
in London on the eighth before starting a three-week stand at the

Olympia Music Hall in Paris, but the political unrest in Algiers in May spilled over into France and ushered in a new government headed by General Charles de Gaulle, which prompted the cancellation of her trip. So Joe Glaser had booked tonight's gig as a last-minute consolation. At the Loew's Sheridan Theatre, a 2,500-seat movie house at Seventh Avenue and Twelfth Street in Greenwich Village that routinely featured live concerts on Saturday nights at midnight, Art D'Lugoff (who had recently opened the Village Gate nightclub, also in the Village) was presenting Billie Holiday and the Dave Brubeck Quartet in, according to press notices, "a program of blues and jazz." Tickets, available at the box office, cost $2.50 or $2.80. This engagement marked the fourth time Billie had played the midnight show, which she could do since the theater did not sell alcohol and she was not required to have a cabaret card. Indeed, because of the moratorium imposed on her performing in nightclubs, Billie relished shows like the one this evening, when she could take the stage in the city she loved, even if its municipal administration in the form of the police department and the mayor's office did not afford her the respect an artist of her caliber deserved. For Billie, that disrespect was a point of contention. "The pretext used to deny me the right to work was my prison record," she wrote. "The police authorities who regulate the local nightclub industry decided that I wasn't fit to be granted a cabaret performer's license although many other nightclub employees with police records are licensed and working."

The band backing Billie would include Mal Waldron, who was a new father. Born three weeks ago, weighing in at seven pounds and nine ounces, was Mala Elaine, a baby girl. Billie was honored Mal asked her to be Mala's godmother. For years, Billie longed to be a mother, but her fervent desire had never been realized. Not having children would be one of the most painful disappointments she had to endure. "There was only one thing in her whole life that she wanted," says Corky Hale, a friend, "and that was to have a baby. That was her life's desire. Yet she could never have a baby. It was heartbreaking." As if to acknowledge her unfulfilled aspiration, over time a litany of friends, not merely Mal, asked Billie to be godmother to their children. It was a role she was always delighted to undertake.

The spotlight pierced the auditorium's darkness to illuminate Billie as she stood at center stage. Dressed in an evening gown, with her jet-black hair pulled back into a ponytail but with no gardenia adorning the side of her head, a decorative detail she had often used in previous years, she swayed gently to the music, quietly snapping her fingers in time with the beat while she stared out onto the standing-room-only audience, blurred by the spotlight's white glow. "Magnificent Billie Holiday . . . looked [like] a pretty picture," one music critic in attendance would write before noting that "so great is her magic that the audience didn't even realize she wasn't singing so much as she was carrying on a husky monologue of reminiscences of the parade of tunes which, over the years, she had made it impossible for anyone to imitate." John S. Wilson of *The New York Times* also reviewed the performance: "Once [Holiday] had loosened up by slashing through 'When Your Lover Has Gone,' she seemed to gain the confidence she needed to show that she can still phrase a song with the smooth, wry skill that once came to her so easily." The *Hartford Courant* critic was even more generous, concluding that "Holiday gave controlled and pulsating treatments to such standards as 'You've Changed,' 'I'm a Fool to Want You,' and 'I Get Along Without You Very Well' "—all songs included on *Lady in Satin,* the album she was there to promote. "[From] her very entrance on stage she had the audience . . . with her completely and by each of her stylistic vocals she answered the audience's faith that Billie is still much to be reckoned with in the art of heart-breaking blues singing."

With passion and honesty, with whatever voice she had available to her that night, Billie sang as she always did, displaying a vulnerability that made her compelling to watch and relatable to the listener. And that *voice*—for years critics and jazz lovers had tried to describe its eccentricity. On first hearing it on a record, poet Owen Dodson wrote: "Here came this voice, so steady, so melancholy, elongated like an El Greco painting; it had nothing to do with reality but everything to do with truth." Critic Leonard Feather commented that Billie possessed "a timbre like that of no other woman," a sentiment echoed by Harry "Sweets" Edison, who believed "she had a sound that when you heard her you knew that's Billie Holiday," and Paul Bowles, who argued that "although many have tried, none can do quite what she does." Oscar Peterson said she had "a voice of pure velvet," while Miles Davis asserted "[she] doesn't need any real horns; she sounds like one anyway." Davis's observation was prescient, since Billie herself contended she fashioned her voice to sound like Louis Armstrong playing the trumpet. Of course, Armstrong influenced Billie with his singing as well, particularly the conversational cadence he employed on "I Can't Give You Anything but Love," from 1929, which he sang as if he were speaking to a lover, not performing for an audience. His idiosyncratic approach to the lyric left an enduring impression on Billie and indelibly affected the way she sang a song.

As for her style, it was unique. She did not belt. She did not scat. She did not use the riffs and runs so popular with some singers. "Her singing is void of any narcissism," saxophonist Charles McPherson says. "There is no ego—nothing—in her voice. You never get the impression she's doing this or that to impress one soul on Planet Earth. It's just pure, 'Help me.' When you hear that human cry expressed, it's as high as you can get in artistic expression. It's an act of humanity; it's not an act of war." At the same time, "her diction was perfect," says musician Loren Schoenberg, who believes "every word she sang was audible and understandable, and in this sense, she's like Ethel Waters." Beyond that, Billie was blessed with what pianist Bobby Tucker called "the greatest conception of a beat I ever heard": "It just didn't matter what kind of song she was singing. She could sing the fastest tune in the world or else something that was like a dirge, but you could take a metronome and she'd be right there."

As for her stage presence, much would be made about how little she moved when she performed. She never stepped away from the standing microphone; her only gestures, besides a tilt of her head, were swaying slightly and snapping her fingers. "When you sing like

Billie Holiday did or play like Louis Armstrong did," Madeleine Peyroux explains, "the whole system locks down to the diaphragm so you are able to go *bop bop bop* hot. You attack at the top of each note. You have to allow the air to go wherever the body is. That's one reason why Billie couldn't move. The body has to lock in because it is pushing the air out. It really makes things swing because it's not just where the note starts; it's also where it ends. If you are forcing the air, it can end more quickly, which makes it a bit more dynamic." And there was nothing like hearing Billie sing live. Charles Mingus, her friend who sometimes accompanied her on bass, believed, according to his son, Eric, "that hearing Billie live was very different from the recordings. She was loud and her vocal tone was focused. [My father] felt the recordings didn't translate that well. He used to laugh about all those singers trying to sing like Billie with their soft mousy voices, mouths swallowing the microphone in order to be heard"—something Billie never did.

Her hallmark style had served her well for nearly three decades, as it did tonight. At the end of her set, while the applause faded following her exit as she ceded the stage to Dave Brubeck and his band—the virtuoso pianist had just returned from a world tour— Billie proceeded backstage to her dressing room, where she gathered her belongings to head home alone.

Outside the theater, while she stood on the sidewalk on Seventh Avenue, she enjoyed an unexpected surprise when she ran into someone she knew—Sonny Rollins. Tall, approachably handsome, often sporting a goatee, he was among the most talented tenor saxophone players on the music scene. A disciple of Charlie Parker, he had recorded fifteen albums and composed pieces like "Doxy," "Oléo," and "Airegin" that were destined to become jazz standards. He was an admirer of Lester Young, with whom Billie enjoyed such a close friendship they had given each other nicknames, or so legend would have it—Lester called her "Lady Day"; Billie called him "Prez," short for "the President of Jazz." Like Billie, Rollins had had brushes with authorities over narcotics. He was even targeted by Harry Anslinger, who, according to Rollins, "racialized what is a medical problem"— drug dependency—"[because] they didn't want white Americans to appreciate black America. They didn't want white Americans to appreciate the *music* of blacks."

Billie had gotten to know Rollins in February when for one weekend midmonth she shared a bill with him and his trio at the Red Hill Inn in Pennsauken, New Jersey, a small town ten miles east of Philadelphia. Owned for two decades by Joe de Luca, the club had become a destination for the jazz set even as it had developed a conspicuous reputation. "[The venue] sat 250 to 300 at its tables," one writer reported, "in a room decorated starkly black. The owner, as did some others in South Jersey, had a history of run-ins with the Internal Revenue Service." Talent performing at the club was provided accommodations at the Walt Whitman Hotel in nearby Camden. While Billie and Rollins spoke to each other at the hotel, while they waited for cars to drive them to the club (when a snowstorm hit one day Billie proclaimed, "The snow is up to my ass!"), and while they mingled backstage between shows, the two of them became friends.

That weekend, Rollins was able to witness the way some people in the industry felt they could treat Billie. What he saw troubled him: "Louis McKay was on the scene at the time [before he left after Memorial Day weekend]. He was there with her at the hotel. He was managing her. There was nothing happening between them of any note. But there was one thing I *did* experience that made me very depressed. We were working for a guy who was castigating Billie about not being on time and saying, 'You don't do this!' He spoke in the most demeaning way. It was very hurtful to me. He was a small-time promoter and he booked her in this engagement she and I were on. I was glad Louis McKay was around because it hurt me hearing this little no-count talking to Billie Holiday that way—in a loud enough voice for everyone to hear. It was a disgrace. In the end, though, Louis McKay did not stop it. I thought about doing something, but it was his place, not mine."

Tonight, as Billie chatted with Rollins in front of the Sheridan Theatre, perhaps he still felt a sense of protection, because once it became clear Billie needed a ride home, he offered to take her. "I was able to give her a ride uptown in a cab. We talked as we rode. At one point she made a comment about the Baroness and Thelonious Monk." The iconoclastic pianist was in the early stages of his twenty-eight-year relationship with Baroness Pannonica de Koenigswarter, a scion of the Rothschild family, who was so devoted to the jazz community—Charlie Parker died from complications of pneumonia and a bleeding ulcer in her suite at the Stanhope Hotel in 1955—she was known as the Baroness of Jazz. Billie shared her thoughts on the couple with Rollins: "The Baroness and Monk were quite the thing at the time. Billie thought it was great all the Baroness was doing for Monk."

When the taxi arrived at her apartment, Billie invited Rollins to come inside, an interlude he would recall as being amiable and pleasant. "We talked for a time. She gave me a copy of her book, *Lady Sings the Blues,* a paperback she signed for me. She said something nice about my music. Maybe it was just to make me feel good. We chatted a bit and then I said good night." While the evening seemed uneventful, Rollins was nevertheless unsettled by the encounter. It was clear her health had deteriorated since February; it was alarming how much she had declined in four months. "She didn't look well. She was being castigated in the newspapers. People were talking about her like she was a criminal. She was ill. You could see she was thin." The image of Billie—unwell, underweight, fragile—haunted Rollins long after he left her in the early-morning hours of what was now the day after the longest day of the year.

His association with Billie had affected Rollins on an artistic level as well. In February and March, he had recorded *Freedom Suite,* his groundbreaking album embracing black consciousness. For the album, Rollins himself wrote liner notes, which would be much discussed following the album's release in late June: "America is deeply rooted in Negro culture: its colloquialisms, its humor, its music. How ironic that the Negro, who more than any other people can claim America's culture as its own, is being persecuted and repressed, that the Negro, who has exemplified the humanities in his very existence, is being rewarded with inhumanity." *Persecuted, repressed, rewarded with inhumanity*—the words hit like blows to the face. Having just spent time with Rollins in February, Billie had loomed in his thinking when he wrote the liner notes: "One reason was 'Strange Fruit.' The song was important to me. I had felt the sting of racial prejudice"—as had Billie Holiday.

After Rollins left, Billie tried to unwind and get ready to go to sleep. Her routine usually involved multiple nightcaps as she chain-smoked cigarettes, often in bed. More than one friend feared she would fall asleep with a lit cigarette burning and set her bed on fire. While Rollins had not mentioned it to her, others close to Billie had started to admonish her about her appearance. Gone was the corpulent yet sensual body that could fill out an evening gown; now her waiflike figure simmered in the glow of the night's spotlight, a pentimento of her former self. But she would not give in; she would not seek proper medical treatment. The last place she wanted to be was in a hospital. Such facilities had not helped her in the past; she had no use for them now. Instead, she would follow what was her custom: get up the next day, book her next gig, make her next appearance, all the while doing what she loved to do—sing. When she was singing, she could keep at bay the soul-crushing loneliness she often felt. When she was singing, she was defying efforts to silence her waged by dark forces determined to undermine her as an artist and diminish her as a woman. When she was singing, she knew she was alive.

CHAPTER 3

𝔔

Lady *in* Satin

Billie Holiday photographed by Don Hunstein. A regular photographer for Columbia Records, Hunstein, later known for shooting the album covers for The Freewheelin' Bob Dylan *and* Bookends *by Simon & Garfunkel, photographed Billie during the recording sessions for* Lady in Satin *in February 1958.*

June 1958

I.

On the day after her appearance at the Sheridan Theatre, Billie awoke at her customary time—midday. Accompanied by Pepe, she went about her everyday routine, sometimes listening to a portable radio she carried with her from room to room. It was good to see Sonny Rollins last night; speaking with him reassured her of the place she had come to hold in the jazz community. They had discussed her new record. Indeed, the more she listened to *Lady in Satin,* the more she believed she had made a consequential album. Its official release date was June 4. When Billie received her first copy, she had sat in her living room and played it on the phonograph. As the melodic music drifted through the small apartment, she felt far removed from the recording sessions in February, when she had been filled with angst and trepidation. She often experienced a numbing sense of insecurity when she was in the studio, but because of the nature of the project, the most ambitious album she had attempted in her career so far, she was particularly unsure during these sessions. So she braced herself with liberal quantities of gin and navigated the recording process as best she could. Throughout June, as she played the album over and over, for herself or friends who stopped by to hear it, she had come to love it. "I've recorded an album called *Lady in Satin* for Columbia recently," she would write to a collector in England, "and I think it is one of the best I've done."

Of all her recordings, *Lady in Satin* engendered a unique reaction, one to which she was frankly unaccustomed. How the project came about, how Billie was able to record it in the first place, was no small feat. And, for Billie, the journey was germane, for ultimately, despite the initial response it received, *Lady in Satin* would come to represent a final capstone in a life that was defined by personal heartbreak eclipsed by a level of artistic achievement rarely witnessed in the world of popular music.

2.

As of 1958, Billie had been recording since 1933, the year she first went into a studio and cut two songs for an imprint of Columbia Records with an up-and-coming front man named Benny Goodman. Between July 2, 1935, and February 10, 1942, Billie and Teddy Wilson and his band completed twenty-two studio sessions in which they recorded seventy-four songs, a number of them featuring Lester Young on tenor saxophone; the Holiday-Wilson collaborations would come to represent a lasting contribution to the history of jazz. From 1933 to 1942, Billie recorded exclusively for Columbia with one exception in 1939, when she cut four songs for Milt Gabler at Commodore Records, a session that was made possible because Columbia refused to record "Strange Fruit," prompting Billie to secure a release that allowed her to cut the song along with three additional numbers for Gabler. Billie recorded again for Commodore in 1944. After Decca Records hired Gabler that same year, she recorded for the label for the next six years. From 1952 until 1957, she recorded for Norman Granz at Clef and Verve records, producing a group of landmark albums that included *Music for Torching* and *Lady Sings the Blues*.

Billie was proud of her oeuvre. It had established her as a seminal recording artist, not merely a legendary live performer with a devoted fan base who would support her whenever and wherever she appeared. Still, she felt she had not been afforded the deference she believed she had earned in the business, given the number of singles and albums she had released and the amount of revenue she had generated for the labels for which she worked. Specifically, she wanted to record an album accompanied by a full orchestra, including a string section. On almost all her previous recordings, she was backed by a small jazz combo, sometimes only a trio. During her time with Decca, she was allowed a modest string section on a few songs, notably "Lover Man" and "You Better Go Now" (the music for the latter was conducted by Percy Faith), but Billie yearned to make an album like Frank Sinatra's *In the Wee Small Hours,* which featured lush orchestrations arranged by Nelson Riddle that beautifully complemented Sinatra's voice. After recording music for twenty-five years, Billie felt she deserved the chance to make such an album.

There had been a recent informal discussion between Columbia Records and Earle Warren Zaidins, Billie's attorney, about her returning to the label, where previously she had enjoyed success. So she instructed her management to set up an appointment in early January 1958 for her to meet with Irving Townsend, an executive producer with the company. In the meeting, she told him she wanted to record a new album, but with one stipulation. "I've got to sing with Ray Ellis," Townsend later recalled her saying that day. "I want this album more than anything else, and I want it to be good." Townsend was receptive to Billie's overture, although he was surprised by her proviso about Ellis, who did not seem to be a probable collaborator for Billie. But the prospect of bringing Billie Holiday back to Columbia Records was too tempting for Townsend to resist. He told her he welcomed her idea. As for Ellis, the only way to determine if he was interested would be to give him a call.

Ray Ellis had learned his craft as a musician and arranger working local gigs in Philadelphia, his hometown, and then playing in military bands in the U.S. Army during World War II. In the late 1940s and early 1950s, he played tenor saxophone with bands headed by Gene Krupa and Paul Whiteman. In 1955, he caught the attention of Mitch Miller, the head of A&R at Columbia, when his arrangement of "Standing on the Corner," a Frank Loesser composition to be recorded by the Four Lads, was selected from an open-call competition for arrangers. The song would go on to become a hit, thanks in part to its whimsical yet memorable arrangement. Miller was looking for innovative new arrangers to bring to the label; now he had one in Ellis, who during the mid-1950s had additional hits with the Four Lads. That success allowed him to make his first album for Columbia under his own name, *Ellis in Wonderland,* which became much talked about in the music industry. It also received excellent notices, with one reviewer observing that Ellis—"talent personified"—created an album emblematic of "his imaginative and creative ability that has made him one of Tin Pan Alley's much sought after arrangers." Another critic implored anyone interested in "nice, easy-going listening [to] try *Ellis in Wonderland* [which features] a fine covey of standards." When Billie listened to the album, she knew she had found her Nelson Riddle. That was why she made her stipulation with Townsend. Ellis, she was convinced, was who she needed to help her make the album of her dreams.

"On January 3," Ellis later wrote, "I received a call from . . . Irving Townsend asking if I was free [in mid-]February. On my reply, he said, 'Great! Billie Holiday is in my office, and she wants you to write the arrangements for the album she's about to record for Columbia.'" Ellis was flabbergasted that Billie Holiday even knew who he *was;* of course, he would be honored to work with her. Soon a contract was drawn up. Columbia agreed to an "unlimited budget" and a thirty-five-piece orchestra featuring a fifteen-piece string section for an album to be recorded in three sessions. Musicians would be paid $60 a session. Billie would receive an advance of $150 a side against a 5 percent royalty. The album would be comprised of songs Billie had not previously recorded. There was one notable legal requirement. "Columbia Records had a provision in her contract," music historian Michael Brooks later wrote, "that made [Holiday's] attorney, Earle Zaidins, personally responsible for her prompt appearance at the recording studios."

Billie first met Ellis when the parties assembled in Townsend's office to sign the contract. In the days after the meeting, Townsend and Ellis went to a local music store and gathered a selection of songs, almost all of them American standards. When Ellis showed the songs to Billie during the week of January 10, she made the final selection of what she wanted to sing. "It didn't dawn on me at the time," Ellis would admit, "but just about every title she picked was the story of her life, unrequited love." Her decisions were based almost exclusively on lyrics. She wanted the songs to form a kind of narrative instead of constituting merely a collection of songs. Sinatra had all but perfected the "concept" album. His contributions to the genre, besides *In the Wee Small Hours,* included *Songs for Young Lovers, Swing Easy!,* and *Songs for Swingin' Lovers!* Billie intended her album to take its place in the same tradition.

With the song list complete, Ellis went off to write his arrangements, which he did by secluding himself in the study at his home in Westchester County, north of Manhattan, where he obsessively labored on the music around the clock, barely sleeping, until he finished. As she waited to record her new album, Billie promoted the paperback release of *Lady Sings the Blues* by appearing on two national radio shows: *Luncheon at Sardi's* at noon on February 4 and *The Barry Gray Show* at midnight on the fifth. She was encouraged by a letter she received from her publisher, which informed her that "250,000 copies of the Popular Library edition went on sale in January on newsstands throughout the country, and from the indications so far, *Lady Sings the Blues* is expected to become one of the biggest paperback bestsellers of 1958." That turned out to be true. By 1959, the book had sold two million copies and had been translated into fifteen languages, including Japanese.

Recording dates for *Lady in Satin* were set for three late-night sessions on February 18, 19, and 20 at the Columbia 30th Street Studio, which pleased Billie. A former Presbyterian church converted into a studio, the reason it was nicknamed "the Church," it was considered by many members of the music industry—from Glenn Gould and Leonard Bernstein to Miles Davis and Charles Mingus—to be among the finest recording facilities in the country because of its superior acoustics. If there were no complications, the album could be released by early summer. After all these years in the music business, after recording more than three hundred songs and logging—literally—countless live performances, Billie Holiday was finally being afforded what she felt she was due—the opportunity to record a studio album accompanied by a full orchestra with strings. As a professional accomplishment, it may not have seemed like much, but for Billie, it was everything she wanted.

———

"Love is funny."

She stood in a small nook that had been created for her to the right of the conductor's stand, where Ellis—clad in dark pants and a long-sleeved shirt and wearing a pair of headphones—hovered before the orchestra playing at full volume. As she sang into the microphone hanging from a boom in front of her, the luxuriant music washing over her in waves of sound, Billie had no sooner sung the line than she was unhappy with it. She stopped.

"Can I get another start?" she said hesitantly into the microphone. "I'm sorry."

It was after midnight on the first recording session for *Lady in Satin,* and Billie was feeling her way through a song. Ellis had scheduled the start time for late in the evening at an hour when Billie would have normally been onstage in a nightclub gig. She was told to arrive at the studio at 10:00 p.m., so she assumed the actual call time was 11:00 p.m. She got there at 11:30. Irving Townsend later remembered she was "all dressed up . . . looking great, as if she were going to perform in public." In fact, she was not wearing an evening gown—the wardrobe choice in which she usually performed, often accented by a mink stole, especially for an outside concert like a jazz festival—but a handsome outfit reminiscent of business attire. Ellis introduced her to the orchestra, more than thirty musicians plus three players she sometimes used to accompany her—Mal Waldron on piano, Osie Johnson on drums, and Milt Hinton on bass. The orchestra gave her a warm round of applause, signifying to Ellis that "the musicians dug her," which was not always the way musicians felt about a singer.

As soon as Billie settled into the studio, she was consumed by the self-doubt she often felt when she performed, a nervous apprehension so powerful that, according to Townsend, "she fortified herself with gin." A cup was placed nearby on a stool when she sang. Gin was often the drug she used when she wanted to avoid something harder; tonight, it was what she needed to get through the session.

With expensive studio time passing, Billie launched into the

first song of the evening—"You Don't Know What Love Is," a melo-
dious tune that Ellis had arranged with an emotive, dramatic introduction followed by, midway through the song, a haunting trumpet
solo played by Mel Davis. But Billie was uncertain of the lyrics, and
it took four takes before Ellis felt they could move on. The session's
second number was "I'll Be Around," an affecting tune about waiting for a lover to be available again ("I'll be around no matter how
you treat me now / So I'll be around when she's gone"). A mournful
violin started the song before a full complement of strings came in
periodically to add to the mood. Once again, Billie was tentative,
this time requiring eight takes before she produced a usable version.

The main problem, Ellis later admitted, was that Billie did not
sound anything like she did on the older records, to which he had
listened studiously as he wrote the arrangements. To Ellis, Billie's
voice, rough and unvarnished, clashed with the rich, luscious sound
of the orchestra. He also mistook her paralyzing nervousness for lack
of preparation and at one point took her aside and berated her. "I
was so mad at her. I was saying, 'You bitch! You sing so great, and
you don't know what you're doing! You're blowing the whole goddam thing!' It was an ego thing with me, because I'd slaved over
the arrangements, picturing the way she was going to say it, and
she wasn't singing it the way I'd thought, and I hated her. I literally
hated her. I think I treated her badly."

Billie did not lash out at Ellis in response. After all, it was *she*
who demanded he become involved in the project; she could hardly
get into a verbal altercation with the one person she insisted work on
the album. She had no choice but to live with his behavior. Even so,
she was hurt by the way he treated her. The session had to proceed,
however, so they moved on to the third number, "For Heaven's Sake,"
a love song about two lovers "alone in the night" who believe "heaven
is here in a kiss." It was the kind of song she had performed numerous
times before—a tune that would have been rendered sentimental by
most singers but, with Billie, evolved into a touching plea for romance.
It required only two takes before Billie fully captured the song.

The final number of the session was "But Beautiful," written
by Johnny Burke and Jimmy Van Heusen. After a string-heavy

introduction, Billie barely finished the first three words—"Love is funny"—when she stopped, unsatisfied with the way she delivered the line. She asked for another take.

Most of the orchestra ceased; some violins played on for a few additional notes.

Billie rehearsed the line amid ambient chatter among the musicians. "Love is fun-ny." A beat. "Love is fun-ny."

"Take two," a voice said from the control booth over the public address system.

"Oh, it's sad," Billie continued. "Love is fun-ny."

More chatter; a handful of musicians practiced several notes; soon it was time to proceed.

"Love is fun-ny," Billie practiced the line one last time.

"Take two," the voice repeated.

There was silence; then the orchestra began.

"Love is funny," Billie sang, as she launched into the song's first section, which built to a climax—"And I'm thinking / If you were mine / I'd never let you go"—when the music reached an emotional peak. An interlude followed first featuring violins, colored by a three-person choir singing faintly in the background, next a melancholy trumpet solo, again played by Mel Davis, before Billie continued with the second vocal portion of the song, concluding with the speaker declaring how she would feel if she had her lover with her: "And that would be / But beautiful / I know." A melodic outro— highlighted by violins and the angelic *ooo*'s of the small choir— completed the song. It was the most successful number of the night.

It was now 2:30 in the morning, and Billie had been drinking gin since the session began. She was noticeably slurring her words, but the gin allowed her to get through four songs. At points during the session, she had gone into the control booth to listen to playbacks, which made her so sensitive about the quality of her voice she refused to allow the playbacks to be shared with the musicians over the speakers in the studio. She did not want the orchestra members to hear what they were playing behind. By the end of the session, she was emotionally drained and physically exhausted. She was more than ready to go home.

Once the session concluded, once Billie left and the musicians packed up their instruments and departed, Ellis remained behind to listen to all the playbacks in the control booth. As he did, he became increasingly upset. "When he heard the playbacks," says Marc Ellis, his son, "he thought, 'Oh, my God, this is going to ruin my career. What am I going to do?' He hated what he heard. He thought he was sold down the river on the project. He didn't know what Billie's condition was. He thought he was going to get the Billie Holiday from 1945. Now he felt this was going to be the end of his musical career"—and it had just started. Ellis was so distraught, so consumed by dread and despondency, he reacted physically to how he was feeling. Abruptly bolting from the booth, he rushed to a nearby bathroom and threw up.

Regardless of any misgivings Billie may have had about the previous night, she returned to the studio the next evening for the second session, again scheduled to start at 11:00 p.m. The first song, "For All We Know," required five takes; the second, "It's Easy to Remember," nine. The best song of the session was the third—"I'm a Fool to Want You"—an evocative ballad about being hopelessly in love with someone who is unfaithful. Written by Frank Sinatra, Joel Herron, and Jack Wolf, the song was Billie's homage to Sinatra, who was, after all, the inspiration for her making the album. Billie poured her heart into the song. "I would say," Ellis wrote, "that the most emotional moment was her listening to the playback of 'I'm a Fool to Want You.' There were tears in her eyes."

For the session's fourth song, Billie attempted to record "The End of a Love Affair." After three tries, plans changed because Billie, as music journalist Phil Schaap later reported, "wasn't comfortable about singing [the song. So] it was decided to give her a day to learn the lyrics, but the band recorded the song without her . . . [an] instrumental version [that would] subsequently be added to by overdubbing." The following night, the final session for the album started out with Billie overdubbing her vocals to the track. Ten takes were required before a finished song was produced. After that, "Glad to Be Unhappy," "I Get Along Without You Very Well," and "Violets for Your Furs" went much better. But the best song of the evening, perhaps the most successful song of all three sessions, was "You've Changed," a last-minute addition Ellis included after he and Billie made a 3:00 a.m. trip to Colony Records the night before to find sheet music for one final song. Ellis finished the arrangement just before the third session started. Still, it had all come together, and Billie's sad ballad about a failed affair was heartbreaking.

With the sessions completed, Ellis had not changed his mind about the recordings. "After we finished the album," he wrote, "I went into the control room and listened to all the takes. I must admit I was unhappy with [Billie's] performance, but I was listening musically instead of emotionally." And the music on the songs was uncommonly beautiful. Over time, the quality of the sound itself would become a topic of discussion; it was the album's engineer, Fred Plaut, more so than Ellis, who created the sound. "The record was recorded differently than most popular records of that period," Marc Ellis says. "The engineer was not a pop engineer. He was a classical engineer. So he recorded the album like he was doing a piece of classical music, which was totally different in sound style. One of the shocking things about *Lady in Satin* is how great it sounds fidelity-wise. Plaut recorded it like he was doing Beethoven. Usually, with pop music, they use a close mike, right up against the instrument. You get a real dry sound, and then they throw echo on it. But, for a classical record, you record from a distance. Plaut grouped the instruments and recorded them as groups. He was able to achieve a lush symphonic shimmering sound."

3·

In the wake of the recording sessions, Billie got on with her life, content to wait for the songs to be mixed as Townsend and Ellis assembled the final album. In March, she found herself back in court—she had been in and out of court on both the East and West Coasts for over a decade now—when she was required to appear in the Court of Common Pleas in Philadelphia for an arrest for narcotics possession in 1956. In February of that year, Billie had been seized by the Philadelphia Police Department while she was in the city appearing at the Showboat. "The arrests of the nightclub singer and her husband-manager Louis McKay," *The Philadelphia Inquirer* reported, "were made during a raid on their room in the Radnor Hotel . . . shortly after 2 a.m. [on the twenty-third. Police] found in the room an ounce and a half of heroin, five hypodermic needles, a syringe, an eye dropper and a spoon. . . . [Detectives] also found a half ounce of cocaine and in McKay's suitcase a .25 caliber automatic pistol." Billie was arrested for narcotics possession, McKay for violation of the Firearms Act. Billie argued there were no drugs in her possession, implying the drugs and paraphernalia were planted; McKay claimed the police planted the weapon before, changing his story, he admitted he carried it for protection. Billie and McKay were released on $7,500 bail, and Billie finished her run at the Showboat playing to what *Down Beat* called "large crowds."

Two years later, on Wednesday, March 12, Billie and McKay faced the consequences of the arrest by appearing before Common Pleas judge Curtis Bok, who was willing to offer probation in exchange for guilty pleas because Billie had cooperated with authorities over the last two years and because she now claimed she had been cured of her drug dependency by a private physician. Described by one newspaper as "looking chic but subdued," Billie was represented by local lawyers; she also had brought along Earle Warren Zaidins as her personal attorney. United Press offered a report detailing key testimony in the hearing: "Captain Clarence Ferguson of the Special Investigation Squad [of the Philadelphia Police Department] testified the songstress enabled his squad to make a number of arrests on dope peddlers and others, particularly on persons who attempted to sell her narcotics. He said she had reported to him every time she made a Philadelphia appearance." With her protracted assistance in mind, Judge Pok placed both Billie and McKay on one-year probation but warned them that they would be sentenced to prison if they "got into trouble in any part of the country."

As probation hung over her head, Billie did her best to enjoy her forty-third birthday in April, which she celebrated on the seventh and then again in May, when Café Bohemia threw a birthday party for her that was written up in the gossip columns. One column item on a different topic published around this time painted a pretty, if misleading, picture of her marriage: "That full-length black diamond mink draped around singer Billie (Lady Day) Holiday is a present from her husband, Louis McKay." In fact, after their court appearance in March, their marriage had remained as tumultuous as it had been for some time. May was a long, forlorn month for Billie with few professional developments to ameliorate the unhappiness brought on by her troubled marriage. It had all come to a head over Memorial Day weekend, which produced the violent clash, complete with Billie bloodied and fainting at her attorney's apartment from the blunt trauma to her head inflicted by McKay, which led to the couple's seemingly inevitable separation.

Finally, June arrived, and Billie was heartened by the release of *Lady in Satin.* The cover featured a memorable portrait of her wearing a satin evening gown with her black hair slicked back and pulled into a ponytail. Billie *was* the lady in satin—so often in real life but now on an album cover. In liner notes, which took up most of the back cover, Irving Townsend prepared listeners for what they were about to encounter—a record that represented a departure for Billie: "She'd heard Ray's work [and] knew better than anyone else that he would be good for her. For there is grace and inspiration unfolding throughout Ray's arrangements which make a singer look her best, and Lady knew it. The use of strings and voice, punctuated with jazz-inspired solos here and there, is a new setting for this jazz singer. The two sounds have never met before."

Perhaps it was the singularity of the album that prompted critics to fall into two decidedly different camps: those who admired the album and those who found it irreparably flawed. The adoring critics gushed, typified by one Canadian reviewer: "The Billie Holiday story, by now a familiar one to jazz fans, seems to be entering a happy new phase . . . and it is certainly good to see her getting back into the swing of things. [Here] is a first-rate jazz recording that you won't want to miss." Echoing that praise, the *Fort Worth Star-Telegram* declared: "This is a somewhat strange conjunction, the rough, throaty croon of one of the great singers of jazz, and the smooth lush strings of an Ellis arrangement. Surprisingly, it blends beautifully." The *Nashville Banner* observed: "Billie Holiday, a famous name to jazz fans, is new and still manages to keep her originality in . . . *Lady in Satin*." And in "Strictly Off the Record," a music column, Larry Devine deemed the album "an outstanding jazz recording," adding that "Miss Holiday finds herself in strange company with Ellis's smooth, satiny string arrangements which are definitely not jazz," but "rather than altering her true jazz style, the strings seem to enhance it."

Such enthusiasm was not shared by all commentators—not by any means. Billie had gotten bad reviews in the past, especially for a live performance on a night when she was not at her best, but the negative response prompted by *Lady in Satin* reflected an animus foreign to her. The vitriol was personal, and it focused on her voice. *The Kansas City Star,* the hometown newspaper of a city known for its jazz, announced that "[Holiday's] voice isn't what it used to be"; another critic claimed that "as a jazz singer [Holiday] has had it"; music writer Polly Cochran declared that Billie's "naturally coarse" voice "breaks often and veers off the melodic track [so badly that it] sometimes is painful to hear the struggle"; the *Los Angeles Times*, calling the album "sad," proclaimed, "No Holiday for Us"; and the *San Francisco Chronicle* noted that it was "a [disturbing] experience for those who heard her when she was really singing to hear this feeble, strained, shaky and sometimes quivering voice." Several reviewers echoed the sentiment of this critic: " 'Lady' is Billie Holiday, and 'satin' is the background-with-strings provided by Ray Ellis and orchestra. However, the dry, husky (sometimes practically toneless) Holiday voice is an odd coupling for [these] tunes."

The New York Times tried to bridge the two critical camps in a review entitled "Billie Holiday—Jazz Singer, Pure and Simple." John S. Wilson offered: "Today Miss Holiday's voice is a rough-surfaced ghost of what had once been a pliant, precise instrument, but its very limitations have brought out additional resources of craft and skill in her use of it. One hears occasional suggestions of this reorientation in [*Lady in Satin*]." Indeed, the push-pull of the critical reception was captured by two reviews appearing in prominent music publications. *Metronome* deemed the album "Holiday-fare of fine quality" while *Down Beat* dismissed the entire enterprise as "a mistake."

In the weeks following the album's release in early June, Billie tried to reconcile the hot-cold nature of the critics. It was not as if the controversy surrounding her voice had been unexpected. In his liner notes, Townsend made sure to put the state of Billie's voice into a broader context in an effort to assuage criticism that might be leveled against her. "Few singers," he wrote, "have suffered so much, paid such penalties for a career, had so few pleasant memories of fame as she. Because we know her so well, we find a more personal meaning in her songs. It's so easy to believe what she sings." That truism is at the heart of *Lady in Satin*. In song after song, Billie emotes about love, often an unrequited love or a failed love affair, and the anguish of her emotions is conveyed in the rawness of her voice. "There is nothing more painful than the expression of unrequited love," Charles McPherson says. "Poets from the beginning of human history have written about it. As such, the tunes on the album are marvelous vehicles for a singer who had her kind of artistry, one that lies in telling stories about the dark aspects of the human condition."

In her private life, which sometimes played itself out on the front pages of newspapers, Billie had lived through dramas involving substance abuse and relationships gone bad. Her pain—and the stress of working in show business—had caused her to drink and at times rely on drugs. All the suffering, all the heartache, was reflected in the damaged, tortured voice captured on the album, the quality of which was only highlighted by Ellis's rich orchestral music. Beyond that, authorities used narcotics to bust her, send her to prison, harm her ability to make a living, and, ultimately, push her to a breaking point. The difficult life she was forced to endure was emulated in the pain displayed on the album. For any artist, the personal is political. No artist could have created a more personal album than Billie Holiday made with *Lady in Satin*—a masterpiece of longing and sorrow.

CHAPTER 4

❧

A Little Jazz History

Young Billie, around age two, in Baltimore. This is the only known photograph of Billie Holiday taken during her childhood.

I.

Once July arrived—a month that saw Alaska become a state, Althea Gibson defend her women's tennis championship at Wimbledon, and Elvis Presley star in a musical motion picture set in New Orleans entitled *King Creole*—Billie came to realize that, despite the mixed reviews, *Lady in Satin* was a hit. The record was selling so well, based on review coverage and her appearances, that word spread through gossip channels that Irving Townsend wanted to sign her to a long-term contract at Columbia. One newspaper reported she was "signed to wax two new albums per year" with *The Afro-American* describing the contract as "lush." Press accounts depicted the deal as a fait accompli, when in fact negotiations were ongoing, so Billie was eager to continue promoting *Lady in Satin* whenever she could. That was one reason why she agreed to make an appearance on *Art Ford's Jazz Party* on July 10.

On that day—a Thursday—she relaxed in her apartment as she listened to music, smoked cigarettes, and did a little cooking, all the while accompanied by Pepe. Of her recent routine, one friend said: "She just sits at home all day and all night." That was true unless she had an obligation to keep like the one she had tonight. This would mark the second time she had been a guest on the show since late May, but with *Lady in Satin* selling well and talk of a new multi-record contract heating up, Billie wanted to appear on television as much as possible. Anyway, she liked Art Ford, as did many singers and musicians in the jazz community.

A radio disc jockey and television personality who often promoted jazz, Ford appeared for fifteen years on the radio station WNEW, where he hosted *Milkman's Matinee* and *Make-Believe Ballroom*. Three months earlier, while he was visiting the World's Fair in Brussels, he was unexpectedly replaced by station management with William B. Williams. Ford took the dismissal in stride, telling *The New York Times,* "I am happiest when the garde is avant. The garde is no longer avant at WNEW." He was content to move on to new endeavors, one of which was *Jazz Party,* a "sublime" program, according to the *Times,* that represented "one of his most impressive achievements." Ford created a mellow, welcoming atmosphere on the show. "Its keynote was informality," jazz author Dan Morgenstern wrote; "station breaks and commercials sometimes were delayed in the heat of the improvised happenings, and Ford never panicked when the musicians took their time deciding what the next number would be. His was a relaxed and unflappable presence, and he had almost as much fun as the players did." The laid-back atmosphere of the show, which was sponsored by Westinghouse and Parliament cigarettes, was contributed to by the bountiful quantities of vodka and orange juice made available before and during the broadcast. Billie was happy to appear on the program whenever she was invited.

As she went about her afternoon, she considered a number of ongoing issues with which she was dealing. One was Louis McKay. She missed having him around, now that he was living in Los Angeles, but obviously if their relationship had devolved to the point where McKay was threatening her with bodily harm—and then making good on his boasts of violence—there was little hope of reconciliation. Dorothy Kilgallen summed up the situation in her column: "Billie Holiday could add a couple more tempestuous chapters to her biography just by recording the things that have happened to her since it was published. Her latest disaster: trouble with the current man in her life, Louis McKay." By this day in July 1958, Billie was considering divorce, although she had not yet taken any demonstrative action. She was still Mrs. Louis McKay, and, for whatever reason, she did not seem to be in a rush to file for divorce. After all, she had not divorced her first husband until she wanted to marry

McKay, and at present there was no new romantic prospect on the horizon.

    For Billie, her deteriorating marriage may have been causing her unhappiness, but more pleasant developments were also taking place. Just this month, Frank Sinatra, a close friend, published an article in *Ebony* entitled "The Way I Look at Race." In a wide-ranging commentary on race in America at the end of the 1950s, a pivotal time for civil rights in the country, Sinatra singled out for its significance to him his friendship with Billie, whom he initially encountered in the 1930s as she was making her early appearances in clubs on Fifty-Second Street. "When I first heard her," Sinatra wrote, "standing in a spotlight in a 52nd Street jazz spot, swinging with the beat, I was dazzled by her soft, breathtaking beauty. It was the kind of face that made a man want to touch it tenderly." But Sinatra did not focus only on her appearance; he assessed her as an artist. "It is Billie Holiday . . . who was and still remains the greatest single musical influence on me. It has been a warm and wonderful influence and I am proud to acknowledge it. [She] is unquestionably the most important influence on American popular singing in the last twenty years. With a few exceptions, every major pop singer in the U.S. during her generation has been touched in some way by her genius."

    Billie had known Sinatra for two decades, and, while she often downplayed her impact on his musical choices, she did acknowledge that she instilled in him a propensity to "bend the note" to enhance his phrasing, what became the hallmark in his singing style. "I told him about notes at the end he should bend," she told a columnist. "Bending those notes—that's all I helped Frankie with." Billie was close to Sinatra during his romance with and marriage to Ava Gardner, who was previously married to Artie Shaw (for whom Billie had worked) and with whom she shared a mutual friend, Lena Horne. Billie once spoke about Ava Gardner to a fan who documented the exchange: "[Billie] had a new Chihuahua called [Pepe]. She had gotten him at an auction and she said, 'Some bitch was bidding against me. She went up to $300.' Billie said, 'I can't afford $300. Who is that bitch? So I looked over and walked toward her and it was Ava Gardner. "Hey bitch," I said, "I can't afford $300." So she said, "Lady, I'm sorry. I didn't know it was you." So Ava bought it and gave it to me as a gift.' " Billie also revealed to her fan "that she had introduced Ava to Frank Sinatra so they were all friends [and] that she had told Sinatra to bend his notes and not sing so 'flat' (meaning straight)."

It was Ava Gardner who was at the heart of the most pressing problem with which Billie was dealing in the summer of 1958: the collapse of the film project based on *Lady Sings the Blues.* As soon as the book was published in 1956, producers in Hollywood expressed interest in purchasing the film rights. In early 1957, Billie received a letter from Lester Cowan, who was an influential figure in Holly-wood, having served in the early 1930s as the executive secretary (later known as the director) of the Academy of Motion Picture Arts and Sciences during the time the organization developed the Acad-emy Awards before setting out on his own to produce such pictures as *You Can't Cheat an Honest Man,* starring W. C. Fields, *My Little Chickadee,* starring Fields and Mae West, and *The Story of G.I. Joe,* starring Burgess Meredith and based on the experiences in World War II of Ernie Pyle. "I want to produce a motion picture version of your autobiography *Lady Sings the Blues,*" Cowan wrote. "And I want to tell you why." He believed, he said, Billie was "the greatest living singer of the blues," on par with performers like Marian Anderson and Maria Callas, who dominated their respective musical genres. Beyond that, Cowan was impressed by the book itself, which he found to be "one of the most gripping, dramatic and moving sagas of survival I had ever read." He could not "put it down until I could find my Emerson's essays on self-reliance." Finally, Cowan touched on an issue vital to Billie—"the staggering cost we pay in this country for the foolish notion of treating the narcotic addict as a criminal and driving sick people through punishment to crime."

The letter worked. In March 1957, Billie signed over film rights to *Lady Sings the Blues* to Cowan, who arranged for William Dufty and Ann Ronell, who was married to Cowan, to write a treatment followed by a screenplay, both based on the book; for Ronell to write three original songs for the picture—"Blue New York," "Hungry for Love," and "Happy Birthday All Year Long"; and for Billie to record the new songs. To play Billie, Cowan approached Dorothy Dandridge, a prominent African-American actress who had won universal acclaim for starring in the 1954 film version of Oscar Hammerstein's *Carmen Jones*. Then, in October 1957, Cowan entered into a financing and distribution deal with United Artists Corporation, with one key requirement spelled out in the contract: "On or before March 1, 1958, [Cowan] agrees to submit to United a final shooting script, a top female star to play the role of Billie Holiday, and a budget for the production of the picture, all of which production items shall be subject to the approval of United, in its absolute discretion."

The requirement proved problematic when Dandridge became disassociated with the project. At once, Cowan replaced her with Ava Gardner, even though she was not African American. Ultimately, Gardner said she was unavailable, although the real reason may have been the fact that she recently divorced Sinatra and moved to Spain, marking her departure from Hollywood in particular and America in general. (After some years in Spain, she settled in London and never moved back to the United States.) Whatever the reason, Gardner would not play the part, so Cowan lined up Lana Turner. As it happened, Turner was unacceptable to United Artists. On February 17, Max Youngstein, a vice president at the company, wrote to Cowan: "I am sorry to say . . . that based on [your] treatment, I cannot accept Lana Turner as a substitute for Ava Gardner. They just aren't in the same class box-office-wise, at the present time. . . . As I see it, you have one of two choices, namely, to get an important male co-star and have the screenplay written to fit, or to work this out so that it suits Ava Gardner's schedule if there is a chance of getting her, because in my opinion she is still by far the best choice for the role. As I told you from the beginning, I don't want to wind up with just another low budget second feature." In the end, arrangements with Gardner could not be facilitated, and by early July 1958, as Billie was making the rounds to promote *Lady in Satin,* the deal between Cowan and United Artists fell apart. As Earl Wilson reported in his column: "Billie Holiday's proposed film bio was canceled." The termination represented a severe blow to Billie, who was looking forward to seeing the film version of her life and enjoying the professional benefits afforded the subject of a major Hollywood picture.

The film project's collapse remained a source of profound disappointment for Billie as she dressed for her appearance on the evening of July 10 on *Art Ford's Jazz Party*. She loved to play music while she was getting ready and tended to prefer classical selections like *Rhapsody in Blue* and *Afternoon of a Faun* and opera pieces like *Porgy and Bess*, one song—"I Loves You, Porgy"—from which she often sang in her shows. Today, she slicked back her hair into a ponytail. She applied ample makeup, hoping to appear as healthy as possible. She made sure she was ready when a private car picked her up in time to travel to the studio in Newark, New Jersey, and get her there sufficiently in advance of a 9:00 p.m. airtime.

2.

When she arrived at her destination in Newark, the Mosque Theatre on Broad Street, Billie got out of the car, entered the building, and took the freight elevator to the second floor (the only elevator to reach that floor) to the cavernous space that was used as a studio from which to broadcast *Art Ford's Jazz Party* live. Stepping off the elevator, she was greeted by Ford's production team, among them Nancy Miller, who was a companion of Buck Clayton, an old friend of Billie's who was one of the musicians appearing on the program that night. (Years later, Miller and Clayton became romantically involved.) Billie visited with the other performers as she prepared for the show, happy to partake of the vodka and orange juice doled out in white paper cups offered by a staff member from a serving cart. Near nine o'clock, Billie stood off to the side in the shadows to watch the top of the show. A group of musicians gathered in the center of the studio awaiting the opening greeting to be made by Ford, who took his place a short distance away from them. A youthful man in a dark suit and tie, he looked more like a corporate executive than the host of a jazz television program.

A reporter described the ambiance Ford created on his show: "The artists assemble in the bare studio; the lighting is very soft, and an infectious informality prevails." That easygoing style permeated from Ford, who spoke into one of the two cameras used to broadcast the program as he got the evening underway.

"Once again," he said to the audience—the one at home, since there was no audience in the studio—"this is Art Ford, here on Channel Thirteen in stereophonic sound. We invite you to listen to the most uninhibited, most inspired, and most unrehearsed American jazz."

With this, the second camera cut to the musicians as they launched into one of two instrumental numbers. At the end of the second song, it was showtime for Billie, who walked out and sat on a stool beside the piano. She was surrounded by musicians. Her regulars—Mal Waldron on piano and Osie Johnson on drums—were joined by Tyree Glenn on trombone, Georgie Auld on tenor saxophone, Mary Osborne on guitar, and Vinnie Burke on bass.

Now came her introduction from Ford, who struck a genial tone when he spoke to the camera: "We'll make a little jazz history—Billie Holiday."

Once the music started and the camera focused on Billie, she stood up from her stool and began to sing a spirited version of "Foolin' Myself," which she had recorded years earlier with Teddy Wilson. The ending of the song was particularly poignant, especially considering the present state of her romantic life: "I'm acting proud / And every time I see you in a crowd / I may pretend / But in the end / I'm just foolin' myself."

When she finished, Billie returned to the side of the studio to allow the musicians to play two instrumental medleys. Then, after Ford introduced her for her second number, she began "It's Easy to Remember," a selection from *Lady in Satin,* the album she was there to promote. At the end of the song, she went back offstage so the musicians could play three more instrumental numbers; then it was time for her final song.

"To twenty-four nations of the world," Ford said calmly to the camera, "the largest jazz audience watching a regular jazz show, we bring you now a moment with Lady Day, Billie Holiday."

After turning her head from the camera to clear her throat, Billie commenced another tune she had recorded with Teddy Wilson— "What a Little Moonlight Can Do." Over the years, she had sung the song so many times it had become a part of her go-to playlist. Tonight, she used an arrangement that built up to an ending she often employed in live shows, where she repeated the word "moonlight" with Waldron answering her by playing the same notes on the piano until she concluded with an emphatic "can do." It was what passed for a "big ending" for Billie, who abhorred anything resembling a gimmick or a stunt in a live performance.

A silence fell over the studio. The ending worked for Art Ford. "Well," he said happily, "if everything is all right with Billie Holiday, everything is all right with jazz." And as the show concluded and she prepared to return to Manhattan, everything *was* all right with Billie because, despite her personal problems and professional setbacks, despite her compromised health, she had put on an entertaining show for an audience one more time.

In the days after her guest spot on *Art Ford's Jazz Party,* Billie continued to deal with the collapse of the *Lady Sings the Blues* movie adaptation, a project she was counting on to bolster her popularity, which was threatened by not only the assault on her carried out by the government but also a change in the country's musical taste as a result of the emerging popularity of rock and roll. She had published *Lady Sings the Blues* for calculatedly commercial reasons, and she was gratified by the mostly good reviews it received, such as those offered by the *New York Herald Tribune,* which concluded it was "one of the most candid self-portraits painted on a typewriter," and *The New Yorker,* which observed that it was "as bitter and uncompromising an autobiography as has been published in a long time, a largely authentic, if almost indigestible, social document." Perhaps, but in the future much attention would be paid to the factual accuracy of her "candid" and "largely authentic" autobiography. For her part, Billie never shied away from the fact that she was more committed to telling a compelling story than to faithfully recording her life. Some of the book's episodes were true, others enhanced or exaggerated; many parts of the book were simply made up. Of the truthfulness of the work, Leonard Feather wrote: "It is a mixture of half-truths, untruths, and events as seen by Billie through a haze of wishful thinking. John Hammond, Teddy Wilson, and others close to her were quick to point out the inaccuracies, as was I."

The opening two sentences of the book would become infamous: "Mom and Pop were just a couple of kids when they got married. He was eighteen, she was sixteen, and I was three." Lester Cowan regarded the "opening . . . of your story" as "classic." He lamented, "I'm still looking for someone who started out with that many strikes against them. I read every sentence after that." Which, of course, was the purpose of the opening offered by Billie and crafted by Dufty: to hook the reader. The sentences were based on two similar sentences included in an article about Billie, on which she had cooperated, that appeared in *PM* in 1945. Unfortunately, the facts in the sentences were all wrong. The ages of her parents were not accurate; her mother was older than her father, not the other way around. Her parents never married; indeed, they never even lived together. Billie went through much of her youth without so much as seeing her father. But Billie didn't care about facts; what was important was entertaining an audience. With that in mind, she maintained the same level of accuracy, or lack thereof, throughout good portions of *Lady Sings the Blues,* which ended up being an enjoyable, if sometimes misleading, experience for the reader.

The unreliability of the book would have a profound effect on future Holiday scholarship. For those charged with chronicling her life, the challenge that emerged was sorting out fact from fiction. Early biographers went so far as to get even her birthplace wrong, primarily because she herself assiduously misrepresented that fact, at first through innocence but later with calculation. Without fail, she informed anyone who asked—friends, fans, even the authorities— that she was born in Baltimore when she was not. For many years, there was a reason why she misrepresented that fact. From her youth until the age of thirty-nine, she was told by her mother and family that she was born in Baltimore, but in 1954 when she needed to get a passport in order to undertake an overseas tour, she learned from the Department of State she was not born there. Despite irrefutable proof of her real birthplace, Billie continued to claim she was born in Baltimore, even in her autobiography, until her death.

Then, after she died, efforts to portray her accurately were harmed substantially by two motion pictures purported to be her "life story," one released in 1972, the other in 2021, that were essentially fantastical accounts that bore little to no resemblance to actual events through which she lived. Still, the facts of her life *were* the facts, regardless of what others—and, for that matter, Billie herself—wanted them to be. And while it was true Billie's imagined account of her biography was a good read, the accurate version was equally as compelling, if for different reasons.

3.

For the record, Billie Holiday was born in Philadelphia, Pennsylvania, at 2:30 a.m. on April 7, 1915, in Philadelphia General Hospital. Her mother was an eighteen-year-old housekeeper named Sarah Julia Harris, who preferred to be called Sadie. Harris was the name of her mother's husband, not her father; eventually, Sadie used the last name of her father, Charles Fagan, who never married her mother. In time, Sadie found herself, as her mother once had, unmarried and pregnant. So, leaving her hometown of Baltimore, she traveled to Philadelphia. In February 1915, as her due date approached, she went to Philadelphia General to negotiate a deal to work at the hospital if she could deliver her baby there. "Sadie Fagan loved me from the time I was just a swift kick in the ribs while she scrubbed floors," Billie wrote. "[At the hospital, she] told them she'd scrub floors and wait on the other bitches laying up there to have their kids so she could pay her way and mine. And she did."

At the time of the delivery, overseen by Dr. Samuel R. Stillman, Sadie was dating a twenty-year-old waiter named Frank DeViese.

On hospital records, while she recorded separate addresses for them, she listed DeViese as the baby's father; in the future, however, she insisted the actual father was Clarence Holiday, a sixteen-year-old musician with whom she had a brief but passionate affair in Baltimore. Coming from West Baltimore, Clarence played the banjo in local groups. The teenagers met at a gig he was working. Clarence never denied his paternity, telling a producer years later that "[Billie] was just something I stole when I was fifteen." Clarence's failure to take responsibility was present from the start. When Sadie told him she was pregnant, hoping the two could set up a home, perhaps even get married, Clarence showed no interest. Marriage was out of the question; Sadie was on her own. Clarence's rejection of a life together was one motivation that drove Sadie to seek brighter prospects in Philadelphia.

Besides listing the wrong father for her new baby, Sadie further confused hospital documents by misspelling her daughter's name. Sadie intended for the child to be named Eleanora, but the hospital recorded the name as "Elinore." Harris was given as the last name, although later the child most often used the name Fagan. Eleanora Fagan—that was the name with which Billie Holiday grew up.

Not long after her baby was born, Sadie moved them back to Baltimore, where they lived with Sadie's half sister, Eva, and her husband, Robert Miller, whose mother, Martha Miller, often cared for Eleanora. In her early years, Eleanora's maternal grandfather loomed as a compelling figure in her life. He was Irish and Roman Catholic, the product of a relationship between a slave and her owner, the sort of arrangement that at one time was not uncommon in certain parts of the American South. This is how Billie described her great-grandmother: "She had been a slave on a big plantation in Virginia. . . . Mr. Charles Fagan, the handsome Irish plantation owner, had his white wife and children in the big house. And he had my great-grandmother out in back. She had sixteen children by him, and all of them were dead . . . except [for my grandfather]." The lone surviving son of a large brood of children made for a dramatic story, but, as she often did, Billie was embellishing the narrative. "Charles Fagan"—Billie's grandfather was named for his father—"had two brothers, John and Guy, and a sister, Rosie [who were all alive]," journalist Linda Kuehl reported. "But the Fagan family was bothered by Eleanora being illegitimate, though other family members were too. Charles did not legitimize Sadie any more than Clarence legitimized Eleanora. Whatever the cause, [there was a] breach, [which] left Billie bitter." Billie preferred to leave her grandfather's siblings out of the picture altogether than to acknowledge their existence.

Billie's grandfather was married to a woman who also did not approve of Sadie—matters were only made worse when she had a child out of wedlock—so, because of his family and his wife, Charles Fagan was forced to limit his involvement with his daughter and granddaughter. Sadie and Eleanora's domestic life changed in October 1920 when Sadie married Philip Gough, a twenty-six-year-old longshoreman who worked in the Port of Baltimore. That fall, five-year-old Eleanora entered public school at Thomas E. Hayes Elementary School before quickly transferring to a Catholic school. In 1922, the family set up home at 209 East Street; then, the following October, Charles Fagan took out a $2,500 mortgage with Sadie to purchase a house at 1421 North Fremont Avenue. If the house was meant to solidify Sadie's marriage, the opposite occurred; in no time, Philip was gone, leaving Sadie and Eleanora on their own. Over the coming months, the mother and child saw their lives became so unstructured that on January 5, 1925, one month before the mortgage company filed a lawsuit for lack of payment on the house, a magistrate in the Juvenile Court in Baltimore determined Eleanora, now a fourth grader at Public School 104 who frequently missed school, was "a minor without proper care and guardianship." The nine-year-old was ordered to reside at the House of Good Shepherd for Colored Girls, a Catholic institution run by the Little Sisters of the Poor. The reform school, an imposing six-story brick building, was located at the corner of Claverton and Franklin Streets.

Assigned the protective pseudonym "Madge," Eleanora lived in the facility, headed by Mother Margaret, for ten months. For the first time in her life, order was imposed on her daily routine. She was steeped in religion and music. Each day, she was required to attend Catholic mass and sing from the *Liber Usualis,* a book of Gre-

gorian chants widely used in Catholic congregations. The book was
the product of Benedictine monks in Solesmes, France, who updated
the chants in such a way that, as one choirmaster wrote, "the rhythm
of material becomes a thing of the spirit." For Eleanora, the cho-
ral sessions represented her first organized encounters with music.
At Good Shepherd, she was baptized twice, in March and August.
For the first service, conducted by Father Edward V. Casserly in the
Sacred Heart Chapel, Oliver Welch, an institution staffer, stood
as Eleanora's godfather, while Christine Scott, another staffer, was
named as her godmother. "Madge was so happy," Scott recalled. "She
was in there with the rest of the girls, all of them in white dresses
and veils. She was grinning from ear to ear. You could almost see her
back teeth. She was light as a feather." Eleanora remained at Good
Shepherd until she was released on October 3—"paroled," according
to official documents—into the custody of her mother.

It was now that Sadie left West Baltimore to move across town
and sublet a room for the two of them from Viola Green, who lived
with her son Freddie in a brick row house at 609 Bond Street, one
block from the Johns Hopkins Hospital. A short tenure there ended
when Sadie and Eleanora moved to Fells Point and assumed residence
in a room on Spring Street before ending up at 219 South Durham
Street, where they lived on the second floor with Sadie's new companion, Wee Wee Hill, whose mother, Lucy, nicknamed Miss Lu,
owned the house. Sadie worked as a housekeeper, often taking well-
paying "transportation" jobs in Philadelphia and New York, while
Eleanora, at age eleven, dropped out of the fifth grade and began
spending less time at home. "She was out and done what she felt like
doing," recalled Pony Kane, who lived in the attic of 217 Durham
Street with her mother, "because she was just don't-care-ish."

Eleanora's newfound sense of freedom was shattered in the early
morning hours of Christmas Eve in 1926 when she was raped by
a twenty-six-year-old neighbor, Wilbert Rich. Sadie and Wee Wee
came home from a night out to discover the sexual assault in progress in their home. Calling the police, Sadie pressed charges and,
after Sadie made a statement and Eleanora was examined by doctors, Rich was taken into custody and charged with six counts of

rape, including the crime of carnal knowledge with a minor. For her part—perhaps for her own protection—Eleanora was sent back to Good Shepherd, now as a state's witness. In January, Rich was found guilty on one count of rape and sentenced to three months in jail. For her second visit at Good Shepherd, where she was baptized a third time, Eleanora stayed until February, when she was once again returned to her mother.

Soon after Eleanora's release, Sadie, who by now was divorced from Philip Gough, realized Wee Wee was never going to marry her. "I was a bad fella," Hill remembered. "I was gambling, running around, running with different women." So, Sadie moved to New York and Eleanora, under the care of Miss Lu, began to work first for Alice Dean and then for Ethel Moore, employment that, besides allowing her to start singing, introduced her to the profession of prostitution. In the winter of 1929, Sadie sent for Eleanora and the pair settled down in Harlem, where Eleanora discovered her mother was working in a bordello at 151 West 140th Street run by Florence Williams. With her past brothel experience, Eleanora joined Sadie, meaning both mother and daughter were working as prostitutes at the same whorehouse. The employment ended when the police raided the establishment in May and arrested a number of the women, including Sadie and Eleanora. Sadie was released, but Eleanora was taken to Jefferson Market Court. There, Judge Jean Hortense Norris sentenced her to one hundred days of hard time in a penitentiary on Welfare Island (now called Roosevelt Island), which is located in the East River running from East Forty-Sixth Street to East Eighty-Fifth Street in the waters between Manhattan and Queens. For Eleanora, the experience was upsetting: "That place was filthy. Fifty girls were packed together in one awful ward, and some of them with TB." The entire interlude, from brothel to prison, unnerved her: "If I thought my childhood in Baltimore was rough, my experiences as a teenage girl in Harlem with no father around to help out were twenty times worse. . . . It meant meeting and getting mixed up with many people and in wrong situations at a time when most young girls are in school." The incarceration on Welfare Island cured Eleanora of any desire to continue a life of prostitution, which prompted Sadie to

move them to Brooklyn, where Sadie returned to work as a maid and
Eleanora, with the help of Kenneth Hollon, redoubled her efforts to
make it as a singer, now with her new stage name—Billie Holiday.

At first, Billie tried to differentiate herself from her father,
because by the early 1930s Clarence Holiday had developed a minor
reputation as a competent sideman in the music industry. In 1918,
after he had joined and then deserted the U.S. Army the year before,
Clarence was inducted a second time near the end of World War I
and assigned as a private to the 54th Company. Because of his music
background, he served as a bugler. He was deployed to France on
October 20 and the war concluded on November 11, but, during his
short time in France, or so Billie later claimed, he was involved in
an incident where he was gassed with mustard gas, which damaged
his lungs. There is no evidence the episode occurred; it was likely
a fiction invented by Billie to make her father—and by extension
herself—appear more sympathetic. Regardless of what actually happened, with the war over, Clarence was given an honorable discharge
in July 1919 and returned stateside to the music scene, joining the
Fletcher Henderson Orchestra as a guitarist who could also play the
banjo. Walter Johnson, a drummer with Henderson, remembered
Clarence as "a very jolly fellow who drank a lot. Whiskey. Straight.
A glass of it. Gulp 'em down. God knows how many he'd drink in
one evening. But I never saw him drunk. Jolly all the time."

As for his romantic life, it was complicated. At twenty-three,
Clarence married eighteen-year-old Helen Bouldin in Baltimore;
even though they never divorced, in 1927, he married Fannie Lee
Taylor of Fredericksburg, Virginia, with whom he moved to Harlem,
where, with Fannie Lee's knowledge, he had a long-term relationship
with a white woman named Atlanta Shepherd. The woman Fannie Lee referred to as her "wife-in-law" was a dime-a-dance dancer
at Remie's Dancehall on Sixty-Sixth Street near Broadway; she and
Clarence had one daughter, Mary, with whom Billie was never close.

While Billie was appearing with Hollon, she and her mother
moved back to Harlem, which in the early 1930s was still in the
throes of the Harlem Renaissance even though, like the rest of
the country, the economics of the community suffered as a result

of the stock market collapse in the autumn of 1929. The Apollo
Theater remained a cultural touchstone; the Cotton Club featured
some of the most accomplished African-American talent in the
music business, from Ethel Waters to Bill "Bojangles" Robinson to
Duke Ellington; and cabarets and after-hours clubs thrived as white
audiences journeyed uptown to take in black artists working in the
smaller venues. In the spring of 1930, Sadie and Billie took a room
on West 127th Street—in time they moved to a larger apartment
in the neighborhood—near where Sadie worked in the kitchen at a
restaurant named Mexico's. Billie worked there as a singing waitress.
Before long, she began to sing at other nightspots as well, among
them Covan's and the Alhambra Bar and Grill. But Billie's fortunes
changed when she started to appear at Pod's and Jerry's, one of the
popular jazz spots in Harlem. Her tenure there, which made her
a "name" in Harlem, established her as an up-and-coming singer
capable of going as far in the business as her considerable talent
would take her.

In her autobiography, Billie described her audition at Pod's and
Jerry's this way: Because her mother couldn't pay the rent, "she got
a notice that the law was going to put us out on the street," which
prompted Billie to go out and get a job. After trying other clubs,
she ended up at Pod's and Jerry's, where "I think I talked to Jerry,"
who, once she danced for him, rejected her as a dancer. But the
piano player, as fate would have it, asked her to sing "Travelin' All
Alone." When she did, "the whole joint quieted down. If someone
had dropped a pin, it would have sounded like a bomb. When I
finished, everybody in the joint was crying in their beer." Jerry had
no choice but to hire her as a singer. And *that's* how she landed the
job that allowed her to earn enough money for her mother to pay the
rent. It was a sensational, a-star-is-born moment worthy of a Hollywood rags-to-riches story. Unfortunately, the episode existed only
in Billie's imagination, until it made its way into the pages of her
autobiography.

The actual turn of events was more down-to-earth. When she

was out barhopping one night in Harlem, she met a young piano player named Bobby Henderson. It was he, impressed by her singing, who took her to Pod's and Jerry's, where he worked. Once she sang for Jerry Preston, the club's owner, he hired her on the spot. It was a simple enough interaction, the way auditions in the nightlife business were normally conducted—much more believable than the fabricated escapade Billie invented. A newspaper columnist provided an accurate picture of her at the club after she had worked there for a while: "She was then about fifteen. She was dressed in a gray skirt and sweater, and she was barefoot. People gave her quarters and change to sing requests. Long after daylight, when I left the place, she left too and ran up the street—still barefoot." By her birthday, she and Henderson were dating. "I never met anybody like her," Henderson said. "She was more of a hip woman than I was a hip young man. I was just a square. She was a *woman,* and it surprised me when I learned she was sixteen years old." Their romance became serious; soon they were engaged. "He was her first real boyfriend," according to a mutual friend, "and a gentleman every which way." With the buzz she received at Pod's and Jerry's, she was offered other gigs. Then everything changed for her in early 1933 thanks to a fortuitous encounter with a jazz fan who had the power to help her in ways few people could.

His name was John Hammond, and he was a son of privilege. His father, John Henry Hammond, sat on the board of ten corporations and served as a partner in a white-shoe law firm; his mother, Emily Vanderbilt Sloane, was the granddaughter of William H. Vanderbilt, the oldest son of magnate Commodore Cornelius Vanderbilt. John grew up in a granite mansion at 9 East Ninety-First Street, graduated preparatory school from the Hotchkiss School, often visited his Vanderbilt grandmother in her mansion on Fifth Avenue, and dropped out of Yale University to pursue his love of music, taking a job at a radio station before being appointed as a recording director at Columbia Records. At twenty-three, he was only a few years older than Billie. Later, Hammond documented their first encounter: "Early in 1933 . . . I dropped in at Monette Moore's place on 133rd Street, a stop on my Harlem rounds. I was expecting to see Monette, a fine blues singer. Instead, a young girl named Billie Holiday was substituting because Monette had gotten a part in a Broadway show with Clifton Webb." (The musical revue, also starring Imogene Coca, was *Flying Colors*.) "Billie's accompanist was Dot Hill, and among the first songs she sang was 'Wouldja for a Big Red Apple?' . . . [Billie] was not a blues singer, but she sang popular songs in a manner that made them completely her own. She had an uncanny ear, an excellent memory for lyrics, and she sang with an exquisite sense of phrasing. . . . Further, she was absolutely beautiful. . . . I decided that night that she was the best jazz singer I had ever heard."

Three weeks later, Monette Moore's club closed, and Billie moved on to sing at other venues. "Night after night," Hammond wrote, "I went to the . . . Harlem speakeasies to hear Billie, who moved around, living off tips and whatever salary she was offered in each place." In April, Hammond gave Billie her first mention in the press, using the alternative spelling of her last name she preferred at first. "This month," he wrote in his column in *Melody Maker,* a weekly British music magazine, "there has been a real find in the person of a singer named Billie Halliday. Although only eighteen she weighs over two hundred pounds, is incredibly beautiful, and sings as well as anybody I ever heard."

Hammond brought others in the industry to hear her— "everybody I knew," he recalled. One was Benny Goodman, who, as Billie remembered, "was not [yet] Benny Goodman; he was just another musician. He worked in the studio band, down at NBC, and he came up one night and he just thought I was wonderful." The decision was made for Goodman and Holiday to record two songs together in a session produced by Hammond. "Benny signed his first contract with American Columbia and dates were set for November [on the twenty-seventh and on December 18]," Hammond wrote. "It was an event in many ways. The titles we recorded were 'Riffin' the Scotch' and 'Your Mother's Son-in-Law.' This was not only Billie's first recording session, but the first time Benny had recorded with a Negro musician—Shirley Clay [on trumpet]—in his band. . . . Goodman and Holiday each had taken a giant step forward." As for Billie, she remembered the trepidation she felt: "I got there and I was afraid to sing in the mic, because I never saw a microphone before, and I said, 'Why do I have to sing in that thing?' Why can't I just sing like I do at the club?' I was scared to death of it."

Around this time, Billie enjoyed another milestone in her career when she made her debut at the Apollo Theater, appearing as a supporting act for one week starting on November 24, 1934. She was accompanied on piano by Bobby Henderson. (In an advertisement for the date, the names of both performers were spelled differently: "Billy Halliday" for Billie, "Bobbie Henderson" for Bobby.) Their romance came to an end when Billie discovered he was already married—to not one woman but two; he soon fled New York City to avoid legal action from the wives. "Now that the engagement between Bobbie Henderson, the pianist, and herself has gone the way of many," a columnist in *The New York Age* reported, "Billie Halliday, the blues singer, is stepping up the pulses of Sugar Hill debs with her pulsating articulation of 'Butterfly' at the Sunset."

As an indication of the strides Billie was making in her nascent career, she appeared in December 1934 in an uncredited role in *Symphony in Black: A Rhapsody of Negro Life,* a nine-minute-and-forty-one-second black-and-white short film directed by Fred Waller with music composed by Duke Ellington. His orchestra was featured in the film, which was shot at the Astoria Studios in Queens for Paramount Pictures. Playing a young woman rejected (and thrown to the sidewalk) by her lover, who is involved with another woman, Billie sings, with palpable poignancy, "The Saddest Tale" (also known as "Blues"). The film was released in 1935. Her appearance in *Symphony in Black,* one journalist noted, "would define her as the unofficial queen of torch songs, typical of the Tin Pan Alley era."

In April 1935, Billie played her second engagement at the Apollo as a featured artist with Ralph Cooper; the lineup, which also included Apollo regular Pigmeat Markham, was extended a second week because of sellout business. In July, Billie forged one of the most significant relationships of her career when John Hammond arranged for her to sing vocals for Teddy Wilson and His Orchestra. On July 2, in a session for Columbia's Brunswick Records produced by Hammond, among the numbers Billie cut were "I Wished on a Moon," "What a Little Moonlight Can Do," and "Miss Brown to You," songs producer George Avakian would later argue constituted "the immortal Billie Holiday." In another session on the thirty-first, the songs included "I'm Painting the Town Red" and "It's Too Hot for Words." These songs were released for play on both radio stations and jukeboxes, the latter of which represented a lucrative business at the time. "Vocals," the *Fort Worth Star-Telegram* observed, "are sung by Miss Billie Holiday, former Harlem nightclub singer, and regarded by Wilson as a 'natural' in presenting the peculiar rhythm of his 'swing' music." The songs became so popular Billie was asked to sing in two additional sessions with Wilson later in 1935 in October and December. "She appeared to have arrived on the scene from nowhere," music journalist Max Jones later wrote, "fully mature as a girl of eighteen, perhaps nineteen, singing with Benny Goodman and then with Teddy Wilson. And, though young, she had a voice that was fresh, but there was something . . . in the way she handled rhythm and in the placement of the notes and timing that was in advance of anything we had heard to that time."

Two years later, she was performing at Clark Monroe's Uptown House on West 134th Street when she received tragic news. On February 23, a telephone call from Texas informed her that, while touring with the Don Redman band, her father had died in a hospital in Dallas. In the future, Billie would describe the events she claimed led to his death: "He had caught a funny kind of pneumonia. It wasn't the pneumonia that killed him, it was Dallas, Texas. That's where he was . . . going from hospital to hospital trying to get help. But none of them would even so much as take his temperature or take him in. . . . Pop finally found a veteran's hospital [and] they finally let him in the Jim Crow ward down there." It was too late, according to Billie; he died soon afterwards. As with other details Billie claimed about her father, these facts were not accurate. To cite his death certificate, Clarence Holiday was admitted on February 21 to St. Paul Sanitarium, where he died two days later of "influenzal pneumonia." He was in Texas only two days before his admission to the hospital. Linda Kuehl documented his death: "[It was] ordinary influenzal pneumonia—nothing 'funny' as Billie had it. [St. Paul was] a white Catholic hospital run by the Daughters of Charity since the 1890s. It was not a veteran's [hospital], and it did not discriminate against his race. The racial aspect entered the picture vis-à-vis the mythical death of Bessie Smith, who died in Clarksdale, Mississippi, almost seven months to the day after Clarence Holiday died in Dallas." It was John Hammond, in fact, who erroneously reported in *Down Beat* that Smith died, after being involved in a serious car crash, because an all-white hospital refused to admit her—a false tale that endured for years until it was ultimately refuted by eyewitnesses. Edward Albee even wrote a play, *The Death of Bessie Smith,* which turned out to be inaccurate in its depiction of events because he based his play on Hammond's misinformation.

As she prepared for her father's funeral, Billie suffered a second blow when she discovered he had two families, a black one with Fannie and a white one with Atlanta. This revelation made the abandonment she and her mother suffered all the more painful. In time, Billie confessed how she felt about her father to Irene Wilson Kitchens: "I know my dad didn't do my mama right. . . . I think things would have been a lot different for me in life if my daddy *did* do my mama right."

All through this ordeal, Billie continued to perform at the Uptown House. One night, Hammond brought in another heavyweight to hear her—Count Basie, who was impressed by what he heard. "She had," Basie believed, "a really strange way of delivering a song. All so wonderful." By March 13, Billie had joined the Count Basie Orchestra, earning seventy-five dollars a week (from which she had to pay all her expenses, including travel). During her time with Basie, Billie formed friendships with fellow musicians—among them Buck Clayton, Jo Jones, Harry "Sweets" Edison, and Lester Young—that would endure for the rest of her life. "Everybody loved her," Basie remembered. "Everybody got along with her. She got along with all the guys. . . . And as for me, I'd look forward for the night to go to work to hear her sing. She just killed me." But Billie's association with the Basie orchestra did not even last a year. On February 11, 1938, a Friday, Billie wrote to a friend: "I've lost my job with Count Basie. I got my three week notice in the mail yesterday. Willard [Alexander] said he had too [sic] let me go because he had too [sic] cut down on expenses but that's not it. I cussed John Hammond out"—Hammond had discovered Basie as well as Billie—"at rehearsal before we went in Iowa State, an[d] after that he gave a party but I wasn't there. We haven't spoke[n]. . . . I could never sing with the band again. . . . Well, honey, right now I'm as low as a snake, don't know what I'm going to do, but I guess something will happen, it's just got too [sic] or else I'll be in the poor house by Tuesday." Eventually, Billie advanced a different story: "Basie had too many managers," she complained to a journalist, "too many guys behind the scenes who told everybody what to do. The Count and I got along fine. . . . But it was this and that, all the time, and I got fed up with it. Basie didn't fire me; I gave him my notice." For whatever reason the separation occurred, Billie made her final appearance with Basie on March 3, 1938, the closing night of a run Basie played at the Apollo Theater.

Six days later, Billie had a tryout with Artie Shaw and His Rhythm Makers at Madison Square Garden in New York City. Shaw was a celebrated clarinet player; his orchestra was a popular touring band. The tryout was so successful Billie was hired at once; she joined Shaw for a three-month stand at the Roseland-State Ballroom in Boston. The move was highly unusual, not to mention controversial, since a black woman would be fronting an all-white orchestra in the era of Jim Crow. "The contract given Billie to act as a part of the outfit is an indefinite one," a press report noted, "and unless racial prejudices intervene, she will remain with the band from now on." She sang with Shaw throughout 1938, but, as it happened, racial prejudices *did* intervene, particularly when the band toured the South, where Billie was not allowed to eat in the same restaurant or sleep in the same hotel as the rest of the band, but also in New York City, where she was discriminated against at the hotel at which the band was appearing—Hotel Lincoln. Owner Maria Kramer worried about Billie encountering the hotel's white patrons. "The hotel management," Billie said, "told me I had to use the back door. . . . I had to ride up and down in the freight elevator"—*this* at a hotel named for the president who signed the Emancipation Proclamation. And when Billie was not allowed to appear on the Old Gold radio show broadcast from the hotel—"Artie said he couldn't let me sing," she claimed—she quit the band on December 10. Afterwards, Shaw attempted to shift the blame, saying at one point, "The bigger our success, the more dissatisfaction there seemed to be in the band. Billie Holiday, who had gotten along fine with [fellow vocalist] Helen Forrest, began to resent her." Shaw failed to point out that Billie's displeasure stemmed from the fact that Forrest, who was white, was treated differently by management and allowed to make media appearances forbidden to Billie because she was black.

Billie was not unemployed for long. On December 18, one week after leaving Shaw, she opened a new club, where her residency changed her life forever. Up until now, nightlife venues in New York had been segregated. Even the Cotton Club, which featured black entertainment, seated an all-white audience on the main floor. In this cultural climate, Barney Josephson, a shoe salesman from New Jersey, came up with the idea of opening a club where integrated entertainment would play to an integrated audience—the first club of its type in the country. To line up his talent, Josephson asked John Hammond to be his musical consultant. The club was Café Society, located in Greenwich Village, and for its first headliner Hammond suggested Billie. "I opened at Café Society as an unknown," she wrote; "I left two years later as a star."

4.

Her years of performing with Basie and Shaw, then at Café Society, were far from her thoughts on this evening in July 1958 as Billie sat in the back seat of a private car on her way to Newark. Tonight, she was en route to make yet another appearance on *Art Ford's Jazz Party,* one week after she had last been on the show. The talent fee of three hundred dollars was incidental, but if sales for *Lady in Satin* were boosted by an additional appearance on the most widely watched jazz program on television, she was happy to do it.

When she arrived at the Mosque Theatre, she went upstairs to the studio, where she saw familiar faces. Among the musicians on the show were Buck Clayton, Osie Johnson, Mary Osborne, and Harry Sheppard. This evening, Billie decided to wear an off-the-shoulder evening gown with a red floral print. Imbibing once again the vodka and orange juice—during an Art Ford broadcast Billie always seemed to be holding a white paper cup when she was not on camera—she stood off to the side to watch the top of the show. When it was time for Billie to perform, she took her place and waited for Ford to introduce her with his usual flair.

"The mood is right tonight," he said in his quiet, soothing tone. "Georgie"—Auld, the tenor saxophonist and tonight's bandleader—"we have the time. There are no rules because when she sings"—meaning Billie—"there's excitement. She sings a song from the heart. . . . [She] might do anything that's on her mind. Whatever it is, I know will be something special."

With that setup—another one of Ford's free-form odes to Billie—the camera cut to her. "Hit it," she ordered matter-of-factly and commenced "Moanin' Low," a love song about a man who is "mean as can be." Dark yet upbeat, the song was a lament about a man who treats his woman "poorly," a man who easily could have been Louis McKay.

For her second number, which she performed after the musicians played a medley of instrumentals, Billie stood beside the piano as Ford spoke to the camera. "I'm going to break the rules and ask for a request tonight," he said warmly. "Billie, because you're sort of a special friend of mine, would you do 'Don't Explain' for Art Ford?"

"You bet," Billie said.

As the camera lingered on her, she allowed herself to slip into the lyrics of the song and sing it with a lilting sadness, a moving gesture for her friend. The number always brought back memories of her failed marriage to Jimmy Monroe, about whom it had been written, but she used that pain to produce an emotion-charged performance.

Finally, when it was time for her last song, Ford gave Billie his customary introduction. "We're especially thrilled to have Billie Holiday," he said, "because when Billie sings, it is jazz history." Billie began "When Your Lover Has Gone," a melancholy tune that con-

cluded with the lines "like faded flowers, life can't mean anything /
When your lover is gone."

With the three songs she sang, Billie left a lasting impression on
the audience at home as well as the musicians and crew in the studio. Among them was vibraphonist Harry Sheppard, who remembers: "Billie was very quiet, very sweet, very nice to everybody, very
together. She was going downhill at the time. It was sad to see. But
she got up there, and she did it. She knocked everybody out." Ford
was gratified by the performance, as his son Arthur Ford, Jr., recalls:
"He knew Billie personally. He was fond of her. He was proud of
getting her on the show. He felt she was someone who didn't get
some of the appreciation she deserved because of her race. That was
not something he agreed with." Yet others noticed Billie was suffering from deteriorating health. Buck Clayton, a friend for many years,
realized that "Billie was more and more in a bad way. She was very
thin, her skin was sallow, and her voice cracked—which was something I never thought I would hear."

It would be one year from that day, on July 17, that Billie Holiday died, in the early morning hours in a hospital room in Manhattan at about the same time of day she was born, only to assume her
place as one of the fabled figures in jazz history.

CHAPTER 5

Bitter Crop

Billie Holiday performing in the studio session during which she recorded "Strange Fruit." The session, which featured eight musicians including Jimmy McLin on guitar, occurred at World Broadcasting Studios in New York City on April 20, 1939. Despite controversies surrounding the song, she sang the groundbreaking anti-lynching anthem for the rest of her life.

I.

It was a pleasant summer evening in Milwaukee, the city on Lake Michigan in the eastern part of Wisconsin known for its breweries, and Billie was waiting to go onstage at the Brass Rail, a modest-sized jazz club located downtown on North Third next to the Princess Theatre. She had played Milwaukee a decade ago when she appeared at the Pabst Theater on an all-star concert bill that included Miles Davis, Fats Navarro, and Max Roach, but she had never worked this room. The nightlife business was full of colorful characters, and the club's owner did not disappoint. At six-eight and more than 320 pounds, Isadore "Izzy" Pogrob was a giant of a man who cruised around Milwaukee in a white Cadillac. One employee remembered that "eating was his favorite thing to do next to flashing his giant roll of cold hard cash." Within two years, Pogrob would be found dead on the side of a country road outside Milwaukee, shot in the head nine times, likely the target of a mob hit. Such were the goings-on in some of the out-of-town clubs Billie was forced to play in the summer of 1958 because government officials in New York City refused to grant her a cabaret card.

To his credit, Pogrob created a welcoming atmosphere at his club, which was one reason why he attracted some of the most prominent names in jazz. Just the previous night, Count Basie and his eighteen-piece band played the room for one night only. Now Billie was set to start a six-night stand from July 29 until August 3. Judging from her schedule, it was hard to believe she was having health issues. On Sunday, July 27, she appeared at the Oakdale Jazz Festival in Wallingford, Connecticut, where she shared the stage with leg-endary sidemen Coleman Hawkins, Buck Clayton, and Henry "Red" Allen. Monday was a travel day; now here she was ready to open at the Brass Rail, backed by Mal Waldron on piano and Tommy Sheri-dan and His Trio, a local combo from Milwaukee.

When she was announced to the eager crowd, Billie took the stage dressed in a sleek, low-cut evening gown and assumed her place at the microphone in the familiar glow of the spotlight. Per-haps she was tired from her travels, perhaps she was not feeling well, but tonight it took her a couple of songs before she fell into a rhythm and was able, as one of the city's music critics observed, "to convince the audience that she still had the blues touch." She connected with "What a Little Moonlight Can Do," and when she completed "God Bless the Child" she delivered it so well "there were sighs from the audience." Afterwards, she "made several other standard blues num-bers sound just right," among them "When Your Lover Has Gone," "Willow Weep for Me," and "I Only Have Eyes for You." As she completed her last number and started to exit the stage, there it was once again, what motivated her to keep going even when she did not feel like it—the resounding ovation from the audience.

After a successful run at the Brass Rail, Billie closed on Sun-day and traveled to Cleveland, where she was scheduled to open at the Modern Jazz Room, in the Central Market area on East Fourth Street, for one week running from August 4 to 10. When she had appeared in Cleveland in 1951 at Lindsay's Sky Bar, the engagement, according to a local musician, helped make Sky Bar Cleveland's "first real jazz club." Now, seven years later, in announcing her run at the Modern Jazz Room, regarded as another one of the city's "legendary rooms," the *Cleveland Plain Dealer* wrote: "Her unique phrasing and earthy emotional voice has influenced most of the current singers since she was discovered by John Hammond and Benny Goodman in the early thirties." That was the case with Marilyn Holderfield, an aspiring jazz singer who came to the Modern Jazz Room to hear Billie—"my idol," as she called her. Following one show, Holderfield was able to speak with Billie. "I couldn't believe it," Holderfield later recalled. "I was trembling. She was beautiful." Seizing the opportu-

nity to ask her for advice, Holderfield, just twenty-one, confided in
Billie that her parents did not want her to sing jazz. Billie reached
out and clutched the young woman's hand.

"Just do it your way!" she said emphatically.

"Billie encouraged me," Holderfield remembered. "She was so
sweet. And this was the last year of her life. I will never forget that."

After she closed in Cleveland, Billie returned home to New
York, where she was gratified by the response she was receiving to
the rerelease afforded a group of her older songs. Earlier in the summer, about a month after *Lady in Satin* came out from Columbia
Records, Commodore Records released *Billie Holiday—Twelve of Her
Greatest Interpretations,* a compilation album comprised of songs Billie originally recorded for the label years ago. From 1939, there were
four songs—"Yesterdays," "Fine and Mellow," "I Gotta Right to Sing
the Blues," and "Strange Fruit"—recorded with Frankie Newton's
band, which featured, among others, Kenneth Hollon on tenor saxophone, Johnny Williams on bass, and Sonny White on piano. Eight
songs—"I'll Get By," "I'll Be Seeing You," "Funny That Way," and
five others—were selected from three recording sessions conducted
in 1944 during which Billie was backed by Eddie Heywood and His
Orchestra, which featured, among others, Doc Cheatham on trumpet, John Simmons on bass, and Sidney "Big Sid" Catlett on drums.
"What you have here," author and musician Carlton Brown wrote
in the album's liner notes, "tell[s] what it is to be (or to have been,
and to always have in your bones) poor and black, hungry and hurt
and in terrible trouble. . . . It is in the bending of melodic lines, the
changing of notes and accents, into a new composition whose color
and design express feelings too deep for words."

If *Lady in Satin* was earning mixed reviews, the critical response
to the Commodore rerelease could not have been more different. The
notices were among the most effusive Billie enjoyed in her career.
Jazz critic C. H. Garrigues, who placed Billie within the context
of "the tragic story of her bitter, hopeless fight against the narcotics
evil," concluded his review by contending that "if jazz had produced

nothing else than these dozen songs (or even the four best of them) it would have justified itself." Of the 1939 songs, *The New York Times* believed Billie "achieved a happy conjunction of originality of conception, matured discipline in performance and a rich and flexible voice that gave the pieces recorded that year . . . a depth and emotional intensity that are paralleled in jazz only in the very best of Bessie Smith's work." And music writer Ralph Gleason gushed in his syndicated column: "These are the great Billie Holiday recordings. . . . The history of jazz singing cannot be written without these records nor can the history of jazz. They are timeless, magnificent, and absolutely unique."

In the August heat, Billie often spent her day in the living room of her apartment listening to albums on the phonograph. Her current favorite of her records remained *Lady in Satin,* but it was hard to ignore the eulogistic reaction the Commodore collection was receiving. The songs on the album, four of them recorded almost two decades ago, were now regarded as classics. Of the songs, there was one, more than the others, that had had a profound effect on her life. She had written songs like "God Bless the Child," "Lady Sings the Blues," and "Don't Explain," with which she became closely associated, and she recorded any number of the popular standards of the day, but one song, with its graphic imagery, emotional honesty, and cultural impact, defined her in a way that could not compare to any other song she recorded. The song was "Strange Fruit." And, as it happened, Billie came into possession of the song only because, after quitting Artie Shaw's band, she agreed to headline at a new nightclub opening in Greenwich Village called Café Society.

2.

The club was the creation of Barney Josephson. Born in Trenton, New Jersey, in 1902, he was the youngest of six children whose parents were Jewish immigrants from Latvia, a small country in eastern Europe on the Baltic Sea. "His father, a cobbler, died shortly after his birth," *The New York Times* later reported. "His mother, a seamstress, worked for a ladies' tailor. Two of his brothers, Leon and

Louis, became lawyers." Graduating from Trenton High School, Barney entered the footwear business, first selling shoes for his brother David in Trenton, then working as a buyer and window trimmer for a store in Atlantic City that paid him forty dollars a week during the Great Depression. But Barney longed for a life in New York City, so in the mid-1930s he moved there with, as the *Times* noted, "a vague notion about opening a nightclub." He had become interested in jazz as a result of trips he made to Harlem to hear Duke Ellington and Ethel Waters at the Cotton Club. What he noticed was that the club, like so many places of business throughout the country, was segregated. The entertainment was almost all black, but, as Josephson later said, "the [black] patrons were seated at the back, in a segregated section—in a *Harlem* nightclub!" The American South operated under the constraints of the Jim Crow laws, yet northern states propagated their own, often more subtle, version of Jim Crow, even in New York, even in Harlem. The nightlife community was no exception to the prevailing prejudice of the day, so Josephson decided to challenge the status quo. "I wanted [to open] a club," he said, "where blacks and whites worked together behind the footlights and sat together out front. There wasn't, so far as I [knew], a place like it in New York or in the whole country."

At that time, while there was sympathy among political progressives to address racial inequality, one organization that was uniquely aggressive in advocating for an agenda of reform on race was the Communist Party of the United States of America. Founded in 1919, by the 1930s, as America languished in the throes of the Depression, it boasted a membership of more than fifty thousand. Naturally, the party was outspoken on issues concerning labor and workers' rights, but also vital to its mission were matters of race. "The Communist Party was one of the main groups that took up the cause of racial desegregation," historian Philip Yale Nicholson says. "It was the Communist Party that took up the case of the Scottsboro Boys in 1932 [when a group of African-American teenagers were wrongly convicted of rape in a trial in Scottsboro, Alabama] with a mixed outcome. The American communists saw racial issues as part of the class struggle in the United States. They saw the way race was used to divide the working class. They were ahead of everyone else on the left in making sure they included black people as members. The American Socialist Party and the labor movement still allowed local chapters to bar black members. The Communist Party was a vanguard on the issue of race."

Its position on racial equality was one reason why Barney Josephson joined the Communist Party, but his enthusiasm for the organization was nothing compared with that of his brother Leon. A lawyer practicing in Trenton, Leon, who would later often be referred to as an "avowed" communist, became so involved in party operations that he found himself a close associate of Gerhart Eisler, whom *The New York Times* described as the "reputed Communist leader in the U.S." The Eisler-Josephson connection was strong enough that at one point Richard Nixon, then a congressman from California, declared that Leon Josephson "is just as important as Eisler." One episode from 1935 revealed, to both the American government and the public, Josephson's true allegiance. "On March 6, 1935," the *Times* reported, "Josephson was one of eight, including three Americans, who were arrested in Copenhagen, Denmark, for possessing fraudulent passports. Josephson was released later, but two of the Americans, George Mink and Nicholas Sherman, alias Shireman, were sentenced to eighteen months in jail for espionage. [A government investigation] said that Mink had been identified by a number of witnesses . . . as a member of the Joint State Political Directorate (OGPU), the Russian secret police organization. . . . Josephson was described by a witness . . . as a member of the OGPU."

The men arrested in Copenhagen were allegedly associated with a Soviet spy ring that was planning to assassinate Adolf Hitler. Barney claimed he was clueless about his brother's involvement with the plot until the arrest hit the newspapers. He would recall reading an article in *The New York Times:* "I read, 'A group of thirty people have been arrested and there are two Americans involved. One of the Americans is Leon Josephson, an attorney from Trenton, New Jersey.' I suddenly became ill and thought, so that's why my brother has been in Europe!" There was little mystery about Leon's politics. "He was a Marxist," his son Lee Josephson says. "He had read the political writings of Karl Marx as a young man, and he believed Marx was correct."

In the fall of 1938, Barney acted on his dream of opening a nightclub. He borrowed six thousand dollars from "two friends of his brother Leon," as it would be reported. While Barney remained a member of the Communist Party for only six months before he withdrew, rumors would persist that the start-up capital for his nightclub came not from Leon's friends but from the Communist Party itself. Whatever the source, Barney leased an L-shaped basement space capable of seating 220 patrons at 2 Sheridan Square in the heart of Greenwich Village at a rent of two hundred dollars a month. He commissioned eight artists, among them Abe Birnbaum and Adolf Dehn, to paint clever murals on the walls. He decided his patrons would be accommodated by a staff that featured, as one reporter noted, "a doorman wearing worn-out gloves [and] waiters clad in tails." He gave the place its own slogan: "The right place for the wrong people." All this was cleverly calculated to set the club apart from venues preferred by the entertainment and political establishment, like El Morocco and the Stork Club. Clare Boothe Luce suggested its name: Café Society. The cover charge would be two dollars during the week and two dollars and fifty cents on weekends. Dinner would cost one dollar and fifty cents, a beer sixty-five cents, and a well drink seventy-five cents.

John Hammond helped Josephson line up the club's initial bill, which included the Frankie Newton Band, Big Joe Turner, and the Boogie Woogie Trio (Meade Lux Lewis, Albert Ammons, Pete Johnson), with Jack Gilford as master of ceremonies and Billie Holiday as the headliner. (Billie's first accompanist, Billy Kyle, was quickly replaced by Sonny White.) When Café Society opened on December 28, 1938, it was instantly de rigueur. "This was what I'd been waiting for," Billie later wrote. "I was so happy."

She was earning one hundred and fifty dollars a week, but, more importantly, she felt as if she was making a social statement by headlining the iconoclastic club. Since Leon Josephson, as Barney's silent partner, was a constant presence there, Billie must have known the club's connection to the Communist Party. After all,

Leon's involvement in the Soviet plot to assassinate Hitler received coverage in the press. Hammond later admitted he was "concerned about [Leon's] role in Barney's new club," but, ultimately, he disregarded his doubts. So did Billie—if she ever had any. In her view, one continuing issue that needed to be confronted in America was racism, however that could be accomplished.

Café Society, according to one reporter, "admitted customers and showcased talent regardless of race, tweaked high society, eliminated chorus lines and cigarette girls, treated its employees well, served good food, and offered pointed political satire." Because of its notoriety, the club attracted a sizable clientele right away. Not surprisingly, the place was frequented by a notable African-American following, particularly members of the black entertainment and intellectual worlds, among them Richard Wright, who was a vocal supporter of the Communist Party. But because of its raison d'être, the club also catered to a large audience of white progressives, from figures like S. J. Perelman and Leonard Bernstein to members of the Roosevelt family, including Eleanor Roosevelt. "Although it was filled virtually every night, mostly with Villagers," *The New York Times* noted, "Mr. Josephson lost money in the first year." His desire to attract even more headline-grabbing attention may have contributed to his decision to consider a new song entitled "Strange Fruit" to be performed in the club when it was brought to him in early 1939.

In her autobiography, Billie described how the song came about: "The germ of the [tune] was in a poem written by Lewis Allan. I first met him [and when] he showed me that poem, I dug it right off. [Allan] suggested that Sonny White, who had been my accompanist, and I turn it into music. So, the three of us got together and did the job in about three weeks. I also got a wonderful assist from Danny Mendelsohn, another writer who had done arrangements for me. He helped me with arranging the song and rehearsing it patiently." That passage may have provided yet another scintillating tale for her audience to relish, but none of the facts were true.

The creator of the song was Abel Meeropol, who was born in

1903 and raised in a Russian Jewish family in Manhattan. He held a bachelor's degree from City College (the college yearbook declared him "a gifted poet" and "the class genius") and a master of arts in English literature from Harvard University. An English teacher at DeWitt Clinton High School in the Bronx, Meeropol was an aspiring writer and a member of the Communist Party, having joined around 1932. He contributed to the Young Communist League, the Theatre Arts Committee, and the Lincoln Brigade, which was why he chose to publish under the pseudonym Lewis Allan (an homage to a stillborn son who would have been given that name); he did not wish his leftist politics to interfere with his ability to earn a living. Still, he was sympathetic to the party's advocacy for racial equality, particularly its support of federal anti-lynching legislation. Throughout the Jim Crow era, lynching posed a danger to blacks, especially in the South. In the 1930s, there was a concerted effort to pass legislation in the U.S. Congress to outlaw the practice. Meeropol saw his opportunity to contribute to the political debate when he ran across a picture in a civil rights magazine. "Way back in the early thirties," he said, "I saw a photograph of a lynching published in a magazine devoted to the exposure and elimination of racial injustice. It was a shocking photograph and haunted me for days." The picture of two black teenagers, Thomas Shipp and Abram Smith, lynched in Marion, Indiana, in 1930, was taken by Lawrence Beitler.

Meeropol was so moved he wrote a poem based on the photograph entitled "Bitter Fruit." It was accepted by *New Masses,* a communist journal, but when the editors failed to run it, Meeropol submitted it to the *New York Teacher,* a publication affiliated with the Teachers Union, where it appeared in January 1937. Soon, he decided to turn the poem into a song and approached musicians, among them Earl Robinson, a Communist Party member known for composing the labor anthem "Joe Hill," until he decided to write the music himself. Because the song consisted of twelve lines that did not follow the traditional verse-chorus progression, the music was intrinsically unique; one musicologist later argued it was based on the Kaddish, the Jewish prayer for the dead. Over the coming months, the song, now entitled "Strange Fruit," was sung at leftist gatherings, often by Meeropol's wife, Anne. In 1938, Laura Duncan, who was African American, sang the song at an anti-fascist festival held at Madison Square Garden. Hoping to find a way for the song to reach a wider audience, Meeropol concluded he needed to get it to well-connected members of the entertainment community. He believed he could trust Barney Josephson, whose profile had been elevated by the successful launch of Café Society, because they were both sympathetic to the Communist Party. Or as Barney's son Edward Josephson puts it, "They traveled in similar left-wing circles." Meeropol and Josephson had a mutual friend in Robert Gordon, who shared their political views; he could easily make the introduction. So, in January 1939, Meeropol stopped by Café Society one afternoon and showed the song to Josephson. When Meeropol played it for him on the piano, Josephson felt immediately it was right for Billie. As soon as she came in for the evening's shows, Josephson had Meeropol play the song for her.

Over the years, some individuals attempted to marginalize Billie by suggesting she did not understand the song, which was untrue. While Meeropol and Josephson were mindful of racism, Billie encountered it all her life, particularly during her tenure with the Artie Shaw band. In addition, Lester Young recounted to her an episode from his youth when, at age fourteen, he was forced to help a friend escape a lynch mob that was out to kill him. The ordeal left a chilling impression on Lester that he carried with him for the rest of his life. Billie knew about the horrors of lynching from friends and press accounts. She experienced Jim Crow firsthand. She more than understood the virulent racism depicted in "Strange Fruit."

Billie was determined to try out the song at Café Society as soon as possible. Since she was performing three sets a night (at eight, midnight, and two) seven nights a week—she committed to such a grueling schedule because she wanted to help the club succeed—she had ample opportunity to see how the song would play to an audience. She had concerns. After all, the song's imagery was stark and disturbing. The opening couplet sets the stage: "Southern trees bear a strange fruit / Blood on the leaves and blood at the root." After an ominous sense of foreboding is created, the central image comes: "Black body swinging in the Southern breeze / Strange fruit hanging from the poplar trees." Next there's a close-up on the body: "Pastoral scene of the gallant South / The bulging eyes and the twisted mouth." And more details: "Scent of magnolia sweet and fresh / And the sudden smell of burning flesh!" The listener learns what will happen to the lynched body: "Here is a fruit for the crows to pluck / For the rain to gather, for the wind to suck / For the sun to rot, for a tree to drop." Finally, the song summarizes the tableau it has painted: "Here is a strange and bitter crop."

"The first time Billie sang the song at the club, the tempo was too fast," says Madeline Lee Gilford, the wife of Jack Gilford, the club's emcee, "and when she came offstage, Jack said, 'It's a dirge, Lady.' When she slowed it down for the next set, Jack had trouble going on after her because the crowd was so broken up. Eventually, she ended each set with the song, and nobody came on after her. Nobody could."

Indeed, once Josephson realized how powerful Billie's performance was, he instituted strict stage directions for the performance. "Before she began," a journalistic account later reported, "all service stopped. Waiters, cashiers, busboys were all immobilized. The room went completely dark, save for a pin spot on Holiday's face." During the intro to the song, played by Sonny White and the Frankie Newton band, she stood silently with her eyes closed as if she were summoning up the ghosts of past victims. Then she sang the song with a simple, haunting delivery. By the end of the song, tears were streaming down her face. "When she finished and the lights went out, she would walk off the stage, and no matter how thunderous the ovation, she was never to return for a bow."

The response to "Strange Fruit" was even more intense than Josephson had anticipated. Word spread quickly that Billie Holiday was ending each set with the performance of a song that had to be seen. Naturally, Billie wanted to record "Strange Fruit" and release it as a single. In March, she approached Columbia Records, who rejected her request to record the song. She received no help from John Hammond. "He disliked 'Strange Fruit,'" jazz historian Michael Brooks wrote, "and, despite Billie's pleas, refused to record it, but he and Columbia had no objection to her doing it [elsewhere]. So she decided to approach a friend who owned a record store, located on East 42nd Street, that was well-known within the jazz community because of its extensive offerings of jazz records."

The friend was Milt Gabler, who as a teenager worked in the Commodore Radio Corporation, a popular radio supply store located in Midtown Manhattan that was owned by his father. As an adult, Milt expanded the store's merchandise to include phonographs and records, renaming it, in 1934, the Commodore Record Shop. The store became, according to *High Fidelity* magazine, "the country's most important source of 78's and a meeting ground for fans and musicians." In 1937, Gabler had started recording music, so when Billie approached him in early 1939 her timing could not have been better. "Billie was very sad," Gabler recalled. "She had this great number that was so important to her, and they wouldn't let her record it. I told her that if she could get a one-session release from her contract I'd like to have her do it for Commodore." Billie secured a release from Columbia that allowed her to record four songs, the standard number recorded in a session.

On April 20, thirteen days after her twenty-fourth birthday, Billie went into a studio at World Broadcasting Studios on Fifth Avenue at Fifty-Fifth Street for the Commodore session. To back her, she asked musicians with whom she had worked: Sonny White on piano, Frankie Newton on trumpet, Jimmy McLin on guitar, Johnny Williams on bass, Eddie Dougherty on drums, Tab Smith on alto saxophone, and Stan Payne and Kenneth Hollon on tenor saxophone. They recorded "Yesterdays," "I Gotta Right to Sing the Blues," and "Fine and Mellow," the last song an original blues number Billie wrote herself, but the session's main focus was "Strange Fruit," which took four hours to record. "Concerned that customers would feel cheated by too short a cut," one report noted, "Gabler had White improvise his now-famous haunting overture; given the song's climactic close, one could hardly tack on anything at the end."

When "Strange Fruit" was released, along with "Fine and Mel-

low" as the B side, about six weeks later, the response was immediate. The *New York Post* declared: "[Holiday] sings with a curious
lack of emphasis, dropping each word slowly and without accent. . . .
The result is a desperate and dreadful intimacy between hearer and
singer. 'I have always been entertaining you,' she seems to say. 'Now
you just listen to me.' The polite conversation between race and
race [is] gone." *The New York Age* observed that "Strange Fruit" "is
believed to be the first phonograph recording in America of a popular song that has lynching as its theme"—"a haunting melody." The
San Francisco Chronicle was blunt in its assessment: "Miss Holiday
sings the brooding tune and the gruesomely descriptive words with
tensity and superb dramatic sense, so that your gorge rises and your
back hairs bristle and you can't bear to live one more little minute. It
may be art." But to understand how the establishment responded to
the song, consider the coverage offered by *Time* in its June 12 issue:
"Billie Holiday is a roly-poly young colored woman with a hump
in her voice. Dance-hall crowds have heard her with Count Basie's
Orchestra, radio audience with Artie Shaw. She does not care enough
about her figure to watch her diet, but she loves to sing." As for
"Strange Fruit," *Time* called it "a prime piece of musical propaganda"
that featured "grim and gripping lyrics." The commentary in *Time*
may have been sexist and disdainful, but there she was—Eleanora
Fagan from Fells Point in Baltimore, now Billie Holiday from Café
Society in Greenwich Village—in the pages of *Time* magazine.

It was ironic that three white Jewish men with leftist political leanings—Josephson, Meeropol, and Gabler—presented Billie
with the chance to record what music producer Ahmet Ertegun later
called "a declaration of war . . . the beginning of the civil rights
movement." But she felt supportive of their politics. She was also
comfortable with Jewish people; after all, her manager, Joe Glaser,
was Jewish and her mentor, Louis Armstrong, was partially raised by
a Jewish family named Karnofsky, spoke fluent Yiddish, and wore
a Star of David around his neck for most of his adulthood. So Billie seized the moment and embraced "Strange Fruit" because she
believed it could contribute to the national discussion raging about
race in general and lynching in particular. The press coverage the

song received proved she was right. Then there was the fact that the song began to post noteworthy record sales, which it was able to do without any airplay because radio stations deemed it too controversial to broadcast. In fact, it was November before the first radio station aired the song when, according to the *New York Daily News,* "WNEW has given its consent to the airing of the brittle song by Billie Holiday, during the Café Society programs, heard nightly."

Ultimately, "Strange Fruit" became Billie's best-selling record—it sold ten thousand copies in the first week of its release, and after three months it reached Number 16 on the popular music charts—and, as she had hoped, it stood as her indefatigable statement about racism at a time when too many people were suffering and too few voices were speaking out. "It was meant as an attack song," Abel's son Robert Meeropol says. "When Abel said he hated lynching and the people who perpetrate it, he meant it. The song was intended to be an attack. It was extremely effective." His brother, Michael Meeropol, adds: "And Billie Holiday's version is what made the song famous."

In 1944, as "Strange Fruit" was well on its way to achieving legendary status as a protest song, Lillian Smith, a young aspiring author from Florida, published a debut novel about a heterosexual interracial couple living in a small town in Georgia, and, after rejecting other titles, named the book *Strange Fruit,* an obvious homage to the song, although in interviews Smith downplayed the connection. Described by J. Donald Adams of *The New York Times* as "the best novel on the theme of miscegenation that I have ever read," the book sold a million copies in hardback, thanks to the provocative nature of its subject matter, which caused the book to suffer various bans—one was the refusal of the U.S. Postal Service to mail it, since it was deemed lewd—and, it could be argued, the familiarity of its title.

The song may have been controversial, but it was among a handful of songs with which Billie was closely associated, which was why when she published her autobiography in 1956 she tried to claim it as her own. That act prompted Abel Meeropol to make a rare appearance in a public forum and state his case. In August, employing his pseudonym, Lewis Allan, he published a letter to the editor in *The New York Times* in which he declared, "Miss Holiday's claim to ownership of my song 'Strange Fruit' is neither new nor in accordance with the truth. . . . The fact is that I wrote both words and the music."

3.

In the latter part of August 1958, as she spent her days and nights suffering through the sweltering summer heat in her apartment, Billie could not help, because of the press coverage the Commodore album was receiving, but reflect back on Café Society and the song she discovered there. In the last year of her life, while she never abandoned "Strange Fruit," she did not sing it as frequently as she once did. In fact, she rarely sang it at all. The reason was simple. Singing "Strange Fruit" had become such a deeply disturbing experience for her, it was hard to summon up the emotional and physical stamina she needed to perform it. The truth was, the song that had become a revered, gut-wrenching cry of protest was too painful for her to sing. The motivation had to be compelling—a deserving audience, an ideal occasion—for her to subject herself to the ordeal of performing the song one more time.

There was another memory of that time that haunted Billie when she allowed herself to think back on it. It did not involve "Strange Fruit" directly but a person she met as a result of performing it at the club that made her famous.

Billie was in residence at Café Society from opening night in December 1938 until the winter of 1940. Her growing popularity allowed her to pick up lucrative gigs at other venues like the Apollo Theater, Off Beat Club in Chicago, Howard Theatre in Washington, D.C., and Kelly's Stable in New York. Her opening at the Stable in December 1939 was, according to music historian Arnold Shaw, "a triumphal appearance and the beginning of her long, thriving association with The Street"—the nickname for West Fifty-Second Street, which, with its string of clubs located almost door-to-door between Fifth and Seventh Avenues, was a prime stop for entertainment, especially jazz, in Manhattan. After engagements elsewhere, Billie always returned to Café Society until late November 1940, when she had a falling-out with John Hammond over her personal life that affected their professional relationship, and she concluded her final engagement at the club.

While those two years at Café Society transformed her career in ways she could never have imagined, Billie also experienced changes in her private life. In the late 1930s, she undertook an affair with Roy Eldridge, one of the preeminent trumpet players on the music scene. He was tall, attractive, talented. Billie felt a connection with him, since he had played on the early songs she recorded with Teddy Wilson. But whatever romance transpired between them was interrupted when, as Eldridge later disclosed to a reporter, "Billie found herself in love with a girlfriend."

She had been involved with women in the past, perhaps going as far back as her teenage years; more recently she was seen with women so often some of her fellow musicians referred to her as "Mr. Holiday." Saxophonist Les Robinson recalled during her Artie Shaw days "there was a little incident when we were in Toronto, when she had a little thing going with a red-haired girl—she did have a little lesbian situation going," while bassist Al McKibbon would never forget the following episode: "One time I was in the men's room, and Billie came in. She went in the urinal standing. What could I do? I thought it was a hell of a thing for a woman to do. I was shocked, but she wasn't. It was like nothing to her. She was another guy." That may have been why Count Basie gave her the nickname "William" (an ironic gesture, since that was his real first name). But any dalliances she experienced had all come to nothing until Billie undertook the romance that ended her affair with Eldridge.

Because of the notoriety Café Society received, Billie had fostered an array of new admirers. There were Manhattan socialites, members of President Roosevelt's family, entertainment figures like Sterling Brown and Paul Robeson. After seeing her perform, people from all areas of society came to admire her. Some became more than fans. "There was a girl," Billie wrote, "I first met at Café Society and got to know pretty well. . . . She was a good-looking chick about my age. . . . She came around night after night. She was crazy about my singing and used to wait for me to finish up. I wasn't blind. . . . It wasn't long before I knew I had become a thing for this girl. . . . Before long she got to depend on seeing me and being around."

Her name was Louise Crane. Chestnut-haired, full faced, with watery blue eyes, she was a ghost when Billie peered out into the darkened audience, a luminous presence in the crowded club. She lingered through the sets until Billie was free to socialize. In their conversations, Billie learned she was a jazz lover from a wealthy, politically connected family. Her father, Winthrop M. Crane, who died when Louise was nearly seven, was a prominent businessman who served as governor of Massachusetts as well as one of its U.S. senators. Her mother, Josephine Porter Boardman, was a philanthropist and proponent of progressive education, who funded the creation of the Dalton School, a private school in Manhattan, and served on the original organizing committee that founded the Museum of Modern Art. Louise was born in Dalton, Massachusetts, where her family maintained an estate, but she and her mother resided in an elegantly appointed eighteen-room apartment at 820 Fifth Avenue. Louise lived in a spacious suite of rooms on one end of the apartment, her mother in an equally capacious suite on the other end. Chester Page, a friend and employee, remembered the Crane apartment as "an oasis of culture, musical and literary, in those days, and Mrs. Crane was its admirable chatelaine." The Cranes' lifestyle was financed by the family business, Crane Paper Company, which, among its myriad commercial enterprises, held a monopoly on supplying the U.S. federal government with the paper used to make currency. When Louise took a twenty-dollar bill from her purse, she was—quite literally—holding Crane paper.

It was not long before Billie learned Louise was in a relationship with an aspiring poet named Elizabeth Bishop. The two young women met in 1930 as coeds at Vassar College. Elizabeth, a former tomboy, was a brilliant fledgling intellectual (she majored in English and cofounded a literary journal entitled *Con Spirito*), while Louise was an underachiever who never acclimated to academia (she was a freshman for three years and did not graduate). "Though Louise had a special proficiency in math and the stock market," Chester Page wrote, "the academic life bored her. She retreated into the dull town of Poughkeepsie to the cinema." A collegiate infatuation between the young women did not result in romance—in part because Elizabeth was secretly in love with her roommate, Margaret Miller—yet they remained friends after college.

Then, in the summer of 1937, the three women traveled together to Europe, where tragedy struck. One day, Louise was driving the girls through the French countryside when a car forced them off the road, causing their car to flip over. Louise and Elizabeth emerged uninjured, but Margaret, who was resting an arm in the open window, had her arm severed from the elbow down. She would have bled to death had a nearby workman not applied a tourniquet before she was rushed to a hospital. Once it was clear Margaret would recover, Louise and Elizabeth, both wracked with guilt, returned to America and settled in Key West. If the two had not already done so, they now set out on a romance, which they memorialized in May 1938 by jointly buying a quaint, coach-style house located at 624 White Street on the beach in Key West. Tragedy, as much as any other factor, had compelled the women to take their relationship beyond their yearslong companionship.

During 1939, as Elizabeth struggled with bouts of depression compounded by a growing dependency on alcohol, Louise often traveled to New York to help her mother, who was in her midsixties, with business and philanthropic affairs. Before long, Louise, a new but enthusiastic devotee of jazz, became a regular at Café Society and soon set out on a mission of pursuing more than a friendship with the unexpected object of her infatuation—Billie Holiday. Louise was not subtle about it. "Then," Billie wrote, "she started buying and sending me presents—slacks and jackets, suits cut and tailored like a man's with butchy accessories. . . . This made no kind of sense. I might not be a lot of things, but one look at me and you can mark me down as a girl-type girl." In actuality, Louise appeared to more than understand that fact, as evidenced by the furs and evening gowns she bought Billie at high-end stores. "[Louise] was good to Billie," according to Irene Wilson Kitchens, Billie's friend whose first husband was Teddy Wilson. "She took her to Bonwit Teller. That's where Billie got her first fox. Lady was so childish about it, like a big kid. 'Renie,' she said, 'look what I got. I got a silver fox.' That was the beginning of Billie getting really nice things to wear, the lovely evening gowns and things. Before it was over, Billie was the most glamorous thing there was. No one in the business looked better than her, and [Louise] had a lot to do with it."

Billie had her own perception of her involvement with Louise. "There we were," she wrote, "a rich white heiress from Fifth Avenue and a Negro girl from uptown. Yet I could hang around on Fifth Avenue with [Louise] and nobody so much as batted an eye—not the uniformed doorman, neighbors, servants, nobody, not even her mother." Kitchens had a different recollection of the way Billie was treated: "[Louise] used to take big groups of rich friends down to hear Billie sing. They all raved about her and afterwards went up to the Crane apartment on Fifth Avenue, but Louise's mother was prejudiced. When she took a woman companion to Europe, she told the doorman to watch who Louise brought up there. When she came back and found out that Louise brought Billie up, she told her daughter that from now on she didn't want any colored folks in the house—she didn't care *who* it was."

While Louise had sporadically returned to Key West, she and Elizabeth lived together in Manhattan in the summer of 1939. It was likely now that Elizabeth first saw Billie perform; beyond this, Elizabeth must have known, judging from the way the two women interacted, that Louise had become more than just a fan to Billie. Louise and Elizabeth never committed themselves to being in a monogamous relationship; still, it was surprising to Elizabeth when she returned home from a social engagement one evening only to discover Louise in bed with Billie. "Elizabeth once told me with a sly laugh," says Lloyd Schwartz, a close friend of Bishop, "how awkward it was to have to ask Billie to leave after finding her in bed with Louise."

Later in 1939, Louise and Elizabeth spent November and December in Florida, but when Louise returned to New York, Elizabeth remained in Key West. Except for a trip south in March, Louise spent much of 1940 in New York, promoting new singers she discovered, among them Ellabelle Davis. She was also seeing Billie. "Louise was very interested in music," Betty Bruce, who knew Louise through Elizabeth, recalled. "Besides [some] Spanish [singers], she was very, very interested in black musicians. She spent a lot of time in Harlem. One time I ran into Louise when I was in New York City. . . . She invited a friend and me to Harlem with her. We went to a nightclub before a performance, and we just sat around at the table and talked to Billie Holiday."

The height of Louise's involvement with Billie came when Louise financed a restaurant for Billie's mother. "Mom," Billie wrote, "had always dreamed of having a real honest-to-God restaurant of her own with a framed license on the wall from the Board of Health. One night Mom was campaigning for her damn restaurant when [Louise] was at the house. Right off she offered to be an angel for the project. It was her way of keeping tight with me, but it was what Mom wanted. So she started planning and eventually ended up with a place of her own. Mom Holiday's on Ninety-ninth Street near Columbus."

In the fall of 1940, Elizabeth visited Louise in Manhattan and realized she was seeing other women besides Billie. When Elizabeth returned to Key West in late December, she knew her relationship with Louise was over. She was distraught. "From Louise I heard about the difficulties of her breakup with Elizabeth," Mary Meigs, a friend of the couple, remembered, "about Elizabeth's despair and her suicide threats. Louise was irresistible to women, she had very blue eyes, full, it seemed, of innocent candor and love of life. She adored people and parties."

Louise left the house in Key West to Elizabeth—either to rent out or to sell—as she got on with her life in New York, which included Billie. Their association reached its most public point in June, when Billie appeared at a Coffee Concert at the Museum of Modern Art, a series of six concerts sponsored by Louise and her mother that featured Benny Carter, Maxine Sullivan, Mary Lou Williams—and now Billie Holiday. During her appearance, which headlined the bill for the evening of June 4, Billie performed a set that included "God Bless the Child," "Fine and Mellow," "I Cried for You," and "Strange Fruit." In reviewing the show, *The New York Times* gushed about Holiday, "of whom the warmly approving crowd could not get enough." In the audience that evening was Marianne Moore, the modernist poet and longtime friend of the Crane family, who was so taken with Billie she conveyed her admiration in a letter to Louise, remarking in particular on "that intimate song of Billie Holiday's about the eyes"—"Them There Eyes."

While all was seemingly going well, it was around this time that John Hammond intervened and derailed Billie's relationship with Louise. Later, he argued Billie's residency at Café Society was "not the success [it] could have been"—a calculated misrepresentation of one of the most celebrated residencies ever conducted by any artist in the history of American nightlife. Hammond claimed that Billie "was heavily involved in narcotics," which in 1939 and 1940 was untrue. Because he so blatantly mischaracterized his motivation, it is not clear why Hammond took the actions he did. But, as he wrote, he went to Louise's family to whom he was related, presumably her mother but perhaps one of her two brothers, maybe all three individuals, and revealed Louise's affair with Billie, warning it could expose the Crane family to being "hurt by unsavory gossip or even blackmailed by gangsters or dope pushers Billie knew." It was not uncommon at the time for prominent figures to be blackmailed for being homosexual. In Louise's case, she was not only a lesbian but also involved with a black woman who was quickly developing a national reputation as a preeminent jazz singer. One could only imagine the scandal that would erupt if the public learned of Louise's interracial lesbian affair with Billie Holiday. Then again, perhaps Hammond was concerned only about himself and how such a scandal could damage him. After all, he and Louise not only traveled in the same social circle, but they were also second cousins, a detail sure to be mentioned in press coverage, since Hammond was generally credited with discovering Billie and then promoting her career.

As it happened, when Mrs. Crane, whose prejudice was no secret, learned about the affair, she did a lot more than "bat an eye,"

despite Billie's claims to the contrary. She ordered Louise to stop seeing Billie at once, a command Louise obeyed. Billie remained bitter
about the end of the affair for years. She dismissed Louise as a "sad"
girl and described her as being "incapable of loving anybody"—an
indication of the love Billie clearly felt for her. Billie also ended her
association with Hammond and never forgave him for what he did.

One person who was not resentful toward Billie was Elizabeth
Bishop. Eventually, she published "Song for a Colored Singer," a
suite of four poems, the last one of which was clearly influenced by
"Strange Fruit." "I was hoping somebody would compose tunes for
them," Bishop said. "I think I had Billie Holiday in mind. I put
in a couple of big words just because she sang big words well—
'conspiring root,' for instance.'"

In the end, Louise Crane was a significant figure in Billie's life.
"They had a long affair," Linda Kuehl wrote. "Billie sang for the
homosexual woman who lived in her. She was the perfect lesbian.
Her stifled cry told of the union forever lost and loneliness that
stayed behind. She ennobled this suffering."

CHAPTER 6

✒

When Your Lover Has Gone

Billie Holiday with Miles Davis at the Persian Room at the Plaza Hotel on the evening of September 9, 1958. Both were appearing at Jazz at the Plaza, an event celebrating the jazz division at Columbia Records. Davis's description of Billie's singing style would become ubiquitous among Holiday fans: "She doesn't need any horns; she sounds like one anyway."

In the waning days of summer in 1958, once August segued into September, Billie enjoyed the success of *Lady in Satin* as she did what she lived to do—play the next gig, then the gig after that. Early in the month, she appeared for two nights, on the fourth and the fifth, at La Ronda Inn in Newtown, Connecticut. The *Westport Town Crier* noted that, backed by her pianist and a trio headed by Joan Marie Cole ("on the organ"), Billie, in presenting her "song stylings," was making "her first appearance in Fairfield County." It was a far cry from the Hollywood Bowl or Carnegie Hall, but it was typical of the dates she played these days. She had no choice but to accept them because she needed the money in order to live. Like so many musicians of her generation, she had rarely been paid her true worth, and when she was, she lost her money to drugs and unscrupulous men who insinuated themselves into her life only to swindle her.

On the night of September 9, however, she found herself in one of her classier recent engagements as she sat at a table in the Persian Room at the Plaza Hotel just south of Central Park on Fifth Avenue in New York City. At the table, covered by a white tablecloth with a small decorative lamp placed in the center, she was joined on one side by Miles Davis, who was dressed in an elegant black suit and tie and sipping a cocktail, and on the other side by Jimmy Rushing, whom she had known since they both sang for Count Basie. The ornate nightclub, featuring Persian murals above the bandstand, was packed with, as one reporter noted, "several hundred [people]— music reviewers, columnists, disc jockeys, feature writers, and critics." The occasion was a celebration hosted by Columbia Records meant to highlight its robust—and lucrative—jazz division. Billie was honored to be included. The invitation was extended because of the popularity of *Lady in Satin.* Wearing a stylish black outfit with a partial headscarf, oversized dangling earrings, and the gold chain and pendant she favored these days, she nursed a cocktail and smoked cigarettes while chatting with Davis and Rushing. She was in her element—in a glamorous room among the heavyweights of jazz—and she was exultant to be there.

Amid the table-hopping and hobnobbing, the music finally started—the reason, after all, such a crowd had shown up. Jimmy Rushing turned in a set backed up by a small band. Duke Ellington, as sophisticated as ever, led his big band through a hard-driving set that included nine tracks, culminating with "Take the A Train." The Miles Davis Sextet—Davis on trumpet, Cannonball Adderley on alto saxophone, John Coltrane on tenor saxophone, Bill Evans on piano, Paul Chambers on bass, and Jimmy Cobb on drums, the same lineup of musicians who the next year would record Davis's groundbreaking album *Kind of Blue*—performed "If I Were a Bell," "Oleo," "My Funny Valentine," and "Straight, No Chaser." The audience may have been impressed with the set, but Ralph Ellison, whom Columbia invited in his capacity as a jazz writer, later sniped in a letter to a friend: "Duke signified on Davis all through his numbers and his trumpeters and saxophonists went after him like a bunch of hustlers in a Georgia skin game fighting with razors. Only Cannonball Adderley sounded as though he might have some of the human quality which sounds unmistakably in the Ellington band."

Finally, it was time for Billie. Onstage, Irving Townsend offered a warm introduction, and Billie made her way to the microphone. Critic Alfred Duckett, who was in the packed room, recorded his impressions of her: "You don't see the picture-book Billie Holiday of the past years. You don't see a lush, lovely woman with the kind of figure that used to make men stare. She's slimmer. She has some of the tragedy of the years written on her face. But she is still beautiful."

After warming up with an opening number, Billie delivered an inspired version of "When Your Lover Has Gone." She sang it with the conviction of someone who was enduring the heartache of a failed affair, an emotion with which she was profoundly familiar at the moment, given her estrangement from McKay. Once she finished, the audience applauded—and applauded. The ovation built to become so animated she had no choice but to sing another song. She had only delivered the first lines—"Hush now! Don't explain!"—when more applause rose up from the room. "She gets into the song," Duckett wrote, "and something chemical, something magic happens between Billie Holiday and her audience. There is no illusion about the way her honey voice drips through, strains through—clear, dripping with heat and astride that beat which is hers exclusively. There is no illusion. She snaps her finger once—in a break—and what happens to the audience with the snap of that finger is the measure of her genius. For she has snapped everyone in the hushed awed room out of one mood level into another. As she finishes up, the musicians on the bandstand—the musicians who are accompanying her—are watching her with great respect and great appreciation." What they heard was what the audience heard. "You listen—and you hear a magnificent performance. You listen and you listen and you hear—an authentic artist."

Following the show, Miles Davis took Billie to Birdland to see Willie Ruff, a bass and French horn player who worked as part of a duo with pianist Dwike Mitchell. Ruff played French horn on *Miles Ahead,* Davis's album released by Columbia Records in October 1957, which featured a twenty-piece band with arrangements by Gil Evans and Davis on flugelhorn. Davis was so taken with Ruff's playing, he wanted Billie to meet him. "After our show," Ruff recalls, "Miles introduced us and Billie sat down right behind Mitchell's piano. We had a nice conversation. People were coming and going in Birdland at that time, everyone from Thurgood Marshall to Jackie Robinson, but Billie Holiday was a big star—one of the reigning legends in our business."

Billie was still on an emotional high when she returned home later that night. The grand affair at the Persian Room would be hard to match for its showmanship and splendor. She had taken her place among the most lauded names in the industry, and, judging from the crowd's reaction, she more than held her own, which made the fact that she was by herself even more painful. Some nights, the loneliness was almost unbearable. She sang about being alone in songs like "Travelin' All Alone, "Deep Song," and "Solitude," but that was only her way of addressing in her art the fear of abandonment she experienced in her life. It seemed she was attracted to men who were not good for her. They abused her emotionally or physically or both; often they also stole her money. The pattern started with her first husband and continued until her current one. A lover would be with her for a period of time—weeks, months, years—and then, inevitably, he was gone. At times like tonight as she lay in bed, her mind sometimes drifted back to all the men for whom she had fallen—a melancholy journey into a past she often tried not to remember.

2.

The spring of 1941 was a good time for Billie. Thanks to the fame she received through her run at Café Society, she was busier than ever with her career. On May 1, she appeared at the May Day celebration held at Union Square to sing "Strange Fruit" and to show her support of the labor movement, if not the Communist Party itself. Currently, she was headlining at Kelly's Stable, sharing the bill with Lester Young and His Band; soon she would move to the Famous Door, another fixture of The Street. She often spent her time off at Clark Monroe's Uptown House, on West 134th Street in Harlem, where she found herself socializing more and more often with Clark's brother, Jimmy, the former husband of Nina Mae McKinney, a Broadway and motion picture star who would come to be known as "the Black Garbo." It was not long before Billie, attracted to his charm and good looks, fixed her full attention on him. If Bobby Henderson had been a youthful dalliance, Jimmy Monroe represented a serious relationship. So, in August 1941, following a brief courtship, "to prove something," Billie later wrote, "to . . . both Mom and Joe Glazer [sic] [who] never stopped telling me I was going to get hurt," she eloped with Monroe to Elkton, Maryland—a "lovers' paradise," as one newspaper described the town—where on the twenty-fifth they were married. "Giving her age as 25 and her name as Billie Eleanor Holiday," the *New York Amsterdam Star-News* reported, "this is the singer's first marriage."

Returning home to discover the surprise elopement sufficiently angered her mother and agent, Billie traveled with Monroe to fulfill club dates in Chicago and Los Angeles. When the L.A. venue abruptly shut down after three weeks, Billie took the train back to New York, while Monroe stayed behind. Her next extended engagement was remembered by Truman Capote: "A wartime jazz joint on West 52nd Street: The Famous Door. Featuring my most beloved American singer—then, now, forever: Miss Billie Holiday. Lady Day. Billie, an orchid in her hair, her drug-dimmed eyes shifting in the cheap lavender light, her mouth twitching out the words." The passage hinted at the legacy of Billie's time with Monroe. She had smoked marijuana since she was a teenager—she particularly enjoyed sneaking off from Café Society between sets to smoke a reefer while driving around the city in a taxi—but Monroe turned her on to hard drugs, specifically opium, which she started to smoke on a regular basis. That fact appeared to be obvious to a devoted fan like Capote.

It was drugs—smuggling drugs, that is—that resulted in Monroe being arrested in May 1942. To be near him, Billie traveled to L.A., where Lester Young convinced Billy Berg to add her to the bill he was headlining at Berg's Trouville Club. When Monroe was found guilty and given a one-year sentence, his imprisonment effectively ended his marriage to Billie, although it was likely over when Billie returned to New York and left Monroe to his own devices. Looking back on their short-lived union, Billie would say the one gift she received from it was a song she later wrote with Arthur Herzog, Jr. Monroe was out one night, and when he came home Billie spotted lipstick on his collar. As he fumbled to come up with an excuse, Billie cut him off. "Don't explain," she said quietly. The song "Don't Explain" became one of her most popular numbers.

With Monroe off to prison, Billie had her liaison with Orson Welles. Then, in November and December, she played Chicago. By

February 1943, she was back in New York at Kelly's Stable before she took up residency at the Onyx Club. It was during this run that she began an affair with a man who made physical mistreatment of her an integral part of their romantic interaction.

One night in 1943, Billie stopped by the Village Vanguard, where the house pianist was Eddie Heywood, a brilliant stylist who earned such glowing accolades touring with Benny Carter that Billie used him and his trio to back her on several dates. Tonight, it was not his crisp, ornate playing style that held Billie's attention but the musical acuity—and the strikingly handsome appearance—of his bass player. Between sets, Billie approached Heywood and asked if she could meet the bass player; she would be in the back having a drink at the bar.

John Simmons later recalled the ensuing encounter: "[So Eddie and I] went back to the back bar [and] Billie Holiday is standing there." Heywood made the introduction. "John Simmons, Billie Holiday." Simmons remembered: "I say [to her], 'I sure have admired your work down through the years. Before I ever became a musician, I admired your work.'" Born in Haskell, Oklahoma, Simmons endured a hard life growing up in Tulsa and California before making a name for himself playing bass for acts like Benny Goodman and Nat "King" Cole.

Standing in the noisy bar, Billie, flattered that Simmons was clearly impressed to meet her, told the bartender to bring her friend a drink. Simmons ordered a Brandy Alexander. As they spoke, Billie paid Simmons a compliment. "I've had a whole lot of bass players," she said, "and I never heard any of them. But I heard you."

After they chatted for a while, Billie told Simmons to pick her up later that night at the Three Deuces, a club owned by the same men who owned the Onyx Club, where she was appearing. When Simmons showed up, Billie was leaving with a woman and could not go with him, but the following night she returned to the Village Vanguard. Years later, Simmons revealed what he thought when he saw her: "Wow! Ain't this something! Here's someone I've admired for years has turned out like this. I've got to go for her. [Even so,] I'm not going to be no Mr. Holiday. I'm still going to maintain myself. My dignity. I'm John Simmons. I mean, I'm not as great a bass player as she is a singer, but I still want to be known as John Simmons, the bassist. Not John Simmons, Lady Day's man."

Though his thoughts remained unspoken at the time, here was a problem with which Billie was all too familiar. Men were drawn to her for her talent, money, and fame, yet they were afraid of living in her shadow. It would have been a unique man who could become involved with her on a long-term basis—independent-minded, sure of himself, confident in his own skin. For Billie, one of the great disappointments of her life was that she never found such a man, at least not one with whom she became romantically involved.

When Billie picked up Simmons the second night, she took him to the apartment she shared with her mother. Simmons was surprised by the modest living conditions: "Where she had to sleep, I just couldn't picture it. It was off the living room; it was a clothes closet with glassed doors. . . . [She] had curtains in there and clothes. A little, small bed, a hospital-size bed." Still, Billie made her intentions clear. "[She] wanted me to go to bed with her. Momma was in the living room, sleeping on the couch. I say I can't make it. She's making preparations, telling me what all I had if I had her. I didn't have to go anyplace to look for anything. I said yeah, okay." But, in the end, Simmons could not bring himself to sleep with her and left.

As it happened, Simmons was already involved with another woman. Dorothy, who was white, came from a prominent family in Chicago; the couple had a daughter, Sue, in 1942. But extraneous obligations were not a topic of concern for Billie, who was resolute in her pursuit of Simmons. Her solution to his reluctance to sleep with her in an apartment he found uninviting was to go out the next day and rent an apartment of her own. Located on 107th Street between Amsterdam Avenue and Central Park West, it was a fourth-floor unit in an elevator building. That night, she went back to the Village Vanguard and, after Simmons got off work, sent him by taxi to the new apartment ahead of her because she was tied up temporarily. When she joined him later, an argument erupted. "She had been

accustomed to whipping her man," Simmons later said. "She scratching them and tearing their clothes off and all. But I doubled up my
fist and knock her out." Many women would have thrown out such
an assailant, but not Billie, which took Simmons off guard: "Come
to find out, she was a masochist." The violence was what she *wanted*.
"She was doing things to make me fight her, to go to bed."

Over the coming weeks, the violence became worse. At one point,
Simmons went to a pet shop in Midtown and bought a whip—a cat
of nine tails but with only three tails. "So, no sooner [did I] get back
home [than] she had to go into her act. And I showed her this whip
when I walked in . . . and I hung it on the doorknob. I [was] tired
of using my hands. And I caught her with this whip. She wanted to
jump out the fourth floor. I hit her everywhere but in her face and
the bottom of her feet." Afterwards, he was sure she would not go in
to work at the Onyx Club. "But before I left home, I run a bathtub
of cold water with a box of table salt in it and put her in it to close up
the welts. [Still,] I just knew she wasn't going to be at work. I took
intermission"—he was now playing on Fifty-Second Street at the
Three Deuces—"and went across the street. There she is under this
pin light with this gardenia in her hair, singing her ass off."

It was while Billie was involved with Simmons that she used
heroin for the first time. Simmons remembered the circumstances:
"A white boy from Dallas called Speck, he was freckle-faced. He
slipped up to her dressing room and made himself acquainted. [He]
introduced her to a hypodermic, showing how many cc's and everything, and, her being adventuresome, she went for it. Every night he
came by he was giving it to her for free until finally she had to have
it. Then he was coming back and getting the money. She'd give him
the money and he'd come back, but he'd take what he wanted first."

Once Billie developed a heroin habit, Simmons ended their relationship. He had been addicted to heroin as a teenager; when he got
off of it, the withdrawal had been so excruciating he vowed never
to risk becoming reliant on the drug again. So, on the day he left,
he packed his belongings and got dressed to go. He finished off his
outfit with a new gaberdine topcoat, but as he was walking out,
Billie grabbed him with such force she tore the coat's back seam.

Simmons beat her so badly he "tried to kill her." The affair may have
been over, but Billie was left with a heroin addiction that plagued
her on and off for the remainder of her life. "She had never thought
of doing [heroin]," Simmons claimed, "until this white boy [from
Dallas] introduced her to it."

Billie was not the only woman with whom John Simmons was
abusive. "He was violent with my mother," says Sue Simmons, who
later became a news broadcaster, "so I'm not surprised he was violent
with Billie. It was a turn-on for Billie. As my father said, '*She* chose
me.' But the violence with my mother was unwanted. It was a frightening thing. Until you've heard the sound of flesh beating flesh—it's
a weird sound and it stays with you. My mother didn't leave my father
because she was very much in love with him. She tolerated it. She also
found out about his affair with Billie, and, as she said, she *still* bought
Billie's records." To his daughter, Simmons had his redeeming quali-
ties. "He was a good dad. He spent a lot of time with me. He taught
me to play softball in Central Park. He was very much in my life."
As the years passed, Simmons was forthcoming with his daughter, to
some degree at least, about his relationship with Billie: "I remember
asking him when I was older if Lady Day was the happiest time in his
life. I did not expect his answer. 'Yes,' he said, 'it was.'"

Not long after her affair with Simmons ended, Billie became
involved, early in 1945, with Joe Guy, a trumpet player from Birmingham, Alabama. He played in bands headed by Fats Waller and
Coleman Hawkins, but Billie was less interested in his musical proficiency than she was in the drug connections he was known to have.
She may have started using heroin while she was with Simmons,
but now, as she sank deeper into addiction, she needed a source who
could get her drugs when she needed them. On that front Guy was
reliable. She was so pleased with him she encouraged people to think
he was her new love interest. On a trip to Los Angeles in April 1945,
she even announced to friends that he was now her husband. There
was only one problem: she was still married to Jimmy Monroe. "Billie Holiday . . . caused commotion," one newspaper reported, "by

news that she had secured a divorce in Mexico and had married
Joe Guy, trumpet with Coleman Hawkins. Friends were puzzled by
Billie's announcement as no one seems to know when Billie visited
Mexico to secure the divorce."

During this time, Billie lived in the Braddock Hotel at 126th
Street and Eighth Avenue, where she was visited by friends like
Elizabeth Hardwick, then a graduate student in English literature
at Columbia University, who would one day become a prominent
novelist and critic, and Greer Johnson, Hardwick's companion, who
forged such a close friendship with Billie he later produced her first
Town Hall concert (one of her more celebrated engagements, where
one thousand people had to be turned away at the door), as well as
other individuals Billie allowed into her inner circle, among them
Frank Harriott, who worked for three months on a profile of her for
PM. Harriott was often accompanied by Owen Dodson, who remembered visiting Billie: "That hotel was the mess of the world. . . .
I knocked on her door, and she poked her head out—filled with
Vaseline (or something), and as I entered, she had on a dilapidated
pink robe. She looked a mess. I had never . . . smoked [marijuana],
but I knew the smell. I knew that she had been smoking it." Dodson
understood the pressure Billie was now under. "Billie was an artist
of so much strength and knew the curse of what she was about. No
wonder that proud girl with the [gardenia] in her hair took to drugs,
because whatever she sang, they could not bear that a black woman
could wear the crown of the Queen of Jazz. . . . Can you imagine a
black woman with the courage to sing songs like ['Strange Fruit']?
She was really a female Paul Robeson everywhere she went."

While Guy supplied Billie with heroin, he also helped her
assemble a sixteen-piece orchestra to tour second-tier, non-marquee
venues in the Midwest and South. In September, Billie was between
gigs in Columbia, South Carolina, and Washington, D.C., when she
received word that her mother had suffered a stroke in New York
on the twenty-third. Rushed to Wadsworth Hospital in Manhattan,
Sadie remained in life-threatening condition for thirteen days until
she died on October 6, while Billie was appearing at the Royal Theatre in Baltimore. Devastated, Billie hurried to New York. At the

hospital, she signed the death certificate for "Sadie Holiday" (a name her mother had come to use even though she never married Clarence Holiday) before she made arrangements with Rodney Dade, a funeral director, for her mother to be buried in St. Raymond's Cemetery in the Bronx. "She was late for her mother's funeral," Elizabeth Hardwick later wrote. "At last she arrived, ferociously appropriate in a black turban. A number of jazz musicians were there. The late morning light fell mercilessly on their unsteady, night faces. In the daytime these people, all except her, had a furtive, suburban aspect, like family men who work the night shift. The marks of a fractured domesticity, signals of a real life that is itself almost a secret existence for the performers, were drifting about the little church, adding to the awkward unreality." Owen Dodson was given an account of the funeral by Frank Harriott: "I remember Frank telling me about how Billie came back from her mother's funeral to find her place emptied of all her gowns, her furs, and her jewels. Evidently, the thieves had known or read in the paper that her mother was dead—and so they robbed her."

After completing her tour following her mother's death, Billie, often accompanied by Guy, returned to Fifty-Second Street, where she headlined at the Downbeat Club throughout November. One notable fan in her Fifty-Second Street days was Malcolm Little, a low-level drug hustler who later, inspired by a religious conversion and a political epiphany, changed his name to Malcolm X. Little recalled Billie's appearance during this engagement: "Her white gown glittered under the spotlight, her face had that coppery, Indianish look, and her hair was in that trademark ponytail." Her singing left a permanent impression: "Lady Day sang with the soul of Negroes from the centuries of sorrow and oppression. What a shame that proud, fine, black woman never lived where the true greatness of the black race was appreciated!" Perhaps, but Billie was still proud of who she was. "I've got two strikes against me," she told a reporter at the time—being a woman and black—"and don't you forget it. [But] I'm proud of those two strikes. I'm as good as a lot of people of all kinds. I'm proud I'm a Negro." Indeed, Mae Weiss, whose husband Sid had played in the Shaw band, believed Billie "was living Black is Beautiful before it was even fashionable. The pride of being black—she did it before we knew what it was. That's the way she lived. She was a trailblazer without being conscious [of it]."

Joe Guy continued to be in the picture—Billie had now fallen in love with him—when she traveled to Los Angeles in September to film *New Orleans,* a motion picture starring Arturo de Córdova and Dorothy Patrick based on a script adapted from a story by Elliot Paul and Herbert Biberman. The origin of the film was a script written by Paul for Orson Welles called *The Story of Jazz,* which was supposed to document the invention of jazz in the Storyville neighborhood of New Orleans, but the script morphed into a love story between a casino owner and a singer from an affluent family, both white, with a secondary love story between a singing maid played by Billie and a bandleader played by Louis Armstrong. "And let me tell you," Armstrong wrote to a friend, "I think it's going to be a pretty good lecture on this music called jazz . . . Billy [*sic*] and I are doing quite a bit of acting (ahem): she's also my sweetheart in the picture. . . . Ump Ump Ump. Now isn't that something? The great Billy Holiday, my sweetheart?" Biberman later remembered the producers became "scared to death that too many Negroes will come to the theatres to see this picture because there will be too many Negro artists in it." So, in the final cut of the picture, much of the emphasis in the second half of the film focuses on Woody Herman and his orchestra—all of whom were white. In what turned out to be an otherwise pedestrian picture, its most inspired moments are the three musical numbers featuring Billie singing with Armstrong and his band—"Do You Know What It Means to Miss New Orleans," "Farewell to Storyville," and "The Blues Are Brewing."

As Guy remained a constant presence in her life, Billie came to know that menacing players were watching her. Even so, she did not kowtow to them no matter how threatening they were. Indeed, at times, it seemed she openly defied them. If there was any doubt about Billie's political beliefs, she made them clear in the *PM* article when it appeared in the fall of 1945. Discussing "Strange Fruit" and the Jim Crow–sanctioned racism that motivated her to sing it, she

offered a stark admission. "That's what made me a communist," she
said. "Everybody should be a communist—not like the communists
you meet at benefits and rallies, though. Not that stuff, at all. But we
should all believe in treating each other as human beings. Everybody
should have the chance to eat and sleep in peace." As for so many
progressives at the time, especially those in the African-American
community, it was the Communist Party's stance on racial equality
that motivated Billie to support the cause. Her life, after all, despite
all her accomplishments, was still defined by her race. "Now when
I'm in the South," she told *PM*, "I . . . stay on the [other] side of
the tracks—in all the stinking little hotel rooms—because I'm not
white. . . . All you need is a white face to be treated like a human,
to be a little more happy."

As long as Guy was with her, Billie was going to remain addicted
to heroin. That was the basis of their relationship. He got her the
drugs she needed, he was dating a woman who had become a prominent jazz figure, and they did love each other. But because of who
she was and the friends and colleagues with whom she associated,
Billie was in a level of danger she did not fully appreciate. Had
she been able to see her current circumstances clearly, had she been
sober enough to understand how her world had become increasingly
perilous, she would have made different choices. However, the heroin
muted her perception, so if she *was* able to see what was happening
around her, she seemed powerless to do anything about it. Still, the
danger that lurked around her in the shadows was real. It took the
form of federal agents who had made Billie their mark.

The surveillance of Billie by the FBI, but more often the Federal Bureau of Narcotics, had commenced not long after she began
her residency at Café Society. That she was working for Barney and
Leon Josephson, considered shills for the Communist Party, initially
focused the government's attention on her; it only intensified when
she started to sing "Strange Fruit." The danger to her was represented
by what was happening to the men around her. Abel Meeropol was
subpoenaed in 1941 to appear before the Rapp-Coudert Committee,

which the New York State Legislature formed to examine the extent to which the education system had been infiltrated by communists. He was asked if the Communist Party paid him to write "Strange Fruit"; his answer was no. That same year, the FBI started a file on John Hammond, whose support of liberal causes made him suspicious. Two years later, the agency opened a file on Barney Josephson, who, in 1944, was included on the Security Index, a list of individuals regarded as a national security risk. Meanwhile, since his involvement in the Soviet plot to assassinate Hitler, Leon Josephson had been monitored by the government. Hoover himself kept an eye on the Josephson brothers, often commenting personally on documents in their FBI files. "Hoover disliked both of them," Lee Josephson says. "He disliked them because they were Reds. He disliked them because they were immigrants. He disliked them because they were Jewish. He disliked them because they refused to cooperate."

All of these men, with their communist connections, were closely associated with Billie. If she was not a primary target before the fall of 1945, she was afterwards—her encouraging "everyone" to become a communist did not help—which was known to Billie's inner circle. "She had a record in the FBI," William Dufty told journalist Joel Lobenthal, "for having sung 'Strange Fruit' in front of the wrong audience, and the FBI had these bulletins, and so she was Red-channeled." Unlike others—Hammond, Meeropol, the Josephsons—Billie had a weapon that could be used against her: her drug dependency. It was an open secret in the jazz community that Billie had a serious heroin habit facilitated by Joe Guy. If the government wanted to silence her, a drug bust and conviction were all that were needed. She could hardly pose a threat from prison.

Then, in early 1947, the saga with the Josephsons and the federal government reached a new level of intensity when Leon Josephson was subpoenaed to appear before the Committee on Un-American Activities of the House of Representatives (HUAC). "The alleged activities of Josephson," *The New York Times* reported on March 6, "involving espionage and the issuance of fraudulent passports, were the subject of a hearing . . . before a subcommittee of [HUAC]"—a hearing Josephson refused to attend. His unwillingness to comply with a subpoena prompted Richard Nixon, a subcommittee member, to recommend Josephson be "cited for contempt of the House and [the] alleged criminal evidence of passport fraud and conspiracy be turned over to the Department of Justice for prosecution." On March 22, J. Parnell Thomas, HUAC chairman, announced a contempt citation was being drawn up for Josephson, who was, according to the *Times,* "named yesterday by two former admitted communists . . . as a member of the Russian secret police." On April 22, almost the entire House voted to hold Josephson in contempt; of the two congressmen voting "nay," one was Adam Clayton Powell, Jr., who represented Harlem. (The Baptist minister–congressman was married to Hazel Scott—one of Billie's dearest friends—who headlined Café Society Uptown, the original club's spinoff located in the East Fifties, where Josephson hosted a reception for two thousand guests to celebrate the Scott-Powell nuptials when they were married.) In arguing for contempt charges, Thomas claimed Josephson and his cohorts represented "a bold and contemptuous challenge of the very sovereignty of our government." In May, Josephson was indicted by a federal grand jury. On May 5, he posted a $2,500 bond to remain free as he awaited trial. Eventually, he was found guilty at trial, and, when he lost an appeals court ruling and the U.S. Supreme Court refused to hear his case, he was sent to prison for a year. The silent partner in Café Society, the club that made Billie famous, was now in prison.

Not surprisingly, the government continued to stalk Billie. "Under the nasty pressure of shifty-eyed Hawkshaws and relentless gumshoe artists from various narcotics bureaus," Billie wrote, "my life has been made miserable. These people have dogged my footsteps from New York to San Francisco and all the territory in between. They have allowed me no peace." It was about this time that Harry Anslinger, head of the FBN, assigned Billie to be trailed by Jimmy Fletcher, one of the few African-American agents employed by the agency, a decidedly white-oriented federal bureau. One peculiar episode unfolded at the Braddock Hotel when Fletcher and a colleague came to bust Billie, only to have her strip nude in front of them to prove she had no drugs in her possession.

The pursuit of Billie finally caught up with her in May 1947, a week after Leon Josephson posted bond in his contempt of Congress case, when she, accompanied by Guy with his ever-present heroin supply, was appearing with the Louis Armstrong Orchestra in Philadelphia at the Earle Theatre. There had been problems during the run. "I was doing 'Strange Fruit' at the Earle," Billie later said, "until they made me stop." Then, after finishing her last show on May 15, Billie was being driven in her car back to the Attucks Hotel when she realized narcotics agents were raiding the premises. "I suppose," Billie later wrote, "my troubled life reached its climax on that early morning in May . . . when [my driver sped away] from my Philadelphia hotel [in] my Cadillac and headed for New York. A federal narcotics agent who had been trailing me fired several shots after my speeding car. But I was scared to death, so [we] kept going. My evil mistakes were catching up with me. In my hotel room they found one and a half grams of heroin—that deadly drug that had me in its clutches for several years. And which was ruining me professionally, physically, and financially." Three prevailing elements in her life— her political leanings, her drug dependency, and her propensity to become involved with men who were bad for her, like Joe Guy—had come together to produce an episode that permanently altered the rest of her life and career.

On May 16, Billie opened for a two-week engagement at Club 18 in New York, where agents, among them Jimmy Fletcher, staked her out. What she did not know was that Fletcher was surreptitiously in communication with Joe Glaser, who, to placate the government, now encouraged Billie to return to Philadelphia, turn herself in, and ask to be sent to a hospital for drug treatment. In the end, Billie decided to listen to Joe Glaser. It was one of the worst mistakes she made in her life.

3.

The drug raid in Philadelphia, and her romance with Joe Guy that led to it, seemed like a lifetime ago to Billie in September 1958, except that it was not. The fallout of that night still plagued her. As a result of the bust and a subsequent conviction, she had no cabaret card and remained under surveillance by the government. She was yet to overcome fully her "evil mistakes"—a reliance on drugs and alcohol—despite her best attempts to stay clean and sober, which both damaged her health and continued to make her vulnerable to the government.

Because she lived under the shadow of her past, all she could do was to get on with her life, which she attempted to do in the early days of autumn by appearing at more events. On the thirteenth, a Saturday evening, she headlined a jazz show at Town Hall in Midtown Manhattan (the scene of her past celebrated performance produced by Greer Johnson); the roster included Jo Jones and His Trio, the Buck Clayton All Stars, Eddie Condon, and J. C. Higginbotham. John S. Wilson reviewed her performance (but not the entire show) for *The New York Times:* "Halfway through a so-called 'All Star Jazz Show' . . . Billie Holiday dragged her way through a slow, slow ballad. Then, as drummer Jo Jones picked up the tempo a bit and Buck Clayton's muted trumpet muttered smoothly behind her, she eased into a swinging version of 'When Your Lover Has Gone' and some of the old Holiday magic began to peep through. . . . But it grew and grew at Town Hall until it seemed to fill the stage as she moved confidently through a short set. . . . By the time she wound up with 'Billie's Blues,' she was singing with more assurance, skill and spirit than this listener has heard from her in years."

Five days later, on the eighteenth, Billie was a guest in the seven o'clock hour of the *Today* show hosted by Dave Garroway. She sang "My Funny Valentine." The following night, members of the audience were still buzzing about her television appearance when she opened at the Flame Show Bar in Detroit, a city she had played numerous times. "A lot of folks saw me on the Dave Garroway show and didn't think I could get up that early," she told one Detroit columnist. "I didn't either." After a successful run in Detroit, Billie returned to New York before, on September 26, she traveled to Wallingford, Connecticut, where she was a houseguest of Irving Townsend as she appeared in a presentation assembled by Leonard Feather entitled "Encyclopedia of Jazz," which featured several

participants—Coleman Hawkins, Buck Clayton, Milt Hinton—
who routinely performed in such cavalcades. For her contribution
to the show, for which she had received an advance on salary of one
hundred dollars two days earlier, a reflection of her current cash flow
problems, Billie sang "I Wished on the Moon" and "Lover Man."
One Connecticut critic was dismissive of her performance: "Billie
Holiday sang straight through two tunes and left forthwith." But
Feather remembered that Billie "sang with a miraculous renewal
of the old timbre and assurance." He also wrote about an offstage
moment that unfolded between Billie and his wife. "I'm so goddam
lonely," Billie confessed, barely able to control her emotions. "Since
Louis and I broke up I got nobody—nothing."

Obviously, she was having trouble coping with the end of her
relationship with McKay, the last of the perilously flawed men with
whom she had become involved. When she returned to New York
from her gig in Connecticut, she received notification from McKay
confirming the fate of their marriage. Presently, McKay was hospitalized in Chicago, fighting a serious illness brought on by the
stress under which he was living. "I suffered a complete physical
breakdown," he later claimed, "and was obligated to interrupt a
business trip to enter a hospital in Chicago for treatment of an acute
ulcer condition." In a telegram dated September 30, 1958, with a
time stamp of 10:21 p.m., which was delivered to Billie's apartment,
McKay updated her on his medical condition before addressing
their marriage. "DEAR MISS HOLIDAY," the telegram read, "I HAVE
BEEN LAYING HERE FLAT ON MY BACK FOR 5 DAYS AND NIGHTS
HAD 3 TRANSFUSIONS UPSHAW CALL YOU I HAVE NOT HEARD ONE
WORD I REALLY WANT TO THANK YOU VERY MUCH FOR A LITTLE
CARD IF I MAKE IT OUT OF HERE YOU CAN ALWAYS CALL ON ME
IF YOU IN TROUBLE I WILL ALWAYS BE IN POSITION ACCEPT YOUR
CALL PS YOU CAN HAVE YOUR DIVORCE FOR NOTHING BECAUSE IT
WAS NOTHING AFTER ALL." The telegram was signed Louis McKay
in care of Billings Hospital. The violent ordeal on Memorial Day
weekend ended up being the ultimate breaking point. Now the tele-
gram summed up what all the years the two of them had spent
together meant to McKay: nothing.

CHAPTER 7

𝒮

It Happened Out West

*Billie Holiday with Tallulah Bankhead and Dickie Wells at Club Ebony, the nightclub
at which Billie enjoyed two extended engagements in the months
after her release from federal prison in 1948. Bankhead, whose yearslong friendship
with Billie became intimate, lobbied J. Edgar Hoover to call off the
federal surveillance of her— to no avail.*

September and October 1958

I.

Billie may have been dissatisfied in her romantic life, but she was buoyed by the fact that her career continued to thrive. At the end of September, she was scheduled to return to a venue she always enjoyed playing, the Blackhawk Club in San Francisco, where she would open a two-week stand on the thirtieth. To assist her on the trip, and to fight off her ever-present feelings of loneliness, Billie arranged for Alice Vrbsky to accompany her. Despite unpleasant events having happened to her there in the past, some of them orchestrated by the government, Billie loved San Francisco. So she was looking forward to her upcoming engagement on the day she boarded the flight from New York joined by, in addition to Alice, her regular traveling companion, Mal Waldron.

"We were on the plane," Waldron remembered, "and we had seven hours to kill. There was nothing to do . . . except sleep or talk. So [Billie] decided she wanted to do a tune. And she wanted it to be autobiographical. She felt she wanted it to be the story of her life." With this in mind, she wrote the lyrics of a song for which Waldron would compose music later. The name of the song—"the story of my life," as she called it—was "Left Alone." "First they hurt me, then desert me," the opening verse concludes. "I'm left alone, all alone."

By the time the airplane landed in San Francisco, the lyrics for the new effort were finished—Billie had now coauthored eleven songs in her career—after which she and her party headed to the hotel to get on with why they had flown out west: the next gig.

Since 1949, the Blackhawk Club, located in the Tenderloin Dis-

trict on the corner of Turk and Hyde Streets, had thrived. A contemporaneous description appeared in *Time* (which affectionately
referred to the club as "a sewer"): "Its dim doorway belches noises
and stale cigarette smoke. Against one wall lies a long dark bar
minus bar stools; a bandstand, just big enough for an underfed quartet, is crammed on the other side; stained, plastic-topped tables and
rachitic chairs crowd the floor. The capacity, when everyone is inhal-
ing, comes close to 200, and strangely, the crowd is always close to
capacity." Despite its run-down condition, the club presented some of
the most acclaimed names in jazz. In 1956, Dave Brubeck recorded
Jazz at the Black Hawk, while just this month Cal Tjader had cut *A
Night at the Blackhawk (Live).* The intimate room featured an oddity:
an area sectioned off with chicken wire where underage minors were
admitted to listen to the music without the possibility of illegally
purchasing liquor. The establishment was owned by Guido Cacci-
enti, a folksy, hands-on manager ("I've struggled for years to keep
this place a sewer") for whom Billie was fond of working. She had
last appeared there in January 1957, a three-day weekend run from
January 11 to 13. It happened to be another performance witnessed
by Truman Capote, her loyal fan, who memorialized his impressions
in his journal: "Went to a small boite to see Billie Holiday. She was
soaked in gin (or something) and her voice is gone. So sad." Eighteen
months later, the voice was still compromised—perhaps even more
so—and Billie had not laid off the gin. If anything, she was *more*
gin-soaked, a reality that may have contributed to what happened
on her opening night.

In her cramped dressing room, Billie sat waiting to go onstage.
A trio including Mal Waldron would back her; she was sharing the
bill with the Leroy Vinnegar Quartet. The jazz scene in San Francisco
was hot at the moment. Red Norvo was playing Easy Street, and
Sonny Rollins was headlining the Jazz Workshop. "Never before,"
the *San Francisco Examiner* observed, "has San Francisco had four top
jazz celebrities playing at three different spots at a single time." But
the longer Billie sat in the claustrophobic room, the more unwell she
felt; perhaps her present spell of heavy drinking was taking a toll. It
was fortunate she had brought along Alice for the trip, which was

to include, halfway through the two-week run at the Blackhawk, a Sunday night star turn at the inaugural Monterey Jazz Festival. The plan was for Billie to finish her last show for the first week, a Sunday afternoon jam session; make the two-hour journey to Monterey to close out the festival that night; then return the next day to San Francisco for her second week at the Blackhawk.

Finally, as showtime approached, Billie made her way to "the powder room," as one local columnist reported. While she was there, either the jet lag from her recent flight or the day's protracted drinking—or both—caught up with her and before she knew it, Billie, as the columnist wrote, "fell down, splat . . . hit her head, crrrrack, and passed out cold." When she came to, she sought assistance and had her head packed in ice. It was some time before she recovered enough to perform, but, determined not to miss her opening night, she pushed herself to go on. As she stared out onto the sold-out room, clouds of cigarette smoke drifting through the shaft of light fixed on her face, she was lucky her backstage ordeal had not been worse. As it happened, the audience was none the wiser. The appreciation they felt for her was reflected in the torrents of applause that followed each song. "Billie Holiday opened at the Blackhawk [on] Tuesday night to a packed house," one newspaper observed, "and the crowd didn't go away disappointed." Nor was Billie dissatisfied. She relished another opening night in another city at a time when, based on what just happened to her, an opening night could no longer be taken for granted.

While she performed her shows during her first week at the Blackhawk, Billie was also dealing with her private life. Word was out that Billie intended to divorce McKay. In his national column on October 1, Walter Winchell reported that "Billie Holiday (Mrs. L. McKay) is expected to file for the final decree soon." *Jet* magazine noted that "singer Billie Holiday plans to file a divorce suit against her estranged husband . . . before she leaves for a Paris nightclub engagement." Another story making the rounds involved Billie moving to Europe and adopting two babies: the proposed exodus from New York was the result of the decade-long cabaret ban, and the adoption was a wish fulfillment meant to satisfy her desire to have children. Apparently, Billie felt so strongly about both of these subjects that she disclosed them one night after a show to a local newspaper columnist named "Chazz" Crawford. "We sobered up considerably," wrote Crawford, referring to himself with the royal "we," "when we learned that Lady Day and her old man, Louis McKay, had split up and that our favorite torch songstress may adopt brown babies in Europe. This is due to a conversation Lady and I had while she was [at the Blackhawk]." With such troubling issues to be dealt with—divorce, frustration over never having children, an endless harassment by the government—it was no wonder Billie was drinking, which she continued to do during her first week in San Francisco. Herbert Henderson, a friend who was a physician, came to see her at the Blackhawk. He was disturbed by what he saw: "She was ill with cirrhosis of the liver, caused by excessive drinking. Alcohol was resorted to in order that she would have no desire for heroin. She had lost much weight and should have been in a hospital instead of a nightclub. When I heard her sing—it was pathetic."

Without question, Billie felt added pressure simply because of where she was. San Francisco had been the site of some painful episodes for her, among them a run-in with authorities that played out in the national press. The source of that ordeal was John H. Levy, a former-mafioso-turned-club-owner with whom Billie became involved after her relationship with Joe Guy ended because of her narcotics conviction in 1947. Now memories of Levy were repellent to her, mostly because his behavior while they were together was frequently so abusive, but it was hard to force him from her mind when she was in the city where their most public episode played out. John Levy—next in the line of men, after Guy, whom Billie should have avoided but didn't—no doubt was in her thoughts as she settled into San Francisco.

The countervailing figure in Billie's life during her time with Levy could not have been more pleasurable. That person was an unconventional woman of style and substance who still confounded Billie even though their affair had ended several years ago. The woman was such an irresistible character, such an undeniable force of nature, that Billie found her impossible to resist. Here was the conundrum about Billie's life. While the men with whom she became involved were destructive, her relationships with women were loving and nurturing. How different her life would have been if her romantic involvements had been exclusively with women, an option that she may not have thought was available to her because of the conservative—and homophobic—times in which she lived.

Still, there was no doubt about how she felt about the woman whom Levy viewed as his competition. Their romance began in the late 1940s in the months after Billie got out of prison, yet sometimes, for Billie, it was as if it had all just happened.

2.

In the cavernous 2,750-seat movie palace, under a beautifully rendered ceiling mural featuring classical figures posed in a heaven-like landscape, under a massive ornate gold-leaf proscenium arch, Billie Holiday stood at a microphone at center stage with Count Basie and His Orchestra behind her. On this night in August 1948, she looked out onto the jam-packed midnight show audience. Dressed in an elegant evening gown, she tilted her head back and swayed seductively as she kept time with the music by snapping her fingers— the same pose she struck when she sang whether she was playing a small venue in Boston or San Francisco or where she was tonight, the Strand Theatre. Located in Times Square on the corner of Broadway and Forty-Seventh Street, it was constructed in 1914 by the same builders who went on to create Radio City Music Hall. Normally, the lavish movie palace merely ran its latest feature motion picture. But for six weeks starting on July 16 to launch the Warner Bros. release of *Key Largo,* the film noir directed by John Huston and starring Humphrey Bogart and Lauren Bacall, Billie Holiday and Count Basie had been booked in what was known as a "flesh-pic combo" to perform before each screening of the picture. With doors opening at nine o'clock in the morning, Billie and Basie, along with a comedy duo, the Two Zephyrs, and a tap-dancing act, Stump and Stumpy, played five forty-five-minute sets a day, seven days a week. Despite New York being in the grip of a historically oppressive heat wave, the extravaganza at the Strand, now well into its run, was doing record-breaking box office. "As very few singers in our time," Barry Ulanov wrote in *Metronome,* "as no uncompromising jazz singer in our time, Billie is a box office attraction. She has her own explanation. 'They come to see me get all fouled up. They're just waiting for that moment. Just waiting. But they're not going to get it. I'm not going to get all fouled up. I'm not!'" Billie's salary was $3,878 a week, a handsome sum for someone who had been released from prison four months earlier.

Among the tens of thousands of people who saw Billie during what ended up being a six-week engagement was Dan Morgenstern, who was new to the jazz scene from Europe: "It was the first time I saw her. I was already in love with her; I knew her records. At the Strand, she was wonderful. One of the things that struck me was her stage presence, because what she did was quite unusual. Instead of moving around the stage and doing things with her body, she pretty much stood still. The only thing she did was snap her fingers and move her head from side to side. Mostly, she was stationary. It was riveting. What she did was so effective, she got you with the song. She held the audience spellbound by her singing." Or, as Ned Rorem later wrote about her performance style: "Holiday scarcely moved, saving until the climax the moment for closing her eyes, tilting back her head, as mountains crumbled."

Tonight, when she stared out into the audience, Billie could see, as she did at numerous midnight shows, the unmistakable silhouette of Tallulah Bankhead in the front row in her "regular" spot staring up at Billie in rapt adoration. It was, as James "Stump" Cross remembered, "as if this were the only show in the world." The two women had known each other since the 1930s—likely starting at the Hot Cha in 1933—when Billie was playing the clubs in Harlem and Tallulah routinely made the rounds of the neighborhood's jazz spots and speakeasies. She had become a theater star in London in the 1920s, cultivating an ardent following of young female fans known as the "gallery girls" who cheered her onstage and attended her performances with such devotion they made her shows commercial hits. So noteworthy—and socially adept—was Bankhead that she became friends with Edward, Prince of Wales, who, after ascending to the throne, abdicated to become the Duke of Windsor. The 1930s saw Bankhead appear in a string of forgettable Paramount Pictures releases with titles like *Tarnished Lady* and *The Cheat* before she left Hollywood for her first love—theater. *The Little Foxes,* Lillian Hellman's family drama set in the South, made her into a marquee name; she followed that success, in 1942, with a star turn in Thornton Wilder's *The Skin of Our Teeth.* Her stage acclaim now made her into a celebrity in the United States, and she became famous for her deep, raspy voice and her habit of using as a salutation the ubiquitous "Dah-ling." She finally made a memorable picture in 1944 when she appeared in *Lifeboat,* directed by Alfred Hitchcock. In 1948, Bankhead had just completed an extensive out-of-town run of Noël Coward's *Private Lives*—a sold-out thirty-week stand in Chicago followed by a five-month national tour that culminated with three weeks at the Biltmore in Los Angeles starting on July 5—in anticipation of opening on Broadway at the Plymouth Theatre in October. August saw her take a hard-earned break from work during which a highlight was her nightly attendance at Billie's midnight show at the Strand. It was not unusual, Tallulah being Tallulah, for her arrival at her reserved front-row seat to be preceded by what could only be described as a grand entrance.

Their childhoods could not have been more different. While Billie survived a youth defined by poverty and abuse, Tallulah was born into privilege in Huntsville, Alabama, and, after her mother died of blood poisoning when she was three weeks old, was raised by her grandparents in the family antebellum mansion named Sunset in Jasper, a small town outside of Birmingham. Billie's father was an aspiring musician she rarely saw; Tallulah's father, William Brockman Bankhead, was a longtime congressman from Alabama who became Speaker of the House and whom Franklin Roosevelt once considered as a potential vice-presidential running mate. Billie's grandfather was the son of a slave; Tallulah's grandfather John Hollis Bankhead was a U.S. senator, as was his namesake, John Bankhead,

Tallulah's uncle. With her mother gone and her father and grandparents often preoccupied with political, social, and business commitments, young Tallulah was cared for by a nanny, who was African American, creating in her an affinity with the black community that stayed with her throughout her life. In fact, even though in 1937 she married fellow actor John Emery in a private ceremony at Sunset (the union lasted four years), perhaps the most significant relationship Tallulah had had so far was with Hattie McDaniel, who won an Academy Award for Best Supporting Actress for playing Mammy in *Gone with the Wind.* "Tallulah was," Linda Kuehl wrote, "a speakeasy habitué notorious for black women loves."

Tallulah's admiration for Billie, who nicknamed her "Banky," was apparent to friends and colleagues during the Strand run. It also became clear they were more than just friends, as a result of Tallulah's propensity to engage in romantic encounters in such a way that others could witness them. At the Strand, when Tallulah visited Billie in her dressing room after the show, they often ended up on the sofa in a compromising position, and Tallulah enjoyed leaving the door to the hallway open enough for anyone passing by to spot them. "My maid . . . was with me at the Strand," Billie later wrote to Tallulah, reminding her of her exhibitionist behavior. "There are plenty of others around who remember how you carried on so you almost got me fired out of the place." Near the end of the run, the two women, clad in dresses appropriate for after-theater dinner and cocktails—they often migrated across the street to the White Rose Bar, where they proceeded to drink the night away—posed on the notorious sofa for a newspaper photographer, each holding one of Billie's two thoroughbred boxers, Mister and Lady. Both women smiled broadly for the camera. The newspaper noted: "Tallulah Bankhead . . . shown above visiting the dressing room of vocalist Billie Holiday, America's Number One Song Stylist. . . . Billie Holiday is one of the greatest [Tallulah] ever heard."

As Billie became close to Tallulah, she came to realize the actress had a propensity for substance abuse. Early on, Tallulah relied on marijuana and cocaine—one reason she was trolling Harlem when she first crossed paths with Billie—before she moved on to an assortment of barbiturates and amphetamines. All the while, she indulged in alcohol, usually whiskey or bourbon. So one commonality Billie and Tallulah shared was an ongoing reliance on drugs and alcohol, dual addictions that over time had a devastating impact on their lives and careers.

But theirs was more than a sexual dalliance. "To Tallulah, Billie was beautiful, a great talent, and a comedienne," William Dufty later told Bankhead's biographer Joel Lobenthal. "For Billie, Tallulah's place was a safe house. She went to stay with Tallulah both at the Hotel Elysee [where she lived] and at Tallulah's house in the country—if she was getting beaten up or she thought she might be set up." The Bankhead estate in the quaint upscale village of Bedford in Westchester County was renowned for its lush beauty. "Billie wasn't impressed by anything—not by furniture or gardens or statues or a view. It was distant and it was white and it was safe." As for the underlying motivations for their romance, Lobenthal believes "they were both childless women who wanted to be a mother. Their longing for a child would have been a bond. They both had a desire to repair, to redo it all. They both loved animals that were substitutes for something else."

For Billie, the current man in her life whose abuse she was often trying to flee was John H. Levy (not to be confused with the respected bass player John Levy, a member of the original George Shearing Quintet who occasionally played in groups backing Billie). Born in 1908 in either Chicago or Arkansas, depending on the press report, this John Levy was raised in Kansas City before coming to New York to pursue business opportunities, most likely in organized crime. He was, according to *The New York Age,* "known for his activities in underworld movements as well as for being the first Negro to own a nightclub in the midtown area." Because of his last name and his light skin tone, it was not always apparent to someone on first meeting him that he was black—a misunderstanding Levy did not go out of his way to correct. "He was," to quote one account, "a tall, balding man with a quiet, knowing smile." The Midtown club of which he was co-owner, along with Dickie Wells and Al Martin, was Club Ebony, a spacious, finely appointed establishment located at 1678 Broadway at Fifty-Second Street. Somehow, in 1948, after Billie was released from prison, despite the fact she did not have a cabaret card, she was able to open at Club Ebony on May 7 and—even more remarkably—perform there in a four-week run without interference from the police, who were well aware of her engagement because the club was frequented by off-duty police officers and federal agents. Here was how Billie described working for Levy: "John Levy ran Club Ebony. . . . There was somebody's money behind him, but everything was run by Mr. Levy. As far as everyone knew, he was the boss. Right then all I knew or cared about was that he could give me a job when no one else dared. He was a big-time operator taking an interest in a chick fresh out of jail."

It was not long into the run before an affair began. At first, Levy lavished Billie with gifts, including jewelry and her first mink coat, until he had secured a place in her life as not only a romantic interest but also her personal manager. The development prompted one newspaper columnist to quip, "There'll be a rumor around your way that John Levy, one of the Club Ebony boys, has taken over Billie Holiday's heart along with her personal managerial contract." The news was made official by *Billboard* in July. So Billie's romance and business involvement with Levy were well underway when Billie opened at the Strand in mid-July and Tallulah was a regular, if not nightly, presence in August. For his part, Levy seemed threatened by Tallulah, who was not a force to be denied. "Banky was about the only person . . . John Levy couldn't scare away," Billie wrote. "She was a brick." The animosity between the two people vying for Billie's attention came to a head one night when Levy tried to force Tallulah to leave Billie's dressing room only to have her slam the door in his face. Charles "Honi" Coles remembered: "I saw Billie in the Strand Theatre on Broadway and Tallulah and Stump were there and Tallulah was furious at John Levy. They had some kind of beef and Tallulah locked the door and wouldn't let Levy in. She called him—you know Tallulah's voice—'Bah-stard'—and all sorts of names."

After the Strand run ended, the two women continued seeing

each other. Tallulah was ringside on the evening of September 17 when Billie opened for her second highly publicized engagement (still with no cabaret card) at Club Ebony, now backed by the Buster Harding Orchestra. Then again, Levy—under new scrutiny since he had become her personal manager—made sure Billie's second opening at his club was a star-studded affair that featured a host of bold-face names, including Marlon Brando, Jessica Tandy, Gene Krupa, Noro Morales, Henry Mills (of the Mills Brothers), Sarah Vaughan, Thelma Carpenter, Lena Horne, Norman Granz, Clark Monroe, and heavyweight boxing champion Joe Louis. The opening was such an event, according to one press report, that traffic was blocked in front of the club on Broadway.

As Billie's involvement with Levy progressed, gifts continued to come in, among them a pea-green Cadillac and a house in St. Albans, Queens, which Billie was led to believe was purchased in her name. (She later discovered it was not; she was misled by Levy into signing the contract as a witness, not an owner.) But, over time, while the gifts arrived, Billie slowly lost control of her finances to Levy, a fact that did not escape Tallulah, who Stump Cross recalled "came to the Ebony every night just to see us." Tallulah was so involved with Billie's daily routine that when Billie came down with laryngitis Tallulah offered a trusted cure—"pancakes, swimming in wild honey"—that became the subject of a gossip column item. As Tallulah grew increasingly suspicious of Levy, a worry she openly shared with Billie, Billie began to press Levy for an accounting of her earnings. She also insisted that if they were going to remain together, she wanted to marry him—a prospect to which he was open, or so he said, even though he was married to another woman with whom he had a son. Tallulah's misgivings were further bolstered by what happened when Billie took a trip out west in December accompanied by Levy. During a four-week run at Billy Berg's in Los Angeles, where she was appearing with Red Norvo and his band, a brawl broke out in the kitchen of the club on New Year's in the early moments of January 1, and somehow Billie ended up in the middle of it.

A group of friends of the owner was gathered in the kitchen when Billie walked through, coming offstage after finishing a set.

A man named Henry Martin bumped into her. A report in the *Los Angeles Daily News* described the ensuring altercation: "Levy . . . demanded to know what happened. [Then he] is alleged to have grabbed a butcher knife and made a lunge at Martin only to miss him and slash at [a man named Robert] Donovan. Donovan was severely cut up." During the fracas, Billie smashed plates onto the floor, presumably trying to force Levy to stop, which he finally did. Now, with the butcher knife still stuck in his shoulder, Donovan stumbled out of the kitchen onto the bandstand, where Red Norvo, alarmed by the wounded intruder, admonished the band to keep playing until the police arrived. When the authorities showed up, Levy was booked on assault with a deadly weapon, but, three days later, Billie was indicted on three counts of felonious assault, even though she had nothing to do with the altercation.

Clearly, something nefarious was at play. Then again, Billie had been trailed by authorities for years. Indeed, Jimmy Fletcher, her nemesis who helped carry out the raid that sent her to prison, had resurfaced recently when Fletcher and a dozen agents and office staff held a birthday celebration for someone in their group by coming to Billie's show at Club Ebony. It turned out that John Levy had a long history with Fletcher, who once arrested him for pimping years ago in Kansas City only to become friends with him when they both ended up in New York. Fletcher was colleagues with FBN agents in California, principal among them Colonel George White, head of the office in San Francisco, who became a key figure in the next suspicious development that happened to Billie in California.

After closing at Billy Berg's, Billie traveled to San Francisco to open at Café Society Uptown, a club owned by Joe Tenner on Fillmore Street. Opening night, January 13, 1949, brought packed houses, thanks to the publicity resulting from the melee at Billy Berg's. Billie settled into her four-week run and enjoyed her accommodations in Room 602 at the Mark Twain Hotel. A week into the engagement, on Saturday, January 22, the following transpired, as recorded by a legal source: "John Levy and Billie were relaxing in pajamas in their hotel suite when the telephone rang. She took the call. It was for Levy. He took the receiver and exchanged a few monosyllables with the person on the other end of the line. . . . He put down the receiver and handed Billie a small package and told her to flush its contents down the toilet. As she neared the bathroom, there was a sharp rap on the door. Levy, who ostensibly had some personal reason for wanting the package to pass from immediate existence, nevertheless took the promptest action to open the door to the hallway, and in rushed Colonel George White with two San Francisco inspectors and several of his agents from the Federal Bureau of Narcotics."

Billie made a mad dash for the bathroom with White right behind her. An ensuing struggle resulted in Billie being able to flush down the toilet most of the contraband—a small quantity of opium and a glass pipe. Still, White succeeded in retaining enough evidence—a few fragments of glass with a brown substance on them—to take Billie and Levy downtown to the Hall of Justice. Although both were arrested, it became clear Billie was the target. Each protested it was a "frame." Much of the resulting press coverage—the arrest made the front page of the *San Francisco Chronicle*—mentioned what Billie wore to the Hall of Justice. One report noted: "Miss Holiday . . . silently hugged her $10,000 silver-blue mink coat around her and chain-smoked cigarettes throughout the formalities." Upon departing the building, Billie proclaimed to reporters: "The show must go on!" And so it did. Only hours after being released on bail (Levy and Billie each posted five hundred dollars), she was onstage at Café Society Uptown singing to another standing-room-only audience. "She [embraced] the mic," one newspaper observed, "and went through her torrid, throaty songs as if nothing had happened at all." Two days later, for her Tuesday evening shows, the *Chronicle* reported that "Chanteuse Billie Holiday . . . had a packed house as usual . . . but the customer who must have intrigued her most was a gent who sat at ringside through two shows and even made a couple of requests—Colonel George H. White, boss of the Federal Narcotics Bureau here."

Back in New York, Tallulah, who was now appearing in *Private Lives* on Broadway, became convinced Billie was being set up by Levy. With Billie in obvious jeopardy, Tallulah decided to use her family's political connections to go directly to what she believed was the source of Billie's problems—J. Edgar Hoover. She set up a three-way telephone call with Hoover in Washington, Tallulah in New York, and Billie in San Francisco. On the day of the call, Billie listened, at first in anticipation and then in horror, as Tallulah became increasingly aggressive with Hoover, who insisted the FBI had nothing to do with what had happened in San Francisco. "But Banky," Billie later wrote, "didn't give up. She begged him to do anything he could for me." When Hoover reiterated that Billie's case was beyond his purview, Tallulah hit back. "What do you mean it's out of your hands? This girl's life was almost ruined once because they sent her to jail. She makes millions of people happy and she never hurts a soul except herself. Sure, she may need a little perking up from time to time, darling, but who doesn't?" The call ended with no promise from Hoover to intercede, and Billie worried Tallulah may have done more harm than good.

On February 2, when Billie and Levy appeared at a preliminary hearing with the lawyer Joe Tenner lined up to make sure Billie could perform at his club—Jake Ehrlich, nicknamed "the Master"—it was clear the government intended to proceed unabated. On February 7, Billie was indicted by a grand jury based on testimony from Colonel White, and the government dropped all charges against Levy. Two days later, Tallulah pressed her case once again with Hoover. She wrote a letter in hopes of convincing Hoover to stop the government's pursuit of Billie by referencing her politically powerful family and by appealing to Hoover's hubris. "I am ashamed," she started, "of my unpardonable delay in writing to thank you a thousand times for the kindness, consideration and courtesy, in fact all of the nicest adjectives in the book, for the trouble you took regarding our telephone conversation in connection with Billie Holiday. . . . I tremble when I think of my audacity in approaching you at all with so little to recommend me, except the esteem, admiration, and high regard my father held for you." (Her father died in 1940; President Roosevelt, thirty senators, and sixty-three congressmen attended his funeral in Jasper, where forty thousand mourners from across the state descended on the sleepy town.) "I would have never asked him or you for a favor for myself but knowing your true humanitarian spirit it seemed quite natural at the time to go to the top man. As my Negro mammy used to say, 'When you pray you pray to God don't you?'" Tallulah could not have been more flagrant in her flattery of Hoover, literally comparing him to God; now she made her appeal. "I have met Billie Holiday but twice in my life"—Hoover surely knew this was not true, since Billie had been under surveillance for years—"but admire her immensely as an artist and feel the most profound compassion for her knowing as I do the unfortunate circumstances of her background. Although my intention is not to condone her weakness"—her inability to kick her drug habit—"I certainly understand the eccentricities of her behavior because she is essentially a child at heart whose troubles have made her psychologically unable to cope with the world in which she finds herself. Her vital need is more medical than the confinement of four walls." Tallulah was making the case that drug addiction should be treated not as a crime but as an illness—a popular position taken by progressives at the time, not necessarily members of law enforcement. "However guilty she may be, whatever penalty she may be required to pay for her frailties, poor thing, you I know did everything within the law to lighten her burden. Bless you for this."

For Billie, for a decade now, Hoover and others working on behalf of the government had done anything but attempt "to lighten her burden." Tallulah hoped her appeal to Hoover might prompt him to call off the government's crusade of mistreatment. It became clear soon enough that her efforts had not worked.

3.

Because of her history with the city, it was no wonder that Billie might have harbored mixed feelings about being in San Francisco in October 1958. Still, she was pleased to be at the Blackhawk—almost one full decade after the events that unfolded around her appearance at Café Society Uptown—and she would have been happy to fulfill her entire two-week engagement, but there was an unexpected development. At the Sahara Hotel in Las Vegas, Louis Prima and

Keely Smith were forced to close two weeks early because of an unanticipated Hollywood commitment, and the hotel management approached Joe Glaser to ask if Billie would consider filling the first of the two weeks. "The Sahara in Vegas sent out an SOS for Billie at $3,000 a week," the *San Francisco Examiner* reported, "so Guido and George"—Guido Caccienti and his partner, George Weiss, at the Blackhawk—"let her off. She'll play the extra week here at a later date." Billie would now close in San Francisco on the fourth and open in Las Vegas on the sixth, but first she had an appearance to which she was looking forward—the Monterey Jazz Festival. On Sunday, Billie, accompanied by Alice Vrbsky and Mal Waldron, headed to Monterey, where she stayed at the Hotel San Carlos.

A chill hung in the night air as Billie stood backstage awaiting her entrance at the first-ever Monterey Jazz Festival, the brainchild of disc jockey Jimmy Lyons—a dream that over the last three days had come true in a spectacular way. A who's who of major acts had appeared, among them Louis Armstrong, Dave Brubeck, Dizzy Gillespie, Harry James, the Modern Jazz Quartet, Max Roach, and Sonny Rollins, only to conclude with the final featured performer— Billie Holiday. A covered stage had been constructed at the Monterey County Fairgrounds; seven thousand chairs were set up to hold the audience, which had been at or near capacity through most of the festival. Tickets cost four or five dollars. For the occasion tonight, Billie wore a chic evening gown featuring a star pattern, oversized dangling earrings, and a snug-fitting mink jacket. Her hair, though not slicked back, was pulled into her customary ponytail. For those who saw her backstage—and eventually some members of the press in the audience—it appeared she had been drinking during the course of the evening. It was sometime after eleven o'clock when Mort Sahl, who was the emcee, stepped up to the microphone at center stage and said, "Here are, simply, Billie Holiday and friends."

The applause washed over her as she took the stage to look out onto a sea of people stretching back into the darkness, a massive crowd surrounded on three sides by tall streetlights creating pools of light on the audience. Mal Waldron concluded his intro vamp and, as the ovation died down, segued into a deliberately paced rendition of "T'ain't Nobody's Business If I Do," a nod to Bessie Smith (who recorded the tune in 1923) that had become Billie's informal theme song. After the opening verse with only piano and bass, Dick Berk, whom Billie had brought with her from San Francisco because she enjoyed his style, came in on drums, but, as he later said, because of Billie's weak voice he chose to use only brushes to back her. The song's end elicited a warm response from the crowd.

When Billie started her second song—"Willow Weep for Me"—the audience clapped in recognition. A dramatic conclusion brought more applause, setting up her third number, "When Your Lover Is Gone," interrupted partway through by a distraction that had plagued the performances throughout the festival—an airplane flying overhead.

Once she finished, Billie spoke to the audience for the first time. "Thank you, ladies and gentlemen. Now I'd like to do a little tune of mine entitled 'God Bless the Child.' I hope you like it." A moving version of the song finished with an ending she used only in concert—a dramatic, slowed-down conclusion—which brought a loud burst of applause punctuated by a scattering of whistles. During the applause, Gerry Mulligan strolled out onto the stage.

"Where's Benny Carter?" Billie said, poking fun at his delayed entrance. "What took you guys so long to get out here? I've been waiting and waiting."

"Benny and Buddy"—Carter and DeFranco—"will be along in a minute," Mulligan said.

"All right," Billie said happily.

"What you going to do in the meantime?" Mulligan asked.

And Billie launched into "I Only Have Eyes for You" with Mulligan complementing her on saxophone, as he did on the next number, "Good Morning Heartache," which was again interrupted by an airplane—much louder than the previous one—flying low overhead. Carter and DeFranco finally entered and joined Mulligan backing her on the next numbers, "Them There Eyes," "Fine and Mellow," and "What a Little Moonlight Can Do."

With her set over, Billie made her exit to the band vamping. After an extended ovation from the audience—there were loud cries of "More!"—Billie returned to the stage. "Thank you very much, ladies and gentlemen," she said. "This was wonderful. What can we do for you? 'Travelin' Light'?"

There were shouts of "Yes!"

As she settled into the song, Carter played brilliant fills on clarinet. It was a beautiful, melodic version of the song. The response from the audience had not ended before she started the up-tempo "Lover Come Back to Me," which ultimately slowed down for a dramatic finish.

An ovation continued as she made her exit, this time for good, a little after midnight in Monterey. Over the years, California had been a place of both heartache and triumph for Billie. Tonight had been a triumph. That fact was not reflected in the responses of the critics, which were mostly unkind to Billie. Writing in the *San Francisco Chronicle,* Ralph Gleason declared: "Her voice is a mere parody of its former beauty." A critic for the *Los Angeles Mirror* was more brutal: "The less said about Billie Holiday the better. I don't know how she made it to the stage. Then she proved what her records have been indicating—she's washed up." A writer for *Down Beat,* who seemed irritated the sidemen appearing with Billie were not afforded significant solos, even misrepresented the ovation given to her, which was easily heard by anyone in the audience, when he wrote: "As Billie finally left the stage, a few persons cheered—whether in praise or derision it was honestly difficult to tell." It had become commonplace for critics to bash Billie. For years, they had been lamenting her loss of voice or pretending surprise when she turned in a successful performance. What they did not seem to understand was that Billie's audience—who never gave up on her—knew her voice was not in the pristine condition it was in during the 1930s when she recorded with Teddy Wilson; the fans were there to hear her performance of the songs, which remained sincere, deeply sensitive, almost confessional. Her audience, including the one who heard her in Monterey, connected with her on an emotional level. Like Judy Garland and Édith Piaf, Billie Holiday may have ended up offering a flawed version of a song, but it was perfect in its authenticity. As the years passed, her performance—her art—became different not only because her voice changed but also because *she* changed. As Miles Davis put it, "You know, she's not thinking now what she was in 1937."

On Monday, October 6, Billie, still accompanied by Alice Vrbsky and Mal Waldron, flew to Las Vegas, where she checked into the Sahara Hotel. She opened later that day in the Lounge Room, but she had plenty of time to relax beforehand, because her first show did not start until 1:20 in the morning, with her final show commencing at 6:20 a.m. Because the hotel wanted gamblers to stay up as late as possible, there was often entertainment throughout the night. Billie was aware of the unusual showtimes in Las Vegas because she had played the city in the summer of 1956. Once again, she had been a last-minute addition, on this occasion to the Jerry Gray Band opening at the Dunes. "The bandleader had just announced . . . that a guest artist was going to be on the bill," to quote an account describing one of the band's rehearsals, "when in walked Billie Holiday." The band's pianist was Corky Hale. "That's the piano player?" Billie scoffed. "You're kidding, right?" But after Billie handed over her sheet music and Hale played a song for her, Billie became so taken with the young pianist—one of the few women piano players working at the time—she blurted out, "Honey, you are my little girl!" and immediately asked her to join her on her next gig headlining at Jazz City in Los Angeles. The two women remained friends as Hale, also a harpist, went on to marry Mike Stoller of Lieber and Stoller, the songwriting team. "For all her fame," according to a biography of Hale, "[Billie] was missing the one thing she really wanted in life—a baby. Instead, she had this little Chihuahua, Pepe, that she diapered and fed from a baby bottle."

There was another reality about Las Vegas of which Billie was sadly aware: an attitude about race that was more in line with the Jim Crow South than other western cities like Los Angeles and San Francisco. Many African Americans, so unwelcome at the hotels on the Strip they instead frequented establishments downtown on what was known as Jackson Street, called Las Vegas "the Mississippi of the West." In 1953, one hotel on the Strip famously drained its swimming pool because Dorothy Dandridge stuck her toe in the water, and Sammy Davis, Jr., was not allowed to stay in the hotel where he performed until Frank Sinatra insisted that he open for him—*and* be afforded accommodations—at the Frontier in 1954. Not much had changed by 1958. "We were staying at the Sahara Hotel," Vrbsky remembered, "but when Lady mentioned to some of her black friends about coming to the show, one said, 'Oh, Lady, they would hire us as a maid or waiter. [But] we can't come to that place [as a guest].' In the club itself, two of her white friends happened to be in the audience one night. I saw her sitting at the bar with the couple, and she said one of the owners came up to her afterwards and said, 'We don't want you sitting at the bar talking to the customers.' That bothered her. She resented that kind of thing. She felt it wasn't anyone's business who bought her a drink at the bar."

The scene was eerily similar to how she was once treated at the Hotel Lincoln in New York City. So much time had passed, yet so little had changed, despite the emergence of a movement advocating for civil rights for black people in America—a grassroots crusade that was long overdue.

4.

On the day she flew from the West Coast back to New York, Billie was leaving behind all that had happened to her out west through the years. She had good memories—her romantic interlude with Orson Welles, shooting *New Orleans* with Louis Armstrong, countless club dates in Los Angeles and San Francisco. But there were disturbing memories too. Her first husband was arrested in L.A. To make matters worse, his eventual conviction and incarceration ended their marriage. But without question, the most frightening ordeal had been her drug bust at the Mark Twain Hotel, which represented the closest she came to facing prison time again since the drug bust and conviction in Philadelphia in 1947. Because of the terror she felt of returning to prison, her past legal ordeal in San Francisco continued to haunt her even as she headed home to New York from Las Vegas. She would never forget the courtroom where the trial took place. Sometimes she could still see the judge on the bench, the prosecutor at the table next to hers, the capacity-sized crowd of onlookers gazing from the gallery. It didn't take much prompting for her to see herself in the courtroom all over again.

The trial had been scheduled for early 1949. To prove that Billie was presently not addicted to narcotics in anticipation of the trial, Jake Ehrlich pursued the unorthodox strategy of having Billie check into a sanatorium. If she was addicted, she would show serious symptoms of withdrawal. "It cost me almost a thousand dollars," Billie wrote, "to pay the doctors to watch me and supervise me down to the last minute so they could go to court and make a statement. I stayed there four days; and when I left everyone in the place was ready to swear on a stack of Bibles that I was clean." Reports later identified her place of confinement as Belmont Sanitorium; her stay was arranged by Herbert Henderson, her friend who was licensed to practice medicine in California. "Holiday willingly underwent urine and blood tests, which proved negative," scholar Sara Ramshaw would write. "After two weeks, Holiday left Belmont." Whether she stayed for four days or two weeks—the record would be unclear—it was apparent Billie was not addicted to narcotics at the time of the drug bust in San Francisco.

After a series of delays, the trial finally began on May 31, 1949, a warm, humid Tuesday in San Francisco. Ehrlich's plan was to paint Billie as someone "unlucky in life" who was wrongly set up by the man who was the equivalent of her husband. Billie confirmed the image when she arrived in the courtroom on the first day looking frazzled as she took her place at the defendant's table. Appearing "somewhat unkempt in a beige suit," one journalistic account noted, "she wore red-and-white-rimmed pixie glasses which did not wholly conceal the evidence of prolonged crying and one eye that was bruised and swollen." Asked about her condition, Billie told a reporter Levy had assaulted her. "You should see my back," she said. "He done it Friday night. It looks better now than what it did. He went off Saturday night—even took my mink—eighteen grand worth of coat. Said he was going to give it to his sister to take care of." Billie looked directly at Ehrlich. "I got nothing now, and I'm scared."

It was, however, her testimony on the stand, during which she came off as sincere and sympathetic, that helped her cause the most. Ehrlich asked her if she had seen Colonel White before. At Café Society Uptown, she answered, "with John Levy. Always with John Levy."

Eventually, Ehrlich requested that Billie explain what she and Levy were doing on the morning the raid occurred. She was pressing him about her earnings, she said. "We had been arguing for a couple of months. I asked him where was the money and what was I making and why didn't he give me some money and what was happening to my money."

"Now," Ehrlich said, "you and Mr. Levy were to get married?"

"Yes, we were. We were sweethearts and I turned my whole life over to him. He took every penny I made. He was supposed to marry me. I never handled any money and I can prove it. We were supposed to get married and we didn't and that is why the argument came up that morning."

"While you were arguing, did Mr. Levy receive a call?"

"Yes, there was a phone call and I answered the phone and it asked for Mr. Levy and it sounded funny to me because it didn't say 'Levy.' It said it different. And I said: 'John, it's for you.'"

Then Billie walked through a step-by-step recitation of the raid that made it obvious, even to the casual observer in the courtroom, that she had been set up.

On cross-examination, Al Weinberger, the prosecutor, was attempting to explore the obviously complicated relationship Billie had with Levy when she blurted out passionately, *"He's my man!"* The irony—one of Billie's best-known songs was entitled "My Man"—was not lost on the courtroom, which, to quote one report, "erupted with spontaneous laughter."

"He has been your man?" Weinberger asked.

"Yes!" Billie exulted, prompting more laugher.

"You handed the phone to him."

"Why, yes! I never did anything without John telling me."

"Was it your intention to throw an object as large as this—"

Billie cut him off: "I didn't ask how large it was! If your wife asked you to throw something away, would you notice how large it was? You would throw it away, wouldn't you?"

The cross-examination was essentially over at this point, as it became evident that on the morning of the raid Billie was merely following the orders of the man she regarded as her spouse even if, as was also apparent, he was doing his best to avoid marrying her.

Despite the effectiveness of her performance on the stand, the line of questioning that sealed the fate of the trial occurred when Ehrlich cross-examined Colonel White. On multiple occasions, White was asked about his association with Levy. How long had he known John Levy? "Since January 22, 1949"—the day of the arrest. Did he know him at any other time? "No." Were he and Levy friends? "No." Did he and Levy visit together? "Subsequent to his arrest I had several conversations with him." But did he know Levy at the time of the arrest? "No, sir. I knew him by description and reputation, but not by sight." Finally, after a lengthy examination affirming his lack of familiarity with Levy, Ehrlich hit White with a piece of evidence Billie had helped him secure: a photograph of Levy and White sitting at a table in the audience at one of Billie's shows *before* the raid. Producing the photograph, Ehrlich said to White, "I show you a photograph and ask whether it is a photograph of you and John Levy?"

Startled, White attempted to deflate the moment by joking it was not a flattering picture of him. Colonel George White, colleague of Jimmy Fletcher, longtime friend of John Levy, had failed in his attempt to frame Billie Holiday. It took the jury of six men and six women—all white—two and a half hours, and two ballots, to return a verdict of not guilty. The jury foreman, Isaac Friedman, told the press after the trial that the jury believed the defense contention that "Miss Holiday had been framed."

In the year after the acquittal, even though it was generally accepted that Levy had set her up, at least for the opium bust if not for the brawl at Billy Berg's as well—Ehrlich openly argued in court that Billie was being victimized by her boyfriend-manager—Billie refused to end her involvement with Levy. His behavior toward her became so appalling—he routinely hit her in the face or stomach in public in front of witnesses—that Bobby Tucker refused to play piano for her as long as Levy was in the picture. During that year, Billie continued to see Tallulah, which infuriated Levy. In February 1950, Billie was playing the Club Riviera in St. Louis at the same time Tallulah was in town appearing in *Private Lives*. One press report observed: "Miss Holiday was happily surprised to note in her audience the presence of her good friend and pal, Tallulah Bankhead, the noted stage star." Stump and Stumpy were part of the variety revue appearing with Billie; Carl Drinkard was accompanying her on piano. "Tallulah came in there with another girl," Drinkard remembered. "Lady goes to their table ringside during intermission, and John [Levy's] saying, 'Look at that bitch, Carl, look at that. That bitch"—meaning Tallulah—"is going out of her fucking mind. She's all over her, she's hugging and kissing Lady." The following month, in March, Tallulah went out of her way to associate herself with Billie publicly, as evidenced by a mention in the *New York Daily News:* "Tallulah Bankhead has joined the Broadway group that is pitching to get Billie Holiday a police license card enabling her again to appear in local clubs."

With Levy, Billie reached her breaking point in late July when she finally ended their personal and professional association. "The split in forces is said to have resulted from a fight which had been brewing for some time," the *New York Amsterdam News* reported. "Miss Holiday will take over her own [personal management]." As it happened, her affair with Tallulah did not last much longer. In 1951, a scandal involving a maid stealing money from Tallulah became front-page news. At a highly publicized trial in December, the maid's lawyer argued his client was advanced money by Tallulah so she could procure for the star "marijuana, cocaine, booze, and gigolos." The maid was convicted, and Tallulah was unnerved by the proceedings. She feared the maid would reveal Tallulah's secrets, such as her heavy drug use and her affairs with women like Billie Holiday. Tallulah became so frightened she completely distanced herself from Billie, who was clearly on Tallulah's mind earlier in the year when she released a recording of her singing "You Go to My Head," a tune closely associated with Billie. One newspaper observed that Tallulah's version of "a song Billie Holiday once made practically immortal" was possibly "the flattest, most unmusical, most painful phonograph record ever made." Billie may have remained in Tallulah's thoughts, but now Tallulah tried to erase Billie from her life altogether. In 1952, when she published *Tallulah: My Autobiography,* the name Billie Holiday did not appear anywhere in its pages. Annie Ross remembers: "Lady and Tallulah had a falling-out. I don't know what it was about. Lady never spoke about it, but she never spoke badly of Tallulah."

As for Levy, in December 1956, he died, according to *The New York Age,* "due to a clot on the brain." He was forty-eight. For some time, he had owned a tavern named Poor John's; he was also facing a trial for income tax evasion, which could have landed him in prison. A press account of his funeral at the Abyssinian Baptist Church in Harlem listed a selection of the numerous mourners who attended; among the nightlife and underworld figures were Mrs. Willie Mays, Oscar Hammerstein, and Count Basie. But included there on the list of mourners was a name not as well-known as some of the others, at least not to the public—federal agent Jimmy Fletcher.

Back home in New York from Las Vegas, Billie tried to recover from her trip out west. Lately, she had been encouraged by a milestone in popular music. At present, the Number 1 single on the *Billboard* Hot 100 was "It's All in the Game" by Tommy Edwards. A slow-paced melodic tune written in the style of a romantic "beat" ballad, the song was important because it represented the first time a black artist had reached the Number 1 position on the *Billboard* charts. The history-making hit stood as encouragement to all black artists aspiring to make it in the music industry.

As for Billie, she did not have much time to rest up from her western engagements. She had accepted two gigs for promoter Lester Isaacs. On October 17, she was featured at the St. Nicholas Arena in

New York City; the following evening, she appeared at the Armory in Elizabeth, New Jersey. For each date, which contained a nine-song set, she was paid five hundred dollars. Next, on the afternoon of the nineteenth, she was scheduled to co-headline with Maynard Ferguson and Pee Wee Russell in the All-Star Package Show of Jazz at the University of Massachusetts. For the event, sponsored by the University Associate Alumni, the school described Billie as one of the "veterans of the jazz world . . . in the 'blues' tradition of Bessie Smith and ranks with such performers as Ella Fitzgerald and Sarah Vaughan." But on the day of the show, neither Pee Wee Russell nor Billie arrived. "The details of the cancellation were not disclosed," one newspaper noted, "but a general feeling of disappointment was prevalent when Russell and Miss Holiday failed to show."

Perhaps the previous events of October coupled with her health issues prevented Billie from making the trip north. Whatever the reason, she felt well enough to appear on *Art Ford's Jazz Party* on the twenty-third, when her fellow performers included Charlie Shavers on trumpet, Mal Waldron on piano, Ben Walter on saxophone, Roy Gaines on guitar, and Harry Sheppard on vibes. "Her voice wasn't the way it was," Sheppard remembers, "but her timing and her performance were great. She was a pro." Still, her missed show was a concern, yet another warning sign of the many she had received—and ignored—for months now.

CHAPTER 8

Goodbye
to the City *of* Lights

Billie Holiday with Hazel Scott and Leonard Feather. Billie and Hazel, a music prodigy who became a master pianist, first met when their mothers became friends in Billie's early days in Harlem. Feather, a writer and presenter, produced Billie's highly successful 1954 European tour. Billie remained close to both friends until the end of her life.

November and December 1958

I.

A decade had passed since Billie lost her cabaret card. It would have been impossible to calculate the amount of money Billie lost during those years because of the obstinacy of the government officials in the city she considered home. Her anger over what she regarded as mistreatment, if not outright censorship, prompted her to question why she continued to live in New York. It made sense for her to relocate to a major European city like London, where she was viewed warmly, or Paris, where Americans often settled for a better life. In the 1920s, Paris played host to the Lost Generation that included figures like Ernest Hemingway, Sara and Gerald Murphy, and Zelda and F. Scott Fitzgerald. In 1925, Josephine Baker escaped the prejudice prevalent in the New York entertainment community and immigrated to Paris; she attracted such attention with her singing and dancing Hemingway called her "the most sensational woman anyone ever saw, or ever will." The relocation of black artists continued over time. In 1948, novelist James Baldwin, exasperated with the racism with which he was forced to deal in America, moved to Paris to carry on with his writing career. In the mid-1950s, Hazel Scott began to live separately from her husband, Adam Clayton Powell, Jr., when she set up a "salon" in Paris that started out as a temporary respite but ended up lasting for seven years. "My . . . years out of America," Scott wrote, "were . . . years of much needed rest, not from work, but from racial tension; and by that I do not mean that I never ran into racism. That would not be true. But whenever I encountered racism in any form [in Paris], it was so rare that it was an exception rather than the rule." Perhaps it was time for Billie to follow the lead of these prominent Americans and seek a home where she would not be punished for being who she was.

So, in the autumn of 1958, when Billie was offered an opportunity to appear in Europe, she leapt at it. The dates came about after she signed with George Treadwell to be her personal manager; he would augment the representation she received from Joe Glaser as her agent. The publicity shots of the mid-October contract signing, showing Billie smiling broadly with pen in hand as an equally delighted Treadwell looked on, had gone out over the wire services. *The Chicago Defender* pointed out that because her "popularity has been at a standstill in recent months," Billie "decided to do something about the lull by engaging George Treadwell . . . former husband-manager of Sarah Vaughan [who] is due much credit for Sarah's rapid climb to the top." For Treadwell, the centerpiece of his revitalization plans for Billie was "a $35,000 four-week European tour." The salary was inflated from the actual number, and it did not appear the bookings added up to four weeks, but to Billie it was all hype for the press anyway. What was important to her was that she had dates in Europe lined up.

The engagements would be presented by Bruno Coquatrix, the French songwriter and music producer who owned the Olympia Music Hall, an esteemed theater in Paris that was originally opened by the creators of the Moulin Rouge. For her engagements, Billie was guaranteed, in a deal bonded with the American Guild of Variety Artists, ten thousand dollars plus transportation costs. So, as October passed, she began to anticipate her upcoming trip to Europe. Despite her health (Harry Sheppard remembers that she had now lost so much weight "her strapless gown was like an inch away from her body"), Billie boarded an airplane, accompanied by Mal Waldron, and departed Idlewild Airport, landing in Paris, where they enjoyed a brief stay, before finally heading on to her first scheduled appearance in Milan, Italy.

No doubt her 1954 European tour, organized and presented by Leonard Feather, during which she played seven countries in four weeks culminating in a final concert in Basel, Switzerland, that was recorded for a live album, was in her thoughts as she prepared to perform on November 3 at the Smeraldo Theatre in Milan. Feather had been meticulous about presenting her in the best possible light. The tour was entitled Jazz Club USA, and Billie shared the bill with top-notch artists such as the Red Norvo Trio and the Buddy DeFranco Quartet. The undertaking had been an unqualified success on both an artistic and a financial level. But Bruno Coquatrix was not nearly as careful in the way he planned to present Billie. Indeed, in her engagement at the Smeraldo, Billie was featured not among other jazz luminaries but, as one publication described the bill, "in the company of pop singers, comedians, acrobats and impressionists." It was a cavalcade of lowbrow entertainment reminiscent of vaudeville, far beneath the dignity of a jazz artist of Billie Holiday's prominence. Needless to say, her set confounded the crowd, who had shown up to see jugglers and slapstick comedians, not songs rendered by a self-described song stylist. The audience response should not have been a surprise. "Billie had to go back to the dressing room after a few pieces," it was later noted, "amidst the whistles." Or as *Melody Maker* reported: "The booing and hissing at second house left the management no alternative but to ask her to forgo the remainder of the week." Coquatrix's obliviousness left Billie stunned and disheartened. She had come all the way from America, with high hopes of being embraced by the Europeans as lovingly as she was in 1954, only to suffer the rare insult of having an engagement canceled partway through the run. It was an unanticipated blow at a time in her life when she had little emotional reserve to cope with such a setback.

Billie's disappointment was softened later in the week when Mario Fattori, the film producer and devoted Holiday admirer, became so upset by Billie's unceremoniously abrupt cancellation that he organized an "invitation only" private concert in La Scala Opera House. Billie was moved by Fattori's generosity and pleased to be presented in such a respected venue, but she remained sour on her trip to Italy. She seemed to have New York in her thoughts when on November 8 she wrote a postcard to Alice Vrbsky, who was keeping Pepe and looking in on her apartment while she was gone.

A performance on November 9 at the Teatro Gerolamo, where she was joined by the Quintetto Basso-Valdambrini, finally saw her enjoy an adoring general-admission audience in Italy. Still, she was more than happy to leave the country, as evidenced by the postcard she sent to Leonard Feather upon her departure. "Just a line to say hello to you and family. What's happening in the Apple[?] this Italy is something else. I was glad to get away. . . . Regards to all, Lady Day."

Billie flew to Paris on November 11, a Tuesday, excited to be in the City of Lights. She began contacting friends in Paris and London. To her friend Max Jones, who wrote for *Melody Maker* in London, she sent a telegram: "At Hotel de Paris till Thursday evening. Love, Billie Holiday." Jones telephoned her on Wednesday and asked her about reports she was considering moving to England. "I'm writing to you," Billie said. "I'll give you the whole story then."

Before any other commitments, Billie was scheduled to appear on Wednesday at the Olympia, which, since it was the home venue of Bruno Coquatrix, was a major engagement for her. Sharing the bill with Jimmy Rushing, her friend from the Basie days, she was looking forward to the show, which was to be broadcast on the radio. The outfit she selected for the occasion was elegant and eye-catching; her strapless long white evening gown was accented by a silk shawl and dangling earrings. Billie cut a stunning appearance when she took the stage, an angelic figure in the soft white of the spotlight, but maybe she was still unsettled by the debacle in Milan—and now she was on the stage of a theater owned by the man who facilitated her embarrassment—or maybe she was not feeling well because of her travels or her bad health, but, regardless of the reason, she gave a performance of her eight-song set that was received almost as poorly as her appearance at the Smeraldo. Gérard "Dave" Pochonet, a drummer who was then a part of the Parisian jazz scene, recalled hearing the performance: "I listened to . . . it on the radio . . . I was quite disgusted by that painful and pitiful caricature of her talent, and the public was also, judging from their reaction and applause."

The crowd was hostile, the press dismissed her performance as a disaster, but a backstage interview with Billie following the show conducted by Henry Kahn for *Melody Maker* indicated she may not have been aware that the concert was a misstep. "Since my separation from my husband," Billie told Kahn, "I do not want to stay in the States. I want to settle in Britain because I love the people. In Britain they do not just call me a singer, they call me an artist and I like that." Billie clung to the hope of moving to Europe, yet Kahn seemed unwilling to ignore the matter at hand. "Lady Day," he wrote, "or the Princess of Harlem, as they call her in France, looked tired. She sat drinking a glass of Vittel water . . . and [spoke] in a meandering voice." As for her performance, he declared: "To be frank, she was a disappointment."

The negative critical reaction to the Olympia show was reported by an American columnist, who disclosed: "Paris critics failed to flip over Billie Holiday's radio debut over there. One of the experts decided her voice was 'scratchy' and several report her indifferent demeanor, which has been more than evident to Yankee observers for some seasons." Justified or not, the general response to the show was uniformly negative. What happened next was unexpected and, for Billie, upsetting. Based on the shows at the Smeraldo and now the Olympia, Coquatrix dropped her. If there were future dates, he canceled them. Even worse, he did not intend to honor the full terms of her contract. In the end, he would pay her only a fraction of what she was due; her agents failed to collect, even though the parties had signed a bonded union contract. Clearly, her new representation, George Treadwell, was not all she had expected; perhaps she did not yet know that when Treadwell and Vaughan divorced the previous year, Vaughan discovered that after she had earned substantial sums each year through the 1950s, her husband-manager claimed they had only sixteen thousand dollars in the bank. Or if Billie *did* know, she was so desperate to reinvigorate her career she overlooked that fact. But Billie now had a larger issue. If her aspiration was to relocate to either London or Paris to pursue a career in nightclubs, as Josephine Baker had done so successfully three decades ago, the decidedly public failure Billie suffered, not to mention the breach she sustained with Coquatrix, represented a potential derailment of a dream she had fostered for some time.

Romance was gone; she was facing divorce. Her career was a struggle in part because of the calculated actions of a vindictive government. And now the one solution to her problems—a move to Europe to find an available and accepting audience—seemed like a long shot if not out of reach altogether.

Her immediate dilemma was obvious. With her sudden break from Coquatrix, she had no prospect of future dates in Europe; nor was she even sure of her travel plans back to America. She was hardly flush with cash, so she decided to try to line up a residency on her own. Back in 1954, after she had completed the European tour dates arranged by Leonard Feather, she made a number of independently booked engagements, among them one night at a club in Paris where she performed with pianist Art Simmons, who was celebrating his birthday. A journalist later described the club: "The rue St. Benoit in Paris begins at the rue Marbeuf and ends a block away in a *cul de sac*. At the end of the little street was the Mars Club which was . . . the gathering place of all the makers and lovers of jazz who lived in Paris or were passing through town. The club had a certain ambiance that Billie Holiday liked." The Mars Club was founded in 1953 by Ben Benjamin, a native New Yorker who managed it with his wife, Etla, until the previous summer, when he sold it so he could open the Blue Note. Currently, the club was managed by Barbara and Barney Butler, a young American couple who, once Billie approached them, were thrilled to host her. In a remarkable development, some would say an indication of the desperate predicament in which she found herself, Billie agreed to perform her unexpected residency not for an accustomed fee but for a percentage of the door. It had been some time since Billie had been forced to make such an arrangement, but she was sure her fans would show up.

Billie's efforts to promote herself in Paris were helped considerably on November 18, when she appeared on a French television show entitled *Music Hall Parade.* On the program, she sang "I Only Have

Eyes for You" and "Travelin' Light." A favorite of hers to sing live,
the second selection was a midtempo nostalgic tune, composed by
Trummy Young and Jimmy Mundy with lyrics by Johnny Mercer,
about a woman who is "travelin' light" because her man is gone. Billie had recorded the song in 1942 for Capitol Records, at the request
of Mercer, but was forced to release the record under the name Lady
Day because she was under contract with Columbia Records. Now
she was singing the song, along with another one of her reliable
tunes, on French television in hopes of reaching her audience.

Billie had begun her dates at the Mars Club by November 20,
when a photographer snapped a picture of her onstage looking right
at home in an elegant thin-strapped black evening gown accented
by a gold necklace and gold earrings. It was near the beginning of
her residency that Billie decided to have dinner one night with a
group of friends at a local establishment named Gabby and Haynes,
a soul food restaurant popular with the jazz set. At the dinner she
was joined by, among others, Mal Waldron and Kenny Clarke, who
in 1949 had a short-lived affair with Annie Ross that produced a
son, Kenny Clarke, Jr., who was being raised by Clarke's brother
and his wife. As it happened, on this evening while she enjoyed her
delicious soul food, children were on Billie's mind. Since she had
been unable to have a child of her own and once had even attempted
an adoption, only to be rejected as an unsuitable candidate because
of her past criminal record, young people often caught Billie's eye,
especially if the person was in the age range to possibly be her child.
Such was the case tonight. When she looked across the restaurant,
she noticed a table where three people were quietly eating dinner.
Along with a handsome young man, there were two young women:
a glamorously beautiful black woman in her midtwenties and an
exotic dark-skinned girl in her midteens. As she ate her meal, Billie
became captivated by the teenager. Finally, she asked Waldron to go
over and invite the girl to join them. The teenager, as Billie learned,
was named Yolande Bavan. A native of Ceylon (later renamed Sri
Lanka), she was an aspiring actress and singer who lived in London
but often came to Paris.

"I was visiting Paris," Bavan remembers, "because my closest friend, Marpessa Dawn—she was an actress who had recently finished filming *Black Orpheus*—was living in Paris and I went to visit her, which I did frequently. I was also singing with a well-known French trio at the Blue Note. Why I thought I could sing I don't know; youth is intrepid. Anyway, Marpessa and I, along with her boyfriend, Eric, went to have dinner at Gabby and Haynes, which was where all of the Americans went to eat soul food. It was a small restaurant but very popular. A lot of Americans were living in Europe at the time. We were having our dinner and talking when suddenly I looked up to see Mal Waldron walking over to our table. I thought he was going to speak to Marpessa because she was famous, but he leaned down and said to me, 'Billie Holiday would like for you to come over and join our table.' I was a very shy young woman, coming from Sri Lanka. Marpessa said, 'Go, go!' But I said, 'No, I'm not going to go.' I just sat there."

When Waldron returned to his table, he told Billie the young woman was too bashful to join them. There was talk among the dinner guests about who the young women were, particularly Bavan, who was singing at the Blue Note. Eventually, when dinner was over, Billie and her party rose to leave, but on her way out Billie said she would join the others momentarily. Then she walked over to Bavan's table. As Bavan glanced up at Billie standing beside her, the sixteen-year-old appeared beautiful and innocent. She gazed at Billie with her dark eyes but did not speak. Finally, Billie said to her, "If I had a daughter, I'd like one like you." And without saying anything else, she turned and left.

Accompanied by Waldron and her party, Billie arrived at the Mars Club in time for her first show at eleven o'clock. It was an intimate space with a welcoming atmosphere, just the sort of place Billie liked to play. Once she took the stage and assumed her place at the microphone, Billie looked out onto the room as she sang. A journalist later recorded what it was like to watch her onstage at the Mars Club: "The incandescence of what was left of her great talent lighted up the place as she stood beside the piano, her voice ravaged by illness, her once-beautiful wine-colored eyes clouded by years of addiction to heroin, communicating her anguish over lost loves, her poignant despair of happiness she had never been quite able to find."

The following night, before she went to the Mars Club, Billie stopped by the Blue Note. Sitting at the bar, she chatted with Ben Benjamin, a good friend, while Yolande Bavan was onstage singing with a trio led by Jimmy Gourley. When the set ended, Yolande spotted Billie at the bar and approached her to say hello.

"You're probably a good singer," Billie said over the hum of the crowd in the club. "You're just not singing well tonight."

"I know," Yolande said.

"You better come to the Mars Club tomorrow at three and I'll listen to you sing and help you."

Yolande was stunned by the overture, and, in a departure from her initial reluctance, she agreed to meet. The next day she went to the club to discover that Billie had brought along Waldron to play the piano for her. After listening to Yolande sing, Billie decided to teach her a couple of songs she often performed. In the way she guided Yolande through "Solitude" and "Don't Explain," running each song numerous times in what became a master class, Billie kept demanding that Yolande adhere to one guiding principle. "Sing the truth!" she said emphatically again and again as Yolande practiced one song, then the other. "Sing the truth!"

What Billie wanted in return for her musical guidance was for Yolande to spend time with her, mostly at her hotel room in the afternoon. Billie always suffered from profound loneliness, and on this trip she had been especially morose. So she asked Yolande to come to the Hotel Crystal, a favorite accommodation among musicians to which Billie had moved when she left the Hotel de Paris, where Coquatrix had been putting her up. On several late autumn afternoons, in the quiet of Billie's hotel room, Yolande sat in a chair to keep Billie company while she went about her ordinary routine. Often Billie lay on the bed and read Superman comic books until it was time to get ready for the evening's show. Then she would cause Yolande to marvel as she straightened her hair with a curling iron.

There were other moments when they drifted into conversation. One subject that seemed to trouble Billie was Louis McKay.

"He hit me," Billie said, "but when he kicked my chihuahua, Pepe, into an empty fireplace, that was the last straw."

"My God," Yolande said. "This man is a monster."

"Yes, he is," Billie replied. "Yes, he is."

But mostly their conversations were upbeat.

"You're going to come to America someday," Billie said at one point, "and I'll buy you twenty-eight flavors of ice cream. We have a place called Howard Johnson's."

"I never heard of twenty-eight flavors of ice cream *or* Howard Johnson's," Yolande said. "It sounds exciting."

And throughout their handful of encounters, during what became a brief but intense friendship, Billie kept looking at Yolande as if she were the daughter she could have had if she had been able to conceive when she met her first husband, all those years ago.

2.

As a gray, wintry evening embraced the city, illuminated by the streetlights and the lights of buildings just coming on, a taxi proceeded through the streets of Paris until it came to a stop in front of a majestic apartment building located at 80 rue Miromesnil in the Eighth Arrondissement, a fashionable neighborhood centered around the Champs-Élysées, the traffic-heavy avenue that links the Arc de Triomphe with the Place de la Concorde. Today was Thanksgiving, a holiday not celebrated in France, unless you were going to the home of an American living abroad, as Billie was.

Billie and Hazel Scott had known each other since their mothers—Sadie Fagan and Alma Scott—became friends during Billie's early days in Harlem. Born in Trinidad and relocated to America when she was four, Hazel was a child prodigy who was accepted to study piano at the Juilliard School when she was eight. At four-

teen, she played hooky from school one day to go hear Billie sing
at the Apollo. By nineteen, she was recommended by Billie to Barney Josephson to headline at Café Society. When Josephson opened
a second Café Society uptown, Hazel was his featured artist. Her
career, not to mention her social life, took off in 1945 when she married Adam Clayton Powell, Jr. A son, Adam III, known as Skipper,
was born the following year. In 1950, *The Hazel Scott Show* became
the first network television program to star an African-American
artist, but a controversial appearance before the House Un-American
Activities Committee, during which Scott defiantly chided committee members by demanding, "Mudslinging and unverified charges
are just the wrong ways to handle this problem," resulted in the
cancellation of her show. Discontent with race relations in America
and problems in her marriage had prompted Scott to come to Paris
last year for what was originally supposed to be three weeks but
had turned into something much longer. Indeed, she had taken this
apartment so Skipper could join her. He was enrolled at the American School of Paris. When Billie telephoned Hazel upon her arrival,
Hazel made sure Billie would come to her home for Thanksgiving
as the evening's honored guest. Hazel loved the holiday and the city
in which they were celebrating it. "My Paris," Hazel later wrote, "is
a pot full of red beans and rice and an apartment full of old friends
and glasses tinkling and the rich, happy sound of people laughing
from the heart. My Paris is the warmth of the big Thanksgiving
dinners I had every year for my old and dear friends." No friend was
dearer to Hazel than Billie.

Emerging from the back seat of the taxi, Billie headed for the
handsome building and, inside, found the door to Hazel's garden-
level apartment. Ringing the bell, she was greeted by her old friend,
who showed her into the apartment, where a handful of guests were
already assembled. They had not been tipped off as to the identity
of the evening's special invitee. One surprised guest remembered
that Billie "had taken off her coat in the vestibule and appeared in
the door of the living room. A big smile illuminated her face, and
wearing a modest black dress with long sleeves, Billie was dressed
beautifully. She arrived alone and was in grand form."

Billie warmly greeted the other guests. She was also thrilled to see Skipper, now twelve years old, who was equally excited to welcome his "Aunt Billie" to his Parisian home. A tour revealed a spacious, comfortable apartment. The living room was dominated by Hazel's Steinway piano, which she had shipped over from America. On a wall near the piano hung a portrait of Hazel's mother, Alma, which no doubt brought back memories for Billie of both Alma and Sadie. Next came Hazel's bedroom followed by a kitchen and a dining room, where the table was already set for dinner. Skipper's room featured a bookcase bed; his walls were adorned with international maps. The apartment was designed oddly, requiring a person to walk through one room to get to the next—there was no main hallway—unless one went outside into the garden. Each room had a door that opened onto the garden.

Billie felt right at home. Music filled the living room, often the songs of Frank Sinatra. A German boxer reminded her of Mister; there was also a Siamese cat named Brigitte (as in Bardot). She was pleased to have a visit with Skipper, who remembers her as being kind and maternal. At one point in a conversation, she spoke to him with passion. "Remember, Skipper," she said. "God bless the child that's got his own. Don't rely on your mother. Don't rely on your father. You have to make your own way."

Before long, it was time for dinner. When the guests took their places at the table, Billie was seated beside Gérard Pochonet, a drummer with whom Hazel had worked on and off since 1950. The guests began to eat the traditional Thanksgiving dinner of stuffed turkey with soul-food trimmings Hazel cooked herself, the preparation of which presented its own small drama, since Hazel, famous for being a virtuoso pianist, had her hands insured by Lloyd's of London and under the terms of her policy was not supposed to cook. As they ate and chatted, Pochonet did not mention to Billie that he had been "quite disgusted" by her performance at the Olympia, which he heard on the radio, but complimented her records solicitously, particularly her early work with Teddy Wilson. "In the midst of the hubbub of various conversations," Pochonet later wrote, "which were going at a considerable pace around the table, I bent my ear close to

Billie. During the story that she was narrating about her personal life, she didn't seem blasé or disillusioned. At that time, she seemed much more satisfied about her musical career, which to her had been a beautiful success. Her personal life seemed to me to have been indeed quite turbulent and somewhat disappointing."

At ten o'clock, the meal having been "demolished because everything was delicious," as Pochonet recalled, the dinner party broke up so Hazel could accompany Billie to the Mars Club for the first show at eleven o'clock. Pochonet joined the two women in a taxi to the venue, which was, he thought, "a most dignified high-class nightclub near the Champs-Élysées, quite friendly and intimate." He stayed to hear Billie sing. "On this night, the audience numbered a good fifty patrons, everyone attentive as Billie sang, the applause most fitting with prolonged cheers. . . . Her engagingly fascinating voice showed in a most favorable light. Her rich, discreet sonority brought out the nuances of her interpretations. My God, it was a . . . pleasure!"

Between sets, as they sat at a table in the club, Billie and Hazel were finally able to visit, just the two of them. As the women drank, they reminisced about how times had been difficult for both of them. For Billie, it was clear her marriage was over; she had no romantic prospects. There were difficulties with her career in America; the response to her show at the Olympia did not bode well for a move to Europe, despite tonight's enthusiastic reaction from the audience. And, of course, there were her health concerns, which was why Hazel implored her to stay in Paris—so she could take care of her. "If you go back," Hazel said, "I may never see you again. You don't have anyone in New York to take care of you." As for Hazel, she had her own problems, which Billie knew. A theater project she desperately wanted to do just fell through; a recent attempt at reconciliation with her husband had ended in turmoil, throwing her into a depression so severe she attempted suicide. The parallel crises in the lives of the two women weighed on Hazel as Billie went onstage to perform her next set.

Nursing a drink, Hazel watched Billie; soon dark emotions took over. "It was a real bitter blues," Hazel would later say, describing what Billie was singing. "And on top of all the problems I was having in my own life at the time, I began thinking about what was happening to Lady Day. Brilliant artist, beautiful person—you could pin all of the superlatives on her, but there she was, having just been misused again by somebody who didn't give a damn about her, having just been given a rough time by the French public because her voice just couldn't do what they wanted it to do on the stage of the Olympia, there she was singing in a little club for whatever percentage she could get."

Watching Billie, Hazel began to drift back to all the years they had known each other and the many occasions they had shared— nights in Harlem, nights at Café Society, outings they had with their mothers. The depth of the moment became too much for her. And from the stage, as Billie looked out into the club, she was close enough to the audience that she could see Hazel had started to cry. Before long, she was weeping so hard audience members could hear her. When her set was over, Billie left the stage, crossed over to Hazel, and, taking her by her arm, pulled her up from her chair and walked her to the back of the club. Pinning her in a corner, Billie stood face-to-face with her. "The next time you feel like this," she said to Hazel, who by now had stopped crying, "just remember that you've got Skipper and Lady only has a little chihuahua and Lady's making it." She paused. "And another thing. No matter what the motherfuckers do to you, never let them see you cry."

As the days passed after Thanksgiving, it became clear to Billie that she was not going to be able to line up additional bookings in Europe. No offers for engagements materialized in London, and prospects for future employment in Paris seemed to have evaporated with the unfriendly response to her performance at the Olympia. She had enjoyed her unplanned residency at the Mars Club. Audiences were enthusiastic; she had been in good voice. It was the type of engagement she liked to play these days, one where the audience, regardless of the size, appreciated her artistry. She had also made enough money to travel home, so she booked a flight for December 2. She would finish out her run at the Mars Club and return to

America. It was not what she wanted to do, but she could not see where she had any alternative.

The rest of her run proceeded smoothly, and when she arrived at the club for her final night she was met with a pleasant surprise. Waiting for her in the club was a French author with whom she had previously become friends in America—Françoise Sagan. In her midtwenties, alluring in her looks, Sagan had first seen Billie perform two years ago in a club in Connecticut when she and a friend named Michel Magne, having flown to New York to see her, drove, as Sagan would write, "nearly two hundred miles in freezing-cold weather before reaching a wild, colorful place that seemed to me far from anywhere—a kind of country-music club with an uninspired-looking clientele that was noisy, rowdy and restless." It was there, not New York City—because Billie was forbidden to perform in clubs there—that Sagan fell in love with her onstage. When Billie met the couple after the show and learned they had come from France to see her, she said, "Oh, dears, how crazy you are." She arranged for them to see her sing in the city after all. Lately, she had been jamming with other musicians at Eddie Condon's after the bar closed. Billie relished the 4:00 a.m. jam sessions where she sang in the empty club accompanied by whichever musicians happened to show up. So she invited her new French friends to come by Eddie Condon's, an invitation they eagerly accepted. "For two weeks," Sagan wrote, "we spent our nights (or rather our dawns, from four a.m. to midday) in that perpetually smoky club, listening to Billie Holiday sing. . . . The audience consisted only of the two of us from France, two or three friends of Lady Day, and her husband, her man of the moment, a big morose fellow with whom she would have violent exchanges."

By the end of the two weeks, Billie had become friends with Françoise, and here she was at the Mars Club. Billie hugged her warmly; Françoise, now married, introduced her to her husband, who did not seem to know how to respond to Billie. Then again, this unease was often an effect Billie had on certain men, especially those who gave off airs of pretension. So, when she joined them at their table before she went onstage, Billie spoke to the husband in a blunt, unassuming voice. "Tell me," she said, "do you beat Françoise?"

When Françoise exclaimed that he did not—and should not start—Billie only laughed.

Finally, it was time for Billie to take the stage. "She sang with eyes lowered," Sagan wrote. "She clung to the piano as if to a ship's rail in stormy seas. No doubt the rest of the audience had come in the same spirit as I had, for they applauded wildly."

Near the end of the night, Billie sat down with her friend one more time. She mentioned her imminent departure for America. "Anyway, darling," she said as if drawing the night to a close, "you know I am going to die very soon in New York between two cops."

"You're wrong," Françoise said. "I don't believe you."

Billie did not respond to her friend's admonition. As for Sagan, what stood out to her about the evening was how much Billie had changed in the two years since she had last seen her: "It was Billie Holiday—and yet it wasn't. She had grown thin; she had aged. . . . She no longer had that innate assurance, that physical equilibrium which had conferred on her such marble-like serenity around the storms and dizzy turbulence of her life."

On Tuesday, December 2, her residency at the Mars Club behind her, Billie settled into her seat on the airplane after it took off headed for LaGuardia Airport in New York City. Accompanied as always by Mal Waldron, who had stood by her throughout this calamitous trip, Billie tried to focus on the good times she had enjoyed, seeing old friends and making new ones. She hoped to put the unpleasantness behind her—the disappointing audiences, the unforgiving rooms, the once-promising business deals gone bad—as she said goodbye to the City of Lights and headed for whatever the future might hold.

CHAPTER 9

The Whole Truth

The mug shot of Billie Holiday taken in May 1947 when she was incarcerated at the Federal Reformatory for Women in Alderson, West Virginia. During her intake interview with a prison official, Billie fabricated stories about her life much as she did nine years later, when she published her autobiography, Lady Sings the Blues.

December 1958 and January 1959

I.

In many ways, 1958 had been a remarkable year for Billie. She recorded and released *Lady in Satin*. She was in her element among other jazz luminaries when she appeared at the Persian Room for Columbia Records. She closed the Monterey Jazz Festival, an event that had been so successful it appeared as if it was going to be presented annually. She played a stream of dates throughout the year from coast to coast in the United States and in Europe. Perhaps it was the fallout of what happened in Italy and France, perhaps it was the relentless pace of the year taking its toll, or perhaps it was her physical condition in general, which had become such a concern she could no longer ignore it; for whatever reason, she slowed down in December. She had only one engagement all month: a week at the Chatterbox Musical Bar in Cleveland, opening on the eighth, where she was greeted with this broadside from the *Call and Post:* "For a singer, who has contributed such a voice to jazz as Billie Holiday, there certainly should be a much happier ending to a brilliant career." It was disconcerting that observers were beginning to describe her as being in the final stage of her career when she had not yet turned forty-four, an age that would be considered midcareer for most artists. Besides the Cleveland gig, she made no public appearances during December. The lack of action stood in stark contrast to the hurly-burly of the previous eleven months. The anxiety she experienced over her idleness was compounded by the continued distress she felt over the failure of her marriage.

It was likely now that she heeded the warnings of her friends who were worried about her health and visited Dr. Eric Caminer, whose office was at 101 East Sixty-Fifth Street. Originally from Berlin, Caminer graduated from the Friedrich Wilhelms Universität Medizinische Fakultät in 1926; he immigrated to New York in March 1939, probably to escape the Nazi regime. He was an internist with a flourishing private practice. When Billie saw him, he confirmed what Herbert Henderson told her in San Francisco: she was suffering from cirrhosis of the liver. Caminer would treat her with vitamin shots, and he insisted that she maintain a healthier diet, but what she had to do first and foremost was stop drinking. The disease had progressed to the point where she had no choice but to quit completely—at once.

Friends like Leonard Feather were hopeful Billie might finally be willing to make the effort to become sober. One evening she dropped by to visit him, his wife, and their daughter, Lorraine—to whom Billie was godmother—at the Feathers' apartment at 340 Riverside Drive, not far from West Eighty-Seventh Street. When Feather offered Billie a drink, she stunned him by requesting a cup of tea instead. "The doctor says I have cirrhosis of the liver," she announced, "and I can't drink." Billie seemed resolved to the reality that, given the severity of her health condition, she had to give up the alcohol she had been drinking since she was a teenager, or at least that was the impression she created.

The solitude of December made Billie realize more than ever the detrimental effect the lack of a cabaret card had had on her life. Were the city to allow her to work in the clubs, any number of them would hire her, and her overall stress level would have been reduced considerably. Others in the nightlife industry were aware of Billie's untenable predicament. Four musicians banned for minor narcotic convictions—trombonist J. J. Johnson, singer Dave Allen, pianist Beryl Rubinstein, and composer Johnny Richards—were challenging the cabaret card law in court; their attorney, Maxwell T. Cohen, had brought a lawsuit before the New York State Supreme Court. "Last year," author Murray Kempton wrote, "under circumstances like these, the police department formally denied identification cards to 328 persons, and thus effectively severed them from an important segment of the exercise of their professions." The court case prompted the American Guild of Variety Artists to pressure the city to end its practice of banning artists from performing. The guild implored club owners to stand up for the banned artists with the threat that, if they did not, guild members would boycott their clubs. Naturally, the figure most often singled out as suffering from a ban was Billie Holiday.

"There's a very serious situation brewing around the New York cafés," *The Philadelphia Inquirer* reported in mid-December. "For years the police department has ruled these clubs by issuing work permits to performers they consider to be 'clean.' Billie Holiday and others who have been picked up on narcotics and other charges have been unable to play New York clubs until their cards were reinstated—sometimes a matter of years." But now AGVA members "have voted to boycott any clubs which require police permits." The boycott could force "owners of every café in town to lobby for removal of the police department's authority."

Those words gave hope to Billie—*removal of the police department's authority.* She had never been able to rationalize the thinking behind a policy that would punish someone like her who made the mistake of taking narcotics by imposing on her a ban that rendered her unable to make a living. Her resentment for being banned fueled the gossip that continued to persist that said she was ready to move to Europe, where the opinions about drug use and addiction were profoundly different from those prevalent in America. *The Pittsburgh Courier* noted that there were "rumors that say Billie Holiday, despondent over being unable to get a work permit in New York City, is seriously thinking of quitting the U.S.A. and settling down in Paris, France." The *New York Daily News* echoed the story, saying that, "unable to work in New York, [Billie] tells friends she may settle in Paris." If the animosity she experienced in Europe on her recent trip had left a permanent scar, it was not evident, as she continued to be open to leaving America.

During the holiday season, Billie received an unanticipated gesture of kindness. Since returning to New York, she had been corresponding with Yolande Bavan, the young woman with whom she had become friends in Paris. In her last letter to her, Billie complained about her ban from the clubs in New York, which meant, for practical purposes, she had little to no money coming in. So, when she received a Christmas card from Yolande, Billie was touched when she opened the envelope to find included in the card a ten-pound note.

With her moratorium on drinking, it was a quiet Christmas season for Billie. In time for holiday shopping, no doubt inspired by the success of her Commodore rerelease, Decca issued *Lover Man,* a compilation of twelve songs Billie had recorded for the label between 1944 and 1950. The collection included, in addition to the title track, some of Billie's most popular songs, among them "My Man," "You're My Thrill," "Crazy They Call Me," "There Is No Greater Love," and "Solitude." The reviews fell more in line with the Commodore rerelease than the mixed notices given to *Lady in Satin.* Calling *Lover Man* a masterpiece, the *Nashville Banner* declared Billie was "a singer's singer"—an accolade "added long ago." A syndicated music column announced "the always dependable Billie Holiday is in top form with a collection of blues songs on *Lover Man.*" The *Deseret News* proclaimed that *Lover Man* "should suit Holiday fans since it catches her at the best in recordings of 1944 to 1950. These are the 'blues' for sure."

It was a mixed blessing for Billie. She loved that people appreciated her older songs, but she had recorded some of the tunes fifteen years ago; a lifetime had passed since then. There was no comparison between the mixed reaction to *Lady in Satin* and the praise lavished on her older work; it was as if the critics wanted her to stay the way she was a decade and a half ago. She could exhibit no change, no growth as an artist. It was a bittersweet accomplishment. At this same time, a problem with royalties from Decca developed. Billie did not believe she had received an honest accounting of record sales from the label over the years. Now the company was releasing another album of her work, yet she had no expectation of seeing accurate royalty statements in the future. As Dorothy Kilgallen reported in November, "Billie Holiday and Decca Records appear to have a problem about disc royalties."

2.

For Billie, January proved to be as quiet as December; she had no bookings or public appearances scheduled for the entire month. She was not yet becoming overly concerned, because Joe Glaser had lined up engagements for the spring and summer. In fact, because of her health, she welcomed the rest. So today—Wednesday, January 14, 1959—was another peaceful winter day in Manhattan. Since waking up, she had spent much of her time puttering around the apartment. She was going about her afternoon when the telephone rang. Answering it, she heard an officious-sounding man on the other end of the line.

"Is this Eleanora Gough McKay?" he said.

Anyone who called her regularly referred to her as either Billie or Lady. The formality took her off guard. "Yes, it is."

"I've been looking for you for over a week," he said. "This is Inspector McVeigh of the United States Customs Service."

Suddenly, Billie became concerned. What could *he* want? She had returned to New York from Europe in early December; too much time had passed for him to be calling about a perfunctory customs matter.

"Could you come down to the Customs House tomorrow afternoon?" The question was posed not as a request but as an order. "I'd like to ask you some questions. There's no need for you to bring an attorney."

Billie had learned not to fall for anyone, particularly a federal official, who said she did not need an attorney when dealing with the government, but she let his comment pass. Upon her pressing him, McVeigh would not reveal anything else about why she was wanted for questioning, so she took down his name, telephone number, and address and ended the call.

Then, in the quietness of her apartment, Billie was seized by a consuming sense of fear. Given her long history with the authorities, she never again wanted to subject herself to questioning by anyone affiliated with a government agency—no matter how nonthreatening the official pretended to be or in what agency he was employed.

With panic taking over, she decided she needed help. She called the Duftys.

She had known Maely Dufty when Maely was married to Freddie Bartholomew, the British actor who as a child moved to Hollywood to appear in such motion pictures as *David Copperfield, Anna Karenina, Little Lord Fauntleroy,* and *Captains Courageous.* After they divorced in 1953, Maely married William Dufty. "Maely Dufty," according to one account, "a Jewish émigré from Germany, was known in Harlem as a fighter for justice, a lover of jazz, and a writer for the *New York Citizen-Call.* She often supported musicians, in part by finding them legal assistance to fight narcotics charges," although she had never performed that function for Billie. The two women met through social circles and became friends well before Maely married Dufty. Once the Duftys set up home on West Ninety-Third Street, Billie was a regular guest, and in 1955 when the couple had their only son, Bevan, they—like so many other friends—asked Billie to be his godmother. That same year, Billie, with the help of William Dufty as her coauthor, began work on her autobiography, *Lady Sings the Blues.* If Billie trusted anyone, it was the Duftys. Years later, Bill Dufty remembered receiving the telephone call from her that day in January: "I could tell from her voice that something serious was afoot. Lady never hollered 'Uncle' until she needed one bad."

When Bill Dufty arrived at her apartment, Billie was hardly able to control her alarm. She could not imagine why an inspector from the Customs Service wanted to question her. Out of caution, Dufty called the Customs House to confirm McVeigh was an agent. He was. So, Billie concluded she had no choice but to attend the meeting. Because she wanted to keep the matter confidential until she knew more, she was unsure who to use as an attorney. She was concerned Earle Warren Zaidins, who represented her on a variety of matters, was too familiar with her; she also worried about his periodic practice of "putting my business on the street." Dufty had an idea. He and Maely had become friends with a young, up-and-coming attorney who was known for being adept with the law and for having a friendly rapport with reporters. The Duftys were guests at the parties she hosted at her cramped but charming apartment on

East Forty-Eighth Street near Fifth Avenue ("there's the dirty room
and the filthy room," she would joke); later in the evening they often
headed for Birdland accompanied by her law partner. Her name was
Florynce Kennedy, but everybody called her Flo.

"Flo was brilliant," Eleanor Pam, a friend and political colleague
says, "feisty and scarily articulate, the originator of the phrase 'a
woman needs a man like a fish needs a bicycle.' She was sharp-
tongued and quick-witted, full of piss and vinegar." Judge Emily
Jane Goodman recalls her as being "forceful and brilliant, [someone
on whom] you could not put anything over." Attorney Edward W.
Hayes remembers that "she looked odd and acted odd, later wearing
a cowboy hat and all that, but she was always perfectly respectable
professionally." Author Sandra Hochman concurs that "she was very
eccentric but in a wonderful way." Her unconventional personality
would emerge even more fully once she joined the women's movement in the 1960s and became, as poet and activist Robin Morgan
says, "her obstreperous, audacious self."

She had come to New York from Kansas City, Missouri, in
1942—the second oldest of five daughters born into a financially
comfortable family (her father was in the taxi business)—to attend
Columbia University, graduating in 1949. She was among the first
black women to enter Columbia Law School, but not without complications. "They said she was being rejected," Goodman recalls,
"not because you're black, they said, but because you're a woman.
She said, 'Well, to my friends at the NAACP it's going to be the
same.'" Suddenly, a place was found for her; she graduated in 1951.
She established a private practice with Don Wilkes, creating Wilkes
and Kennedy. Because of her life experiences concerning race and
because of her media and political savvy, Kennedy was the ideal
attorney for Billie Holiday. She also happened to be a fan who had
seen Billie sing "Strange Fruit" in 1955 at a benefit honoring Emmett
Till in Harlem.

Billie asked Dufty to call Kennedy at once. When Dufty explained
the situation to her, she had no idea why the Customs Service might

want to question Billie. "As we talked," Dufty would write, "I had a sudden recall of an old story I had read in the papers about a pair of narcotic addicts put under arrest for failure to register with the Treasury Department." Quickly researching the topic, Kennedy discovered the problem: the Narcotic Control Act of 1956, which stipulated that "no citizen of the United States shall depart from the U.S. if he is addicted to or uses narcotics as defined by the Internal Revenue Code of 1954 unless such person registers with Customs prior to departure and upon his return to the country. Penalty for failure to register will subject the offender to fine and imprisonment." Potential violators included "anyone convicted of violation of the narcotics or marijuana laws of the U.S. or any state, the penalty for which is imprisonment for more than one year." Because Billie's previous conviction carried a sentence of one year and one day—"what a difference a day makes," Dufty wrote—Billie risked being sent back to prison, all because she did not know she was required to register with Customs when she left and reentered the country. The mere thought of returning to prison filled her with trepidation and despair.

When Dufty hung up the telephone, Billie, knowing tomorrow held another harrowing encounter with a government hell-bent on destroying her, was overcome with anxiety. She could barely cope with the terror she felt. "She called the liquor store and ordered full quarts of Gordon's gin," Dufty wrote, "and she started looking for a home for the dog." After all, for two decades now, once she had made herself a target of the authorities by appearing at Café Society, Billie Holiday, one of the most accomplished artists in the music industry, had to face the constant threat that at any time she could leave home and, through no fault of her own, end up arrested and in jail. The damage the omnipresent threat inflicted on her psyche over the years would be impossible to measure. If she had been following the advice of her doctor to stop drinking, as she told Leonard Feather she was, the day's disturbing news short-circuited that effort. Once the delivery arrived from the liquor store, the rest of the day and night became one long blur of dread dulled by gin.

When the surveillance started during her Café Society residency, Billie initially became a suspect because she was working

at a club that challenged prevailing racial prejudices and because
the powers-that-be behind the club appeared to have communist
connections, but scrutiny grew worse—Billie and Jack Gilford, the
club's emcee with whom she had become friends, often saw police
watching them when they got off work—once Billie began to sing
"Strange Fruit." What she did not know but would soon find out
was that she had caught the attention of Harry Anslinger, who in
1930 had been instrumental in the creation of the Federal Bureau
of Narcotics, whose mission of cracking down on narcotics use and
trafficking could be traced back to the Harrison Narcotics Act in
1914. "With Harry Anslinger," Sonny Rollins says, "it had a racial
aspect with it. It was *Mexicans* who smoked marijuana; we should
stay away from marijuana and *Reefer Madness* and all of that. It was
all very political."

Anslinger appeared fixated on the African-American community in general and the jazz world in particular. In one memoran-
dum he described jazz this way: "It sounded like the jungles in the
dead of the night." So he relished the FBN going after jazz musicians for their narcotics use, including figures like Rollins, Dexter
Gordon, Charlie Parker, and—perhaps the score he wanted most—
Billie Holiday. Annie Ross says: "'Strange Fruit' was a factor in why
they went after Lady, but the greater reason was that she was successful, and people loved her and they loved her singing. She had to
be brought down a notch." Or as Colonel George White, representative of the mindset at the investigative agencies, put it, "She flaunted
her way of living, with her fancy coats and fancy automobiles and her
jewelry and her gowns—she was the big lady wherever she went."
The implication was clear: Billie needed to be put in her place. "It
was her brazenness and her attitude," David Margolick says. "She
was unbowed. She was defiant. That's what made her a target, and
Hoover's men were absolutely ruthless."

The opportunity for the government to bring down Billie had
come in May 1947 once she and Joe Guy were busted for narcotics
possession in Philadelphia. No matter how hard she tried, she could
never forget that day in court when—at the recommendation of Joe
Glaser—she showed up without representation, a decision that made

her a sitting duck for the prosecution. The rigged court appearance and the months in prison that followed were the reason why she was filled with fear over becoming entangled with the actions of another government agency. Before she knew it, her fate could be sealed, just as it was in a courtroom in Philadelphia a dozen years ago.

3.

On May 27, 1947, as Billie took her seat at the defendant's table in the District Court of the United States for the Eastern District of Pennsylvania, she felt confident, because of Joe Glaser's advice, that if she asked the court for help she would be sent for treatment at a hospital. From the bench, the Honorable J. Cullen Ganey peered down on Billie sitting alone. When Joseph Hildenberger, an assistant district attorney, asked Billie if she wanted to be represented by an attorney, she gave her fateful answer.

"No," she said.

"How do you plead?" the deputy clerk asked.

"I would like to plead guilty and be sent to a hospital," she replied.

With this, Hildenberger recounted for Ganey the details of Billie's case—"the case of a drug addict." He depicted Billie as a victim of her fame. "We have learned that in the past three years she has earned almost a quarter million dollars . . . and she doesn't have any of that money. These fellows who have been traveling with her, sweethearts, would go out and get these drugs and would pay $5 or $10 and they would charge her $100 or $200 for the same amount of drug. It is our opinion that the best thing that can be done for her would be to put her in a hospital where she will be properly treated and perhaps cured of this addiction."

Judge Ganey asked Billie a series of questions about her show business background and her now-chronic drug use. Answering each question as best she could about her career, Billie also confirmed she had started using heroin three years ago.

"Didn't you know it was wrong to have narcotics in your possession?" Ganey asked.

"I knew it was wrong," Billie said, "but I couldn't help it once [I] got started, sir."

When Ganey asked about what quantity she was taking, Max H. Roder, an agent, responded by saying she was taking "fifteen to twenty grains a day."

"Is fifteen to twenty grains a large amount of heroin to use?" Ganey inquired.

"It surely is. If you or I would use one shot, we would be dead immediately." That was how much Billie's system had become acclimated to the drug.

As soon as Hildenberger brought up Joe Guy, Billie tried to change the subject by suddenly interjecting, "I am willing to go to the hospital, Your Honor. I want the cure."

When the court appearance had gone on for about fifteen minutes, Ganey appeared to be ready to hand down his decision. It was not what Glaser told Billie it would be. "You," the judge announced sternly, "stand here indicted criminally as a user of narcotics."

To underscore the severity of Billie's drug addiction, Ganey asked her how much money she made last year.

"I don't know exactly," she said. "Forty to fifty thousand, I imagine."

"Forty to fifty thousand," the judge said bluntly, "all gone?"

"Yes, sir," Billie said, and then, as she seemed to realize the momentousness of what had happened to her, she broke down sobbing.

Ganey called a sidebar to confer with the prosecution team. Afterwards, he continued his remarks to Billie. "I want you to understand," he said, "that you stand here as a criminal defendant. . . . I want you to know you are being committed as a criminal defendant; you are not being sent to a hospital alone primarily for treatment. You will get treatment, but I want you to know you stand convicted as a wrongdoer. . . . In your imprisonment you are going to find that you are going to get the very best medical treatment which can be accorded to you; that is the beneficial part of the government's position in this case." Finally, Ganey concluded by saying, "You, Billie Holiday, under information, March Term, 1947, [must] undergo imprisonment for the period of one year and one day."

Without being allowed to go through a proper withdrawal period, Billie was given one shot of heroin to keep her from getting sick on the trip when officials placed her on a train to be taken to the Federal Reformatory for Women in Alderson, West Virginia. At one point during the nineteen days that she endured hellish withdrawal symptoms, she sat for an interview as part of the prison's intake process to provide biographical information about herself. But even as she spoke with the prison officer, she could not resist fabricating details about her life. She told the officer she was born in 1919, not 1915; she claimed her real name was Billie Holiday Monroe when it actually was Eleanora Harris Monroe; she indicated she completed the sixth grade at Public School 36 in Harlem before she dropped out of school, whereas years later in her autobiography she would say she "finished the fifth grade in school in Baltimore and I hadn't been back." Upon Billie's representation, one passage of the admission summary describes her youth as follows: "She is the only child of Clarence and Sadie Holiday. She appears to have been deeply attached to her parents, and states her childhood was happy, though economic circumstances were not good. . . . Her father was a musician, and in 1928 or 1929 moved his family to New York City, where opportunities for employment were better. Subject was raised in Harlem's teeming tenements and is a product of that section." This, clearly, was the childhood Billie longed to have—nice family, loving parents, living conditions that were the urban equivalent of a house with a white picket fence. So powerful was her desire to have an ordinary—and happy—childhood that even now, at the age of thirty-two, she was manipulating the facts to the way she wanted them to be—to a federal government officer, no less.

The uneventful time she spent in prison was agonizing in its mundanity. Still, she tried to maintain an upbeat outlook, as evidenced by this citation from a progress report: "Subject is a wholesome influence with a good attitude. She spends her time knitting (extremely well) and listening to records. She reads a lot in the evening and prefers the better magazines." During her stay, she never sang one note, despite numerous requests from inmates and staff. Inmates were allowed to possess, according to a prison rules sheet, "books, novelty pins, *plain* combs to wear in the hair, *small plain* gold or silver colored crosses on chains, victrola records, sheet music or music books (semi-classical and classical numbers, popular songs, but no blues or hill-billy numbers), photographs and snapshots of the immediate family." Billie got along well with inmates; a prison romance was rumored. She received and sent mail. One person with whom she corresponded was Leonard Feather. "Leonard," she wrote in a letter dated July 19, 1947, "if it's not asking too much please call Joe Glaser and see what he intends to do about some good publicity for me. I've had so much bad stuff written about me and I do think we should do something so that people won't forget me. After all, a year is a long time for the public to wait." Lorraine Feather says: "Billie wrote letters to my father from prison. She said she needed money in prison too. [At one point], she wrote to him on toilet paper."

Billie also corresponded with Joe Guy, who was in jail in Philadelphia on similar charges to hers. "Joe," Billie wrote on August 5, "I know you don't like to write but can't you write just a little more? I have your picture in a frame right here before me as I write this. . . . The picture really makes me happy now. . . . Sweetheart, I can't answer you about the girl here as it's against the rules to write about inmates and officers and what you wrote was censored. I told your mother that she should have your Dad go to Phila [*sic*] to see about your case and she agrees with me because I don't want it to be like it was for me. I didn't even have a lawyer and it's awful to go through things like that alone. . . . Well, darling, I guess that's all for now except I never wanted time to pass so bad in my life and it just seems to crawl and creep along. But my day is coming and we will be together again. . . ." As it happened, despite the romantic overtures she made toward him, Billie's time in prison marked the end of her relationship with Joe Guy, who eventually returned to Birmingham and stopped playing music.

One element of prison life especially disturbed her. "Jim Crow was the rule everywhere," Billie wrote. "We ate separately, slept separately, and went to church at different times. That . . . was a real drag." The racial disparity, as she would later reveal, instilled in her "a greater determination to fight against discrimination." Her confinement came to an end on March 16, 1948, when she was released early for being a superior prisoner. But the months in Alderson affected her deeply. "The most lonely sound in the world," she later confessed to a friend, "is a train whistle at night when you're lying in bed, locked up. It can really fuck up your mind."

Upon her release, Billie traveled to New Jersey to stay with Bobby Tucker, her pianist, to prepare for her first post-imprisonment engagement, a solo show at Carnegie Hall on the evening of March 27 arranged by promoter Ernest Anderson, who was himself a character, with one reporter describing him as "a scholarly, bespectacled little man who . . . has acquired the reputation as an entrepreneur and impresario." Demand for tickets was so strong sales set a box-office record for the historic venue. The show was a stunning success, as Billie proceeded through the playlist with such power and precision her audience was left dazzled. The *New York Daily News* declared that "[Billie Holiday] is probably the most highly styled singer we have [who is so beloved] there were times Saturday night when her concert took on the atmosphere of a revival meeting with her fans rocking and shouting at her from all over the house. [It was] something of a show business landmark." Meanwhile, *Time* observed that "her voice, a petulant, sex-edged moan, was stronger than ever." Due to popular demand, a second show was arranged for April 17; it too sold out. If the goal of the government had been to destroy Billie's career by sending her off to prison, the ploy had failed spectacularly, which only made matters worse for Billie. "The police have been particularly vindictive," she wrote, "hounding, buckling, and harassing me beyond endurance."

In the immediate year after Carnegie Hall, she enjoyed continued success exemplified by a return engagement at the Strand Theatre in Manhattan ("The ovations were so great that she was unable to include her recent original compositions," one newspaper reported) and an appearance in a Universal-International short film featuring Count Basie interacting with and then playing with his orchestra for

Frank "Sugar Chile" Robinson, a twelve-year-old piano prodigy, and Billie, who sang "God Bless the Child" and "Now, Baby, or Never." Still, Billie remained a target, and in the summer of 1953 her profile was raised even higher by events beyond her control when on June 19 Julius and Ethel Rosenberg were executed following a trial for espionage for allegedly supplying top-secret government nuclear design documents to the Soviet Union. In the wake of their deaths, condemned by an international amalgam of defenders, who questioned the government's treatment of them before, during, and after the trial—in the future, new evidence would implicate Julius, but not Ethel—it was revealed that their two sons, Michael and Robert, were being adopted not by family members but by Abel Meeropol, the author of "Strange Fruit," and his wife, Anne. Though he did not know them, Abel Meeropol was even a pallbearer at the Rosenbergs' funeral. Then, in 1955, Gloria Agrin, who assisted Emanuel "Manny" Bloch in defending the Rosenbergs, married Barney Josephson. Now two of the men who had helped Billie become a prominent figure in the entertainment industry—Meeropol and Josephson—were connected to one of the most notorious cases of presumed communist sympathizers in American history. If she could be viewed as guilty by association—a not uncommon occurrence in the world of Hoover and his acolytes—Billie was seen as even more suspicious now.

4.

It was a hazy January afternoon, with the temperature hovering in the midforties, as the taxi sped along amid the towering buildings in downtown Manhattan. In the clamor of the Wall Street district, the car came to a halt at 201 Varick Street. Bundled up in a coat and scarf and accompanied by her new lawyer, Florynce Kennedy, whom she had already nicknamed "the hip kitty from Kansas City," Billie emerged from the taxi and headed for the entrance of the Customs House. Going inside, the two women took the elevator up to the fourth floor, where they were shown into the office of the supervising customs agent, room 405, a banal, nondescript space reminiscent of so many government offices. The pair were greeted by Inspector

Martin McVeigh, the agent who had called Billie the day before, and his partner, Agent Mario Cozzi. The women sat on one side of a conference table; the men on the other. Like the vast majority of federal agents Billie had encountered over the years, the men were buttoned-up, all business, total squares.

"Mrs. McKay," McVeigh said, starting the inquiry at 3:40 p.m., "Agent Cozzi and I are Customs agents of the United States Treasury Department. You are here at our invitation in connection with an investigation we are conducting relative to your having departed from and reentered the United States without having registered in accordance with the narcotic registration law, about which we desire to ask you certain questions. Are you willing to answer our questions?"

"Yes," Billie said.

So Kennedy was right. All of this was the result of Billie not registering with the government when she recently departed for and returned from Europe—requirements of which she was completely unaware.

"I want to advise you," McVeigh continued, "that under the Constitution of the United States you are not compelled to answer any questions, but if you do, and the government desires, they may use your answers against you. Is that clear, and in the circumstances are you willing to answer our questions truthfully?"

"Yes," Billie replied.

"Will you stand and raise your right hand, please?"

Billie did as she was requested.

"Do you solemnly swear that the statements you are about to make," McVeigh said, "will be the truth, the whole truth, and nothing but the truth, so help you God?"

"I do," Billie said, sitting back down.

"What is your name, age, and occupation?"

"My name is Billie Holiday," she said. "I am forty-one. I am a singer. That's my occupation."

Of the three pieces of information she offered, only one was true. Yes, she was a singer. But she had never legally changed her name to Billie Holiday, and she was forty-three.

McVeigh let the age pass for the moment; he corrected her name. "Is your true name Eleanora Gough McKay?"

"Yes."

"Billie Holiday is your—"

"Stage name."

McVeigh established her address, her citizenship, and her passport number before he offered a warning: "In the event you don't fully understand any of our questions, will you please refer to your attorney, Miss Kennedy." Then he asked, "Where were you born?"

Without hesitating, Billie answered, "Baltimore, Maryland."

"Did you say Baltimore, Maryland?" McVeigh said. "Your passport lists Philadelphia, Pennsylvania, as the place of your birth on April 7, 1915. What is the correct—?"

Billie interrupted. "I went to school in Baltimore. I always say Baltimore." It was clear she was nervous and uncertain. "I went to school in Baltimore," she repeated. "It's a mistake. I'm sorry."

"Then you want to correct that answer?"

"Yes, that's right."

"Were you born in Philadelphia, Pennsylvania, on April 7, 1915?"

"April 7, 1915."

"That would make you forty-three years of age," he said.

Billie acquiesced on the issue of her age. Then McVeigh confirmed her travel itinerary—she had flown from Idlewild Airport to Paris in late October 1958 and returned from Paris to LaGuardia Airport on December 2—after which he shifted the focus of the questioning to a more ominous line of inquiry.

"Have you ever been convicted for any narcotic offenses—?"

"Yes, I have."

"—of the federal government or any state thereof?"

"The federal government once."

"Were you convicted or did you plead guilty?"

"I wanted to go away for a cure," Billie said, "and they gave me—"

McVeigh stopped her. "I have a copy of your record from the Federal Bureau of Investigation, which indicates that on May 26,

1947, as Billie Holiday, you received a sentence of one year and one day at the Federal Reformatory for Women in Alderson, West Virginia. Is that a true record?"

If Billie held any doubts that these two agents had been in contact with, or perhaps were even directed by, the FBI, McVeigh confirmed her worst fears.

"Yes, that's right," she said, verifying her record.

Suddenly, Cozzi spoke up. "Were you arrested in Philadelphia by federal narcotics agents?"

"No, I wasn't really arrested," Billie explained. "They were sort of like you people. They were very nice to me."

McVeigh pointed out that a law was passed in 1956 that required a person convicted of narcotics possession to register with the government upon leaving and reentering the United States. Was she aware of the law?

"I didn't know anything about it at all," Billie said.

"What was the purpose in leaving the United States?"

"I went there to sing," she said. "Just myself and my piano player. And my agent gave me the tickets . . . and he never [told] us about registering. I never saw any sign, so I didn't know. I went to the doctor, I did everything else I should have done, so why shouldn't I have done this? I did not know."

After asking who her pianist was—Mal Waldron, Billie said—they questioned her once again as to whether she registered upon leaving and reentering the country.

"Nobody asked me to. I never did it before. This must be something new because wouldn't they ask me?"

"No," Cozzi interjected. "It's not the government's responsibility to ask every individual passenger or person leaving the United States if they have a narcotics record. . . . You'd be insulting a lot of people."

Clearly, Cozzi meant the comment to be a not-so-veiled insult.

"Oh," Billie said. "I suppose so. I didn't see any sign. I'm awfully sorry about it."

In response, the agents produced a small sign—seven by eleven inches—warning narcotics users and violators to register upon leaving and reentering the United States. Signs like this one, they claimed, were posted in the airport. "Have you ever seen any similar sign before this?"

"No," Billie said. "If I had, I would have noticed it and I would have asked [my agent] about it, and I would have done something about it. Really, I don't know anything about it." She paused. "They took pictures of me standing on the ramp with a little bag, the newspapers. . . . I couldn't have been trying to sneak away. . . . They kept me out there in the cold for half an hour."

The federal agents had accomplished what they set out to do— they proved she was in violation of the 1956 law—but they were not finished.

"Mrs. McKay," McVeigh said, "have you ever been arrested for narcotics violations other than in May 1947?"

"Yes. About a year ago. But it was all wrong."

"Would that have been an arrest on or about February 23, 1956, in Philadelphia, Pennsylvania, by their police department for narcotics drugs?"

"Something like that. There was nothing to it."

"You were acquitted?"

"Yes."

"Was there any other time you were arrested for any other narcotics violation?"

"Not that I remember."

McVeigh challenged her. "Were you arrested in San Francisco on or about January 22, 1949?"

"With John Levy, yes."

"And the record shows that the charges were dismissed?"

"That's right."

Finally, they had done it—listed her trail of legal woes, although they had gotten their facts wrong: she was found not guilty at trial in San Francisco in 1949, and she had pled guilty in lieu of parole in Philadelphia in 1958. Still, the customs agents had made their point. Billie was a felon who found herself repeatedly in trouble with law enforcement. Was there anything else she wanted to add?

All the years of harassment—surveillance by agents, court

appearances, prison time and probation, not to mention being unable to earn a living because of a cabaret card ban—came crashing down on her. "Well," she said, "it just seems that a little thing like this I didn't know about, and nobody cared enough about me—my agents, and I got management for this and that—to tell me about it. I have been trying my best to be a good girl, and a little thing like this, I have to come down here and go through all this. That's all I have to say. It's terrible; that's all. Once you get in trouble for narcotics, it's the end. I think it's the worst thing that could happen to anybody in the wide world. That's all I got to add."

Billie felt some sense of satisfaction from being able to unload on the agents. What she could have said was that the government's torment of her had hampered her career and harmed her emotional and physical well-being. But she left it with what she said, which was more than she usually offered to someone from the government. The agents did not respond to her but, instead, invited Kennedy to issue a lawyer's statement.

"I hope we make it entirely clear," Kennedy began, "that Miss Holiday's intention has been at all times to comply with whatever rules and regulations there are, and inasmuch as this law was enacted rather recently, 1956, it had not come to her attention. Apparently, her attorney did not know of it. I, personally—although we were not representing her at this time—we were not aware of it. . . . And I can only say it's a clear case of not being responsible to a law which she had already been acquainted with. That's about all I can say." Kennedy moved to end the meeting. "I think it can be seen that it has been Miss Holiday's intention to abide by the law."

As the interview concluded, Billie realized her legal jeopardy was anything but over when McVeigh made his concluding pronouncement. "I'm going to refer this matter with all these statements to the United States Attorney for the Eastern District of New York at Brooklyn, and I necessarily will be guided by his decision in the matter."

It had gone as well as could have been expected. Billie never lost her composure; nor did she reveal any information the government did not already have. For what it was worth, she had the truth on her side: she had not registered because she was not aware of the law, and no one—not her agent, not her attorney, not any government official at either Idlewild or LaGuardia Airport—informed her of it. The meeting ended, but the matter was not resolved, leaving Billie in a legal limbo that only exacerbated her fragile emotional state.

"Billie came out of the hearing shaken," William Dufty wrote. "It had gone well, she felt, but she was still scared. Kennedy complimented [her] on being an excellent witness. 'I should be a good witness by now, honey,' Lady snapped. 'I've had enough experience on the damn stand.'"

A transcript of the hearing was produced, which, at a later date in Kennedy's office, was signed by Billie and the two agents as being accurate and authentic. The document was entitled "Statement of Mrs. Eleanora Gough McKay, Also Known as Miss Billie Holiday."

CHAPTER 10

"I'm Billie Holiday!"

*Billie Holiday with Yolande Bavan at the after-party at
Humphrey Lyttelton's 100 Club following her appearance on a taping of the
British variety television show* Chelsea at Nine *on February 24, 1959. Billie
had first met the sixteen-year-old singer and actress three months earlier when
she spotted her in a restaurant in Paris. On her way out, Billie stopped
by Bavan's table and said, "If I had a daughter, I'd like one like you."*

I.

"This, then, is my complaint," Billie wrote. "When will the police lay off me and allow me to earn a living, and in a dignified way?" The answer was clear. It was not just the police in pursuit of her but all areas of the government, including, as unlikely as it may have seemed, the U.S. Customs Service. The meeting at the Customs House may have transpired without incident, but, for Billie, because of what she had been through, because of all the pain and suffering she had been forced to endure, she had to assume the worst might happen. With the real prospect of prison looming, terror set in. Memories of Alderson weighed down on her—the loneliness, the tedious labor, the degrading segregation. She could not survive going back to prison, not now, not at this point in her life. She was not in the best of health; another prison sentence would kill her.

After the meeting at the Customs House, the waiting began. The uncertainty was unnerving. If the U.S. attorney decided to prosecute her, there would be a trial; if there was a trial, her fate would be in the hands of a jury. Her only hope was that a jury in New York would view her as sympathetically as the jury in San Francisco had a decade earlier, but she could not count on it. Her feelings of fear and apprehension were not helped when during the last two weeks of January and the early days of February she had on her schedule no gigs and only one public engagement, a brief appearance on a telethon for children with disabilities—the bill featured an array of stars like Steve Allen, Judy Holliday, and Elaine Stritch—that was broadcast live, with Martha Raye as host, which started on Sunday,

February 7, at five in the afternoon and ran for nineteen hours. Billie was happy to perform on the show because of the cause—she was sympathetic to its support of children—and Martha Raye, who had been a faithful advocate of hers for years. The appearance, however, did not go without incident.

Dressed in a stunning white strapless evening gown set off by earrings and a necklace featuring a six-point star, Billie sang "My Man." Memories of Louis McKay likely beset her, but no doubt her pending legal troubles weighed on her mind just as strongly, and by the end of the song, live on television, Billie began to cry as she sang. When she finished, she abruptly bolted from the stage. "There is nothing unique about La Holiday shedding tears after a perfor-mance," one newspaper observed, "but there is usually an explanation when requested. 'I just felt like crying,' she told reporters following the telecast. . . . Was Miss Holiday brooding over 'My Man' or was it something else? This question may never be answered." That was true, because except for a handful of people—her closest friends and her attorneys—no one knew the debilitating pressure under which she was living as a result of her ongoing legal problems.

Mostly, these days, what Billie did was sit in her apartment, too paralyzed to undertake anything besides watching television. Lately, she began to shoot heroin again from time to time—more "chip-ping" than outright using. Miles Davis would remember her coming to Birdland one night in early 1959 to borrow money for heroin; he gave her what he had—about one hundred dollars. "She was look-ing real bad by this time," he later wrote, "worn out, worn down, and haggard around the face and all. Thin. Mouth sagging at both corners. She was scratching a lot. Before she was such a well-built woman, but now she had lost all that weight and her face was bloated from all that drinking. Man, I felt bad for her." But at this time what Billie relied on most was Gordon's gin, her old standby that had got-ten her through so many live gigs and studio sessions. Straight gin cut her hunger for heroin and numbed the anxiety she felt about her future. Her precarious mental and physical state became concern-ing. "Lady," Alice Vrbsky remembered, "was mainly drinking Gor-don's gin and Seven Up [and] that was what she was living on and that was why she started losing so much weight." When Bill Dufty mentioned her heavy drinking, Billie snapped back, "If you had the government breathing down your neck, you'd be drinking too."

She could not sleep. She was not eating. She was losing weight, and she was already thin. She saw Dr. Caminer, who, on February 10, wrote her a prescription for retinoic acid, which could counteract some of the damage heavy alcohol consumption had done to her body's organs, particularly her liver, yet his main directive remained the one she did not seem to be able to follow: stop drinking. As pressure built because of the pending hearing, Billie drank gin from the time she got up until she went to bed to try to sleep, usually with little success.

A date was set in early February for Billie to appear at the U.S. attorney's office, but as the day approached she could not force herself to go to it. Her lawyers succeeded in delaying the appearance, arguing that their client was sick, which was true. Day after day, Billie existed on gin and Pall Malls; her trip to Caminer did not seem to improve her emotional condition. Finally, a new date for the hearing—February 12, 1959—could not be postponed. So, her lawyers, Don Wilkes and Florynce Kennedy, picked her up at her apartment and drove with her in a car headed for a federal building in Brooklyn where she was scheduled to make her appearance. As they proceeded down the West Side Highway, around Midtown, Billie became so consumed with fear she tried to force the driver to stop so she could get out. Her lawyers prevailed upon her to remain in the car, insisting she had an excellent chance of having potential charges dismissed. She forced herself to believe them and, despite her apprehension, they drove on.

At last, in a government building in Brooklyn, Billie sat before a panel of three U.S. attorneys who questioned her on the events surrounding her departure from and return to New York in the autumn of 1958. With her lawyers by her side, Billie answered questions in a hearing that dragged on for ninety grueling minutes. For Billie, it was an overwhelming experience. Almost one month had passed since she received the telephone call from Agent McVeigh. During that time, the fear of being sent back to prison was a constant presence in her life. Now it came down to the decision of the three-person panel, who, after her testimony was concluded, went into private deliberation to decide whether or not to prosecute. When the panel returned, a decision was announced; it was not unanimous. It was, however, in her favor. The attorneys decided, in a two-to-one vote, not to proceed with a prosecution. In her perennial drama with the government, it was rare when fortune went her way, although, because it was obvious neither she nor her representation was aware of the new registration law, it was questionable whether a case should have been pursued against her in the first place. Regardless of the circumstances, Billie was overcome with relief. Her mood changed instantly when she heard the decision; she and her attorneys celebrated following the hearing. That night, with fears of prison time now ameliorated, Billie slept well for the first time in a month. Such was the nature of her life in the first weeks of 1959.

Several days after the hearing, Billie received good news—a welcome reprieve from the doldrums that had consumed her since her return from Paris in early December. Billie's management had been approached by an English television producer to see if she would appear on *Chelsea at Nine,* a popular weekly variety show hosted by Bernard Braden and broadcast throughout Great Britain. She would perform three songs on a show that would be taped in February for broadcast in March. She was being given short notice—she had to fly to London on Sunday, February 22, for a taping on Tuesday—so obviously she was replacing a guest who had dropped out at the last minute. But concerns of this sort did not matter to Billie, who was excited to accept the offer. She was thrilled to be returning to London.

2.

It was a chilly evening in London when Billie exited the Jet Clipper and entered the Pan Am terminal at Heathrow Airport. She was traveling alone because during January, Mal Waldron, worried about a lack of dates to play for Billie, took a regular gig at the Five Spot Café. The trendy club on Cooper Square popular with the jazz set and contemporary art crowd was famous for legendary residencies from performers like Thelonious Monk and John Coltrane. For the gig, Waldron was accompanied by Peck Morrison on bass and Jimmy Wormworth on drums. He was going to play his gig at the Five Spot on Monday night, then fly to London on Tuesday in time to accompany Billie at the show's taping.

Upon her arrival at Heathrow, Billie assumed she would take a taxi to her hotel; instead, when she stepped into the terminal, she was met by an old friend—Max Jones, a writer for *Melody Maker*. It was not the first time Jones had greeted her at Heathrow. Back in 1954, when she arrived in London for an engagement after completing her Leonard Feather–produced European tour, Jones, at the direction of his publication, welcomed Billie at the airport. He had never met her before—she was traveling with Louis McKay and Carl Drinkard—but he brightened her day by slipping her a half-finished bottle of whiskey, which she happily stashed in her mink coat. Then, at an ensuing press conference, he watched as the British newspaper reporters pelted her with questions about drugs. "I'm trying to get my police card back," Billie said at one point. "You know I'm not the only one: *some* kids have been in trouble two or three times and are still working. So why pick on me? Somebody's got a hand in it somewhere, some kind of politics. That's what I'm squawking about." It was then that Jones had further endeared himself to Billie by changing the subject and asking her about jazz.

Tonight, almost five years later, Jones welcomed her to London again, only this time without the whiskey.

"The whole thing was a rush," Billie said. "We just heard about this TV date two or three days ago. That's why I couldn't let you know in time. I knew damn well you'd be here anyway."

Jones told her he had heard about her television booking from the office of Harold Davison, the producer who presented Billie in London in 1954, and checked with the airline to determine when she was due to arrive—and now here he was.

On their way out of the airport, Billie said she needed to stop and make a telephone call. At a pay phone, she dialed the number of Yolande Bavan.

"Where the hell are you?" Billie said when Bavan answered. "I'm here."

"Where?" Yolande said.

"At Heathrow."

"Who are you with?" she asked.

"Max," Billie said. "We'll call you tomorrow."

As planned, Max telephoned Yolande the next morning and arranged for her to spend the day with Billie on Tuesday as she rehearsed for and then taped the television show. On Monday, and for the rest of Billie's visit, Max spent, as he later wrote, "most of my waking hours with [Billie]." He would document one memorable interlude that likely occurred on Monday: "[An] event I cannot forget was taking Billie to the Downbeat, a musicians' hangout in Soho. She wanted to sing, and a spontaneously formed group accompanied her on several songs. The club telephone rang in mid-song, and when a Hooray Henry customer prolonged his phone conversation, an enraged Kenny Graham (bandleader, tenor man, and Holiday worshiper) moved swiftly towards him and carried the protesting Hooray bodily away to enforced silence. The act somehow typified the hold Billie exercised on all *her* people."

But it was a conversation Jones had with Billie at Club Caribe in Leicester Square that, once he wrote it up for *Melody Maker,* made news. When Jones asked about a recent interview Miles Davis gave in which he made his comment that would become notorious in Holiday lore—"[Billie] doesn't need any horns; she sounds like one anyway"—Billie responded to Jones by saying, as she smiled sheepishly, "That's how I try to sound; I didn't know I succeeded." The conversation then turned to Billie relocating to Europe, possibly London. Earlier, in November, Jones had written that she wanted to buy a house in London and perform in Britain, France, Sweden— "wherever the opportunities arise." Was relocation still a possibility?

Billie confirmed a potential move. "I can't get my police card to work in New York," she said, "so how can I make it there? America won't let me work, so I'm going to make it in Europe or somewhere."

Billie presented to Jones an argument she had advanced for a decade: she had made a mistake, she paid her dues to society, so why would the government not allow her to earn a living with dignity?

"I'm Billie Holiday!" she exclaimed pointedly, her voice swelling with emotion. "Singing's the only thing I know how to do, and they won't let me do it. Do they expect me to go back to scrubbing steps—the way I started out?"

The "scrubbing steps" comment was a reference to a passage in *Lady Sings the Blues* where she described making money as a young child in Baltimore by washing the front steps for the owners of row houses—a practice remembered by no one who knew Billie when she was growing up. But it made for a good story.

It was nine o'clock in the morning of the twenty-fourth and Billie sat in another dressing room waiting for another gig. It seemed she had spent her life in dressing rooms, but at least this one, in Granada's Studio 10 in what was once the Chelsea Palace Theatre on King's Road, was comfortable and well-appointed. The Palace Theatre was opened in 1903 with a seating capacity of 2,524 seats on two levels. For many years, the theater served as a home to burlesque. John Osborne was inspired to write *The Entertainer*, his three-act play that starred Laurence Olivier in its original production, after watching Max Wall perform at the Palace. By the 1950s, as the live entertainment business moved away from vaudeville-like performance, the theater was purchased by Granada, which turned it into a television studio. Still, when you stood before the audience you could almost feel the ghosts in the Chelsea Palace around you—the old vaudevillians doing their best song and dance in the pastel glow of the footlights.

Today, as she settled into her dressing room, Billie enjoyed pleasant companionship. Before Max collected her at her hotel, he had picked up Yolande Bavan, who was excited to accompany Billie for the day. "She had nobody else close to her to come," Bavan says. "Hazel Scott was in Paris. I knew Max wanted me to spend the day with her. Maybe he was concerned she was getting towards the edge by then. Maybe he was concerned she wouldn't be able to do the show."

With Bavan to keep Billie company—Beryl Bryden, the jazz singer, also dropped in—Max was free to run errands for Billie. At some point during the day, someone mailed Alice a postcard Billie had written upon her arrival in London. "Hi Alice," the postcard read. "Well I made it[.] hope you receive this card before me[.] the trip was crazy six hours"—the Jet Clipper flight time from New York to London. "Kiss Pepe Regards to family Lady Day." She also sent Leonard Feather a postcard: "Hi Leonard: Just here for a quick TV show. Thinking of you. See you next week. Regards to family, Lady Day." But the main errand Billie asked Max to run was to go shopping for vodka, for which she reimbursed him in dollars when he returned with her order. Mixing the vodka with orange juice, which she drank on the rocks, Billie spent the rest of the day until showtime nursing one cocktail after another.

"We had a bottle of vodka," Bavan recalls, "and orange juice and a little bag of ice that Max had bought. Lady would ask me for another vodka, and I'd pour her a vodka and orange juice, then add the ice. She wouldn't drink it without the ice. She was drinking all day. Around one p.m., I started melting the ice. She never caught me. It was the only way to stop her drinking. She almost went through a whole bottle of vodka."

The reason she needed to be at the studio all day was not only for hair and makeup but mostly for rehearsals with the orchestra. Peter Knight had written arrangements for two songs—"I Loves You, Porgy" and "Please Don't Talk About Me When I'm Gone"— that she was going to perform with the orchestra he was conducting. Her final song would be "Strange Fruit," which she would sing accompanied on piano by Mal Waldron, who was en route to London. Billie was making a political statement by singing the final selection. Appearing before the House Committee on Un-American Activities in September 1950, folk singer Josh White, who began singing "Strange Fruit" after Billie established it as a groundbreaking protest song, assured the congressmen that he had not—and would not—sing the song abroad because "it's our family affair, to be solved by Americans in the peaceful, democratic American way." Obviously, Billie did not share his sentiments. Her position was embraced by an emerging segment of the civil rights community, who believed that ignoring racial inequality was effectively endorsing it. Still, singing the song in a foreign country would be viewed as criticism of her homeland. So her decision to sing "Strange Fruit" on British television coupled with the comments she made to Max Jones made it clear that Billie was coming to the end of her patience with how she was being treated by the American government. She was now willing to speak out even more forcefully than she had in the past.

After all, the campaign of persecution—as exemplified by her recent ordeal with the Customs Service—had taken its toll. "Billie was very jumpy," Bavan recalls. "She was frightened of everything. She was suspicious, as well she ought to be. By then, she had had so many things happen to her. She was getting slightly paranoid. At one point I had to go to the bathroom, and she said, 'Why?' I was in the bathroom in a stall, and she came in and said, 'Are you in there? Are you coming out?' We went back to the dressing room together."

Finally, in the early evening, it was showtime. Mal had arrived to play for all three songs. Billie finished hair and makeup. She selected a striking outfit for the show—a silver-gray, knee-length form-fitting dress made from a shimmering knit fabric. She wore an ornate bracelet on her left wrist, silver dangling earrings, and a pair of matching high-heel shoes adorned with bows. She was the picture of class and sophistication—a lady.

Wearing a conservative suit and tie, Bernard Braden, the host, spoke to the camera with a soft, studied detachment as he made his introduction. "She's a jazz legend," he said. "She sang with Benny Goodman's old band, most of the big bands since. She's written a book. She appeared in films, and her records sell like hotcakes. I give you Billie Holiday."

Billie emerged from the wings to arrive at center stage. She looked out onto an audience seated before her in the darkened studio. Behind her Mal sat at a baby grand piano; behind him hung a curtain concealing a full orchestra.

As the music complemented her, Billie began an emotional, deliberately paced rendition of "I Loves You, Porgy." She was careful always to pronounce the word "love" without an "s," eliminating the original intent of George Gershwin to affect a black dialect, which did not seem necessary outside the context of the show for which it was written, *Porgy and Bess*. Tonight, the tone of the performance became particularly poignant in a slowed-down middle section during which Billie was accompanied only by Waldron on piano. When the orchestra resumed, she returned to an almost confessional tone until she reached the climactic "I got my man." There was a crescendo of music signaling the song's end as applause swelled from the audience. Billie could not see Yolande, but, as she watched from the wings, she had become so affected by the performance that she began to cry.

When the applause died down, Billie spoke to the audience. "Thank you," she said, "and I'd like to do a little tune entitled 'Please Don't Talk About Me When I'm Gone' "—a deeply ironic selection given her declining health. After a brassy introduction, she moved into the swinging upbeat tune, hanging just behind the beat and gesturing subtly with her hands. There was a "big" ending— "Please don't talk about me"—pause for effect—"when I'm gone." Then more applause.

Finally, it was time for "Strange Fruit." Because of the kind of dates she had performed lately featuring shorter, more upbeat sets, and because of the emotional toll the song now took on her when she sang it, Billie had rarely performed "Strange Fruit" over the last year. She had not abandoned the song; she just needed a reason to sing it. Appearing on a television program broadcast across Great Britain— which would send a signal to her adversaries back home—seemed to be such an occasion.

"And now," Billie said, "a little tune written especially for me— 'Strange Fruit.' "

Once the studio lights dimmed to highlight Billie's face and Waldron played a short introduction, Billie began a plotted, passion-

ate version of the song. Each word was delivered with careful enun-
ciation, as if she were reciting an indictment. And when she slowed
down for the ending—"And here is a strange and bitter crop"—
she delivered "crop" as if she were emitting a wail of mourning.
There was an explosion of music from the orchestra, underscoring the
song's conclusion, and Billie stood motionless at center stage as the
applause swelled.

It was, without question, the most impressive television appearance she had made in her career. It was a deeply personal performance. The average viewer would not have suspected the angst and
apprehension that filled her during the day prior to the taping of the
show. But she was now what she had always been: the consummate
performer whose gift was her ability to make a listener experience
the emotion she was feeling as she sang a song. Given everything she
had endured in her life, it was fitting somehow that the last song she
sang on her final appearance on television would be "Strange Fruit."
The last words she would say on television would be "bitter crop."
The words were important to her. She wanted to entitle her autobiography *Bitter Crop* before Doubleday insisted on using what was
presumed to be the more commercial alternative *Lady Sings the Blues.*

"Lady Day," the announcer said in a voice-over to end her portion
of the show. "Billie Holiday."

After the taping, Max escorted Billie and a party that included
Yolande Bavan to Humphrey Lyttelton's 100 Club. "We were all sitting together," Bavan remembers. "There were goodbyes at the end
of the night. Max returned Billie to her hotel; the following day he
took her to the airport." As she headed back to New York, Billie
had a forthcoming project she was anticipating with excitement. In
a little over a week, she was scheduled to record a new album. No
doubt it was that project—the next gig—that was on her mind as
she departed London for what would be the final time.

3.

The negotiations that had been underway that would have allowed
Billie to record two albums a year for Irving Townsend at Colum-

bia Records—the prospects for which were real enough that they had been reported in the gossip columns—had finally collapsed when the two sides could not agree on the length of the contract. Columbia wanted a one-year contract with four one-year renewable options executed at the sole discretion of the company, but Billie would agree to no more than one one-year renewable option. So no contract was signed. As a result, when MGM Records hired Ray Ellis as a producer, Billie, who was always keenly aware of the comings and goings in the music industry, decided to approach Ellis to see if he would be interested in making another album with her. To Billie, the reteaming made sense because as the months passed, *Lady in Satin* remained a favorite of hers from her substantial body of work. Billie took matters into her own hands—as she was thoroughly capable of doing—and dropped by Ellis's office unannounced only to encounter an obstinate receptionist who did not know who she was. A scene was avoided when Ellis's assistant happened to pass by, spotted Billie, recognized the problem, and took her back to see Ellis. When Billie suggested recording another album of standards, Ellis seized the opportunity. He would not only write the arrangements for the album but produce it as well. Details of the financial agreement (she would receive an advance of one hundred dollars per side against a future royalty of 5 percent) were included in a standard contract negotiated by Earle Warren Zaidins, who was, echoing the demand made by Columbia Records for *Lady in Satin,* required to deliver Billie to the recording studio on time for each session. Most importantly, Billie was once again given what she wanted: an orchestra with strings.

Billie had not even recovered from her whirlwind trip to London when the article by Max Jones entitled "I'm Settling in London" appeared in *Melody Maker* on February 28. The story confirmed what Billie had been saying for some time. If New York was not going to allow her to earn a living working in the clubs, she had no choice but to relocate elsewhere. London was a logical choice. The topic was certainly in the air when Billie arrived at eleven o'clock in the evening on March 3 for her first MGM recording session at the Pathé Studios at Park Avenue and 106th Street. Leonard Feather later described her entrance: "Many singers come to record dates in sweatshirts and slippers, running for cover every time a photographer appears. Not Lady. She walked into the studio statuesque and sharp as ever, as attractively made up [as ever]."

But the discussion among the musicians quickly turned from any pending move to London to a more disconcerting topic—her obvious failing health. If Billie had appeared weak and fragile before, now she was visibly ill. During the session, which featured Hank Jones on piano (instead of Mal Waldron) as well as a midsized band including four violins, Billie struggled through four numbers. "All the Way" ended up sounding unfinished; "It's Not for Me to Say," "I'll Never Smile Again," and "Just One More Chance" were closer to being complete recordings but lacked the magic of the *Lady in Satin* tracks. Part of the problem was Billie's weakness. She had trouble sustaining an adequate level of engagement with the material to complete a song from start to finish. Later, Ellis was brutal in his assessment of the situation: "It was one take and if you didn't get it, that was it, baby! I was the producer on this one and trying to keep everything going and hoping she will not pass out." Still, the session stretched from the evening of the third into the early morning hours of the fourth before Ellis got four songs recorded well enough to attempt to include them on an album.

For the second session, which began on the evening of the fourth, a twelve-string section complemented a large band that included Harry "Sweets" Edison on trumpet and, once again, Hank Jones on piano. On bass, the band was joined by Milt Hinton, a longtime friend of Billie. (He would have played on the first session, but he had a previously booked session at Columbia Records.) Perhaps because of their closeness, Hinton, also a gifted photographer, snapped shots of Billie that are disturbing in the extent to which they capture her deterioration. In the shots she appears as elegant as always, wearing a pair of plaid slacks, a black blouse, and a black sweater. Her favorite gold chain and pendant hang around her neck. But the photographs reveal a woman who was thin, ill, unsteady. It was clear she was not well enough to be recording an album. In one shot, she holds in her right hand what appears to be a vodka on the rocks. As the session once again stretched into the early morning hours, Billie was able to make it through four more songs—"When It's Sleepy Time Down South," "Don't Worry 'Bout Me" (a title that seemed a bitter commentary on her, considering her health), "Sometimes I'm Happy," and "You Took Advantage of Me."

"She was sick," Milt Hinton later remembered about the session. "She had asked for all the musicians on this date, people who had been associated with her before. They were all there. She wasn't feeling well. Her voice was very bad, and the band played just marvelously and she enjoyed it and when she listened to the playback, she was very unhappy with the way she sounded. Our hearts were bleeding for her. She wanted to do it, but it wasn't there. And that can happen. We wouldn't dare mention it to her. We tried to encourage her and said, 'You want to do another one?' One time she said, 'Yeah, let's try another one.' And we tried another one, and it was the same thing."

A decision was made to delay the third session a week until the evening of March 11. Perhaps Billie could rebound somewhat with much-needed rest. It was likely during the week off that Billie and Edison dropped in one night at the Five Spot to see Mal Waldron, who on this night was playing with Donald Byrd on trumpet and Pepper Adams on saxophone. John Handy, a tenor saxophonist who had just played the club with Charles Mingus, was having a drink at the bar: "Billie came in with Harry Edison. They walked in together and sat right next to the bandstand. At one point Donald Byrd handed her a mic so she could sing from the table"—Byrd may have understood Billie's compromised condition and did not want to bring her up onstage—"and Harry borrowed Byrd's trumpet to play along with her. I first heard Billie as a little kid, when I was six years old, but I had never seen her—and there she was. I was anti-drug, but I realized a talented, attractive woman like Billie Holiday shouldn't have to live like she did. I respected her."

As it happened, Ellis also used the week off to rethink the musicians for the final session. He eliminated the string section and assembled a band featuring Edison with Al Cohn on tenor saxophone and Danny Bank on baritone saxophone. On the eleventh, when Bank first saw Billie, whom he admired but did not know, he was stunned by her physical condition. Bank remembered Billie "was so sick, she had no balance. . . . I don't know why she recorded that day. Maybe because the session was already booked, and she needed the money." Bank mistook Alice, who was there to assist Billie at all three sessions, as her nurse. Billie had declined to the point where it appeared that she needed to be under medical care. Somehow, she managed to record "There'll Be Some Changes Made," " 'Deed I Do," and "All of You," which was the most successful song she recorded for the album. For the final song of the night, Billie sang "Baby Won't You Please Come Home?"—an appropriately ironic selection, given her history with romantic relationships. It would be the final song she recorded in a studio.

Ellis was uncertain about what they had been able to record in the sessions. "It did not go well," remembers Ray Ellis's son, Marc. "She may have knocked out on a few of the tunes. My father never talked about it." Nor did MGM know when the album would be released, although a decision was made about the title. It would be called *Billie Holiday*.

CHAPTER 11

The Death *of the* President

Billie Holiday performing "Fine and Mellow" with Lester Young, Coleman Hawkins, and Gerry Mulligan during a rehearsal for the episode of The Seven Lively Arts entitled "The Sound of Jazz" in December 1957. Lady Day and Prez had been friends and musical soul mates since 1934. "They were the epitome of partnership and harmonious musicmaking," composer David Amram says. "There is nothing like working with another musician to tell a story together."

March 1959

In the early hours of Sunday, March 15, 1959, around the time when the crowds in the bars in New York City were thinning out as bartenders announced last call, word began to spread that what many in the jazz community had feared for some time had happened: Lester Young had died. He had been living in a modest room at the Alvin Hotel, located at Fifty-Second Street and Broadway across from Birdland, so it did not take long for news to reach the club scene that he had suffered a fatal heart attack in his hotel room. Patrons coming and going at Birdland could easily see the emergency personnel at the hotel.

Down in Greenwich Village at the Half Note Club, Charles Mingus—the mercurial musician known as much for his volatile temperament as he was for his unique bass playing style—was onstage when a son of one of the owners told him the news. John Handy, a young sideman who would go on to become an accomplished saxophonist, was playing in the Mingus band that night: "We were still onstage when we heard Lester had died. Charles wanted to go into a minor blues, a twelve-bar minor blues, and he had me play. I played a long time. I played several choruses in the minor blues in C minor. Then other people played. Finally, we took it out and got off the stand and talked about the loss. Charles knew Lester. I had met him once at a concert where I played. But the first time I ever picked up a saxophone and tried to play a song it was 'Jumpin' at Mesner's' and it was the Lester Young solo." Subsequently, Mingus composed, based on the impromptu dirge the band improvised that night, "Goodbye

Pork Pie Hat," which he included on his masterwork *Mingus Ah Um*. (A fashion enthusiast, Young often topped off his look with a black porkpie hat, which he ordered, one source noted, "from a Victorian women's magazine.") Reports of the death of Lester Young, the most influential tenor saxophone player in the modern jazz era, had not even been published in the newspapers yet, but already he was being lionized.

At the end of 1958, Benny Carter told Young he could get work in Europe, so in early 1959 Young decided to pursue opportunities there and accepted an eight-week engagement at the Blue Note Club in Paris. Dan Morgenstern saw Young right before he left: "I had written something about him that he liked, and he wanted to see me. He was at the Five Spot and I visited him backstage. There was no dressing room. He was in the kitchen actually. We talked for a while, and he said, 'I'm going to Paris, but when I come back I want to see you.' As I was leaving, he said, 'When I get back, we have a date. Now don't forget.' I walked out; there was a step down. And he said, 'Don't stumble. You might fall.' It was the last thing he ever said to me."

Young also made future plans with other people at this time. "I ran into Lester one night at Birdland," Willie Ruff remembers, "and he invited me to come up to his room at the Alvin Hotel with my French horn to play some duets. He was going to play the bass clarinet. He wanted to see how the two instruments blended together. I wish I could have but I didn't get the chance to play with him. It was shortly before he died."

In Paris, Young opened at the Blue Note on Friday, January 23, backed by René Urtreger on piano, Kenny Clarke on drums, Jamil Nasser on bass, and Jimmy Gourley on guitar. While he worked at the Blue Note and lived at the Hotel de la Louisiane, located in Rue de Seine, he battled depression, a chronic condition that had only gotten worse since his departure from New York. He began to drink even more heavily than he normally did. "Prez is as bad as you," drummer Carl "Kansas" Fields, who was also playing in Paris, wrote to Billie. "He wants me around most of the time. I am 'cause I dig him. He sure is blowing." He may have been performing well, but Young's behavior in Paris suggested a troubled mental state. On February 6, at the end of his second week at the Blue Note, he granted a rare interview at six o'clock in the evening to journalist François Postif, which was conducted in Young's hotel room—he had moved to the Hotel d'Angleterre, perhaps for reasons of companionship—where, Postif remembered, "Lester was lying quite nude on his bed, unshaven and ill-looking. He was drinking port wine, and . . . he was not quite in his normal attitude." His drink of choice in Paris was absinthe, a powerful liquor so strong it was not sold in America; it was a dangerous drink for someone afflicted with cirrhosis of the liver, which Young was. His liver had become hardened from years of drinking, and in Paris, where it was likely agitated by the absinthe, he began periodically to bleed internally. However, an irrational fear of doctors prevented him from seeking medical attention.

During his stay in Paris, Young had sometimes visited Hazel Scott, who just had her own health scare that required a major operation, at the apartment where Billie celebrated Thanksgiving. "I remember Lester coming over," Adam Clayton Powell III says. "On one occasion, he was sitting on the sofa in the living room waiting for my mother. He was leaning against the corner of the couch. I joined him and talked to him a little bit. There was natural light coming in from the courtyard in the late afternoon. To me, he looked old and world-weary; then again, I was twelve years old." At one point, Adam glanced down at a satchel Young had with him. "He had some things that I recognized were related to drugs. I could see a rubber tourniquet. He looked at me and he looked down and said, 'Don't you do this.'" Perhaps his stomach pain had become so severe he needed to self-medicate with something stronger than absinthe.

On March 4, Young agreed to record a session for Eddie Barclay at Studio Barclay; the session, during which Young's brilliance shone through his obviously diminished physical state, ended up being his last. Then, as he approached the end of his seventh week at the Blue Note, he realized he could not continue. Ben Benjamin recalled that "he wanted to go home because he said he couldn't talk to a French doctor." So Young decided to end his gig one week early and fly back to New York. He played his final set on Friday, March 13, the last time he ever appeared before an audience. By Saturday, March 14, he was in such distress he headed home. He packed his belongings and prepared to go to Orly Airport. Hazel Scott later recalled him stopping at her apartment to say goodbye on his way to the airport: "It pains me to remember that he went from my apartment to an airplane which took him to America and death."

On the flight home, Young experienced excruciating pain—"to the point where he bit his lip," according to one account, "causing it, too, to bleed." When he landed after an agonizing eight-hour flight, he was met at Idlewild Airport by Elaine Swain, a young woman with whom he had become close friends. She suggested he go to the hospital, but he insisted on returning to the Alvin Hotel, where, sep-arated from his wife and family, he had lived for the past year. Back at the Alvin, he was relieved to sit once again in a chair in his room and stare out the window at the lights on Broadway as he drank. Finally, he lay down on the bed and fell asleep, coming to at one point long enough to form his lips into an embouchure and start to move his fingers as if he were playing an invisible horn. Swain called a doctor, who arrived only to discover there was little that could be done. Lester Young died around three o'clock on Sunday morning in a rented room in a run-down Midtown hotel favored by musicians. He was forty-nine years old.

News reports identified the cause of death as a heart attack, but Dr. Luther Cloud, a psychiatrist and physician whom Lester had come to trust enough to allow him to treat him—Cloud was out of town that weekend, so he could not see Lester—concluded Young's hardened liver severed a vein or an artery in his esophagus, causing acute bleeding, which likely triggered his cardiac arrest. In short, Young may have died of heart failure, but the underlying condition that caused his death was cirrhosis of the liver. He died from years of alcohol abuse.

As word of Young's death was announced in clubs across the city, the telephone in Billie's apartment began to ring with friends

calling to break the news to her. She had finished her final recording session for MGM only four days ago, and she was still exhausted
from the experience, which had proven to be much more challenging
for her than she had anticipated. In recent years, Billie and Lester
had not been as close as they once were, but still his death had a
profound effect on her. For two decades now, in the collective consciousness of the jazz world, because of their friendship and their
musical collaboration—from January 25, 1937, to March 21, 1941,
in fifteen different sessions with three different bands, they recorded
fifty-two songs—they had been inexorably intertwined: Prez and
Lady Day. "They were the epitome of partnership and harmonious
musicmaking," David Amram says. "There is nothing like working
with another musician to tell a story *together.*"

They had met in 1934 after Young replaced Coleman Hawkins in
the Fletcher Henderson Orchestra, for whom Billie's father had once
played guitar. For most of Young's tenure with the band, they were
on tour, but during a sit-down in New York, Young found himself
hitting the late-night clubs in Harlem looking for a jam session to
join, and one night he ran across Billie at a club. She would remember the magic she felt when they initially played together. "From
then on," Billie wrote, "Lester knew how I used to love to have him
come around and blow pretty solos behind me. So, whenever he could
he'd come by the joints where I was singing to hear me or sit in."
    Born in Woodville, Mississippi, in 1909—Lester was almost six
years older than Billie—he grew up, according to one source, "in and
around New Orleans in a musical family that performed in min-
strel shows and carnivals." His father, Willis Handy Young, "was an
accomplished music educator [who] doted on Lester but also often
belt-whipped the boy," prompting him to run away ten or twelve
times. Moving to Minnesota, the performing family toured around
the country; in Kentucky, they were almost lynched by an angry
white mob. Young left the family permanently when he was eighteen, playing with local Midwest bands like the Blue Devils, a group
led by Walter Page. Ralph Ellison remembered seeing Young in

Oklahoma City in 1929. "A tall, intense young musician . . . arrived in Oklahoma City," Ellison wrote. "With his heavy white sweater, blue stocking cap and up-and-out-thrust silver saxophone, [he] left absolutely no reed player and few young players of any instrument unstirred by the wild, excitingly original flights of his imagination. . . . Lester Young . . . with his battered horn upset the entire Negro section of town. . . . I first heard Lester Young in a shine chair, his head thrown back, his horn even then outthrust, his feet working the footrests, as he played with and against Lem Johnson, Ben Webster . . . and members of the old Blue Devils Orchestra."

Before long, Young joined Count Basie in Kansas City. In these years, Young began to develop his unique stage presence. "Young was the first jazz musician to wear sunglasses on stage (indoors and outdoors)," scholar Joel Dinerstein wrote. "Long before Charlie Parker and Miles Davis became famous for turning their backs on the audience, Young recognized the use of shades as a mask to deflect the gaze of others without causing conflict, and to create an air of mystery." He left Basie for Fletcher Henderson for more money—"bread," as he called it before the word became acknowledged slang—seventy-five dollars a week.

"Bread" was not the only unique expression Lester used. Friends and colleagues noted that he spoke in an idiosyncratic language of his own invention. Favorite expressions were "You dig?," "I feel a draft" (something bad is about to happen), or "That's cool" (*Smithsonian* later contended the term "was probably coined by him"). "Bing and Bob Crosby" meant the police. "Grays" were white people; "Oxford grays" were black people. It was a language that sounded foreign to those who were unfamiliar with the lingo. Bassist Bill Crow remembers sitting next to Young years later in the audience at Birdland: "He was a seat over from me and soon Jo Jones"—the drummer from the Basie band when Young was a featured saxophonist—"sat down on the other side of him. So, I was eavesdropping on what they were talking about. I could not understand anything they were saying. They were talking in code. There were all kinds of weird words they were using. It was like a hipster's language."

Young also had a habit of nicknaming fellow musicians. Trumpet player Harry Edison was "Sweets"; saxophonist Buddy Tate was "Lady Tate." Then again, Lester called many of his friends "Lady," both men and women. It made sense, then, as he began to meet up with Billie regularly on those Harlem nights to sit in with her at the clubs where she was working, that he started calling her "Lady" too. Shortening her last name, he came up with his personal nickname for her—Lady Day. Later, Billie claimed she gave him a nickname as well. "I always felt he was the greatest," Billie wrote, "so his name had to be the greatest. . . . The greatest man around then was Franklin D. Roosevelt and he was the President. So, I started calling him the President. It got shortened to Prez." But members of the Blue Devils would recall that in the band, long before he met Billie, Young was often referred to as the President. More than likely, Billie adopted the moniker that was already being used, but as their careers took off and they became public figures, the myth that surrounded their friendship contained the fiction that Billie invented the nickname—a misconception she co-opted in the same way she reinvented details of her own life to make them more to her liking.

In time, at the end of a night of jamming, Young would go home with Billie, who was sharing a railroad apartment in Harlem with her mother. Young decided Sadie also needed a nickname, so she became the "Duchess" to Billie's "Lady." When Young found "an unregistered guest," as Billie called it—"a big dirty old rat the size of my dog"—in the dresser drawer in his hotel room, Lester became "almost a nervous wreck" and moved into a spare room in Billie's apartment. "When I first came to New York in thirty-four," Young would say, "I used to live there for a long time. She was teaching me about the city . . . which way to go, you know, where everything is shitty." He remained with Billie until the Fletcher Henderson band left New York.

Because he had replaced Hawkins, Young was constantly being compared to him—and not necessarily favorably. "Fletcher's wife, Leora," Linda Kuehl wrote, "used to wake [Lester] up every morning to play Hawk's records and nag him, 'Lester, can't you play like this?' Finally, [Lester] got tired of hearing 'that bitch' try to teach him to play like somebody else, and he got tired of 'those motherfuckers in the band whispering on me, Jesus!' He said: 'I had in my mind what I wanted to play, and I was going to play that way.' "

Eventually, he left Henderson and returned to Count Basie. He was still with the band when Billie joined in 1937. With Basie, Young was encouraged to develop his style; fellow band members may have kidded him at times, but they understood the genius of what he was doing. Billie later remembered a friendly competition Young shared with tenor saxophonist Herschel "Tex" Evans. "Prez and Herschel," Billie recalled, "were forever thinking up ways of cutting the other one. You'd find them in the band room hacking away at reeds, trying out all kinds of new ones, anything to get ahead of the other one. Once Herschel asked Lester, 'Why don't you play alto, man? You've got the alto *tone.*' Lester tapped his head. 'There's things going on up there, man,' he told Herschel. 'Some of you guys are all belly.' " The bottom line was Young had an unshakable conviction to pursue what he wanted to achieve. "One of the things he was fond of saying," according to his son, Lester Young, Jr., "was that playing music was like telling a story. You have to know how to tell *your* story. Some people tell their stories better than others. That's what improvisation is [all] about."

Young remained with Basie when Billie left, but the two stayed in touch and worked together whenever possible. In 1943, Young starred in *Jammin' the Blues,* a ten-minute black-and-white short film directed by *Life* photographer Gjon Mili. The elegantly shot picture, which was nominated for an Academy Award, showcased the idiosyncratic playing style for which Young was known. "Lester had an odd way of holding his horn," Linda Kuehl wrote, "at a forty-five-degree angle, with his shoulders hunched over, his fleshy-lidded hound dog eyes closed . . . a cigarette between his fingers, blowing euphorically, utterly detached, pouring his heart in his horn."

For Young, the most disturbing period of his life began in 1944. "Drafted in September," Dinerstein wrote, "by an undercover agent who followed the Basie band in a zoot suit, [Young] was denied a musician assignment at a base band by a middle-class African-American bandleader who thought he lacked proper musical education. His inability to submit to discipline drew the attention and hostility of his commanding officer, who soon found marijuana and barbiturates in his trunk. Young was court-martialed in a Kafkaesque trial in which he calmly admitted his long-term drug use and proudly claimed he had never harmed a man; he was sentenced to nearly a year in solitary at [Camp] Gordon, Georgia, where he was often beaten." Because of his individuality, Young, already one of the most original artists on the music scene, was treated by the U.S. Army like a common criminal—or worse. After his eventual release from military service, Young rarely, if ever, discussed the experience. "A nightmare, man, one mad nightmare," he later confessed to a fellow musician who asked him about his time in the army. "They sent me down South—Georgia. That was enough to make me blow my top. It was a drag, Jack."

Billie relished the months she spent with Lester during her stint with Basie—they often sat next to each other on the tour bus—but it was the fifty-two songs they recorded together in the studio, with Young backing her using riffs and "pretty" solos played in his trademark understated delivery, what journalist Whitney Balliett called "a perfect balance between tension and relaxation," that allowed their collaboration to take its place in jazz history.

In the legend of Lady Day and Prez, there was the inevitable complication. In the first week of February 1951, years into their friendship, the two had a falling-out when they were both appearing in Philadelphia. Billie was at the Rendezvous for a week; Lester and his band were playing the Showboat. Hanging out in a bar one night, as they had done on so many occasions since 1934, they got into a disagreement when Lester admonished Billie for her continued periodic reliance on heroin and, less life-threatening but still important to him, her insistence on referring to him in the past tense when she spoke about him to reporters ("Lester was my favorite tenor player," she often said). As disciples of Young had emerged in the business—Stan Getz, Paul Quinichette, Al Cohn, Zoot Sims, and Gerry Mulligan all seemed indebted to the Young style to some extent—Lester became increasingly sensitive to the fact that they were sharing a spotlight that once shone only on him. He believed these "ladies"—"my children," as he often called them—were taking attention—and, importantly, work—that would have gone to him. As he told a friend, "They're picking the bones while the body is still warm." Billie's propensity to place Lester in the past tense in the press only solidified the notion that he was among the old guard who had now been replaced by the young newcomers.

Their argument was bad enough—although there was evidence Lester was more upset than Billie when she later said, "You can hurt his feelings in two seconds. I know because I found out once that I had"—that the two close friends did not speak for three years. It became so apparent that it was a topic acknowledged not only among their fans but also in the jazz community in general. Then, in July 1954, the two of them were both booked to appear at the inaugural Newport Jazz Festival in Rhode Island. George Wein, the festival presenter, orchestrated what became a reunion. "I had lined up Teddy Wilson, Jo Jones, and Milt Hinton to back up Billie," Wein says, "and I asked Lester to play with her too. It was one of the most moving things I've seen because Billie went on without Lester. I was standing next to Prez offstage. He hadn't played with her [in many years]. Finally, Prez muttered to himself, 'I guess I'll have to go up and help the Lady out.' I'll never forget those words. And he went out—and that was a good set. Looking back, I think he wanted to make an entrance. He wanted to see what kind of shape she was in. That was during the period when they had had the falling-out. But he went on anyway. For any jazz fan, like myself and those in the audience, it was thrilling to see."

It marked the end of the feud. "[Young] shuffled onstage," one music publication reported, "and once again was a part of a Billie presentation. They later embraced in the dressing room, and the feud was over."

The coverage of the death of Lester Young was extensive, from *Billboard* ("[he was] one of the most influential instrumentalists on the jazz scene") to the *South Bend Tribune* ("[his] lazy tenor saxophone style made him famous in jazz circles") to the *New York Daily News* ("[he was] a leading exponent of 'cool' music") to *The New York Times* ("[his] playing was shaped around a languorous, breathing tone that gave rise to a whole generation of followers"). The ubiquity of his death underscored his lasting achievement. But Billie grieved on a personal, not merely artistic, level. She had lost one of her dearest friends; no one in the music business was more closely associated with her than Lester. It was a heartbreak she had hoped she would never have to endure, but now it had happened.

The funeral was scheduled for Thursday, March 19, at 1:30 in the afternoon at Universal Chapel at Lexington Avenue and Fifty-Second Street—not far from the clubs where Lester and Billie had spent so many nights of their lives. Billie did not want to attend the funeral alone—she knew the day would be emotional for her—so she arranged for Leonard Feather to accompany her. When he came by to pick her up, he noticed her mental and physical condition; the last time she had visited him, she refused a cocktail because her doctor had ordered her to stop drinking. "The abstinence probably lasted a few weeks," Feather wrote, "but I remember when I dropped by her apartment to take her to Lester Young's funeral, she took along a small flask of gin as protection." Then, in the taxi ride on the way to the funeral, Billie stunned Feather with a comment. "You know," she said, "these things happen in threes. I'll be the next one to go."

The funeral was well attended. Lester's wife, Mary, planned the affair with the help of Count Basie's wife, Catherine. Lester's children were there (he had two—Lester, Jr., and Yvette); his elderly mother, Lizetta Gray, had flown in from California. Naturally, there was a large contingent from the Count Basie Orchestra, including Jo Jones, Jimmy Rushing, Buddy Tate, and Dickie Wells. Billie had expected to sing, but it was made clear to her that Lester's widow, from whom he was estranged when he died, did not want her to participate in the service. Future accounts would contend Mary believed Billie was "in no state" to sing, which was not true, but perhaps Mary knew Billie was friends with Elaine Swain, Lester's companion for the last year who was barred by the family from attending his funeral. Regardless of what the motivation was, Mary did not want Billie to sing in the funeral service.

The somber ceremony got underway. As it progressed, the reality of what was happening, compounded by the depth of her loss, began to weigh down on Billie. Consumed by sadness, she became enraged by the fact that she was being excluded from the funeral of her musical soul mate. Al Hibbler rose to sing "In the Garden," a song he composed for the occasion. And Billie, as she sat on a pew in the crowded chapel, could no longer control her emotions.

"They won't let me sing," she said out loud. "The motherfuckers won't let me sing for Prez."

After Hibbler, Tyree Glenn, the trombonist, took the stage to play a doleful version of "Just A-Wearyin' for You," a parlor song Lester admired.

"They won't let me sing," Billie repeated, now louder. "The motherfuckers won't let me sing for Prez."

Then, as Glenn played the final notes of the song and it was apparent the service was going to conclude soon, Billie became disconsolate. "They won't let me sing!" she said, sobbing. "The motherfuckers won't let me sing!"

Dan Morgenstern was seated beside Billie. "She kept saying, 'The motherfuckers won't let me sing,' meaning the family," he remembers. "She said it numerous times. She started saying it when it was clear to her she was not going to be asked to sing. She was so upset she was crying. She repeated it until it was obvious something had to be done. So, we left before the final prayer. Budd Johnson and Paul Quinichette"—both saxophonists who were friends with Billie—"took her each under an arm. We went out onto the street. There was a bar nearby. We took her there to get her a drink. She calmed down, although she was still upset—and rightly so."

As the friends drank at the bar, it was hard to believe someone as vital and enigmatic as Lester Young was gone. His presence remained with them; you could almost hear him speak. *Ding dong!* he might have said. *Paul—Lady Q—you're one of my children. Sound just like me. Thanks for giving some love to Lady Day. That's cool, Q. You dig? She'll always be my Lady Day.*

———

The last time Billie and Lester appeared together was fifteen months earlier, when they were both included in a television program featuring some of the most revered figures in jazz. "The best thing that ever happened to television," author Eric Larrabee wrote in *Harper's Magazine* at the time, "happened on CBS between 5 and 6 in the afternoon on December 8, [1957]. It was an installment in *The Seven Lively Arts* series called 'The Sound of Jazz,' and as far as I'm concerned you can throw away all previous standards of comparison." Critics and fans shared the sentiment, marveling at the lineup of talent. Among the thirty-two prominent names were Thelonious Monk, Count Basie, Mal Waldron, Roy Eldridge, Doc Cheatham, Coleman Hawkins, Ben Webster, Gerry Mulligan, Danny Barker, Milt Hinton, Osie Johnson, Jo Jones, Vic Dickenson, Jim Atlas, Jimmy Giuffre, Lester Young—and, the only woman included on the show, Billie Holiday. Producer Robert Herridge had hired as executive producers for the program Nat Hentoff, Whitney Balliett, and Charles H. Schultz, who were instrumental in bringing together the stellar assortment of talent.

Lester was supposed to be featured on the program, but when the musicians gathered for a rehearsal on the fifth, which was recorded by Columbia Records for release in February, Lester showed up looking run-down and ill. "[Young] was waiting, alone and weak, in an empty room next to the studio," Hentoff wrote. "I told him that he didn't have to be, as scheduled, in the reed section of the Count Basie/All-Star Orchestra. . . . He nodded and told me he was up to the small group session, later in the show, featuring Billie Holiday."

On the day of the show, which was broadcast live from the CBS Studio 58 in Manhattan, a problem emerged. "Only one of the [musicians] caused trouble," Hentoff wrote. "During a sound check, Herridge received a note from a representative of the sponsor, read it, and tore it up. He paraphrased the message for me and Whitney: 'We must not put into America's homes, especially on Sunday, someone who's been imprisoned for drug use.' Herridge told the bearer of the note that if Billie Holiday could not go on, he, Whitney, and I would leave." The show proceeded as planned, but once again Billie had been singled out as a target for derision.

The show began, and when it came time for the segment devoted to Billie, John Crosby, a writer with the *New York Herald Tribune* who served as host—he wore an understated suit and tie—spoke to the camera in a studied, deadpan tone. "Billie Holiday," he said, "is one of a handful of really great jazz singers. Her blues are poetic, highly intense. Playing with her today are some of the musicians who accompanied her back in the thirties on some of the greatest jazz records ever made."

Then, in a prerecorded voice-over, Billie began talking: "The blues to me is like being very sad, very sick, going to church, being very happy. There's two kinds of blues. There's happy blues, and there's sad blues." Wearing slacks and a matching white blouse and sweater, her hair pulled back in her usual ponytail, she walked out and sat on a stool in the middle of the musicians, many of whom over the years had become close friends and confidants. As she prepared for her performance, the voice-over continued. "I don't think I ever sing the same way twice. I don't think I ever sing the same tempo. I don't know—the blues is just sort of a mixed-up thing. You have to feel it. Anything I do sing, it's part of my life."

The musicians started with the instrumental opening of "Fine and Mellow." After Billie sang the first verse—slow and emotive— Ben Webster launched into a smooth, melodic chorus. Then came the moment when Lester, who was seated on a stool because of his health, stood and stepped forward and blew, with a deliberate and elegant tone, a hypnotic chorus which so enthralled Billie she looked on with wonderment and affection. When their eyes met for a brief magical instant that could have only come from the love they felt for each other, the expression on Billie's face was that of someone transfixed by the moment, the music, the musician making it. All the "pretty solos" he had played behind her in the past seemed to be contained in this one effervescent interlude of music. She nodded with approval as she listened, and when the solo ended—it lasted only thirty-five seconds, but it told the story of a musical romance that had gone on now for almost a quarter of a century—Billie segued into her next verse. There would be additional solos in the performance—from Coleman Hawkins, Gerry Mulligan, Vic Dickenson—yet the most memorable one was when Prez played for Billie for what turned out to be the final time. After the show, they visited with each other in the dressing room; then they said goodbye.

CHAPTER 12

Memory *and* Desire

Billie Holiday photographed by Dennis Stock. In her last year,
there were two constants in Billie's life: a cigarette in one hand and Pepe,
her beloved Chihuahua, at her feet.

April 1959

I.

She spent her life waiting in the wings. Tonight was no different. Billie had traveled from New York to Philadelphia. In the dressing room before the show, she applied her makeup as she always did, straightened her hair with a curling iron, after which she pulled it into a ponytail, and slipped into her evening gown. As she waited for showtime, she visited with old friends, since she was sharing the bill with Duke Ellington and His Orchestra and Dizzy Gillespie and His Band. They were appearing on the evening of Friday, April 3, at a benefit performance given by Devon Jazz Committee for Bryn Mawr Hospital held at the Academy of Music, one of the most prestigious venues in which she had appeared in her career. Located downtown on Broad Street, it opened in 1857, making it the oldest opera house in the United States. The 2,509-seat hall, known as the "Grand Old Lady of Broad Street," was modeled on La Scala in Milan, where Billie had played in November. The hall had been home to past productions of some of history's great operas and presented singers such as Enrico Caruso and Édith Piaf. It was said that in 1865, from windows on the balcony level, mourners looked down onto the street to watch the coffin of Abraham Lincoln pass by as his funeral cortege made its way to Independence Hall, where he would lie in state, during which time three hundred thousand people filed past to pay their respects. Seven years later, Ulysses S. Grant, Lincoln's general, accepted his nomination for reelection as president in the hall, where that year the Republican Party held its convention. Walk into the Academy of Music and you are stepping into history.

For Billie, it was a time of memory and desire. It had been only a little over two weeks since Lester died, and she remained consumed with memories of the times they shared—enjoying meals cooked by the Duchess, playing in the Basie band, visiting with each other during countless nights out over the years. Billie cherished memories of Prez; they also filled her with a desire to keep singing. Friends had told her she needed to slow down and take better care of herself because of her health, but she wanted to continue working. Anyway, she had played only a few gigs since she returned to New York from Paris. Besides headlining Cleveland in December, she appeared on Easter Sunday, March 29, in concert with Al Belletto and his sextet at the Magnolia Ballroom in Atlanta in what press reports promised would allow "the celebrated song stylist" to present her "superb vocal renditions." In short, over the last four months, she had sung twice on television and recorded an album, but she had appeared in only one nightclub and one concert hall. When she went through a dormant period—to be sure, they had been scarce since her release from prison—she always yearned to return to the stage.

Standing in the wings tonight, she was filled with exuberance. When her entrance was announced, she crossed the stage to take her place in the spotlight once again. This evening, looking out into the theater was like peering into days of yore—President Grant sitting in his box, the mourners gazing down from the balcony windows onto the coffin containing the body of President Lincoln passing by on the street out front. And as the music consumed her, she lost herself in the emotions of the songs, which tonight she sang with sureness and ardor.

"She was really frail," says Philip Yale Nicholson, who, then a college student, was in the audience, seated in the orchestra section, "but what an imposing presence she was on the stage. She stood tall and on her rickety legs she was really not the force she had been as a performer or as a person. Her voice was becoming reedy and delicate. She shifted her weight from one foot to the other while standing, but her posture was being affected by her frailty. She had a bleached out, faded look to her. We knew she had been through a lot in her career. It was not a secret she had been in prison and struggled with drugs—all of that. We were seeing a woman who had been through a lot, yet there she was. She still had her voice."

Four days later, on the early evening of April 7, her forty-fourth birthday, Billie was getting dressed in her bedroom. She applied her makeup, fixed her hair, and selected her outfit for the night—a pair of torpedo pants set off by a leopard-skin blouse. The occasion was a birthday party she was hosting for herself at her apartment. It had been fifteen years since she had thrown a birthday party, she told friends, so now seemed like a good time to have one. Alice Vrbsky came over to help with the food, which Billie spent the afternoon cooking. One guest remembered having chicken, ribs, and potato salad; another recalled fish stuffed with hamburger and peppers, greens, and black-eyed peas prepared in the style of the soul food Billie's mother used to cook. Billie set up tables in front of the picture window overlooking the courtyard, so the food could be laid out and served buffet-style. Annie Ross, an old friend with whom Billie had recently reconnected, volunteered to help with the drinks in the kitchen.

As the guests arrived, with a record always playing on the phonograph, Billie eventually could look out onto her crowded living room and see the people who were then most important to her. There was Flo Kennedy, who had helped her elude the government's latest attempt to bust her on—it still sounded crazy to say—customs violations. There were the Duftys, Maely, a friend for years, and Bill, Billie's coauthor. There were two friends from her Count Basie days—Ed Lewis, who still played when he was not working as a motorman on the subway, and Jo Jones, the drummer who now toured with his own band. The Basie veterans reminisced about Lester Young, who, Jones said, had been haunted by the death of Herschel Evans. ("Lester practically didn't drink or smoke until around the time Herschel died in 1939.") There was Tony Scott, the clarinetist, with whom Billie had played on numerous occasions, who came with his wife, Fran; Tony snapped photographs of Billie and the guests. There was Elaine Lorillard, the socialite who founded the

Newport Jazz Festival, who came alone. There was Barrie Thorne, who worked in the New York office of the British Broadcasting Corporation; Billie implored her to pass on her "undying love" to Max Jones, their mutual friend in London. There was Leonard Feather, her close friend; Feather made a point of challenging Billie about her health. She had never looked so frail, he believed; she was, as he put it, "skinny rather than slender." "You need to check into the hospital and get some rest," Feather told her. But Billie would have nothing of it. "I have gigs to do," she said, "and a new recording coming out."

All of which was true. After a long fallow period (for her), Billie had gigs scheduled from April to June, and Ray Ellis was currently mixing her new album. She was grateful she had much to celebrate. At some point in the evening, the party moved from Billie's apartment to Birdland, where the festivities continued well into the night. "Lady never stopped toasting herself," Feather wrote. "Bottles were emptied with alarming speed. Many of us wondered whether there would be any more birthdays to celebrate."

2.

During much of 1958, Billie enjoyed a steady stream of visitors who dropped in when she was in town and not on the road, but by the early months of 1959 fewer and fewer people came by to see her. McKay remained in Los Angeles, and Billie had not developed an interest in anyone else for romantic companionship. Many nights, she sat in her living room alone, smoking a joint and watching television—an unsettling departure from the norm for someone who was used to being in the spotlight, the center of attention, celebrated. Loneliness had always been a challenge for Billie, so one night not long after her birthday party, she called Annie Ross, whom she had known since Annie arrived in New York City six years earlier and arranged to be represented by Joe Glaser.

Born in London to Scottish vaudevillians, Annie was raised in Los Angeles by her aunt, the actress and singer Ella Logan, starting from the age of four when she won a contract as a child actor with Metro-Goldwyn-Mayer. Annie appeared in an *Our Gang* short film in 1938 and played Judy Garland's sister in *Presenting Lily Mars* in 1943; at fourteen, she wrote a song, "Let's Fly," recorded by Johnny Mercer and the Pied Pipers. She then wrote a song for herself entitled "Twisted," a vocalese based on a saxophone instrumental by Wardell Gray, and recorded it in 1952; afterwards, she toured Europe with Lionel Hampton. She sought out Glaser as her agent the following summer because she was determined to forge a career for herself as a singer and because, fifteen years younger than Billie, she regarded her as her role model and hoped to be represented by her agent.

The day after she signed with Glaser, he called her at nine o'clock in the morning. "Can you get hold of a piano player and can you get up to the Apollo right away?" he asked. "Yes," Annie said, "I think I probably can." Glaser said, "Well, get your gown, get your music, get the piano player, and I want you to be up there by ten o'clock." Annie was thrilled. "Oh, that's marvelous. By the way . . . who am I replacing?" Glaser said, "Billie Holiday."

Billie was opening for a weeklong run at the Apollo Theater on August 14, 1953. Press reports indicated she was suffering from an abscessed tooth—her jaw was severely swollen—but, more likely, someone had hit her. Her jaw hurt so badly she did not believe she could sing the first of her multiple shows on her opening day; the show started at 10:00 a.m. When Annie learned whom she was replacing, she was, as she would recall, "scared out of my wits. Number One, it was the Apollo, and, Number Two, I was replacing my idol." Annie called her pianist and, with her secondhand evening gown in tow, headed for the Apollo, where she discovered the day's talent included Duke Ellington, whom she had first met at her aunt's house in Brentwood when she was fourteen. Right away, Ellington realized she was nervous, so he took her to meet Billie. Annie would recall their first encounter: "So [Duke and I] went down to the dressing room and Lady was there with her dogs and her piano player and [Duke] introduced me and she said, 'Hey, baby, how are you doing?' And I said, 'Oh, I'm a little nervous.' And she said, 'Why? You don't have to be nervous. . . . You'll be fine.' She asked if I needed a gown, a piano player, and so on. She was truly lovely to me. The time came for me to sing"—Annie was introduced by Ellington—"[and] it's a tough audience at the Apollo. There were lots of hollers and hoots when I walked out, but I was singing advanced stuff like 'Twisted' and 'Farmer's Market' and that saved my bacon." Billie watched Annie's set from the wings. "I came off the stage and the audience was applauding and Lady was on the other side waiting for me as I came off. And she put her arm around me, and I put my arm round her and I started to cry. And Duke came off and said, 'What are you two beautiful ladies doing wrapped up in each other's arms crying? Come on out.' The three of us went out and took a bow. That was my personal introduction to Billie Holiday."

The women remained in touch and met up in Paris in early 1954. Billie was on her first European tour; Annie happened to be in Paris at the same time. When they rendezvoused in the city, Billie said she wanted to go shopping for underwear. Annie Ross remembers: "Once Lady and I go out, she decided she wanted to buy some jewelry. I said, 'Okay.' We went down to the Champs-Élysées and we went into a shop. The guy brought out his wares—cases and cases of jewelry. And Lady said after a while, 'No, I don't see anything I like. Forget it.' So we leave the shop and start walking down the Champs-Élysées and she brought out a handful of stuff she had stolen. I didn't know what to do so I did nothing. And Lady laughed! She thought it was hysterical."

More recently, Annie had had a peculiar run-in with Billie, when Dorothy Kilgallen published an item in her column suggesting Lana Turner was being considered to play Billie in the film adaptation of *Lady Sings the Blues* Lester Cowan was developing for United Artists. For some reason, Billie assumed Annie leaked the information to Kilgallen. Furious, she confronted Annie in a nightclub where she was appearing, but Annie was so startled by the tirade Billie realized at once she had targeted the wrong person and apologized.

Since the run-in back in the summer, they had remained in touch. Billie was especially happy for Annie, who was beginning to enjoy much acclaim when she teamed up with Dave Lambert and Jon Hendricks to form Lambert, Hendricks, & Ross. After recording their debut album, *Sing a Song of Basie,* in 1957, the trio, often specializing in vocalese, would go on to become what *The New York*

Times later called "probably the most successful vocal group in the history of jazz." In 1958 and 1959, Annie was in the beginning stretch of her rise to fame. Since Annie's name was currently at the forefront of the jazz community, it made sense for Billie to pick up the telephone and call her one night after her birthday party, a moment Ross recalls: "Lady rang me and said, 'Would you come up and see me?' She hated being alone. I was honored to go be with her."

That first evening led to more visits. It all started out innocently enough, as evidenced by the cute nickname Billie gave her: "Annie-Banannie." Annie Ross remembers: "We would cook together. We would listen to music together. We would talk." As Billie chain-smoked cigarettes, they talked about whatever was on Billie's mind, like her estranged husband: "He was horrible to her. He had beat her. She told me about it. 'And that motherfucker came up and hit me,' she'd say. Or, 'Girl, I had a black eye.'" They talked about Billie's past friends, like Tallulah Bankhead: "She was very close to Tallulah. She admired her craft as an actress." They talked about Billie's repeated run-ins with authorities: "She felt as if the FBI was out to get her. She was right, of course. It all came from Hoover, the motherfucker! And, yes, race was an issue. She felt race was an issue. They hated her. They wanted to kill her."

But, as the visitations continued, it was not long before an activity far different from cooking or listening to music entered into their nighttime routine. In recent months, Billie had slipped back onto an old crutch and started using heroin from time to time. When the subject of heroin was brought up, Billie was surprised to learn Annie was using with the person she was currently dating—Lenny Bruce.

Annie had dabbled with drugs in her past but had been clean until she met Bruce, the cutting-edge stand-up comedian who was known for his dark side, both in his comedy routine and in his private life. In early 1959, he was still married to Honey Harlow, a professional stripper, even though she was serving a federal prison sentence in California. Because of the nightclub circuit where he

worked to make a living, Bruce often found himself in the company of jazz musicians, so it was not unusual when he started seeing
Annie in Chicago in February while he was working at the Cloister.
They had met because Annie was in town appearing with Lambert,
Hendricks & Ross and friends took her to see Bruce one night after
her show. What *was* unusual was that, once they hit it off, Bruce,
normally the epitome of cool detachment, fell for her badly. From
the start, drugs were a part of the romance.

After the Chicago gig, Bruce moved to New York to be near
Annie. Working at a club called the Den, he lived in Hotel America, and he and Annie began fantasizing about getting married one
day—*if* Bruce ever divorced Honey. "Lenny's engagement ring was a
hypodermic needle," one observer would note about Bruce. "[Annie]
had been] off drugs when Lenny met her. He turned her right back
on again. That was one of his tricks with women. If he really liked
them, he always turned them on."

On April 5, Lenny Bruce made his first appearance on *The Steve
Allen Show* on NBC. He concluded what would become a legendary television performance—thirteen minutes of stand-up, which
included a brief dialogue with Allen—with a rendition of "All
Alone," a song, written by Bruce, about living alone after a romance
has failed. The poignant song is sung to his "wife," who has left him,
the reason he is alone. And the name of his wife, the object of his
intense emotion, is Annie. "I can see her in about twenty years from
now," Bruce says in the sketch, setting up the end of the song by
addressing her directly. "How you doing, Annie? You're still washing your hair with Dutch cleanser, I see." Then he closes the song by
describing how his former love is living in a rented room while he
resides in a Knob Hill mansion—all alone.

Perhaps Bruce's mention of Annie in the television monologue
tipped off some people to their budding romance. On April 15,
Dorothy Kilgallen reported in her column: "New twosome, quite
understandable: cool Singer Annie Ross and cool Comedian Lenny
Bruce." One of the elements that brought the couple together—and
kept them together—was heroin. Annie became an expert with the
drug. A friend of Bruce recalled: "[Annie] would take the clumsy

geezer and shoot herself in the thigh with the sure, neat efficiency of a diabetic taking an insulin injection."

So, on those nights Annie visited Billie in her apartment, it was inevitable that they began to shoot up together. "Lady was using a lot," Ross says. "My idol did, so I was using with her. It was the only solace she had. She tried to stop many times. She found comfort in using. The straight gin was not enough. She believed there was no hope. The government was winning. What could she do? We would get high and do the things you do when you're stoned."

Perhaps the shared using was one reason why Billie felt an intimacy with Annie she experienced with few others in her life at the time. Because she was so comfortable with her, Billie revealed to Annie notions she normally kept to herself.

"Annie-Banannie," she said one night out of the blue, "I need my hair washed."

"Of course, Lady."

Then, taking her into the bathroom, Annie had Billie undress and climb into the bathtub. Once she was undressed, the thinness of her body was painfully apparent. Her propensity to rely on gin and heroin, instead of the down-home soul food she loved to cook, was showing its effect. In the past, Billie had been a stout, imposing woman capable of easily mastering Mister, her boxer, whom she had to give up because she could no longer handle him, the reason her companion became the petite Pepe, who now looked on as Annie leaned over the tub to shampoo Billie's hair. When she finished soaping it, instead of just washing out the suds with water, Annie left for the kitchen and returned with a bottle of vinegar. Once the suds were washed out, she used the vinegar as a rinse on Billie's hair. Billie had never had a vinegar rinse before. She thought it was wonderful. It made her feel taken care of. It made her feel special. Her peals of laughter filled the bathroom as Annie applied the vinegar rinse until Billie's hair was smooth and silky.

They were singers, after all, a mentor and her protégé. They could spend hours relaxing in the living room as they listened to albums Billie played on her phonograph. Billie enjoyed playing *Sing a Song of Basie,* a matchless experience for Annie, since she was listening to her songs with her idol. Of her own albums, Billie continued to play *Lady in Satin,* which remained a favorite of hers. And, on some nights, after listening to music, they sang. The heroin creating a dreamy state they shared, they blended their voices together effortlessly. Just the two of them, singing, a cappella. "Them that's got shall get," they harmonized, sitting on the sofa in the dimly lit room, all that was important to them in that moment contained in the lyrics of the song, Billie's song. "Them that's not shall lose. / So the Bible said, and it still is news. / Mama may have, Papa may have / But God bless the child that's got his own."

CHAPTER 13

❧

Farewell *to* Storyville

Billie Holiday photographed by jazz aficionado Mel Levine as she performed at Storyville in Boston during an evening show on April 24, 1959. Owned by George Wein, who founded the Newport Jazz Festival where Billie also performed, Storyville was one of her favorite nightclubs to play.

April and May 1959

From where she stood, Billie could hear the excited buzz of another audience. At the piano onstage, Mal Waldron was vamping in a moderate but lively tempo, the perfect background music to bring on a singer. She had been in the business since she was a teenager—for over a quarter of a century now she had appeared in countless venues across America and throughout Europe while recording over three hundred songs contained on a wide range of albums—yet she still felt a rush of anticipation before she took the stage, just as she did on this cold April evening in Boston. She was partway through a week-long run at Storyville, a club she loved so much she had appeared here four times before. Tonight's first set was special because it was being broadcast live on WMEX, one of Boston's popular AM radio stations.

"Now, ladies and gentlemen," an announcer said in a faintly animated voice over the club public address system, "accompanied by Mal Waldron on piano, Champ Jones on bass, and Roy Haynes on drums, it's Storyville's pleasure to welcome for her first performance this evening"—a slight pause for effect—"the great Billie Holiday!"

In the small jam-packed club the applause rose up as Billie made her way onto the stage. As she arrived at the microphone to stare out onto the club, Waldron segued into the opening of the first song. "Holding hands at midnight," Billie sang into the microphone, "'Neath the starry sky." And while she progressed through "Nice Work If You Can Get It," she improvised on the song's melody more than she usually did, perhaps because she felt so at home in the club.

Storyville was named for the neighborhood in New Orleans that between 1897 and 1917 city officials zoned as the nation's first red-light district; it was here, during roughly the same time period, that a new genre of music indigenous to America called jazz was created and began to flourish. The namesake Boston nightclub, owned by music impresario George Wein, opened in 1950 downstairs in the Copley Square Hotel. In early 1951, it moved to the Hotel Buckminster on Kenmore Square, but two years later it returned to the Copley Square Hotel, now on the street level.

When Billie finished "Nice Work," the room burst into applause, and Waldron began her next song, one she routinely performed live. (She was friends with the composer, Ann Ronell, whose husband, Lester Cowan, had attempted to adapt *Lady Sings the Blues* into a motion picture.) "Willow weep for me," Billie sang, then later, "Sad as I can be. / Hear me willow and weep"—a long pause—"for me." The sadness in her voice reflected the melancholy of the song, so, when the number ended and the audience again began to applaud, Waldron picked up the beat as Billie launched into "When Your Lover Has Gone."

Her fourth song, "Billie's Blues," was her most inspired performance of the night. "I've been your slave, baby," she sang stoically, "ever since I've been your babe." Of course, the song sounded like a confession in part because she had written it. "But before I'll be your dog / I'll see you in your grave." A litany of men could have come to her mind as she sang her song—John Simmons, John Levy, Louis McKay. "My man won't give me no breakfast / Won't give me no dinner. / Squawked about my supper / then he put me outdoors."

Billie changed the tone with "Too Marvelous for Words"; then there was an upbeat finale, "Lover Come Back to Me," a song often favored by Billie, which Waldron concluded by slowing down the tempo for a climactic ending—"This heart of mine is singing / Lover, come back to me."

When the set was over, Billie turned to leave the stage amid a flood of applause. And even though she could not hear it in the club, the radio station made an announcement as the ovation continued. "You've been listening," the announcer said, "to the vocal stylings of

Billie Holiday. With the Roy Haynes Trio in George Wein's Story-ville in the Back Bay section of Boston."

In her dressing room, Billie sat down in a chair. She had been able to get through the set, shortened to six songs because of the radio broadcast, without any incident. She did not sound like a singer whose medical condition was continuing to falter as she suffered the ravages of an advanced case of cirrhosis of the liver.

Billie had been making appearances in Boston for almost all her career. She first sang in the city in August 1937 when she appeared with the Count Basie Orchestra at the Ritz Hotel. Seven months later, in March 1938, she had changed orchestras to work for Artie Shaw. Their engagement at the Roseland-State Ballroom marked the first time Boston audiences had witnessed an African-American singer appear with an all-white orchestra. "The sight of sixteen men on a bandstand with a Negro girl singer," Billie wrote, "had never been seen before—in Boston or anywhere."

She played in Boston during the 1940s. A highlight came in April 1947 when she appeared at Symphony Hall as a special guest in an all-star revue performing with Louis Armstrong and his band. The concert, entitled "Birth of the Blues," was meant to be an overview of the history of jazz, and *The Boston Globe* singled out Billie when its critic noted that "the real star of the evening was vocal stylist Billie Holiday who, along with the incomparable Armstrong, is a jazz artist of real stature." Billie continued to appear in Boston after her release from prison in 1948 when New York City revoked her cabaret card and nearby cities like Boston became an economic lifeline for her.

In February 1951, Billie, whom the *Globe* described as "[a] sepia singer of jazz songs," enjoyed a weeklong stint at the Latin Quarter. After that, she mainly appeared in Boston's two most respected jazz venues—the Hi-Hat and Storyville. Between 1951 and 1955, she appeared at each venue four times. Because of the club itself, and because of her connection with George Wein, who also ran the Newport Jazz Festival, where she had appeared, Billie maintained a special feeling for Storyville. Of her inaugural run in October 1952 *Down Beat* observed: "A new Lady Day calmly conquered the jazz-oriented citizenry of Boston in the course of a rewardingly successful week. [She was] singing better than anyone here had heard her sing in the last few years." But during the engagement it was an event outside the club that Wein would remember: "One night, we took Billie for a dinner at Durgin-Park, down by the Old State House. An old, old restaurant in Boston. And we take her for lobster dinner. But the next thing I know she says, 'Well, I want a female lobster.' I had never heard anyone ask for a female lobster. Afterwards, I understood. Female lobsters had the eggs. She knew that. Still, it made for an interesting experience calling over the chef at Durgin-Park and saying, 'Miss Holiday wants a *female* lobster.' "

The next weeklong engagement at Storyville, in October 1953, started out under unfortunate circumstances. For the run Billie was to be backed up by Jimmy Woode on bass and Peter Littman on drums, but her pianist, Carl Drinkard, failed to show up for opening night. Wein was called on to save the occasion: "So, I had to play opening night. It was a disaster because I didn't know her songs. I *knew* the songs, but I had never played them. Even so, Billie made it through the night and sang the tunes. Then again, she was always correct with me. She made every show. She was never temperamental in any way." This was remarkable, since during the run she was suffering from an abscess in her jaw, a medical condition noted by the *Globe* critic, who remarked that "she had the house rocking despite that abscessed jaw."

She next appeared at Storyville in November 1954 and October 1955. Then, in August 1957, she starred alongside a host of jazz luminaries, including Sarah Vaughan, Count Basie, Maynard Ferguson, and Dizzy Gillespie, at the North Shore Jazz Festival in nearby Lynn, Massachusetts. So it had been more than a year and a half since she sang in the Boston area when she opened at Storyville on April 20, earning a weekly fee of $1,700, a much smaller salary than she made in her heyday but money she needed badly now that she was living on her own and headed for a divorce.

For most of the run, George Wein had been traveling in Europe.

He returned to Boston in time to see Billie's final day of shows. "In those days," Wein recalls, "we did five shows on Sunday. They weren't long shows—twenty-five or thirty-minutes—from two in the afternoon until three at night. That Sunday, I sat through all five shows, and I was totally mesmerized. I thought I had been transported back to the thirties. There was a lightness to her voice. She sang the old standards. It was one of the most fantastic musical experiences I ever had."

After one set, Wein went backstage to see her. The two hugged warmly.

"Billie," Wein said. "I haven't heard you sing like that in years. What's happening with you?"

Billie was full of emotion. "I'm straight now, George. I'm straight now. You've got to help me."

Wein was more than ready to help. "I'll call Joe Glaser right away," he said. "We'll put on a festival. I've never heard anything like this."

Billie took Wein's hand and placed it on her chest so he could feel her heartbeat. "Her heart," Wein remembers, "was beating like a drum."

George Wein was not the only observer profoundly moved by Billie's appearance at Storyville. In "The Jazz Scene," which ran in *The Boston Traveler,* a local daily publication, critic John McLellan entitled his April 27 column "Billie Holiday Can Teach 'Em." He praised Billie, arguing that the new singers should study her. "They just don't swing. Billie Holiday does. . . . [Her songs] are bittersweet, but not saccharine, they are lonely, but not self-pitying. They are particularly appropriate for her voice and style. The . . . ease of the young girl is gone. The voice now cuts through like a painful knife. But there is a ripe, mature beauty to her singing. . . . As Nat Hentoff once wrote, 'other singers sing about emotion, Billie actually projects the emotion itself.' It is this sound in her music that is perhaps most important in making Billie Holiday a true jazz singer. Even more than the craft of swinging which she does so effortlessly. The others can't even seem to manage this first step of learning the craft, never mind the art of singing jazz."

Though her body was being debilitated by an insidious disease, Billie remained a singular presence in jazz. Her engagement at Storyville, a week of dazzling performances those who saw them would remember for years, even decades, was a testament to the singer she was and the master artist she had become. Indeed, it had been a remarkable week for Billie. She was in good form; she had a level of voice control she did not always enjoy in those days. The rooms were full, the audiences effusive. While she was not her youthful self, she did not necessarily appear unhealthy to the general public. In black-and-white photographs, snapped during an evening show on April 24 by jazz enthusiast Mel Levine, Billie looks commanding, sophisticated, regal. She wears a dark, elegantly designed gown; her long chain and pendant hangs around her neck. Black, oversized earrings adorn her ears. Her black hair is slicked back into her customary ponytail. Tasteful makeup highlights her soft, dramatic face. "My father loved her as a jazz singer," Oren Levine says. "She was so far removed to what people were doing at the time. She was unique."

There was no way an ordinary audience member would have looked at her during her run at Storyville and known that the years of periodic heroin abuse and the more than two decades of chronic alcohol consumption had compromised her health to the point where her condition was proving to be life-threatening. An audience member at Storyville would have seen what George Wein thought he saw—a consummate artist enjoying a resurgence of her talent that allowed her to sing as she had not sung in some time. "Of course," Wein recalls, "it was her curtain call because she was *not* straight as she had promised me. In fact, it was the end."

2.

Saying farewell to Storyville once again, Billie returned to New York, where she addressed issues involving her career and her health. She continued to resist going to the hospital or even allowing her doctor to make a concerted effort to address her ill health. And while the response to her engagement at Storyville had been heartening, more and more she was having to endure the type of feedback exemplified by one critic who was responding to a rerelease of an old Commodore Records album she made accompanied by jazz pianist Eddie Heywood. The record was entitled *An Evening with Eddie Heywood and Billie Holiday.* "The Billie Holiday-Eddie Heywood contains, simply," Ralph J. Gleason wrote in the *San Francisco Chronicle* in May, "some of the greatest jazz vocals ever recorded. Aside from Billie Holiday's own efforts, there are no jazz vocals in history that have this incredible quality of smoldering fire in ballad singing. Even the classic Ma Rainey and Bessie Smith blues sides and the more recent soaring improvisations of Sarah Vaughan seem slightly tepid by comparison. Into Billie Holiday's voice at that time on these records there was concentrated more emotion, more fire and more burning sadness than in any other jazz singing ever put on record." It was astonishing praise, almost unheard of for a singer to hear in her own lifetime, but then came the blow to her spirit: "One has only to compare these to her current release to realize that today's Billie Holiday is a sad, tragic and crippled figure, her talent hardly a ghostly echo of its former greatness. That's why those of us who were lucky enough to hear her then can't listen to her now and instead must turn to these records happily available once again." It was as if Billie were reading death notices written about her art; it was an unnerving and disheartening experience.

With critics savaging her and the government continuing to harass her, it was no wonder that Billie was occasionally consumed by bouts of paranoia, such as those she had suffered on the trip to London in February to appear on *Chelsea at Nine,* which were only made worse by her habitual drinking. Friends were sometimes the target of her suspicion. One night soon after her run at Storyville, following a long night of drinking gin, she decided to lash out at Leonard Feather, who, she had been told, was making disparaging comments about her conduct in Boston.

Even though it was two o'clock in the morning, Billie telephoned Feather, waking him from a sound sleep. "Come over here right now," she said angrily.

Later, Feather remembered that "she made it sound so urgent that I dressed and rushed over."

After she let him in the apartment, Billie sat down at her kitchen table where she, according to Feather, "[had been] nursing the bottle."

"I hear you've been saying I was drunk in Boston," Billie said, accusingly. "What's all this shit going on? I don't want people putting my motherfucking business in the street. I made every show and you can ask anybody."

"I didn't have to ask," Feather would write. "Charlie Bourgeois, of Storyville, had already told me what a good week she had done, and this was the only story I was spreading." Once Feather corrected her misinformation, it did not take long for Billie, as she had with Annie previously, to become angry not with Feather but with the person who had misrepresented what he was supposedly saying about her.

Around this time, Billie spent an evening visiting with a friend that produced decidedly less drama. Tony Scott was among the finest clarinet players in the field of jazz. Born Anthony Sciacca in Morristown, New Jersey, he attended the Juilliard School, changed his name, established himself as an essential jazz clarinet player, and, in the 1950s, recorded a series of albums for RCA. Billie had known him for years. Back in the 1940s, he had even accompanied her on piano on gigs, but they both liked it when he backed her on clarinet. He had worked with Sarah Vaughan and was friends with Lester Young and Charlie Parker. Billie always enjoyed spending time with him because of his wit and charm, not to mention his extensive knowledge of music. On the evening she called on Tony and his wife, Fran, at their apartment on Seventy-First Street near Central Park, she was joined by another guest, Bill Attaway, the novelist who had also written songs in the Calypso style, among them "Day-O," which was a hit for Harry Belafonte. The get-together was filled with drink and laugher, but mostly Billie indulged Tony, a passionate amateur photographer, who convinced her to pose for a series of pictures. She "put on all kinds of faces for me," Scott recalled, allowing him to create a portfolio of images that displayed an array of emotions—

anger, impatience, surprise, joy. Billie also arranged for Tony to play clarinet with her at a benefit concert at which she was appearing in Greenwich Village near the end of May. Scott was happy to do so. And when she left that night to go home, Scott decided Billie was in good form—"the real Lady."

As May passed, Billie saw her health continue to decline. Her weight loss was alarming. She was advised by her doctor not to keep her upcoming nightclub dates and to stay home, where she needed to stop drinking and focus on improving her health, but she refused to listen. She had been fine during her engagement at Storyville; indeed, she received some of the most effusive feedback she had been given in years. She was sure she could perform her next gig, which was scheduled to start for one week on May 11 at the Flamingo Lounge, a club in Lowell, Massachusetts, not far from Boston, a venue she had never played before. Ignoring all warnings, she traveled to Lowell. During the first two nights of the run, she was so ill she could not complete a set, but on the third day she rebounded and then turned in four days of shows as good as those she had performed at Storyville. When she finished her last set at the Flamingo Lounge, it would be the final time she appeared in a nightclub, the forum in which she had worked most often in her career since she ventured onto the stage as a teenager in goodtime houses in Baltimore before moving on to the dive bars in Brooklyn and Queens and then the jazz clubs of Harlem and beyond. It was here, on the nightclub stage, that Billie practiced her craft and perfected her art to become the quintessential live entertainer.

Back in New York from Lowell, Billie did what she had done for so long. She began looking forward to the next booking. At present, she was scheduled to appear in Los Angeles, starting on May 29, along with the Dave Pell Octet; after that, she would proceed to a run in Montreal. To keep the bookings coming in, Billie now had to deal with a narrative in the press—one she herself had encouraged—that said she was moving to Europe, where she felt she would be treated more hospitably. But her recent unfortunate experiences in Milan and Paris had damaged her prospects of relocating to Europe. A new narrative needed to be advanced. So while she was in Lowell, a gossip item was leaked, no doubt by her management, to Dorothy Kilgallen: "Billie Holiday plans to buy a home in Long Island, refuting the reports that she intends on settling permanently in Europe. She still has hopes of getting her nightclub card renewed, as Billy Daniels did." A popular singer whose trademark song was "That Old Black Magic," Daniels temporarily lost his card because he shot a man, prompting felonious assault charges. At least Billie's illicit actions were directed toward herself, not anyone else; indeed, the only person she ever harmed was herself.

On the business front, Billie initiated the process to sign with Broadcast Music Incorporated, a music rights management company. It was an effort to maximize her revenue as a songwriter, since she had written, usually with a coauthor, some of her most popular songs, among them "Fine and Mellow," "Billie's Blues," "Don't Explain," and "God Bless the Child." Several jazz figures including Miles Davis, Sonny Rollins, and Dinah Washington were signing with BMI as well. Considering the range of issues with which she was dealing—future club bookings, song royalties, and, most happily, a renewed interest in the film rights to *Lady Sings the Blues*—it was hard to imagine that Billie was also coping with her failing health. The severity of her condition was made evident to her in mid-May as a result of a visit from some old friends.

She had met Terkild Vinding and his wife, Pearl, during the Copenhagen stop on her 1954 European tour. Vinding was a psychiatrist who also had a keen interest in listening to and performing jazz, which accounted for his nickname—"Doctor Jazz." Through a radio program he hosted, he met most of the major jazz figures who played Copenhagen, so he was excited to attend, along with his twelve-year-old daughter, Lone, Jazz Club USA when it came to the K.B. Hall. Following the show, he went backstage to visit with the artists. As he spoke with Billie, they hit it off so well he invited her to his home for an after-concert gathering. Once there, Billie, given her constant interest in children, naturally gravitated toward Lone, who found her to be, as she says, "very sweet, very nice."

After they spoke for a few minutes, Lone said, "I know how to sing 'God Bless the Child.'"

"You do?" Billie said warmly. "Sing it for me."

And as Lone made her way through the song, her soft, innocent voice hitting the notes beautifully, tears slowly welled up in Billie's eyes.

Since that night, Lone's father and Billie had remained in touch. In 1956, Vinding and his family immigrated to America. After living in Virginia for two years, they had recently relocated to Cedar Grove, New Jersey. Now that they were nearby, it was easy for the Vindings to drop in on Billie for a visit, as they did today. Sitting in her living room, Billie listened while Terkild caught her up on what was new with him and his family. Then Billie played them *Lady in Satin,* after which she gave them an autographed copy of the album. But as the afternoon wore on, Vinding could no longer remain silent about Billie's physical condition. He was deeply worried about her health. Because of her liver cirrhosis, her legs and stomach were swollen to a degree he had never seen before.

"You must go at once to a hospital," he finally said, "and get the fluid drained out."

As she had for months, Billie refused to go.

"I do not have a New York license to treat you," he continued, "but we will drive you to a hospital of your choice."

Again, Billie refused.

So Vinding abandoned his medical recommendations as the three of them got on with their visit. And when the Vindings left that day, Billie had been successful—as she was with all of her friends—in stonewalling them in their attempt to persuade her to seek treatment for what was now clearly an alarming condition.

On the evening of Monday, May 25, Billie had agreed to appear at Jazz at the Phoenix, an all-star benefit concert for the Lower East Side Playhouse hosted by Leonard Feather and Steve Allen at the Phoenix

Theatre in Greenwich Village. As the day passed, Billie was not feeling well, but she was loath to renege on the commitment, especially one associated with her friend. There was also the fee—three hundred dollars. It was a small sum, but until she sold the film rights to *Lady Sings the Blues,* which would once again make her flush with cash, money was tight and every check helped. So she got dressed and took a taxi down to the Village. She made sure to go early to give herself time to prepare for the show. She made her way to her dressing room and was seated before a large oval mirror encircled with twenty light bulbs, all burning brightly, when Feather—who was producing the show, along with Elaine Lorillard, Bob Bach, and Allan Morrison—dropped by to see her. He was not prepared for what he saw; she had worsened in the time that had passed since he last saw her: "[She was] seated at the makeup table coughing, spittle running unchecked down her chin. Looking at her, I was on the verge of tears, and she knew it. 'What the matter, Leonard? You seen a ghost or something?' Indeed, I had; a ghost so emaciated, so weak and sick, that it was impossible for me to hide my feelings. She had lost at least twenty pounds in the few weeks since I had seen her." Feather left her alone in her dressing room, disturbed by his encounter.

Before long, Steve Allen, on whose television show Billie had appeared, came into the dressing room and, literally, did not recognize her. "There was a little old Negro lady sitting [there]," Allen wrote. "And just to be polite, I said, 'Hello, how are you?' She said, 'Fine, how's it going?' Something like that. I said, 'Okay.' And since I didn't know her, I walked to the other end of the room and just looked at my fingernails for a few minutes. And suddenly I had a very creepy feeling. And I did a very slow doubletake, and the little old lady was Billie, looking forty years older than I expected to see her. The last time she had been fifty pounds heavier and a lovely looking person. . . . So suddenly seeing her skinny as a rail—looking like someone you see in pictures out of Dachau, looking very skinny, very skinny arms, very old." Soon, Allen departed as well, again leaving Billie alone in the dressing room.

Before long, Tony Scott stopped by to tell her he would not be able to play clarinet tonight because he had broken his finger. He later recorded the alarm he experienced over how much her condition had deteriorated in the three weeks since she came to his apartment: "When I went to her dressing room, I got the shock of my life. Since I had seen her last, she had lost so much weight that she looked like a skeleton. Her nose was dripping water, her arms were the size of what her wrists used to be, and her wrists were only bones, no meat." He asked her what was wrong; she said she had not eaten in three weeks but was being given B_{12} shots by her doctor. "She spoke with an effort, slowly, husky and drawling like she did when she was really high, only now she wasn't high. . . . I looked at her skin. It was flaccid, and a gray color had seeped in where before it was always a beautiful chocolate brown."

Once he overcame his shock, Scott, wondering why no one in her daily life had noticed this disturbing change, asked her, "Where's Louis?"

"I don't know," Billie said. "I'm all alone."

No sooner had she said the words than tears came to her eyes. Then, though she tried not to, she started to cry.

Once he learned McKay was gone, a development Billie had not mentioned in their last visit, Scott reminded her she always had her friends. "You got me," he said.

Now she began to sob. "I got nobody," she said, taking Kleenex from a box to dry her eyes. "I'm all alone."

She shook her head slowly from side to side and repeated as if it were an incantation, "I'm all alone. I got nobody. I'm all alone. I got nobody. I'm all alone. I got nobody."

Billie faced the mirror with Scott standing behind her. To soothe her, he gently placed his hands on her shoulders. He had always known Billie as tough, sure of what she wanted, in charge, the way she was onstage. But something had broken; he had never seen her in such a state. Her heartache was so complete he could do little but try to comfort her: "All I could do was to keep my hands on her shoulders and feel a sinking feeling in my body like my soul was shriveling up, as I realized I was listening to a person I had never really known."

———

Later, as the show got underway, Steve Allen introduced Billie when it was time for her to go on. "Ladies and gentlemen," he said to the audience, "and now, the one you've been waiting for, the one and only Billie Holiday, Lady Day."

But, as Mal Waldron played for her to make an entrance, as she had done so many times before, no one appeared. It finally became apparent Billie was having trouble walking from the wings to the stage. Realizing he was going to have to help her, Allen moved the microphone closer to the wings so her entrance would be shorter. Then he and Feather, one on either side of her, escorted her onto the stage to the microphone. The resounding wave of applause from the audience combined with that familiar sensation— the feel of the spotlight on her face—gave her a jolt of excitement. She snapped her fingers loudly to set the tempo for the song, and it was likely the energy she was receiving from the audience that allowed her to make it through "T'aint Nobody's Business If I Do," which over the years had become her anthem of defiance sung for all those who wanted to tell her how to live her life. More applause; another burst of inspiration; and she was able to sing "When Your Lover Has Gone," one of her most reliable numbers. But when she was finished, even though she had planned to sing five more tunes, even though she desperately wanted to sing the next number, she simply could not force herself to go on. The spirit was there, but the body failed to respond. Once it seemed like she might collapse, she turned to leave as Allen rushed out onto the stage to help her walk off.

Tony Scott was watching from the wings. When Billie reached him, he opened his arms and she fell into his embrace to keep from collapsing to the floor. By now, Waldron had come over from the piano. Scott and Waldron both realized Billie needed to go home at once, so, along with Scott's wife, they escorted her from the theater and helped her into Scott's car. After the Scotts got in and they headed out, Billie continued to feel weak and unwell on the way uptown. And as she sat in the back seat of the car while Scott sped through the city, the lights from the passing buildings and streetlights flashing into the car, there was no way Billie would allow herself to contemplate that the evening's songs were the last she would ever sing onstage.

CHAPTER 14

⅋

Fade Out

*Billie Holiday with Tony Scott, the virtuoso clarinetist who was a close friend.
It was to Scott that she confessed, "I am all alone," which created in her a profound
sense of loneliness that permeated the last year of her life.*

May, June, July 1959

When Billie woke up on Tuesday, she still felt ill from the night before. After experiencing similar problems on the first two nights of the engagement at the Flamingo Lounge, she had recovered sufficiently that she was able to turn in an excellent run, so she was hopeful she could rebound once again. She believed the vitamin shots Caminer was giving her were helping; if anyone asked, she contended she had decreased her drinking. With this plan in place, she decided to take it easy for a few days to get her energy back. After all, she had gigs coming up; she wanted to cancel as few of them as possible. As it happened, Billie's friends, particularly Leonard Feather, had a different course of action in mind. They believed it was long past time for them to take a more aggressive posture with her, which she discovered when three of them arrived at her apartment that Tuesday for an emergency visit, an episode that took on the unmistakable tone and feel of an intervention.

It was organized by Feather, who was profoundly worried about her after the incident at the Phoenix Theatre. "The next morning," he later wrote, "I called Joe Glaser and Allan Morrison, then the New York editor of *Ebony* [and a producer of the previous night's show], with the suggestion that the three of us as a delegation might be able to break down [Billie's] long resistance to hospitalization." The two men were more than willing to accompany Feather, but once they arrived at Billie's apartment and she escorted them in, they encountered her familiar reluctance. "As we sat in [the living room of] her apartment," Feather wrote, "Glaser did most of the talking, guaranteeing all her hospital expenses and begging her to call off [her upcoming gigs]." But, lying on the sofa, Billie remained steadfast. She had bounced back in Lowell; she was sure she could do it again. "No, I'll be all right," she assured them. "The doctor said these shots he's giving me will do it." As the conversation continued, Billie showed no signs that she would agree to admitting herself to the hospital. After an hour, the three men gave up, having failed in their mission, and, as Feather recalled, they left "in a mood of frustration and despair." Meanwhile, Billie went about her day, unwilling to accept that by ignoring her friends who were pleading with her to get more urgent medical care, she was endangering her life.

In the end Billie did decide not to travel to California for shows at Club Jazz Seville, a small venue in Los Angeles, even though advertisements announcing her appearance had already made it into the press. While she remained in New York, she followed a recommendation made by Caminer to eat a light diet, and she had a new young friend, Frankie Freedom, who had been spending time at the apartment to watch after her. Alice Vrbsky, who visited only in the evenings now because she had taken a day job, later described Freedom: "[He was a] young Negro boy [who] was staying there for the last weeks and helping her. I don't know where he came from. He was tall and thin and young, about seventeen or eighteen. [Press accounts later placed his age at twenty-two.] He had ambitions to be in the theatre and I don't know how Lady got to know him that well." Annie Ross remembered "he was housekeeper for blues singer [LaVern Baker]," and he was "a marvelous cook" who "adored Lady."

Frankie often did Billie's hair and nails and cooked for her, which he did for the rest of the week. Around two o'clock in the afternoon on Sunday, May 31, it was as she sat down at the kitchen table to eat a meal of oatmeal and custard he had prepared that she began to feel faint. Seeing she was in trouble, Frankie suggested they go to the hospital. "She was fighting with me," Freedom would say, "and wouldn't let me take her to the hospital in a cab." Then, after pushing ahead for month upon month while denying the severity of her condition, the inevitable finally happened and Billie passed out. One moment she was focused on the food in front of her as she spoke with Frankie; the next she lost consciousness and everything went black. Later, it was determined she slipped into a coma.

Terrified over what to do, Frankie rushed to the telephone and called Caminer, who immediately contacted the police to arrange for an ambulance to take Billie to Knickerbocker Hospital, a private facility located at Convent Avenue and West 131st Street. Frankie stayed with her until the police ambulance arrived and emergency workers carried her out on a stretcher and placed her in the back of the ambulance. Once Frankie got in to ride with Billie, who was unconscious, the ambulance sped off, heading for Knickerbocker Hospital. There, as Freedom later said, some time passed—"damn near an hour"—before any medical attention was given to her. Records indicated that Billie was admitted in the emergency room at 3:40 p.m., but after hospital personnel smelled alcohol on her breath and saw needle track marks on her arm, they diagnosed her as suffering from "drug addiction and alcoholism," refused to admit her to the general hospital, and sent her by ambulance, now apparently without Freedom, to Metropolitan Hospital, a public facility located in East Harlem at First Avenue and Ninety-Seventh Street, which had a more lenient policy concerning the treatment of patients afflicted with substance abuse. Billie was admitted at 5:30 p.m. When Caminer arrived twenty minutes later, having first gone to Knickerbocker Hospital only to discover his patient had been denied admission and sent to Metropolitan Hospital, he found her unattended, lying on a stretcher in the hallway, still unconscious. Part of the problem was her name. She was registered under Mrs. Eleanora McKay. The staff did not seem to realize they were ignoring America's preeminent jazz singer.

Once Caminer saw Billie was not being treated—while in a "cardiac emergency," no less—he exploded. Demanding to see the doctor in charge, he was told he had left for dinner. In his reporting, William Dufty documented what followed: "Caminer kicked up such a storm, according to witnesses, that Miss Holiday was finally rushed into an oxygen tent. Hospital records do not show what time these 'internal orders' were carried out—'that evening,' said the supervisor of nurses. Well over three hours had passed, Caminer estimated, between the time the ambulance picked Miss Holiday up and her admission to an oxygen tent."

At first, Billie was placed in a public ward, perhaps because Caminer demanded immediate attention and a bed there was what was available, but, once word began to circulate that Billie Holiday had been admitted, reporters and photographers tried to gain access to her, so for better security hospital officials moved her to a private room on the twelfth floor, Room 6A12, where she remained in an oxygen tent. It was not long before she also started to be fed intravenously.

She was in Room 6A12 the next day when Earle Warren Zaidins, who had received a telephone call telling him Billie had been hospitalized, arrived at Metropolitan Hospital and introduced himself to the hospital superintendent. The first order of business was to make sure Zaidins was actually Billie's attorney. To do so, the superintendent accompanied Zaidins to Billie's modest gray room, where, now barely conscious, she lay in an oxygen tent. Approaching the bed with Zaidins beside him, the superintendent asked Billie if she knew who the man was. Looking Zaidins over, Billie shot back, as best as she could in her diminished state, "What do you mean? That's my fucking lawyer, Earle."

That Monday, Zaidins began working with hospital officials to develop the message that could be given to reporters, who were demanding information. A problem had arisen. Hospital doctors were not prepared to rule out the possibility that Billie was suffering from complications due to narcotics use—perhaps an overdose— even though Caminer insisted Billie's immediate medical emergency was not produced by an episode involving drugs but by malnutrition, liver cirrhosis, and a compromised heart. Caminer was emphatic that Billie's condition, which was listed as critical, did not stem from recent drug use. In fact, as time passed and she showed no signs of narcotics withdrawal, which would have occurred if she had been relying on heroin on an ongoing basis, it became clear that any drug use in which she might have engaged over the past few months was recreational, not habitual. In short, at the present time Billie was not addicted to narcotics, heroin in particular.

On Tuesday, hospital doctors remained unwilling to rule out drug use as the cause of illness. As a result, a spokesperson refused to disclose any cause when information about Billie was finally released to the press. The hospital would only confirm that she was in critical condition. For his part, Caminer offered an assessment of her state: "Billie was in very bad shape yesterday, but her condition is improving, although still critical. She is in an oxygen tent." On Wednesday, with this limited information, news of Billie's health was splashed across the country when the two major wire services, Associated Press and United Press International, ran the story. "Billie Holiday in Hospital," read the UPI headline, while the AP warned, "Billie Holiday Ill, Condition Critical." Both services noted that hospital officials refused to disclose "the nature of her illness."

Naturally, the press continued to demand information, since it was obvious the hospital was obfuscating on the cause of Billie's sickness. As Wednesday passed and Billie continued to show no signs of narcotics withdrawal, hospital officials finally ruled out drugs as the source of her immediate health crisis. So the hospital agreed to allow Zaidins to speak for Billie, and in essence the hospital, when he met with reporters late Wednesday. He first disclosed the cause of illness: hepatitis, a severe liver inflammation, and heart failure. He added: "Her response to treatment has caused her attending physicians to be greatly encouraged and hopeful—in the absence of further complication—of a recovery." The resulting explosion of publicity, which hit on Thursday, announced the seriousness of her state of health. The UPI headline blared, "Negro Blues Singer Battles for Her Life," while the *Daily Defender,* published in Chicago, announced in a banner headline, "Billie Holiday Seriously Ill."

The Duftys were out of town when Billie collapsed on Sunday but returned to New York as soon as possible, in part because Bill wanted to write about her for his newspaper. Since he was a friend, he was able to gain access to her, unlike the rest of the reporters who were forced to run with statements from Billie's lawyer and doctor. So, when Dufty's article appeared in the *New York Post* amid the flood of articles nationwide, his had a decidedly personal feel to it, which was conveyed in the article's opening sentence: "Billie Holiday sat up in her sunny Metropolitan Hospital room today, sniffing bouquets from Ella, Lena and Sinatra, Basie, Belafonte and Bankhead, grinning at the Page One stories forecasting her demise and saying philosophically to a crony, 'Some damnbody is always trying to embalm me.'" As he had with *Lady Sings the Blues,* Dufty was intent on telling a good story—one of which Billie approved, if she herself had not orchestrated it—and not necessarily on disclosing actual facts. In truth, Billie was still deathly ill; she was not sitting up in bed but remained in an oxygen tent. What's more, her room was not flooded with bouquets of flowers sent by famous friends. When Dufty visited her on Wednesday, virtually no one had sent flowers. As he later revealed, "My notion was not to present a picture of a dying woman. The business I wrote about the flowers was a lie; she was receiving calls but there wasn't a thing arriving. I put in the names to shame people into sending things." In a subsequent article, Dufty also claimed Gary Cooper "sent a yard long telegram full of the Holy Ghost and his newly discovered Catholicism." Maria Cooper Janis, his daughter, says: "I know my father saw Billie Holiday perform and admired her, but they were not friends." As he often did when remaking the events in Billie's life for calculated effect, Dufty was determined to create a compelling story in which Billie appeared as the sympathetic heroine. In short, Billie was in critical condition in an oxygen tent, but that was not what she wanted the public to know. She was still shaping her image, through the writer with whom she had collaborated now for three years, in the way *she* wanted herself to be seen, regardless of what the truth might be.

As her illness became headline news nationwide, Billie focused on getting better. On Thursday, Caminer described her condition as "slightly improved." By Saturday, it was reported that, still in an oxygen tent, she had so far received four blood transfusions. On Sunday, one week into her hospital stay, her condition was considered critical but improving. On Monday, however, Dr. Ferdinand Piazza, the hospital's senior medical superintendent, was less optimistic, telling reporters, "She is not making much progress."

During her second week in the hospital, Billie began, rather miraculously, to improve. She was allowed visitors, and a steady stream of friends came by to see her, among them Alice Vrbsky, Frankie Freedom, the Duftys, Joe Glaser, and Mal Waldron. She had rebounded enough to make a request of Waldron; because she felt bad about what happened at the Flamingo Lounge, she wanted Mal to write to Jimmy Makris, who ran the club, and apologize again, which he did, saying in his letter, "As soon as Billie is able, she wants to come back to Lowell and make up for those two nights." To spur on her recovery, her friends brought into her hospital room a radio, a phonograph, and records. As she regained her strength, she listened to music while reading her favorite comic books and magazines. When Zaidins received a copy of her unreleased MGM album, he played it for her one evening, much to her delight. He also reported that MGM had sent a registered letter informing him that the company was exercising the option in Billie's contract to record another album. Billie was ecstatic, suggesting, only half-jokingly, that they should record the album in the hospital. Not missing a beat, she quipped, "We can call it *Lady at the Met.*"

Zaidins was doing all he could to line up work for her with the hope that the promise of upcoming creative endeavors might motivate her to fight harder to regain her health. He wanted to give her something to live for. To that end, he arranged for her to sign with Shaw Artists Corporation as a booking agent. More significantly, he received an offer from, and negotiated a contract with, a company called Valor Productions to make a motion picture based on *Lady Sings the Blues.* Bill Dufty was also involved, no doubt at Billie's insistence, in developing future projects for her, and his were of a more immediate nature. Billie now felt well enough that she devised a scheme to make some quick cash. She had Dufty come in so she could dictate to him a tell-all article about her drug addiction, the perfect piece to capitalize on the publicity she was receiving for her illness. Subsequently entitled "I Needed Heroin to Live," the article, after being rejected by *Playboy* and *Esquire,* sold to *Confidential* for $1,500, a fee she and Dufty split. Billie kept her share of the money, $750 in fifty-dollar bills, taped to her inner thigh.

At one point while Maely Dufty was visiting, Billie made a pronouncement to her that at first seemed unrealistic but would soon prove prophetic. The comment was based, of course, on the years of harassment Billie had suffered at the hands of the government. She was now, after all, easy prey. "You watch, baby," Billie said to Maely, "they're going to arrest me in this damn bed." Friends who knew her best understood what could have been viewed as paranoia. "The motherfuckers really were out to get her," Annie Ross says. "Lady felt she was a target of the government because of the nature of the arrests and how they were carried out. She felt there was a plot to destroy her. She was right."

As it turned out, Billie's prediction *was* right.

Here was the relevant sequence of events, according to authorities: On Thursday, June 11, an unidentified nurse—her last name would subsequently be revealed as Figueroa—was making her morning rounds when she saw white powder on Billie's nose. Becoming suspicious, she looked around the room and discovered a silver foil envelope containing white powder—and now versions of the story vary—either in Billie's right hand or in a Kleenex box beside Billie's bed. The nurse called in a hospital guard—likely to be a witness—before she spoke to Billie. "What's that?" the nurse supposedly asked Billie, indicating the powder on her nose, to which Billie replied, "Mind your own damn business." Billie was said to have retrieved the envelope from her purse, which hung on a hook on the wall across the room. The nurse confiscated the foil envelope and turned it over to Dr. Piazza, the hospital superintendent, who submitted it for analysis to Dr. Harold Appleton, the chief chemist. When the powder was revealed to be heroin, Piazza contacted the New York Police Department. On Friday, police descended on Billie's hospital room, where she was arrested for possessing narcotics—"a deck of pure heroin," they claimed, enough for two "rides." Police alleged she admitted that she "sniffed it"—heroin—from time to time and that she "found" the foil envelope in the bottom of her handbag from when she entered the hospital nearly two weeks ago. Police claimed they were skeptical; they believed a friend of Billie's smuggled the heroin into her room. Regardless, police indicated Billie would be arraigned at a later date. Meanwhile, she would remain confined in her hospital room as a prisoner and police guards would be stationed outside her door.

This may have been the story put forward by the government in the form of the NYPD, but there were problems with it. Because Billie was unconscious when she was taken from her apartment to the hospital, she did not carry in with her the handbag that allegedly contained the heroin. Once the handbag *did* make it into the hospital room, perhaps brought to Billie by a friend, it was kept on a hook away from her bed. Maely Dufty recalled: "Billie's handbag was hanging on a nail on the wall—six feet away from the bottom of her bed. It was virtually impossible for Billie—with hundreds of pounds of equipment strapped to her legs and arms for transfusions—to have moved one inch towards the wall." Maely was not the only friend who believed Billie was framed for drug possession in much the same way she had been in San Francisco years earlier. Alice Vrbsky remembered: "When they said in the paper that they found heroin on her, I don't know how she could have taken a hit of heroin in the hospital. She did not mention anything to me about the heroin in the hospital." Florynce Kennedy wrote: "It was obviously a setup. I don't believe that if heroin had been smuggled into the hospital it would have been left sitting in a Kleenex box, which was where Nurse Figueroa claimed to have found it." William Dufty informed Adam Clayton Powell, Jr., at the time of the arrest that he was suspicious of the nurse, who had disappeared, he said, for four days only to return to work and find Billie in possession of heroin. Dufty later told a journalist: "Certainly the [drugs] that were used as evidence were planted on her." And Annie Ross believes: "The drugs were clearly planted in the hospital room by the nurse. After all, it had happened to Lady before."

Regardless of what led up to the event, Billie was arrested in her hospital bed on Friday, June 12, and booked by telephone at the East 104th police station. Afterwards, because she was being held in police custody, officers removed from her room her radio, records, phonograph, and comic books. Three police officers were stationed outside her room to prevent her from receiving guests. Inspector Edward F. Carey announced to the press that she had been arrested and would be arraigned in her hospital bed when she was well enough to face the proceedings. Soon after the arrest, the NYPD also arrested Frankie Freedom, charging him with possession of sleeping pills; he was arraigned before Magistrate T. Vincent Quinn in Manhattan Felony Court and held on $1,500 bond. It was a classic move made by authorities to pressure a potential witness, through legal exposure that could result in prison time, to inform on a high-profile target like Billie Holiday.

As a result of the announcement from police, another wave of national publicity hit on Saturday. Now with the added detail of narcotics possession, the coverage was even more widespread, not to mention lurid, than earlier coverage of her illness. The headlines depicted her as a criminal—"Billie Caught with Heroin in Hospital," "Billie Holiday Arrested on Dope Charge," "Charge Billie Holiday Used Narcotics While in Hospital," "Billie Holiday, Critically Sick, Put Under Arrest," "Singer Held in Dope Case." Her portrayal in the press was disturbing and sensational; it was as if she were presumed guilty merely because of the allegation. "The persecution she was going through [was terrible]," Sonny Rollins says. "She was being persecuted in the press." Others, like Mal Waldron, believed the press coverage reflected the ill-informed way with which the government had been dealing with Billie for years. "My father," Mala Waldron says, "was angry because he felt the police were on her so much. He hated that. He felt if she had been treated like someone with an illness instead of being treated like a criminal, she would not have ended up the way she did. He was very angry about it."

In the coming days, more details about the arrest emerged, facts the government may not have wanted the public to know. On the day Nurse Figueroa made her discovery, here was Billie's physical state, as later described by William Dufty: "Her wrists and ankles were slit, and her arms and legs stretched out akimbo so that glucose could pour into her veins. Her back was rimmed with running sores. She had a six-inch incision in her mid-section. The hollows in her temples made her look seventy. She was down to ninety-nine pounds. She had been on the critical list for twelve days, receiving oxygen [much of] the time. Her condition was described as terminal—the end of the line." Even so, on Thursday, Billie was supposedly sniffing heroin, and, on Friday, despite her grave condition, her hospital room was raided and she was interrogated, without being allowed to have an attorney present, by first two, then three, police detectives, who threatened to haul her to the Women's House of Detention—even though she was bedridden—unless she confessed and named her supplier. It was when she refused to cooperate that Detective Michael Coenan placed her under arrest and informed her that, going forward, no one would be allowed past police guards unless the visitor secured written permission from the 23rd Precinct.

Before this ordeal, Billie had been improving. She was doing well enough that the oxygen tent had been removed, although she was still being given nutrition intravenously, which had contributed to her gaining a modest amount of weight. She felt well enough that she welcomed the chance for Frankie Freedom to come in and fix her hair and paint her fingernails, which were covered with a double coat of crimson-red polish. Alice Vrbsky also stopped by to help her answer the hundreds of cards and letters that were pouring in as a result of the press coverage of her illness. In every way, Billie seemed to be rebounding as she attempted to get back to some semblance of everyday order concerning her appearance and the way she dealt with her fans. Then the police raided her room, and even though she had suspected the government would make such a move, the actual event was, for Billie, a profound shock to the system, a debilitating blow to her recovery. Now she was a prisoner with officers guarding her door. The police, quite literally, turned her hospital room—normally an oasis of healing and recovery—into a prison cell. Billie felt unsettled, fearful, and depressed. Whatever modest improvement she had experienced was blunted by the raid. It was a sinister—and intentional—tactic of intimidation. It was not long before her physical and emotional well-being began to deteriorate.

As Hazel Scott watched the press coverage of Billie's unfolding ordeal from Paris, she sent her a letter, which arrived around this time. "I love you," Scott wrote, "and I think that you are one of the special people. Prez sure [was] pure. So are you. Guess the mother-fuckers never will understand! Pray for you baby. I always pray for you." She signed it, "Love, Hazel."

On Saturday, with Billie's approval, Joe Glaser met in his office with Florynce Kennedy and Don Wilkes, who were retained as Billie's criminal lawyers, to determine how they could counteract the moves made by the police. The first order of business was to remove the guards. So the lawyers prepared a writ of habeas corpus, a constitutional provision that protects a citizen from unlawful imprisonment, and, searching around for a judge on the weekend, located New York State Supreme Court Justice Arthur Markewich, who signed the writ and scheduled a hearing for Tuesday. Despite the lawyers having secured a signed writ of habeas corpus, the police refused to remove the guards.

Meanwhile, Kennedy and Wilkes discovered the Manhattan district attorney intended to proceed with an indictment, which meant that Billie risked being relocated to the Bellevue Hospital Prison Ward. The idea that an entertainer of Billie's renown would be taken from her hospital bed—while still in critical condition—and placed in a prison ward was unacceptable to her lawyers. They decided to make an unconventional legal maneuver. "Wilkes," Kennedy later wrote, "came up with the stratagem of offering to have [Billie] testify before the Grand Jury. This tactic saved her from being indicted for the felony of possessing narcotics, which would have meant moving her to the prison ward. But she was still under arrest." In legal circles, the maneuver was controversial. "It's highly unusual," Judge Emily Jane Goodman says, "but if you feel you have the right case to be effective and if you believe the Grand Jury will hear your case and not indict, you can do it. Usually, you can't use such a tactic because you know your client is guilty. It's a difficult move."

On Tuesday, June 16, Wilkes and Kennedy and an assistant district attorney representing the NYPD appeared before Justice Henry Epstein in the New York Supreme Court to argue the matter of the writ of habeas corpus. The assistant DA contended police officers were merely protecting Billie from anyone who might want to sneak drugs to her, while Wilkes countered that the guards were a form of harassment of a seriously ill woman who "may never leave her bed"—an indication of just how sick Billie was. "If she ever becomes able to face arraignment," Wilkes told Epstein, "I'll see that she is there. She can't leave her bed." With this assurance in mind, Epstein granted the writ, paroled Billie into the custody of her attorneys, and ordered the removal of the guards. Later that day, after Epstein made his ruling, Billie quipped to a police officer at her bedside, "Looks like everyone is waiting for me to kick the bucket, but I am going to fool them."

In an act of defiance, the NYPD *still* refused to remove the guards. It was not until later in the week when Wilkes threatened to return to court seeking a second writ that the guards were finally removed, almost one full week after Billie was arrested. The effect of the obstinate maneuverings of the NYPD meant that during the week Billie, now at a vulnerable juncture in her recovery, was effectively isolated from her friends, colleagues, and support staff. The Duftys were prevented from seeing her, as was Leonard Feather. Annie Ross remembered: "[While] she was very ill and in hospital I was working at the Apollo, and J. C. Heard, the drummer, was on the bill with Lambert, Hendricks, & Ross, and J.C. said, 'You know, I hear Lady is very, very bad. Let's go down to the hospital between shows and see her.' So, we tore down to the hospital, and we couldn't get upstairs because there was a complete ban on any visitors in case they were bringing her any stuff or anything. So, we wrote a note, and we then found out she was absolutely livid when she found out we'd been downstairs and hadn't been allowed up."

Then, on Sunday, June 21, two detectives showed up in Billie's hospital room and, in an act of retaliation by the NYPD for having the guards removed, fingerprinted her and took mug shots while she lay in her hospital bed. To get into the hospital, the detectives had to pass a gathering of protesters on the sidewalk near the front entrance led by Reverend Eugene Callender, a Presbyterian minister who had become an advocate for the humane treatment of people suffering from substance abuse. The protesters were picketing the

NYPD's treatment of Billie. "Let Billie Live," read a sign held by one of them. The public may have been coming to her defense, but the government seemed as determined as ever in its persecution of her.

Despite the public outcry, the district attorney appeared determined to force Billie to make an appearance before the grand jury, which he scheduled for June 26. The absurdity of trying to require a bedridden patient to appear before a grand jury was not lost on Wilkes. On June 24, in an effort to delay the appearance, he wrote to Assistant District Attorney Melvin Glass. "Suffering from a condition so grave that at the time she was considered beyond recovery," Wilkes wrote, "she was none the less given a bit of a going over, first by two, and then by three detectives. Her books, flowers, record player and radio were taken away from her, and in general she was dealt with as if she were a reincarnation of Ma Barker (a gang leader of the 1930s), rather than one of the most gifted, brilliant and creative artists in the history of American music." That seemed to be the crux of the injustice: an artist who should have been celebrated as a national treasure was being hounded by a government dead set on destroying her. To underscore his point, Wilkes wrote: "On June 21, two detectives descended on her room to 'mug' and fingerprint her while she was still in her hospital bed, without permission, knowledge or consent." Now the DA wanted her to appear before a grand jury when she was not able even to get out of her bed. Ultimately, only because it would have been physically impossible for her to do so, the district attorney agreed to postpone her grand jury appearance, and the legal ordeal that had unfolded over almost two weeks temporarily came to a halt.

Even so, the government's actions had taken their toll. Any progress Billie had shown came to an end, and a new level of concern seized her friends. "I had never given up hope that she would be able to come out of it alive," Alice Vrbsky said, "until all this happened. It was the last straw."

Despite the setback, Billie remained hopeful about the future. She continued to line up work for when she was released from the hospital. On July 8, she signed a contract, negotiated by Flo Kennedy, to appear for a fee of $750 in a motion picture entitled *No Honor Among Thieves* to be produced by Vinod International Films. Around this time, Joe Glaser visited her to explain the problems that would develop if she had two booking agents, so she called Milt Shaw, owner of the Shaw agency, to withdraw from her contract and, unable to reach him, sent him a letter explaining that she had made her decision when she was ill and "in no position to know what I was doing." She had signed with Shaw to placate Zaidins, who represented the agency, because he had an offer for the film rights to *Lady Sings the Blues*. Billie badly wanted to sell the film rights, but Valor Productions was offering $50,000 and she wanted twice that amount. So she was holding out for more money, even though on June 30 Zaidins had sent a telegram to Louis McKay at the West Eighty-Seventh Street apartment that stated: MOVIE CONTRACT READY CONTACT IMMEDIATELY.

But Billie was perhaps most pleased on the day she looked up from her bed to see an old friend walk through the doorway to her room. Fortunately, she had had her hair and nails done that day, so she was looking her best as she lay in bed. Naturally, she was smoking a cigarette—which she did throughout her hospital stay, particularly when she was not in an oxygen tent—as Frank Sinatra approached her accompanied by his longtime personal valet, George Jacobs. Sinatra did not comment on Billie's appearance—so different from what it had been when she headlined on Fifty-Second Street and he often sat in the audience in the front row to watch her—although Jacobs later did: "Her body was defeated. Her once plump form was wasted away. She was skin and bones, and barely that. The hard life that had made her music so great and true had literally eaten her alive. All the booze had rotted out her insides."

Billie was thrilled to see Sinatra, who was equally happy to see her. He looked as debonair as ever as he stood beside her bed, his familiar voice filling the room, much to the surprise of the hospital staff who happened to come by.

"I can't tell you how much I love *Lady in Satin*," Sinatra said to Billie.

For Billie, it was heartening to hear his praise, especially since he had been her inspiration for making the album in the first place.

Now, sensing the severity of her condition, Sinatra tried to get her to talk about future projects. If she had something to look forward to, perhaps she would be more motivated to rally.

Finally, Sinatra acknowledged what he owed her for teaching him phrasing back when he was breaking away from singing with the big bands. As she had for years, Billie downplayed her contribution to his singing.

"I may have showed you how to bend a note, Frankie," she said modestly, the years of their friendship coming full circle in the moment. "That's all."

Louis McKay was staying in Billie's apartment because, during the first week after she had fallen ill, he flew in from California and for most of her hospitalization visited her daily. During the week when the police guarded her room, he was required to secure a written notice of admission from the 23rd Precinct each day to see her. Considering their long history together, Billie did not appear to care one way or the other that McKay was on the scene. Mostly, he seemed concerned about business. He encouraged her to sign the film deal Zaidins had negotiated with Valor without waiting for a larger fee for the option. Indeed, to many of Billie's friends, what McKay seemed to be keenly aware of was the fact that, because he and Billie were still legally married and because Billie had never made a will, he stood to be the sole heir to her estate. While Billie was not currently flush with liquid assets—in part because McKay had handled her money for years and kept much of it for himself—the royalties generated by her records would potentially be worth a fortune. McKay was, in a real sense, on a death watch.

On July 10, doctors ordered that Billie was allowed to receive candy, ice cream, or fruit but no salty foods, an indication that there was a slight improvement in her condition. And there was. In the forty days she had spent in the hospital, she had gained thirty pounds, an encouraging sign for her ongoing recovery. Then, even though the symptoms of the liver cirrhosis had lessened, an unanticipated complication occurred when she was struck with a new ailment—an intense kidney infection. Perhaps this additional infection was a mitigating factor, or perhaps her system was simply giving in to the stress under which she had lived since her collapse on May 31, the severity of which was only intensified by the torment through which the NYPD was putting her, but on Saturday, July 11, Billie began to experience problems with her heart. Immediately, doctors placed her back under an oxygen tent, her contempt for which she showed by sneaking a cigarette as she lay in the tent and nearly setting herself on fire. When a nurse caught her with the cigarette, she quipped, "They already arrested me a month ago. What are they going to do for an encore?" In her general disposition, Billie appeared to remain hopeful, yet over the next three days her physical state deteriorated considerably. By early Wednesday, July 15, her condition had become so dire that doctors allowed Billie, a lifelong Catholic, to receive the last rites of the Roman Catholic Church administered to her by a priest.

Those who saw her during this time remarked on her beauty, which shone through despite the ravages of her illness. "She was still rather beautiful," Florynce Kennedy recalled, "especially when she smiled. She had a very sweet, almost childlike smile." William Dufty wrote: "She was beautiful; no one who saw her exquisite brown head against the hospital white pillow would dare talk of her loveliness in bygone days."

On Wednesday, she remained conscious. In the morning, Joe Glaser visited; the Duftys saw her in the evening. Louis McKay was a constant presence. Alice Vrbsky spent time with her as well but later recalled her deep concern: "I saw death in her face. . . . I saw the same thing in my father's face." When Alice left that Wednesday night, she picked up a strong feeling from Billie about her visiting the next day: "I felt almost that she didn't want me to come."

Thursday saw Billie decline as she began to lapse from consciousness. McKay was often at her bedside, as was Bill Dufty, who later said that "she was in extremis for something like twenty-four hours [where she] was above and beyond consciousness, where the body goes on and the will to live is there, and the will to live was there until the end." But, as afternoon turned into evening, it was apparent that death was approaching. She had come so far in her life, traveling from the downtrodden areas of Baltimore to Harlem in the throes of a creative and cultural renaissance to some of the most esteemed stages in Europe and America, but here she was, in a time-worn room in a public hospital in East Harlem with the prospect of yet another arduous legal battle looming before her. For twenty years, she had been in open combat with the government; the idea of going through another fight was too much for her to bear. The will to live remained, but the forces out to crush her were more powerful than ever, and in her compromised state she no longer had what she needed to fight them.

As Thursday night passed into Friday morning, she was unconscious. Her breathing became increasingly labored. Around 2:40 a.m., McKay left her bedside to go make a telephone call. Dufty took his place to carry on the vigil. A private nurse was also present. In the quietness of the darkened room, around the time of night when she was often exiting the stage after her final set, Billie—dignified, noble, beautiful even in this moment—lay in repose in her hospital bed. She continued to breathe until 3:20 a.m., when she stopped. Her face relaxed. Her body went limp. The nurse felt her pulse, but there was none. Quietly, she told Dufty, "She's gone."

CHAPTER 15

ℒ

Angel *of* Harlem

The funeral for Billie Holiday was held at St. Paul the Apostle Roman Catholic
Church on Columbus Avenue at Sixtieth Street at 11:00 a.m. on July 21, 1959.
The solemn requiem mass was conducted by Reverend Joseph Troy, who was
assisted by Fathers Lawrence McDonnell and Robert Nugent.

July 1959 and Afterwards

I.

In the wake of Billie Holiday's death, those who knew her were profoundly affected by the loss. Having been with her when she died, Bill Dufty went home to channel his grief into a moving obituary, which appeared later in the day on Friday in the *New York Post*. "Billie Holiday died . . . as simply and regally as she had lived," he wrote. "She was poor [but] with a $50,000 movie contract for her life story waiting for her signature she was holding out for double or nothing. She was triumphant; for . . . years the government had paraded her throughout a whirligig of courts, jail, bail. . . . She was alone. When her fighting heart gave out . . . only her special nurse and this reporter were at her bedside."

The news of her death traveled quickly through the jazz community, just as word had spread four months earlier when Lester Young died. Leonard Feather, Billie's friend and intermittent concert promoter, was distraught. "I can still remember," Lorraine Feather says, "my father sitting on the side of the bed crying. Someone had called to tell him what happened. He was deeply upset." Louis Armstrong—who had recently survived his own health scare in Italy, where he came down with pneumonia that resulted in him developing a heart condition—was moved by Billie's death, commenting, "She had the most unique voice and style I'd ever heard. What she felt when she sang, she felt with all she was." But no one was more devastated than Frank Sinatra, who was inconsolable. "He locked himself in [his] 72nd Street penthouse and wept for two days," George Jacobs wrote, "playing songs like 'Autumn in New

York,' drinking, and crying. I had never seen him hurt so much . . . but [what] else could match this horrible waste? Mr. S told me something that she had said, that you don't know what enough is until you've had more than enough. Now she knew, but it was too late, and it killed him a little bit as well."

In Paris, Hazel Scott was devastated. "When she last visited us," Adam Clayton Powell III says, "my mother didn't want her to go back. She was worried that there wasn't anyone in New York who would take care of her." As it turned out, there was not, and now she was gone. "I was overcome by all the tragedy," Scott wrote, "all the greatness and all the beauty of her life." Naturally, one person who took the death especially hard was the man who had spent much of the last two years with her; Mal Waldron lost his collaborator and his friend. "After Billie passed," Mala Waldron says, "it was really difficult for my father. It was hard to get him to talk about her because it was so painful for him—he was never open about his emotions anyway—and because he was very protective of her memory. Eventually, he survived a potential tragic episode. He said it was a mental breakdown, but years later he admitted it was a heroin overdose. In hindsight, I think Billie's death was a contributing factor in what happened to him."

Few who knew Billie expressed their grief more eloquently than Dexter Gordon, the tenor saxophone devotee of Lester Young and Billie—when asked once what about her singing influenced him so profoundly, his one-word answer was "phrasing"—with whom Billie had socialized in New York in the mid-1940s, when they often found themselves in Harlem in after-hours clubs like Mae's. Now deeply moved by Billie's death, he conveyed his emotions in a letter to *Down Beat,* which he composed while he was confined in a minimum-security prison near Los Angeles; like so many other jazz artists, he was serving a sentence for narcotics possession. "Tragedy surrounded Billie Holiday," Gordon wrote, "as an octopus surrounds the victims with its tentacles. . . . [But] she wore it, tragedy, like a cloak of honor. . . . Even in the songs she sang pathos reared its sentient head. The theme was inevitably one of misuse: 'My man, he beats me, too.' 'Jim never brings me pretty flowers.' 'Lover man, someday he'll come and he'll dry my tears.' The heart-rending 'Gloomy Sunday' and 'Strange Fruit.' . . . Sure, she sung them, but even these had an aura of gloom.

"Lady sang out for all the world to bear witness to the suffering of womankind. Moreover, men and women both received her message. Someone I know, very dear to me, while suffering in a hospital, heard repeatedly in her delirium the voice of Billie Holiday—her only consolation.

"After entering the hospital and being put on the critical list for complications, Billie was said to have been found with a bundle of heroin by a nurse, who was 'happening by.' From this, I deduce she was still fighting for her life. However, after the police, the notoriety, the inevitable court hassle to follow, she seems to have given up, and unlike old generals, just faded away. This, to me, is a sad note of our times, our society, in which something as heinous as this is allowed to happen. A thinking person can denote many other intangibles in a situation such as this.

"Billie's contribution will always be near, for many singers carry her style on today. . . . Lady's voice, while very sophisticated, was coarse, soft, yet earthy. Her style and delivery were unique, all her own. The contribution she made in the American art form, jazz, was infinite and immeasurable and meant many things to many people. . . . Generous to a fault, Billie was misused by people, many people. Loving well but not wisely, that is the story of Billie Holiday's life. Although regal, but not 'pale,' Lady to me was a queen."

The coverage of Billie's death was extensive. A banner headline and photograph of her took up the entire front page of the *New York Post,* which outsold all other newspapers in New York on Friday. Inside, readers found Dufty's obituary, entitled "Billie Holiday Died After Relapse; First Lady of the Blues was 44." Obituaries sent out over the two wire services appeared in newspapers across the country. The AP obituary, "Singer Billie Holiday Dies," described her as "a wasted shadow of the once great blues singer who packed nightclubs from coast to coast" and reported her "immediate cause

of death . . . as congestion of the lungs complicated by heart failure."
The AP noted that at the time of her death "she was under arrest—
charged with possession of a pack of heroin in her bed." The UPI
obituary, also entitled "Singer Billie Holiday Dies," played up her
history of narcotics use as well: "The Negro singer, who had hit the
top of her profession, then fell to the depths in the throes of narcotics
addiction, was said to have licked the habit and to have been on her
way back when, in the words of her booking agent, 'her motor just
wore out.'" Indeed, in most of the coverage of her death, especially
in that generated by mainstream news organizations, the emphasis
was placed on her narcotics addiction, which, it was pointed out, had
brought on repeated encounters with the criminal justice system.

The *New York Times* obituary, entitled "Billie Holiday Dies Here
at 44; Jazz Singer Had Wide Influence," which ran on Saturday, fell
in line with other coverage by playing up her drug use. "She had
been under arrest in her hospital bed since June 12 for illegal possession of narcotics," the newspaper observed, noting later: "In 1947,
a cloud that had been gathering over Miss Holiday and which was
to cover the rest of her career, burst on her [and she] was arrested
for a narcotics violation." The newspaper did, however, attempt to
document her importance as a singer: "Miss Holiday set a pattern
during her most fruitful years that has proved more influential than
that of almost any other jazz singer, except the two who inspired
her, Louis Armstrong and the late Bessie Smith." Meanwhile, the
obituary in *Time* was minimal in its coverage and callous in its sentiment. The entire obituary read: "Died. Billie Holiday, 44, Negro
blues singer, whose husky, melancholy voice reflected the tragedy of
her own life; in Manhattan. Born of indigent teenagers, schooled in
a Baltimore brothel, she stubbornly nursed her resentment, poured
it out in songs that reached their height of popularity in the early
'40s—'Billie's Blues,' 'The Man I Love,' above all, 'Strange Fruit,' a
description of a Negro lynching in the South—succumbed to the
dope addiction which dogged her to its end." In the country's most
widely circulated newsmagazine, the death of America's foremost jazz
artist was afforded two sentences, which contained an array of code
words and phrases—"Negro blues singer," "tragedy of her own life,"

"stubbornly nursed her resentment," "dope addiction." The obituary was not a recapitulation of what Billie achieved in her life and career but an effort by the establishment to marginalize her as an artist and deride her as a woman, all with a not-so-subtle undertone of racial animus.

Some urban newspapers were more sympathetic in their coverage. The *New York Daily News* observed: "Death, at 44, put blues singer Billie Holiday under the spotlight of world attention for the last time. Whenever performers gathered, the comment was much the same: Billie was a trouper, they said. Billie had it rough, but Billie played it game." And this from the *Globe and Mail* in Canada: "Even in death Billie Holiday is misunderstood. Every obituary . . . calls her a blues singer . . . when, in fact, a blues singer is one of the few things she was not. . . . Billie Holiday was a jazz singer, the best ever of her sex, and ballads, not blues, were her bread and butter. She probably sang fewer honest-to-goodness blues than any other major singer in jazz."

Most sympathetic were industry publications. "Few others could ever sing the blues like Billie Holiday," *Billboard* proclaimed; "few other singers will ever be remembered as affectionately or as compassionately as Lady. . . . In spite of all [that happened to her] or perhaps because of it, everyone finally realized that Lady Day was touched with greatness."

On Friday, in the hours after her death, the handful of family, friends, and advisers who were helping Billie make decisions at the end of her life—the Duftys, Joe Glaser, Earle Warren Zaidins, Louis McKay—conferred to discuss funeral plans. Dufty felt strongly that he did not want a "jazz" funeral, as he called it, an emotional affair, likely held in Harlem, used to air grievances and engage in political posturing—to which he believed Billie would have been opposed—so he argued that because Billie was a lifelong Roman Catholic and because she was internationally famous he was certain that the Archdiocese of New York would be willing to hold a funeral at St. Patrick's Cathedral presided over by Cardinal Francis Spellman. McKay was too tempted by the status that such a funeral could bestow on Billie—and by extension the Estate of Billie Holiday, of which he was the sole heir—and, based on Dufty's assurances, went along with the plan. But when Dufty contacted the Archdiocese, neither St. Patrick's Cathedral nor Cardinal Spellman was available on such short notice. Given Billie's fame, however, the Archdiocese was loath to ignore Dufty's wishes. As such, church officials offered what they said were second-best accommodations. The funeral could be held at St. Paul the Apostle Roman Catholic Church on Columbus Avenue at Sixtieth Street with a solemn requiem mass conducted by Reverend Joseph Troy, who was pastor of the church, and assisted by Fathers Lawrence McDonnell and Robert Nugent. McKay was agreeable with the arrangements, and the funeral time was set for 11:00 a.m. on Tuesday, July 21. First, though, the body of Billie Holiday would lie in state for viewing by the public at Universal Funeral Chapel—the site of the recent funeral of Lester Young—on Sunday from 2:00 until 10:00 p.m. and Monday from 9:00 a.m. until 10:00 p.m.

In anticipation of mourners passing by to see her lying in state in a heavy bronze coffin, Billie was dressed as if she were about to take the stage. She wore one of her favorite evening gowns—a rose Chantilly lace gown with long sleeves—and pink gloves. Around her neck was a five-strand pearl necklace. Each ear was adorned with a cluster pearl earring. There was a halo of white gardenias in her hair. She appeared to be, as she always did onstage, the epitome of style and grace—a lady.

When the funeral chapel opened its doors on Sunday afternoon, a crowd of mourners had already gathered. People passed by steadily all afternoon and into the evening, hundreds an hour. A reporter described those who had come to offer their last respects: "[There] stretched a line of people, the poor, the rich, the famous, the unknown, all there to pay tribute to the lady who sang the blues and lived the blues." When the viewing concluded at 10:00 p.m., four thousand mourners had filed past the coffin. On Monday, another six thousand people passed through the chapel, as exemplified by one "middle-aged woman," according to one account, who "stood near the heavy bronze coffin [and] wept as these words came brokenly from her lips"—"Lady Day will sing the blues no more."

Among the ten thousand mourners, there was one who lingered at the coffin longer than most. Tallulah Bankhead had remained distant from Billie since 1951. The two had been in communication, of a fashion, in 1956 when Billie was preparing to publish *Lady Sings the Blues*. A copy of the manuscript was sent to Tallulah. Once she discovered the book contained passages about her, Tallulah made sure that Doubleday knew she wanted them removed. "The book indicated a very close friendship between two women," according to Lee Barker, the book's editor, "and that Tallulah had gone to Billie's apartment many times for spaghetti dinners. [Theirs] was a very close friendship [that] spanned a period of several years . . . maybe about five or six years." Hurt and angry over Tallulah's rebuff, Billie sent her a letter. "I thought I was a friend of yours," Billie wrote, addressing her as "Miss Bankhead." "That's why there was nothing in my book that was unfriendly to you. . . . Read my book over again. . . . There's nothing in it to hurt you. If you think so, let's talk about it." Tallulah never wrote back, nor did she call; the book was edited, with most of the pertinent passages removed, and published. As time passed, the unfinished business between them haunted Billie. They had been so close; then it all ended. Yet, Billie never fully understood why.

As for Tallulah, in recent months, through press reports and gossip from friends, she had kept up with Billie's worsening health crisis compounded by new legal woes. If her true feelings for Billie remained unclear, they were revealed as she visited the funeral home. Fellow mourners remarked the Broadway star when she approached the coffin and then, after gazing at Billie for some time, leaned down and started whispering to Billie as if she were still alive. No one could hear what Tallulah said; the silent words were for Billie alone. But the bond that existed between the two of them seemed to linger on after Billie's death. It was some time before Tallulah finally left. It would be the last time she was with Billie, because she did not attend her funeral. Instead, as a gesture of her affection, she sent to the church twelve dozen long-stem roses. A card read: "God bless you. Love. From Tallulah."

When the hearse pulled to a stop in front of St. Paul the Apostle Catholic Church shortly before eleven o'clock, six pallbearers carried the heavy bronze coffin up the church's front steps as crowds of people—five hundred or more—lining both sides of the street looked on. Inside, three thousand people were packed into the church, making it the largest funeral ever held there. "The throng at the church and outside," according to *The New York Times,* "was so heavy that ten policemen were detailed to the scene. Traffic was disrupted in front of the church at Columbus Avenue and [Sixtieth] Street." Among the forty honorary pallbearers who attended the funeral were Teddy Wilson, Mary Lou Williams, Gene Krupa, Benny Goodman, Roy Eldridge, Charlie Shavers, Henry "Red" Allen, Joe Williams, Juanita Hall, Leonard Feather, Ray Ellis, Mal Waldron, and Joe Glaser. Indeed, the audience was replete with jazz stalwarts, from John Hammond and Jo Jones to Tony Scott and Michael Peter Grace, the latter one of Billie's most devoted admirers.

Once the coffin was placed on a catafalque at the head of the center aisle, the service began. The solemn requiem mass was conducted by Reverend Troy with responses rendered in Latin chants by the church's ten-man choir. The stately service kept the focus of the occasion on the loss of Billie Holiday and not Louis McKay, who arrived at the ceremony with a woman named Kay Kelly, who claimed to be Billie's half sister even though she was not. (She was the daughter of Phil Gough by a woman other than Sadie Fagan, making her Billie's stepsister by marriage.) The ceremony was a fitting final tribute to Billie Holiday, who had spent her life attempting to rise above her modest beginnings; now here she was honored by the somber figures in the Roman Catholic Church with the elite of the jazz community looking on from the audience. "There was no eulogy to the lady of song," *Newsday* noted, "only music as the church resounded to the refrains of a solemn requiem mass." It was all too appropriate that the transcendent sound of music, not the voice of a reverend, best conveyed the loss represented by the death of Billie Holiday.

After the service, five limousines headed up a lengthy procession of cars that proceeded from St. Paul the Apostle to St. Raymond's Cemetery in the Bronx, where Billie was to be buried alongside her mother. One reporter observed: "The morning ritual deviated only once, but in the direction of another tradition. On its way from [the church to the cemetery], the funeral procession detoured eastward to 110th Street and snaked slowly through Harlem. There had been no advance notice of this and few of the passersby in the street were aware of its meaning. It was as much Billie Holiday's farewell as Harlem's farewell."

In the weeks and months ahead, commentators began to place Billie Holiday into historical perspective and, in doing so, evaluate her accomplishments as a musician. The tone of the assessments changed now that she was dead; a longing for the "Billie of the past" was replaced by an ability to view what looked to be her complete oeuvre. Typical of many of those appraisals was one offered by British jazz critic Benny Green: "And the conclusion I eventually came to was that Billie Holiday is one of the most significant jazz artists who ever lived . . . that she was one of the most remarkable natural musicians jazz has seen, so natural in fact that it is very doubtful whether she was fully aware of it, and that . . . her unqualified artistic triumph was all the more remarkable because it required her, almost inadvertently, to prove the universality of jazz in a way no instrumentalist could possibly have done." At the same time, there were essay-length memoirs of Billie published by friends like Leonard Feather and tribute programs broadcast on the radio. But perhaps the most enduring homage to Billie Holiday was not an essay or a radio broadcast but a poem written on the day she died by someone she never met.

2.

In 1959, Monday was jazz-poetry night at the Five Spot, the café on Cooper Square where the creative crowd—painters, poets, novelists, journalists—could listen to some of the most eminent names in jazz, among them John Coltrane, Thelonious Monk, Ornette Coleman, and Charles Mingus, all of whom held residencies at the club. Mal Waldron, who had started working at the Five Spot in January, often played for jazz-poetry night. "Kenneth Koch and Larry Rivers had begun staging jazz-and-poetry evenings there," author Brad Gooch wrote, "in response to similar events in San Francisco initiated by Allen Ginsberg and Kenneth Rexroth."

Near the end of her life, Billie came into the Five Spot alone one night around 1:00 a.m. to visit with Mal on a jazz-poetry night. On this occasion, Mal was accompanying Kenneth Koch, a member of the New York School, the group of painters and poets working in downtown Manhattan that included, among others, painters Larry Rivers and Robert Motherwell and poets John Ashbery and Barbara Guest. As Koch read his poems, with Waldron improvising on the piano behind him, Billie sat at the bar and listened. A table of friends of Koch, including Rivers, was among the audience, which, at capacity as it was tonight, numbered between eighty and one hundred customers. Once the set was over, Koch and Waldron left the stage to appreciative applause and made their way to the bar, where Billie sat on a stool. Mal introduced her. "Man," Billie said to Koch, "your stuff is just crazy!" Koch took it to mean that she enjoyed his poetry.

Later, Billie had taken a table with Mal when Joe Termini, an imposing yet friendly man who owned the club with his brother Iggy, approached her.

"Hey, Lady," Joe said. "You gonna sing for us tonight?"

Billie looked around the room and spotted an off-duty policeman at the bar. "I'd love to," she said, "but the fuzz is standing over there."

Termini knew to whom Billie was referring; he was an off-duty policeman—a precinct captain no less. "But, Lady," Joe said, "that's who wants to hear you sing."

So Billie gladly accepted the invitation, and before long she took the stage, where, accompanied by Waldron, as she had been now for two years, she sang three songs. Kenneth Koch remembered: "It was very close to the end of her life, with her voice almost gone, just like a whisper, just like the taste of very old wine, but full of spirit.

Everyone was crazy about her. She sang the songs in this very whis-
pery beautiful voice. The place was quite crowded. She sang these
songs, and it was very moving."

What Billie did not know was that among Koch's friends that
evening was the poet Frank O'Hara, who had just come out of the
restroom when she took the stage. That's where he stood to watch
her set. O'Hara had seen Billie once before, in June 1957, when she
played a midnight show—then called Music for Night People—at
Loew's Sheridan Theatre along with the Charles Mingus Quintet,
the Randy Weston Trio, and Barbara Lea. Billie had been performing in Philadelphia, so she was late arriving to the midnight show.
But O'Hara stayed until he heard her. "We didn't leave," said Irma
Hurley, one of four friends who accompanied O'Hara to the concert. "She finally arrived pretty zonked out. But she did sing." Brad
Gooch wrote: "O'Hara's reaction to her performance was as exhila-
rated as his reaction to Judy Garland's show at the Palace Theatre,
after which he had commented . . . "Well, I guess she's better than
Picasso.'" As he watched Billie the second time, O'Hara was not in
the cavernous Sheridan Theatre but the claustrophobic Five Spot,
and Billie Holiday was *right there.* The moment stayed with him long
after Billie finished her final song.

Memories of the performance came flooding back to O'Hara on
July 17 when he was walking down the sidewalk in Manhattan and
saw the front-cover headline on the *New York Post:* "Billie Holiday
Dies." During his lunch hour back in his office at the Museum of
Modern Art, where he was a curator, O'Hara wrote one of his "I do
this, I do that" poems. That evening, after traveling to East Hampton, where he visited friends, he read them the poem:

THE DAY LADY DIED

It is 12:20 in New York a Friday
three days after Bastille day, yes
it is 1959 and I go get a shoeshine
because I will get off the 4:19 in Easthampton
at 7:15 and then go straight to dinner
and I don't know the people who will feed me

I walk up the muggy street beginning to sun
and have a hamburger and a malted and buy
an ugly NEW WORLD WRITING to see what the poets
in Ghana are doing these days
                                        I go on to the bank
and Miss Stillwagon (first name Linda I once heard)
doesn't even look up my balance for once in her life
and in the GOLDEN GRIFFIN I get a little Verlaine
for Patsy with drawings by Bonnard although I do
think of Hesiod, trans. Richmond Lattimore or
Brendan Behan's new play or *Le Balcon* or *Les Nègres*
of Genet, but I don't, I stick with Verlaine
after practically going to sleep with quandariness

and for Mike I just stroll into the PARK LANE
Liquor Store and ask for a bottle of Strega and
then I go back where I came from to 6th Avenue
and the tobacconist in the Ziegfeld Theatre and
casually ask for a carton of Gauloises and a carton
of Picayunes, and a NEW YORK POST with her face on it

and I am sweating a lot by now and think of
leaning on the john door at the 5 SPOT
while she whispered a song along the keyboard
to Mal Waldron and everyone and I stopped breathing

3·

The coverage of Billie's death was still resonating with the public when, one week after she died, MGM released *Billie Holiday,* what was now her final album, with music provided by Ray Ellis and His Orchestra. As expected, the critics focused on the album's place in her career, not merely its relative merit. In the *Nashville Banner,* Bob Battle, describing the effort as her "memorial album," noted: "The high-fidelity album is her last and often termed greatest recording."

The Indianapolis Star's Lynn Hopper wrote: "More of a tombstone than a memorial, the album nevertheless proves that when it comes to blues, the real test of a jazz singer, Miss Holiday has no peers, even in this decayed stage." In his syndicated column, "On the Record," Henry C. Schwartz observed: "Tragic *Billie Holiday* shows the results of her addiction but the style is similar to that which made her a great jazz personality." Years later, Ray Ellis revealed that in post-recording editing Billie's voice was "accidentally" modified electronically, no doubt to overcome some of the deficiencies that emerged during the recording sessions. The weakness of the voice, in some ways made more obvious by the manipulation during editing, kept the album from being the achievement it could have been. The physical deterioration that had taken place from February 1958, when she recorded *Lady in Satin,* to March 1959, when she recorded *Billie Holiday,* prevented her from producing the album she hoped to make. Sadly, the album was a missed opportunity, a tragedy made all the worse by the fact that it was her final recording effort.

On July 21, 1959, because Billie died without a will, Louis McKay filed with the Surrogate's Court in the County of New York a petition for Letters of Administration on the Goods, Chattels, and Credits of Eleanora McKay, also known as Billie Holiday. (Interestingly, he misspelled her last name as "Holliday.") Subsequently, Judge Samuel DiFalco issued letters of administration setting up the Estate of Eleanora McKay A/K/A Billie Holiday, whose beneficiary, because he was the sole heir, was Louis McKay. The man she had intended to divorce would now receive all the financial advantages generated by her estate, a bitter irony that was not lost on friends who were close to Billie. As Annie Ross says, "Louis McKay was only there for the money." And now he had it. Reportedly, in the year following Billie's death, her record sales resulted in $100,000 in royalties.

Not long after Billie's death, McKay retained Florynce Kennedy as the lawyer for the estate. Kennedy immediately came to believe that Billie had been cheated by entertainment companies, who routinely underreported royalties, and mounted a crusade to collect some of the money she believed Billie was owed. Her early actions were so noteworthy Kennedy was soon hired to represent the Estate of Charlie Parker as well. "One of the first things I did," Kennedy wrote, "was to affiliate both artists with BMI, and we were at last able to get a few thousand dollars as an advance, which of course was an outrage, because these artists had made millions for the record companies and music publishers. These companies had almost entirely stopped paying royalties to them or their estates." (Apparently, efforts to affiliate Billie with BMI had not been completed before she died.) Such royalties would have been extremely beneficial to Billie at the end of her life, when she was experiencing diminished income because of her illness; just as helpful would have been sickness benefits that she was due from the American Guild of Variety Artists union. According to Kennedy, "Billie Holiday never got her sickness . . . benefits, which she had paid into for probably 25 years."

During the decade of the 1960s, Kennedy waged a war with entertainment companies on behalf of the Holiday and Parker estates, her representation of which was announced by a large gold plaque that was mounted on the front door of her apartment, which was also her office. "We did finally manage to collect a fair amount from the record companies," Kennedy wrote, "but the story of the exploitation of Black performers by the people who make fortunes from them has yet to be told." In the end, the Estate of Billie Holiday was conclusively settled in 1971, more than a decade after Billie died. Sometime before that, Kennedy had moved on with her life and career, focusing instead on helping to advance feminist issues so ardently she became a significant figure in the women's movement. "She didn't [talk about Billie] because of the distant time," Gloria Steinem says. "I'm not sure I would have known about her past connection had it not been for the sign on Flo's office door."

By the early 1970s, enough time had passed since Billie's death that it was possible to look back on her life and place it in the context of the times. The first artistic homage to Billie came in 1971, when Frank Sinatra included "Lady Day," a tribute to Billie, on his album *Sinatra & Company.* "Poor Lady Day," Sinatra sang, "could use some love. / Lady Day has too much pain." In 1972, Mal Waldron released a tribute album entitled *Blues for Lady Day.* But, at this time, the vehicle about Billie that garnered the most attention—for better or worse, it helped to define the broader commentary about her following her death—was a motion picture released with considerable fanfare by Paramount Pictures.

After numerous attempts to turn *Lady Sings the Blues* into a picture, both during Billie's lifetime and following her death, the adaptation finally reached movie screens in October 1972. Produced by Jay Weston and Berry Gordy, among others, and directed by Sidney J. Furie, the picture starred Diana Ross, the former lead singer of the Supremes. However, because Louis McKay controlled the film rights to the book, the resulting screenplay bore little resemblance to Billie's autobiography, much less the truth. The McKay character, played with sophistication and charm by Billy Dee Williams, is a savior figure to Billie, who is depicted as often lost and consumed by drug addiction; a man who routinely abused her, both verbally and physically, is portrayed as her knight in shining armor. The picture was a profoundly dishonest enterprise. Yet while reviews were resoundingly negative, the reception afforded Diana Ross was guardedly kind. Consider Vincent Canby writing in *The New York Times*: "*Lady Sings the Blues* . . . poses a tough question: How is it possible for a movie that is otherwise so dreadful to contain such a singularly attractive performance in the title role? [The director and three screenwriters] made trite and meaningless such things as the child rape, indentured servitude in a Harlem whorehouse and an addiction to drugs that eventually contributed to Lady Day's death at age 44. It all becomes ridiculous. . . . Under such imbecilic circumstances, it's not yet possible to tell whether Miss Ross is a good actress, but she's an actress of exceptional beauty and wit, who is very much involved in trying to make a bad movie work."

Other critics concurred. In the *Chicago Tribune*, Gene Siskel announced: "The fact that *Lady Sings the Blues* is a failure as a biography of legendary jazz singer Billie Holiday doesn't mean it can't be an entertaining movie . . . because of an old-fashioned *grande dame* performance by Diana Ross, late of the pop-rock scene, in the title role." In *Newsday,* Joseph Gelmis was even more forthcoming: "I'm told by fans of Miss Holiday that the movie has virtually nothing to do with her real life. If you can accept that premise at the outset, you may be able to enjoy the picture for what it is: The first genuine Hollywood love story with black stars." Apparently, the entertainment industry *was* able to accept such a premise. Diana Ross was nominated for Best Actress in a Motion Picture for both the Golden Globe Awards and the Academy Awards. She won neither, although the Golden Globes named her Most Promising Newcomer—Female. More to the point, since the goal of the picture was to create a commercial vehicle for Ross and the producers, Berry Gordy released on Motown Records a double album soundtrack with Diana Ross singing Billie Holiday songs, which went to Number 1 on the *Billboard* album charts.

The persona of Billie Holiday appeared again in two novels at the end of the decade. In 1978, *Listening to Billie* by Alice Adams starts off, to quote *The Philadelphia Inquirer,* "with a richly evocative incident—it's the early '50s and a gleaming Billie Holiday makes a dazzling entrance into a mid-Manhattan club where blond, young, and inattentive Eliza Hamilton is preoccupied with her future husband." As the story unfolds, "Billie Holiday becomes the novel's ironic, telling emblem of sorrow and despair as her tragic muse hovers over the lives of Eliza and her 'eastern prep school types.' "

Then, in 1979, Elizabeth Hardwick incorporated Billie into her novel *Sleepless Nights.* Her portrayal of Billie was unflinching yet poignant, as exemplified by a description of the first time Hardwick met Billie, around 1943, singing in a club on Fifty-Second Street: "She was fat the first time [I] saw her, large, brilliantly beautiful, fat. She seemed for this moment that never again returned to be almost a matron, someone real and sensible who carried money to the bank, signed papers, had curtains made to match, dresses hung and shoes in pairs, gold and silver, black and white, ready. What a strange, betraying apparition that was, madness, because never was any woman less a wife or mother, less attached; not even a daughter

could she easily appear to be. Little called to mind the pitiful sweetness of a young girl. No, she was glittering, somber, and solitary,
although of course never alone, never. Stately, sinister, and absolutely
determined." Later, Hardwick wrote about the end of Billie's life:
"Her work took on, gradually, a destructive cast, as it so often does
with the greatly gifted who are doomed to repeat endlessly their own
heights of inspiration. . . . She lived to be forty-four; or should it better be said she died at forty-four. Of 'enormous complications.' Was
it a long or a short life? The 'highs' she sought with such concentra-
tion of cause remained a mystery. . . . Her whole life had taken place
in the dark. The spotlight shone down on the black, hushed circle
in a café, the moon slowly slid through the clouds. Night—working,
smiling, in makeup, in long, silky dresses, singing over and over,
again and again."

Three years later, it was the music and not the persona of Billie
Holiday that appeared in a work of fiction. In *The Women of Brewster Place*, a debut novel comprised of a series of interlocking narra-
tives featuring African-American women, Gloria Naylor, according
to *The New York Times*, "bravely risks sentimentality and melodrama
to write her compassion and outrage large, and she pulls it off tri-
umphantly." One character, Etta Mae Johnson, loves her Billie Holiday albums and, at one point, "clutched [them] in front of her chest
like cardboard armor." In the magical novel, the lyrics of Billie's
tunes appear to Etta Mae as if the songs were signposts guiding her
through life.

On March 10, 1981, Louis McKay died of a heart attack in New
York City at the age of seventy-two. Six years earlier, he had married Bernice Yancey. In his will he left 20 percent of his estate—
essentially the estate of Billie Holiday—to Yancey and the remainder
to Louis McKay III, a son he had during a marriage four years after
Billie died but before he married Yancey. When Yancey challenged
the will in court, she was awarded a statutory elective one-third
of the estate because she was McKay's wife at the time of his death.
In the mid-1980s, most of the revenue of the Billie Holiday estate

came from record royalties, now averaging between fifteen and twenty thousand dollars a year. It was ironic that Billie's money, which she worked so hard to earn in her lifetime, was now going to two people with whom she had no connection.

Cultural references to Billie Holiday continued over the years. In 1988, on *Rattle and Hum,* their hybrid album of live and studio performances, U2, one of the most popular rock and roll bands in the music industry, included "Angel of Harlem," their homage to Billie Holiday. "Lady Day got diamond eyes," Bono sang. "She sees the truth behind the lies." Two years earlier, Warner Bros. released *'Round Midnight,* a motion picture directed by Bertrand Tavernier and centered on the fictional Dale Turner, a character inspired by saxophonist Lester Young and pianist Bud Powell. A singer reminiscent of Billie Holiday, played by Lonette McKee, makes a memorable impression in the picture, but it is the mesmerizing portrayal of Turner by Dexter Gordon, who was nominated for an Academy Award for Best Actor, that elevates the entire creative effort to make *'Round Midnight,* as *The New Yorker* would later proclaim, "the film that jazz deserves." In 1997, Tony Bennett—who once described Billie Holiday as "the most perfect singer in America"—released *Tony Bennett on Holiday: A Tribute to Billie Holiday,* an homage containing nineteen songs associated with Billie. "Billie Holiday was the goddess of musicians," Bennett said at the time of the album's release. "They played their instruments from her voice." Chris Parker, who played drums on the album, says: "Tony and Billie traveled in the same circles. He talked about her with some familiarity. He was sad to see her taken advantage of. She was such a talent. How different it would have been if she had been able to stay off drugs or if the people who pushed them on her had stayed away. He was visibly upset." In 2014, Annie Ross, collaborating with John and Bucky Pizzarelli, made *To Lady with Love,* her tribute to Billie, which began with a spoken-word rhyme: "She became my idol, my mentor, my friend. / She remained my favorite until the very end." On April 13, 2014, Audra McDonald opened at the Circle in the

Square Theatre on Broadway in *Lady Day at Emerson's Bar and Grill,*
a play with music supposedly inspired by Billie's final performances;
for her portrayal, McDonald won the Tony Award for Best Actress in
a Play, marking her history-making sixth Tony Award. In 2019, *Billie,* a documentary directed by James Erskine, began streaming on
various outlets. The picture, based on the research archive of Linda
Lipnack Kuehl, who undertook a biography of Billie Holiday in the
early 1970s but never completed it, began with, according to *The
New York Times,* "one of the most unusual and . . . disturbing hooks
for a documentary in some time": the fact that Kuehl did not finish
her biography because she fell to her death from a window of a hotel
in Washington, D.C., in what police ruled a suicide, an opinion not
shared by Kuehl's family. In February 2021, *The United States vs. Billie Holiday,* directed by Lee Daniels, began streaming on Hulu; it is
a profoundly flawed portrayal of Billie, even less factually accurate
than *Lady Sings the Blues* (a feat Billie Holiday fans did not believe
was possible). "The most problematic aspect," *The Boston Globe*
noted, "is the introduction of the semi-fictional Jimmy Fletcher who
was indeed a Black FB[N] agent instrumental in Holiday's arrests
and bureaucratic harassment but was in no way a starstruck Lady
Day fan who became her lover later in life." Musician and author
Lewis Porter questioned the worthiness of the entire enterprise, writing, "If you believe this film . . . you have been the victim of one
of the worst instances of rewriting history in the annals of Hollywood. . . . There are so many . . . errors in the film I barely know
where to begin." Again, the entertainment industry ignored the
faulty vehicle in which the actress playing Billie appeared, and, like
Diana Ross before her, Andra Day, who portrayed Billie with decidedly less wit than Ross, was nevertheless nominated for Best Actress
in a Motion Picture by the Golden Globe Awards (which she won)
and the Academy Awards (which she did not). In April 2021, the
Dallas Symphony Orchestra premiered *Partners: A Double Concerto*
by David Amram; in the three-part piece inspired by musical pairs,
the second portion focused on Billie Holiday and Lester Young in
a movement *The Dallas Morning News* said "conjures up the atmo-

sphere of a 1940s nightclub." Lyrical and melodic, the movement was a poignant paean to their enduring musical partnership.

During her lifetime, especially during the 1950s, a decade defined by conservatism in the multiple forms of sexism, racism, and homophobia, Billie Holiday was devalued as a woman and minimalized as a singer and musician. She was rarely honored by the music industry; her entire collection of awards was four citations for Best Leading Female Vocalist given to her between 1944 and 1947 by *Esquire* magazine. When the first Grammy Awards were presented in 1959 for work released the year before, *Lady in Satin* was ignored. Moreover, for the last two decades of her life, because she represented a perceived threat to the status quo, she was methodically harassed by the government. The marginalization continued after her death. Federal and local governments refused to release documents related to how she was treated while she was alive. The City of New York, the New York Police Department, and Metropolitan Hospital never made a full disclosure concerning the events of the summer of 1959 that eventually resulted in her death. The FBI would attempt to downplay its involvement in the two-decade crusade carried out against her. "There is no evidence that the Federal Bureau of Investigation took much notice of Billie Holiday between 1939, when she started performing 'Strange Fruits' [*sic*], and her 1949 [*sic*] arrest on narcotics charges by the Federal Bureau of Narcotics," FBI spokesperson Ray Hall writes. "The only known main FBI file is the short narcotics violation file [concerning the San Francisco arrest]." The twelve pages in Billie's FBI file compare dramatically with the FBI files gathered on Leon Josephson and Barney Josephson, each of which numbered approximately two thousand pages. "Nor is there any evidence the Bureau ever maintained surveillance on her. The only known federal surveillance . . . was that of the Federal Bureau of Narcotics." That is now the official position of the FBI, even though customs agents Martin McVeigh and Mario Cozzi admitted a file existed, as of early 1959, with McVeigh saying to Billie, "I have a copy of your record with the Federal Bureau of Investigation," before mentioning information regarding events *besides* the San Francisco arrest.

Over time, in various forms of media, Billie Holiday was portrayed as a drug-addicted victim who happened to sing even as her contribution to American culture was downplayed or ignored. But a more suitable assessment of her would result from viewing her as she was—an iconoclastic artist who made a timeless contribution to American art in the tradition of innovators like Walt Whitman or Georgia O'Keeffe or Aaron Copland or D. W. Griffith. She has earned her place as a figure afforded reverence and admiration in the continuing American story. As journalist Philip Martin wrote: "She made her slim, spare voice into a line as confident, proud and indelible as those of Edgar Degas or Wallace Stevens. She transcended her material, turned performance into art. . . . How is still a mystery that argues for her genius."

Those who knew her or know her work can speak to her legacy. George Wein believes "Billie was the ultimate jazz singer. . . . She was the purest of all jazz singers that I ever heard." Singers concur, as noted by Sheila Jordan: "Lady was a beauty in looks and in voice—an incredible and deep singer. There was no one quite like her. She was a great, great singer and storyteller." Annie Ross agrees: "She was the best. She was jazz. She was blues. She was someone who just lost someone. She was someone who lost her whole world. She sang the truth. Her feelings, the lyrics she sang, were honest. She never sang a false note." Camille Thurman feels indebted to Billie: "She was the epitome of beauty, grace, strength, dignity, and integrity. It's unfortunate that people focus on [her struggle with drugs] rather than the beautiful contributions she made. She deserves to be respected and acknowledged for what she did. As an African-American woman, it's unfair for her to be represented as a victim. What other woman at that time was performing the way she did?" Madeleine Peyroux contends that "she was one of the reasons that recorded music is a wonderful thing. I know she knew how great she was and how important her approach to her work was. But did she know she was changing the musical landscape? I don't think anyone ever told her that, but she did. By using the vernacular as she did, she created a new style of singing." Yolande Bavan notes: "She spoke from experience with such eloquence. If you hear her you want to cry, you want to scream, you want to laugh. The gamut of emotions was elicited by the way she presented herself."

She was also the musician's singer. Bassist Chuck Israels says: "Billie absolutely made you understand her connection to what she was singing, which affected all of the singers and musicians who followed her. We've all been affected by that." Charles McPherson believes Billie was "the greatest": "She is a real artist in the true sense of the word. That kind of talent with that kind of depth is not often handed out. It's providence. When you listen to her, you can hear everything that woman is trying to convey to you." Bassist Larry Ridley argues: "She's a stylist all on her own. Her contribution as an artist, there's no question about her prominence. She contributed to the jazz tradition." Loren Schoenberg concurs: "I'd use the word 'mystery'; there was something with her that was not explicitly stated, in a way that's elusive. Still, she is immediately identifiable. Her musical legacy will be that she is one of the great musicians of her era. She is one of the giants." To Sonny Rollins, "Billie was a consummate artist. She used her voice as an instrument. She improvised with the melody the way musicians improvised with their instruments. That's what makes her completely different from other singers. Sometimes when I listen to her it brings me to my knees the way she improvises on a song. She was at least a genius." And David Amram proclaims: "She had the uncanny ability to make you, the listener, feel as if she were singing right to you. She was a communicator on a soul-to-soul level, which is the highest achievement any human being can offer. Even when she was going through hell, she made it heaven on earth for everyone who knew her or saw her or heard her—and still does."

Acknowledgments

For providing interviews, research material, or other help while I undertook my work on Billie Holiday, I am grateful to Mehmed Ali, David Amram, Anne Anderson, Nancy Baker, Yolande Bavan, David G. Berger, Peggy Biever, Edith Lorillard Cowley, Bill Crow, Douglas Henry Daniels, Jordan Davis, Maya Days, Joel Dinerstein, the late Ervin Drake, Ken Druker, Rune Egenes, Emile Elliott, Vincent Elliott, Marc Ellis, Dennis Fairchild, Lorraine Feather, Arthur Ford, Jr., Will Friedwald, Dave Gelly, the late Madeline Lee Gilford, Brad Gooch, Judge Emily Jane Goodman, Maxine (Mrs. Dexter) Gordon, Corky Hale, John Handy, Edward W. Hayes, Cynthia Herbst, Terri Hinte, Sandra Hochman, Harold Holzer, Aaron Howard, Dick Hyman, Chuck Israels, Lawrence Jackson, Maria Cooper Janis, Sheila Jordan, Edward Josephson, Lee Josephson, Louis Josephson, Barry Kernfeld, Karen (Mrs. Kenneth) Koch, John Leite, Oren Levine, Joel Lobenthal, Mike Lubbers, Jay Maisel, Gerard Malanga, Lone Malast, David Margolick, Ted Mase, Holly Maxson, Charles McPherson, Lynn McPherson, Michael Meeropol, Robert Meeropol, Gary Meltz, Eric Mingus, Robin Morgan, Dan Morgenstern, Philip Yale Nicholson, Maureen O'Hara, Erik Svinding Olsen, Ron Padgett, Chester Page, Eleanor Pam, Chris Parker, Madeleine Peyroux, Letty Cottin Pogrebin, Lewis Porter, Adam Clayton Powell III, Mary Reinholz, Ricky Riccardi, Larry Ridley, Frank "Sugar Chile" Robinson, Victoria Robinson, Sonny Rollins, Clint Rosemond, the late Annie Ross, Deborah Ross, Monk Rowe, Willie Ruff, Shane Salerno, Anthony Sampas, Larry Sandberg, the late Phil Schaap, the late Marina Sampas Schell, Lawrence Schiller, Loren Schoenberg, Lloyd Schwartz, Mary Scott, Monica Shaka, the late Harry

Sheppard, George Shipley, Alyn Shipton, Sue Simmons, David "Chet" Williamson Sneade, Gloria Steinem, Michael Steinman, Guy Sterling, Andrea Stern, Sady Sullivan, Adam Swanson, Camille Thurman, Mala Waldron, the late George Wein, Sarah M. Williams, and Alice Zaidins.

I want to thank Ken Schwartz, who granted me access to his private collection of Billie Holiday material at his Detour Gallery in Red Bank, New Jersey; Norman Saks, who provided me a copy of his interview with Alice Vrbsky; Joel Lobenthal, who supplied me with a copy of his interview with William Dufty; and Myra Luftman, who gave me permission to use the substantial file containing the work of her sister, Linda Lipnack Kuehl.

Significant archives devoted to Billie Holiday are available at two universities. At the Stuart A. Rose Manuscript, Archives, and Rare Book Library at Emory University, I am indebted to Kathleen Shoemaker, who answered countless research inquiries with efficiency and professionalism; her staff, including Gabrielle M. Dudley, were always helpful. At the Institute of Jazz Studies at Rutgers University–Newark, Elizabeth Surles could not have been more accommodating in supplying research for my book; her assistance was invaluable. At Rutgers, I also want to thank Vincent Pelote.

I received additional research assistance from Christian McWhirter at the Abraham Lincoln Presidential Library and Museum; Lee Arnold and Jack McCarthy at the Academy of Music Archives; Michael Scotland at the Addisleigh Park Civic Organization; Sean Dickerson at the African American Museum and Library at Oakland; Katie Ankers at the British Broadcasting Corporation Archives; Emma Davidson at the Henry W. and Albert A. Berg Collection of English and American Literature, New York Public Library; Rob Hudson and Emily Walsh at Carnegie Hall; Jacey Kepich at the Kelvin Smith Library, Case Western Reserve University; Patrick Scheg at CBS Broadcasting; Center for Brooklyn History; Mike Mathis at the Cherry Hill, New Jersey Historical Society; Peter Klarnet at Christie's; City of New York Department of Records and Information Services; Andrew Kaplan at the Cleveland Public Library; Michele Smith at the Estate of Billie Holiday; Raymond Hall and John Fox at the Federal Bureau of Investigation; Leanne Fallon at the Free Library of Philadelphia; Ayanna Woods at the Gloria Naylor Archive; Anthony DiGiovanni at the Historical Society of Pennsylvania; Christopher Bruhn and Jennifer Newman at Hunter College Libraries, City University of

New York; the Hamilton College Jazz Archive; Raymond Maxwell at Howard University; Sarah Williams at the Jazz Workshop; Brooke Shilling at the Special Collections Archives, Johns Hopkins University; Las Vegas–Clark County Library; Lowell Historical Society; Bridget Cooley at the Lowell Library; Beverly Corum at the *Lowell Sun;* Michael D. Schulman at Magnum Photos; Natalie Kelsey and Sandra Bennett at the Medical Society of the State of New York; Melissa Shriver at the Milwaukee Public Library; Scott Wenzel at Mosaic Records; Michael J. Hancock at the National Archives and Records Administration; Stephen Carla at the National Archives at Philadelphia; Arlene Shaner and Paul Theeman at the New York Academy of Medicine; Cheryl Malone at the New York County Medical Society; Bridgett Pride and A. J. Muhammad at the New York Public Library; Alice Standin at the Jerome Robbins Dance Division, New York Public Library for the Performing Arts; Larry Rivers Archives, Special Collections, New York University; Kimberly Sulik at the New York County Surrogate's Court; Beth Zak-Cohen at the Newark Public Library; Joshua K. Blay at the Department of Records, City Archives, City of Philadelphia; Philadelphia County Court of Common Pleas; Schomburg Center for Research in Black Culture, New York Public Library; Tim Noakes at the Department of Special Collections, Stanford University; Toby Silver at Sony Music Entertainment; Tenderloin Museum; Amy Thompson at the Library Special Collections & Archives, University of Idaho; John Davis at the Special Collections in Performing Arts, University of Maryland; Jeremy Smith at the Special Collections and University Archives, University of Massachusetts Amherst; Carisa Kolias at the Center for Lowell History, University of Massachusetts Lowell; Lindy Smith and Chuck Haddix at Special Collections, University of Missouri–Kansas City; Ken Druker at Verve Label Group; Rebecca Aldi at the Beinecke Rare Book and Manuscript Library, Yale University; Christopher Ciemniewski at the Wallingford Public Library; and Kristen Chinery at Wayne State University.

For their research assistance, I want to thank Karen Needles and Dominique Rocker but especially Kira Jones, whose skills in all areas of research are unmatched. At Hunter College, I want to acknowledge for their collegiality and support Jennifer Raab, Sarah Chinn, Angela Reyes, Paul McPherron, Stephen Wetta, Donna Masini, Angelo Nikolopoulos, Andrew Polsky, Suzanne Farrin, and Richard Kaye. At Alfred A. Knopf, I have been pleased to work with Brian Etling, Belinda Yong, Nicholas

Latimer, Kathy Zuckerman, Elka Roderick, and Rita Madrigal, and I am fortunate to have as an editor Erroll McDonald, whose belief in this book has been a constant source of encouragement and whose keen editorial eye helped shape its narrative.

For their friendship and support, I am grateful to Erika Fortgang Casriel, Cara Erdheim Kilgallen, Eva Salzman, Mitch Corrado, Cynthia Scott, and Elaine Henderson. For her care and generosity of spirit through years of friendship, I would like to thank Sandra Cisneros. Finally, I want to acknowledge my attorney, Timothy Holden, and my agent, Tony Outhwaite, a consummate professional and friend who first proposed that I write *Bitter Crop*.

Notes

CHAPTER 1: THE LAST NIGHT AT THE FLAMINGO LOUNGE

4   Mal Waldron: For biographical information about Mal Waldron, see *A Portrait of Mal Waldron,* a television documentary directed by Tom Van Overberghe and produced by Minerva Pictures in 1997.

5   Taking a sip: Much of the information about Billie Holiday's appearance at the Flamingo Lounge comes from articles written by Mary Sampas for her column in *The Lowell Sun*—"Lady Sings the Blues," May 18, 1959; ". . . And Walked Off Singing," Sept. 15, 1959; and "The Song Is Ended," Dec. 5, 1972—as well as Mary Sampas Schell, interviews by the author, 2020, and Anthony Sampas, correspondence with the author, 2023.

5   Lowell, Massachusetts: Lowell Historical Society.

6   Billie had played Lowell: advertisement, *Lowell Sun,* Apr. 15, 1938, 120.

6   Flamingo Lounge: John Leite, interview by the author, Jan. 2021.

6   a local observer: Mary Sampas, "Lady Sings the Blues," *Lowell Sun,* May 18, 1959.

6   In mid-April: Dorothy Kilgallen, "Voice of Broadway," national syndicated column, Apr. 13, 1959.

6   Another columnist: "Memo from John Miller," *San Francisco Chronicle*, May 3, 1959.

7   Jimmy Makris: Mary Sampas, "The Song Is Ended," *Lowell Sun,* Dec. 5, 1972.

7   Norm Crosby: Mary Sampas, "Lady Sings the Blues," *Lowell Sun,* May 18, 1959.

7   "The fabled Billie Holiday": Sampas.

8   Billie proceeded: Sampas.

8   "Now," she said softly: Sampas.

8   Back in her dressing room: Sampas.

9   Russell Banks: Russell Banks, "The Myth of Billie Holiday," *Transition,* no. 57 (1992): 88.

9   Frank Harriott: Frank Harriott, "The Hard Life of Billie Holiday," *PM,* Sept. 2, 1945.

10   She was especially fond: Billie Holiday with William Dufty, *Lady Sings the Blues* (New York: Doubleday, 1956; repr., Harlem Moon/Broadway Books, 2006), 9.

10   "She was a tall girl": Julia Blackburn, *With Billie: A New Look at the Unforgettable Lady Day* (New York: Vintage Books, 2006), 42.

10   Sleepy recalled: Linda Kuehl book manuscript, Institute of Jazz Studies, Rutgers University Libraries, Archives and Special Collections.

10   she "was known": Kuehl.

10   "Ethel used": Kuehl.

10   Pony Kane recalled: Kuehl.

10   Skinny remembered: Kuehl.

11   "After Sadie left": Kuehl.

11   "I'll never forget": Kuehl.

11   "Her mentors": Kuehl.

11   small apartment at 7 Glenada Place: Johnny Simmen, "Kenneth L. Hollon: Portrait of an Unsung Musician," *Coda,* May 1974, 4–5.

11   Kenneth Hollon: Simmen, 4–5.

11   "I used to take": Simmen, 4–5.

12   Billie Dove: John Chilton, *Billie's Blues: The Billie Holiday Story 1933–1959* (New York: Da Capo Press, 1975), 7.

12   whose pictures included: Billie Dove entry, IMDb.

12   Her name was Mary Sampas: Obituary, *Lowell Sun,* Jan. 15–17, 2011; and my interviews with Mary Sampas Schell, 2020.

12   She affected a professional: Leite interview.

13   As they spoke: The remainder of the section is based on Mary Sampas's column for *The Lowell Sun.*

14   in late March: "New Loew's State Reopens Tonight: Will Bow with *Some Like It Hot*," *New York Times,* Mar. 28, 1959, 11.

14   from May 11 to 17: *Boston Daily Record,* May 11, 1959.

14   Proof was comments: Sampas, "Lady Sings the Blues."

14   along with the Dave Pell Octet: *Los Angeles Sentinel*, May 21, 1959, C4; *Los Angeles Tribune,* May 22, 1959.

15   As one friend put it: William Dufty, interview by Joel Lobenthal, Aug. 22, 1994.

CHAPTER 2: A WOMAN OF THE WORLD

18   Hazel Scott would contend: Charles L. Sanders, "Lady Didn't Always Sing the Blues," *Ebony,* Jan. 1973, 112.

18   "She didn't complain": Alice Vrbsky, interview by Norman Saks, Feb. 8, 1985.

19   "casting rumors": Dorothy Kilgallen, "Voice of Broadway," national syndicated column, May 29, 1958.

19   Barris released: The advertisement for *Lady Sings the Blues* appeared in *The Observer* (London) on June 8, 1958.

19   Philip Larkin: Philip Larkin, "Harsh and Bitter-sweet," *Guardian,* June 13, 1958, 4.

19   Her first engagement: Entry for *Club Oasis* on IMDb.

19   On the twenty-ninth: Phil Schaap and Ben Young with Matt Herman, *WKCR Billie Holiday Festival Handbook* (New York: WKCR Books, 2005), 145.

20   but presently she resided: The information about the lease is taken from a Municipal Court of the City of New York summons contained in the Billie Holiday

collection, Stuart A. Rose Manuscript, Archives, and Rare Book Library, Emory University.

21 Her friend Annie Ross: Annie Ross, interview by the author, Dec. 2019.

21 when they met in Detroit: Donald Clarke, *Wishing on the Moon* (New York: Da Capo Press, 2000), 333.

21 Club Juana: Billie Holiday with William Dufty, *Lady Sings the Blues* (New York: Doubleday, 1956; repr., Harlem Moon/Broadway Books, 2006), 193.

21 they were arrested in Philadelphia: "Billie Holiday Arrested in Raid," *New York Times,* Feb. 24, 1956, 51.

22 "She had to marry him": William Dufty, interview by Joel Lobenthal, Aug. 22, 1994.

22 So, in March 1957: Ken Vail, *Lady Day's Diary: The Life of Billie Holiday 1937–1959* (Chessington, UK: Castle Communications, 1996), 184.

22 The situation had come to a head: Affidavit of Earle Warren Zaidins filed in New York County Surrogate's Court, Jan. 26, 1965.

22 He later admitted: Affidavit of Louis McKay filed in New York County Surrogate's Court, Feb. 26, 1965.

22 Annie Ross would hold: Ross interview.

22 A telephone call: A partial transcript of the conversation appears in Julia Blackburn, *With Billie: A New Look at the Unforgettable Lady Day* (New York: Vintage Books, 2006), 278–82.

23 As for the Memorial Day weekend: Zaidins affidavit, Jan. 26, 1965.

24 Alice was a fan: The autographed album is in the private collection of Ken Schwartz.

24 "Louis paid me once": Vrbsky interview.

24 "Billie liked to cook Baltimore specials": Vrbsky.

24 "all of her nightgowns": Vrbsky.

24 "Billie didn't care for Ethel Waters": Vrbsky.

25 all of which she readily acknowledged: Holiday with Dufty, *Lady Sings the Blues.*

25 a friend later said: Dufty interview.

25 "There was an elegance about her": David Amram, interview by the author, June 2021.

26 "if that evil motherfucker": Clarke, *Wishing on the Moon,* 441.

26 "She had antennae": Dufty interview.

26 Her friend Greer Johnson: Blackburn, *With Billie,* 159.

26 Irene Wilson Kitchens: Linda Kuehl book manuscript, Institute of Jazz Studies, Rutgers University Libraries, Archives and Special Collections.

27 Sherman Adams: "Eisenhower Continues to Back Top Aide," *Democrat and Chronicle* (Rochester, NY), Oct. 27, 1956, 35.

27 Nixon at a civic rally: "Nixon at Theresa October 31, Rally," *New York Age,* Oct. 27, 1956, 35.

27 Sputnik 3: "Sputnik Visible," *Standard Star* (New Rochelle, NY), June 21, 1958, 1.

27 founded in July: Nasa.gov.

27 "The Purple People Eater": CHUM's Weekly Hit Parade, week of June 16, 1958.

27 Orson Welles: Barbara Leaming, *Orson Welles: A Biography* (New York: Penguin Books, 1983), 507–26.

27   Billie enjoyed: Holiday with Dufty, *Lady Sings the Blues,* 106.

28   "I liked him and he liked me, and jazz": Holiday with Dufty, 106.

28   In the wake: "Negroes 'Out' for 2½ Years," *Star-Gazette* (Elmira, NY), June 21, 1958, 1.

28   Billie had experienced: Billie discusses the racial mistreatment she faced in *Lady Sings the Blues.*

28   Harry Anslinger: For a history of the Federal Bureau of Narcotics, see Matthew R. Pembleton, "The Voice of the Bureau: How Frederic Sondern and the Bureau of Narcotics Crafted a Drug War and Shaped Popular Understanding of Drugs, Addiction, and Organized Crime in the 1950s," *Journal of American Culture* 38, no. 2 (June 2015): 113–29.

29   Dorothy Kilgallen to report: Kilgallen, "Voice of Broadway," May 1958.

29   "Strange Fruit": For a history of "Strange Fruit," see David Margolick, *Strange Fruit: The Biography of a Song* (New York: The Ecco Press, 2001).

29   Originally, she was: "Billie Holiday in London for Concert," *Afro-American,* June 7, 1958, 7.

30   So Joe Glaser: Jesse H. Walker, "Theatricals," *New York Amsterdam News,* June 14, 1958, 15.

30   "The pretext used to deny me": Billie Holiday, "I'm Cured for Good Now," *Ebony,* July 1949.

30   "There was only one thing": Corky Hale, interview by the author, July 2020.

31   "Magnificent Billie Holiday": Alfred Duckett, "Showbiz," *New York Age,* June 28, 1958, 20.

31   John S. Wilson: John S. Wilson, "Brubeck Quartet Heard in Concert," *New York Times,* June 23, 1958.

31   The *Hartford Courant:* Jack Bishop, "Jazz Concerts Enliven Summer in New England," *Hartford Courant,* June 29, 1958, 39.

31   "Here came this voice": Draft manuscript by Owen Dodson, Owen Dodson papers, Stuart A. Rose Manuscript, Archives, and Rare Book Library, Emory University.

32   Critic Leonard Feather: Leonard Feather, *From Satchmo to Miles* (New York: Stein and Day, 1972), 73.

32   Harry "Sweets" Edison: Harry "Sweets" Edison, interview by Mark Rowe, Sept. 3, 1995, transcript in the Fillius Jazz Archive, Hamilton College.

32   Paul Bowles: Paul Bowles, "Billie Holiday: Singer Presents a Concert in Town Hall," *New York Herald Tribune,* Feb. 17, 1946.

32   Oscar Peterson: Martin Chilton, "Billie Holiday: The Wild Lady of Jazz Who Adored England," *Independent,* July 17, 2019.

32   Miles Davis: Miles Davis made the comment in "An Afternoon with Miles Davis," an interview conducted by Nat Hentoff, *The Jazz Review,* December 1958.

32   "Her singing is void": Charles McPherson, interview by the author, July 2021.

32   At the same time: Loren Schoenberg, interview by the author, May 2023.

32   Beyond that: Robert O'Meally, *Lady Day: The Many Faces of Billie Holiday* (New York: Da Capo Press, 1991), 37.

32   "When you sing like Billie Holiday": Madeleine Peyroux, interview by the author, Feb. 2023.

33   And there was nothing: Eric Mingus, correspondence with the author, June 2023.

33 Outside the theater: Sonny Rollins, interviews by the author, 2020.

33 Sonny Rollins: For a biography of Sonny Rollins, see Aidan Levy, *Saxophone Colossus* (New York: Hachette Books, 2022).

33 He was even targeted: Rollins interviews.

33 Red Hill Inn: "Billie Holiday at Red Hill Inn," *Philadelphia Tribune,* Feb. 15, 1958, 14.

33 Joe de Luca: Richard J. Salvucci, "Harvey Husten Presents 'Jazz in Jersey': The Red Hill Inn," All About Jazz (website), June 24, 2020.

34 "[The venue] sat": Salvucci.

34 What he saw troubled him: Rollins interviews.

34 "I was able to give her": Rollins.

35 "The Baroness": Rollins.

35 "We talked for a time": Rollins.

35 "She didn't look well": Rollins.

35 *Freedom Suite,* his groundbreaking album: Riverside Records released the album on June 30, 1958.

36 "One reason was": Rollins interviews.

CHAPTER 3: LADY IN SATIN

38 Accompanied by Pepe: Billie's everyday routine is described in Alice Vrbsky interviews by Norman Saks and by Linda Kuehl, excerpted in Julia Blackburn, *With Billie: A New Look at the Unforgettable Lady Day* (New York: Vintage Books, 2006).

38 "I've recorded an album": Ken Vail, *Lady Day's Diary: The Life of Billie Holiday 1937–1959* (Chessington, UK: Castle Communications, 1996), 195.

39 As of 1958: The information in the paragraph comes from Phil Schaap and Ben Young with Matt Herman, *WKCR Billie Holiday Festival Handbook* (New York: WKCR Books, 2005).

40 During her time with Decca: Schaap and Young with Herman.

40 "I've got to sing with Ray Ellis": The quote, included on the back of the album in liner notes written by Irving Townsend, also appears in press accounts such as the one in the *Richmond Times Dispatch,* June 29, 1958, 90.

40 Ray Ellis: Mike Barnes, "Composer Ray Ellis Dies at 85," Associated Press, Oct. 31, 2008.

40 In the late 1940s: Barnes.

40 In 1955, he caught the attention: Barnes.

41 with one reviewer observing that Ellis: Al Wolfe, "Record Review," *Tyrone (Pa.) Daily Herald,* Sept. 12, 1957, 6.

41 Another critic implored: Bob Goddard, "In Our Town," *St. Louis Globe-Democrat,* Sept. 13, 1957, 10.

41 "On January 3": The quote comes from the liner notes that appeared on the original *Lady in Satin,* Columbia Records, June 4, 1958.

41 Columbia agreed: Blackburn, *With Billie,* 269.

41 Musicians would be paid: Blackburn.

41 Billie would receive: Blackburn.

41 "It didn't dawn on me at the time": The quote comes from the liner notes that appear on *Lady in Satin,* Legacy Edition, Columbia Records, 1997.

42   As she waited to record: Letter from Pines Publications, Inc., to Billie Holiday,
      Billie Holiday collection, Stuart A. Rose Manuscript, Archives, and Rare Book
      Library, Emory University.

42   She was encouraged: Pines to Holiday.

42   Recording dates for *Lady in Satin:* Schaap and Young with Herman, *Festival Hand-
      book*, 138–44.

43   "Love is funny": The episode of the recording session is based on Schaap and Young
      with Herman and on *Lady in Satin,* Centennial Edition, Columbia Records, 2015.

43   She got there: Blackburn, *With Billie,* 271.

43   Irving Townsend later remembered: Blackburn, 271.

43   As soon as Billie settled: Blackburn, 271.

44   "I was so mad at her": Blackburn, 271.

46   "When he heard the playbacks": Marc Ellis, interview by the author, June 2020.

46   Ellis was so distraught: Ellis.

46   "I would say," Ellis wrote: Liner notes, *Lady in Satin,* Legacy Edition.

46   After three tries: Schaap and Young with Herman, *Festival Handbook,* 141.

47   "After we finished the album": Liner notes, *Lady in Satin,* Legacy Edition.

47   "The record was recorded": Ellis interview.

47   In February of that year: "Billie Holiday Seized for Dope," *Philadelphia Inquirer,*
      Feb. 24, 1956, 27.

48   "The arrests of the nightclub singer": "Billie Holiday Seized for Dope."

48   March 12, Billie and McKay: "Billie Holiday Guilty," *New York Times,* Mar. 13,
      1958.

48   Described by one newspaper: "Billie Holiday Placed on Probation in Dope Case,"
      Afro-American, Mar. 22, 1958, 7.

48   "Captain Clarence Ferguson": "Singer Billie Holiday Is Placed on Probation,"
      United Press International, Mar. 12, 1958.

49   "That full-length black diamond mink": *Pittsburgh Courier,* Apr. 5, 1958.

49   Irving Townsend prepared listeners: Liner notes, *Lady in Satin,* 1958.

49   Canadian reviewer: *Saskatoon (Saskatchewan) Star-Phoenix,* June 20, 1958, 4.

50   Echoing this praise: Jack Butler, "In Record Time," *Fort Worth Star-Telegram,* July 6,
      1958, 28.

50   The *Nashville Banner* observed: Pinckney Keel, "Disc Data" column, *Nashville Ban-
      ner,* July 7, 1958, 24.

50   And in "Strictly Off the Record": Larry Devine, "Strictly Off the Record," *Salt Lake
      Tribune,* July 27, 1958, 96.

50   *The Kansas City Star:* "Recorded Music," *Kansas City Star,* July 6, 1958, 69.

50   another critic claimed: "Look and Listen . . . with Rowe," *Richmond Times-Dispatch,*
      June 29, 1958, 90.

50   Polly Cochran: Polly Cochran, "Lady Day Cuts New Columbia Record," *Indianapo-
      lis Star,* July 6, 1958, 90.

50   the *Los Angeles Times:* "No Holiday for Us," *Los Angeles Times,* Sept. 28, 1958.

50   the *San Francisco Chronicle* noted: "DISCognizant," *San Francisco Chronicle,* June 22,
      1958.

50   the sentiment of this critic: "Record Roundup," *San Diego Union-Tribune,* Sept. 7,
      1958.

50 *The New York Times* tried: John S. Wilson, "Billie Holiday—Jazz Singer, Pure and Simple," *New York Times,* July 6, 1958.

51 Metronome deemed: Bill Cross, "The Singers and Their Records," *Metronome,* Oct. 1958, 26.

51 *Down Beat* dismissed: Martin Williams, "Reviews," *Down Beat,* Aug. 7, 1958, 24.

51 "Few singers," he wrote: Liner notes, *Lady in Satin,* 1958.

51 "There is nothing more painful": Charles McPherson, interview by the author, July 2021.

CHAPTER 4: A LITTLE JAZZ HISTORY

54 One newspaper reported: Art Sears, Jr., "Star Dust," *Cleveland Call and Post,* Aug. 9, 1958, C2.

54 with *The Afro-American* describing: "Hits Wax Jackpot," *Afro-American,* Aug. 2, 1958, 7.

54 Press accounts depicted the deal: Alfred Duckett, "Showbiz," *New York Age,* July 19, 1958, 26; and "Lady Day, Jazzman in Columbia Pacts," *New Journal and Guide,* July 12, 1958, 18.

54 That was one reason: Ken Vail, *Lady Day's Diary: The Life of Billie Holiday 1937–1959* (Chessington, UK: Castle Communications, 1996), 195.

54 Of her recent routine: Julia Blackburn, *With Billie: A New Look at the Unforgettable Lady Day* (New York: Vintage Books, 2006), 279.

54 A radio disc jockey: John P. Shanley, "Executive at Work," *New York Times,* May 18, 1958.

55 Three months earlier: Shanley.

55 "I am happiest": Shanley.

55 a "sublime" program: Shanley.

55 "Its keynote was informality": Dan Morgenstern, *Living with Jazz: A Reader,* ed. Sheldon Meyer (New York: Pantheon Books, 2004), 644.

55 Dorothy Kilgallen summed up: Dorothy Kilgallen, "Voice of Broadway," national syndicated column, July 24, 1957.

56 "The Way I Look at Race": Frank Sinatra as told to Allan Morrison, "The Way I Look at Race," *Ebony,* July 1958.

56 "When I first heard her": Sinatra.

56 "It is Billie Holiday": Sinatra.

56 "I told him about notes": The comment Billie Holiday originally made to Earl Wilson is included in Jody Rosen, "Frank Sinatra and Billie Holiday: They Did It Their Way," *New York Times Magazine,* Oct. 19, 2015.

56 Billie once spoke about Ava Gardner: Gene Chronopoulos, *It All Started with Billie Holiday: A Memoir of Jazz* (New York: iUniverse, 2010), 184.

57 from Lester Cowan: Burt A. Folkart, "Lester Cowan, 83; Movie Producer," *Los Angeles Times,* Oct. 25, 1990.

57 "I want to produce": A draft of the letter Lester Cowan wrote to Billie Holiday is in the Lester Cowan and Ann Ronell "Trial of Billie Holiday" collection, Special Collections in Performing Arts, University of Maryland Libraries.

57 He believed, he said: Cowan and Ronell.

57 Beyond that, Cowan: Cowan and Ronell.

57 He could not "put it down": Cowan and Ronell.

57 Finally, Cowan touched on: Cowan and Ronell.

57 In March 1957, Billie signed over: Multiple contracts are held in Cowan and Ronell.

58 To play Billie: *Chicago Tribune,* Mar. 15, 1957, 16.

58 Then, in October 1957: The contract is contained in the Cowan and Ronell collection, Maryland.

58 Ultimately, Gardner: For an autobiography of Ava Gardner, see Ava Gardner, *Ava: My Story* (New York: Bantam Books, 1990).

58 On February 17, Max Youngstein: The letter is contained in the Cowan and Ronell collection, Maryland.

58 As Earl Wilson reported: Earl Wilson, "It Happened Last Night," a nationally syndicated column, July 29, 1958.

59 When she arrived: Information about the Mosque Theatre, the recording studio contained therein, and the broadcasting of *Art Ford's Jazz Party* comes from Harry Sheppard, interview by the author, Mar. 2021.

59 Stepping off the elevator: Information is taken from Linda A. Fowler, "A 'Jazz Party' to Remember," NJ.com, May 8, 2008.

60 "The artists assemble": Jack Gould, "Time to Relax: Art Ford's TV Jazz Show Exemplifies Television without Tension," *New York Times,* May 25, 1958, X13.

60 "Once again," he said: A complete listing of the episodes of *Art Ford's Jazz Party* is found at the Institute of Jazz Studies, Rutgers University Libraries, Archives and Special Collections, in "Art Ford's Jazz Party 1958 TV & Radio Broadcasts," compiled and edited by Bob Weir. Portions of numerous episodes of the program are available on YouTube, details from which inform the rest of the scene.

61 "one of the most candid": The quote is included in an advertisement in the *Chicago Tribune,* May 24, 1958.

61 *The New Yorker:* The quote appears in William Dufty, "The True Story of Billie Holiday," article 1 of series, *New York Post,* July 20, 1959, 14. It is further discussed in John Szwed, *Billie Holiday: The Musician and the Myth* (New York: Penguin Books, 2015), 23.

62 Leonard Feather wrote: Leonard Feather, *From Satchmo to Miles* (New York: Stein and Day, 1972), 80–81.

62 "Mom and Pop": Billie Holiday with William Dufty, *Lady Sings the Blues* (New York: Doubleday, 1956; repr., Harlem Moon/Broadway Books, 2006), 3.

62 Lester Cowan regarded: Cowan and Ronell collection, Maryland.

63 For the record, Billie Holiday: Birth certificate of Billie Holiday, the Bureau of Vital Statics, the Commonwealth of Pennsylvania.

63 "Sadie Fagan loved me": Holiday with Dufty, *Lady Sings the Blues,* 3.

63 At the time of the delivery: Birth certificate of Billie Holiday.

63 On hospital records: Birth certificate.

64 Clarence never denied his paternity: Nat Hentoff, "Billie Holiday: Jazz's Aching Songbird," *Daily Beast,* Feb. 14, 2015.

64 Sadie further confused: Birth certificate of Billie Holiday.

64 Harris was given as the last name: Birth certificate.

64 Not long after her baby was born: Stuart Nicholson, *Billie Holiday* (Boston: Northeastern University Press, 1995), 19.

64 "She had been a slave": Holiday with Dufty, *Lady Sings the Blues*, 7.

64 "Charles Fagan"—Billie's grandfather: Linda Kuehl book manuscript, Institute of Jazz Studies, Rutgers University Libraries, Archives and Special Collections.

65 October 1920 when Sadie married: Nicholson, *Billie Holiday*, 21.

65 That fall, five-year-old Eleanora: Nicholson, 21.

65 In 1922, the family: Nicholson, 21.

65 Charles Fagan took out: Robert O'Meally, *Lady Day: The Many Faces of Billie Holiday* (New York: Da Capo Press, 1991), 72.

65 January 5, 1925: Tracy Fessenden, "Billie Full of Grace: How Billie Holiday Learned to Sing at the House of the Good Shepherd," NPR.org, Aug. 20, 2019.

65 The nine-year-old: Fessenden.

65 The reform school: Blackburn, *With Billie*, 23.

65 Assigned the protective pseudonym "Madge": Fessenden, "Billie Full of Grace."

65 Each day, she was required: Fessenden.

66 The book was the product: Fessenden.

66 For the first service: Nicholson, *Billie Holiday*, 24.

66 "Madge was so happy": Kuehl manuscript.

66 A short tenure there: O'Meally, *Lady Day*, 67.

66 "She was out and done": Kuehl manuscript.

66 Eleanora's newfound sense of freedom: Nicholson, *Billie Holiday*, 25.

66 Sadie and Wee Wee: Nicholson, 25.

67 For her part: Fessenden, "Billie Full of Grace."

67 Soon after Eleanora's release: Kuehl manuscript.

67 In the winter of 1929: Nicholson, *Billie Holiday*, 32.

67 "That place was filthy": Holiday with Dufty, *Lady Sings the Blues*, 29.

67 "If I thought my childhood": Billie Holiday, "Can a Dope Addict Come Back?," *Tan*, Feb. 1953, 34.

68 In 1918, after he had joined: The original draft registration card of Clarence Holiday is dated July 5, 1917.

68 Clarence was inducted: Nicholson, *Billie Holiday*, 18–19.

68 Because of his music background: Nicholson, 18–19.

68 he was involved in an incident: Holiday with Dufty, *Lady Sings the Blues*, 4.

68 Clarence was given: Nicholson, *Billie Holiday*, 19.

68 At twenty-three, Clarence married: Donald Clarke, *Wishing on the Moon* (New York: Da Capo Press, 2000), 43–44.

68 The woman Fannie Lee referred to: Clarke, 43–44.

69 In her autobiography: Details in the following paragraph are from Holiday with Dufty, *Lady Sings the Blues*, 37–38.

70 "She was then about fifteen": Robert Sylvester, "Dream Street" column, *New York Daily News*, June 4, 1959, 78.

70 "I never met anybody like her": Rebecca Carey Rohan, *Billie Holiday* (New York: Cavendish Square Publishing, 2016), 31.

70 His father, John Henry Hammond: "John Hammond, 76, Critic and Discoverer of Pop Talent, Dies," *New York Times*, July 11, 1987, 1.

70 John grew up: Hammond obituary.

70 Later, Hammond documented: John Hammond with Irving Townsend, *John Hammond on Record* (New York: Summit Books, 1977), 91.

71 The musical revue: Entry for *Flying Colors,* Internet Broadway Database.

71 "Billie's accompanist was Dot Hill": Hammond with Townsend, *John Hammond on Record,* 92.

71 "Night after night": Hammond with Townsend, 92.

71 "This month," he wrote: The column appeared in *Melody Maker,* Apr. 1933.

71 "Benny signed his first contract": Hammond with Townsend, *John Hammond on Record,* 119.

71 In an advertisement: The advertisement appeared in *The New York Age,* Nov. 24, 1934.

72 "Now that the engagement": Marcus Wright, "The Talk of the Town," *New York Age,* Dec. 1, 1934, 5.

72 December 1934: Phil Schaap and Ben Young with Matt Herman, *WKCR Billie Holiday Festival Handbook* (New York: WKCR Books, 2005), 25.

72 Playing a young woman: Schaap and Young, 25.

72 The film was released: Szwed, *Billie Holiday,* 55.

72 Her appearance: Khanya Mtshali, ed., *Billie Holiday: The Last Interview and Other Conversations* (Brooklyn: Melville House, 2018), ix.

72 In July, Billie forged: Hammond with Townsend, *John Hammond on Record,* 147–48.

72 On July 2, in a session: Hammond with Townsend, 147–48.

73 "Vocals," the *Fort Worth Star-Telegram* observed: *Fort Worth Star-Telegram,* Sept. 8, 1935, 19.

73 On February 23, a telephone call: Death certificate of Clarence Holiday, Bureau of Vital Statistics, State of Texas.

73 Billie would describe the events: Holiday with Dufty, *Lady Sings the Blues,* 77.

73 It was too late: Holiday with Dufty, 78.

73 To cite his death certificate: Death certificate of Clarence Holiday.

73 Linda Kuehl documented: Kuehl manuscript.

74 The racial aspect entered the picture: The misrepresentation of the death of Bessie Smith by John Hammond is corrected in Chris Albertson, *Bessie* (New York: Stein and Day, 1973). For a review of *Bessie,* see George David, "Bessie," *New York Times Book Review,* Feb. 18, 1973, 25.

74 "I know my dad": Kuehl manuscript.

74 "She had," Basie believed: Count Basie oral history interview by Linda Kuehl, Jazz Oral History Project, Institute of Jazz Studies, Rutgers University Libraries, Archives and Special Collections.

74 "Everybody loved her": Basie oral history interview.

74 On February 11, 1938: The letter is held in a private collection.

75 "Basie had too many managers": Dave Dexter, "Billie Holiday: I'll Never Sing with a Dance Band Again," *Down Beat,* Nov. 1, 1939.

75 Shaw was a celebrated clarinet player: John Chilton, *Billie's Blues: The Billie Holiday Story 1933–1959* (New York: Da Capo Press, 1975), 51.

75 "The contract given Billie": "Billie Holiday to Be Featured in All-White Band," *Pittsburgh Courier,* Mar. 19, 1938, 21.

75   "The hotel management": Dexter, "Billie Holiday."

76   "The bigger our success": Nat Shapiro and Nat Hentoff, eds., *Hear Me Talkin' to Ya* (New York: Dover Publications, 1966), 323.

76   "I opened at Café Society": Holiday with Dufty, *Lady Sings the Blues,* 104.

76   this evening in July 1958: Vail, *Lady Day's Diary,* 195.

77   Among the musicians: Vail, 195.

77   "The mood is right tonight": Portions of some episodes of *Art Ford's Jazz Party* are available on YouTube.

78   Harry Sheppard, who remembers: Sheppard interview.

78   Arthur Ford, Jr., recalls: Arthur Ford, Jr., interview by the author, 2021.

CHAPTER 5: BITTER CROP

80   Isadore "Izzy" Pogrob: "The Brass Rail Files," Tea's Weird Week (website), January 9, 2019, https://teakrulos.com/2019/01/09/the-brass-rail-files/.

80   Count Basie and his eighteen-piece band: advertisement, *Milwaukee Journal,* July 28, 1958.

81   as one of the city's music critics observed: "Billie Holiday Still Has Touch with the Blues," *Milwaukee Journal,* July 30, 1958.

81   Afterwards, she "made several other standard": "Billie Holiday Still Has Touch."

81   As she completed: "Billie Holiday Still Has Touch."

81   Lindsay's Sky Bar: Joe Mosbrook, *Cleveland Jazz History* (Northeast Ohio Jazz Society, 2003), 126.

81   "Her unique phrasing": *Cleveland Plain Dealer,* Aug. 3, 1958, 150.

81   Marilyn Holderfield: Marilyn Holderfield's meeting with Billie Holiday is recounted in Mosbrook, *Cleveland Jazz History,* 131–32.

82   Commodore Records released: Information about the album is in the Milt Gabler Papers, 1927–2001, Archives Center, National Museum of American History, Smithsonian Institution.

82   "What you have here": Liner notes quoted in C. H. Garrigues, "A Dozen Billie Holiday Songs in Reissue Album," *San Francisco Examiner,* July 27, 1958, 146.

83   *The New York Times* believed Billie: John S. Wilson, "Billie Holiday: Jazz Singer, Pure and Simple," *New York Times,* July 6, 1958, X13.

83   And music writer Ralph Gleason: Ralph Gleason, "Album of the Week," Times Mirror Syndicate, 1958.

83   Born in Trenton: John S. Wilson, "Barney Josephson, Owner of Café Society Jazz Club, Is Dead at 86," *New York Times,* Sept. 30, 1988.

83   "His father, a cobbler": Wilson.

84   Graduating from Trenton High School: Wilson.

84   But Barney longed for: Wilson.

84   He had become interested in jazz: Whitney Balliett, "Night Clubs," *New Yorker,* Oct. 9, 1971, 75.

84   "the [black] patrons": Balliett, 75.

84   "I wanted [to open]": Wilson, "Barney Josephson."

84   "The Communist Party": Philip Yale Nicholson, interview by the author, 2020.

85   The Eisler-Josephson connection: "Key Witness Balks at Hearing as Red," *New York Times,* Mar. 6, 1947.

85 "On March 6, 1935": The contents of the article are later echoed in "Beal Says Soviet Let Him Fake Name," *New York Times,* Oct. 21, 1939.

85 The men arrested: David W. Stowe, "The Politics of Café Society," *Journal of American History* 84, no. 4 (Mar. 1988), 1397.

85 He would recall reading: Stowe.

85 "He was a Marxist": Lee Josephson, interview by the author, May 2020.

86 While Barney remained a member: According to Stowe, "Politics of Café Society," 1398, "FBI officials clearly believed there were direct links between the Communist party and Café Society."

86 Barney leased: Balliett, "Night Clubs," 69.

86 "The right place for the wrong people": Stowe, "Politics of Café Society," 1387.

86 "This was what I'd been waiting for": Billie Holiday with William Dufty, *Lady Sings the Blues* (New York: Doubleday, 1956; repr., Harlem Moon/Broadway Books, 2006), 93.

87 "concerned about [Leon's] role": John Hammond with Irving Townsend, *John Hammond on Record* (New York: Summit Books, 1977), 207.

87 according to one reporter: Stowe, "Politics of Café Society," 1384.

87 "Although it was filled": Wilson, "Barney Josephson."

87 "The germ of the [tune]": Holiday with Dufty, *Lady Sings the Blues,* 94.

87 The creator of the song: Nancy Kovaleff Baker, "Abel Meeropol (a.k.a. Lewis Allan): Political Commentator and Social Conscience," *American Music* 20 (Spring 2002): 26.

88 He held a bachelor's degree: Baker, 26.

88 An English teacher: Baker, 26.

88 He contributed to the Young Communist League: Baker, 26.

88 Throughout the Jim Crow era: David Margolick, *Strange Fruit: The Biography of a Song* (New York: The Ecco Press, 2001), 19.

88 "Way back in the early thirties": Baker, "Abel Meeropol," 45.

88 The picture of two black teenagers: Bryan Pietsch, "Behind 'Strange Fruit,' Billie Holiday's Anti-Lynching Anthem," *New York Times,* Apr. 25, 2021.

88 Meeropol was so moved: Baker, "Abel Meeropol," 45.

88 based on the Kaddish: Larry Sandberg, interview by the author, June 2020.

89 Meeropol's wife, Anne: Baker, "Abel Meeropol," 48.

89 In 1938, Laura Duncan: Dorian Lynskey, " 'Strange Fruit': The First Great Protest Song," *Guardian,* Feb. 16, 2011.

89 "They traveled in similar left-wing circles": Edward Josephson, interview by the author, May 2020.

89 So, in January 1939, Meeropol: Margolick, *Strange Fruit,* 27.

89 Since she was performing: Holiday with Dufty, *Lady Sings the Blues,* 102.

90 "The first time Billie sang": Madeline Lee Gilford, interview by the author, July 2007.

90 "Before she began": Margolick, *Strange Fruit,* 33.

90 "When she finished": Margolick, 33.

91 The friend was Milt Gabler: Douglas Martin, "Milt Gabler, Storekeeper of the Jazz World, Dies at 90," *New York Times,* July 25, 2001.

91 according to *High Fidelity* magazine: Martin.

91 "Billie was very sad": Meg Greene, *Billie Holiday: A Biography* (Westport, CT: Greenwood Press, 2006), 61.

91   On April 20: Information in the paragraph, including the quote, comes from Margolick, *Strange Fruit,* 46.

91   "Concerned that customers": David Margolick, "Performance as a Force for Change: The Case of Billie Holiday and 'Strange Fruit,'" *Cardozo Studies in Law and Literature* 11, no. 1 (Summer 1999): 100.

92   The *New York Post* declared: Margolick, *Strange Fruit,* 56.

92   *The New York Age* observed: "Night Club Singer Records Song About Lynchings in the South," *New York Age,* June 17, 1939, 1.

92   The *San Francisco Chronicle* was blunt: Jive, "A Homeopathic Dose of Horror," *San Francisco Chronicle,* June 25, 1939, 22.

92   *Time* in its June 12 issue: "Strange Record," *Time,* June 12, 1939.

92   Ahmet Ertegun later called: Pietsch, "Behind 'Strange Fruit.'"

92   Louis Armstrong: Terry Teachout, *Pops: A Life of Louis Armstrong* (New York: Houghton Mifflin, 2009), 31–33.

93   In fact, it was: Ben Gross, "Listening In," *New York Daily News,* Nov. 3, 1939, 67.

93   "It was meant as an attack song": Robert Meeropol, interview by the author, May 2020.

93   His brother, Michael Meeropol: Michael Meeropol, interview by the author, May 2020.

93   Described by J. Donald Adams: J. Donald Adams, "Speaking of Books," *New York Times Book Review,* May 28, 1944, 2.

93   That act prompted: Lewis Allan, "Strange Fruit," *New York Times,* Aug. 12, 1956.

94   "a triumphal appearance": Arnold Shaw, *The Street That Never Slept* (New York: Coward, McCann, & Geoghegan, 1971), 202.

95   But whatever romance: Martin Chilton, "Billie Holiday: The Wild Lady of Jazz Who Adored England," *Independent,* July 17, 2019.

95   "There was a girl": Holiday with Dufty, *Lady Sings the Blues,* 97.

96   Her father, Winthrop M. Crane: National Governors Association website.

96   Her mother, Josephine Porter Boardman: Jennifer Huberdeau, "Josephine Porter Crane: A Socialite Who Tackled Social Issues," *Berkshire Eagle,* Mar. 29, 2019.

96   Chester Page, a friend and employee: Chester Page, *Memoirs of a Charmed Life in New York* (New York: iUniverse, 2007), 67.

96   The Cranes' lifestyle: Page, 68.

97   "Though Louise had a special proficiency": Page, 71.

97   Then, in the summer of 1937: Facts in the paragraph come from Marilyn May Lombardi, "The Closet of Breath: Elizabeth Bishop, Her Body and Her Art," *Twentieth Century Literature* 38, no. 2 (Summer 1992): 152. Details of the car crash are also contained in Frank Bidart, "Elizabeth Bishop," *Threepenny Review,* no. 58 (Summer 1994): 6–7.

97   "Then," Billie wrote: Holiday with Dufty, *Lady Sings the Blues,* 98.

97   "[Louise] was good to Billie": Linda Kuehl book manuscript, Institute of Jazz Studies, Rutgers University Libraries, Archives and Special Collections.

98   "There we were": Holiday with Dufty, *Lady Sings the Blues,* 98.

98   Kitchens had a different recollection: Kuehl manuscript.

98   "Elizabeth once told me": Lloyd Schwartz, interview by the author, June 2020.

99   "Louise was very interested": Gary Fountain and Peter Brazeau, *Remembering Eliza-beth Bishop* (Amherst: University of Massachusetts Press, 1994), 84.

99   "Mom," Billie wrote: Holiday with Dufty, *Lady Sings the Blues,* 99.

99   "From Louise I heard": Fountain and Brazeau, *Remembering Elizabeth Bishop,* 86.

99   During her appearance: "Coffee Concerts Close," *New York Times,* June 5, 1941.

100   In reviewing the show: "Coffee Concerts Close."

100   Later, he argued: Hammond with Townsend, *John Hammond on Record,* 208.

100   Hammond claimed that Billie: Hammond with Townsend, 208.

100   But, as he wrote: Hammond with Townsend, 208.

100   As it happened, when Mrs. Crane: Facts in the paragraph come from Holiday with Dufty, *Lady Sings the Blues,* 99.

101   One person who was not resentful: Information and the quote in the paragraph come from Anne R. Newman, "Elizabeth Bishop's 'Song for a Colored Singer,'" *World Literature Today* 51, no. 1 (Winter 1977): 37–40. A longer version of the quote appears in Ashley Brown, "An Interview with Elizabeth Bishop," *Shenandoah* 17 (Winter 1966).

101   In the end, Louise Crane: Kuehl manuscript.

CHAPTER 6: WHEN YOUR LOVER HAS GONE

104   Early in the month: "Billie Holiday Stars at the La Ronda Inn," *Westport (Conn.) Town Crier,* Sept. 4, 1958, 17.

104   The *Westport Town Crier:* "Billie Holiday Stars."

104   On the night of September 9: Alfred Duckett, "Showbiz," *New York Age,* Sept. 20, 1958, 47.

104   as one reporter noted: Duckett.

105   Jimmy Rushing turned in: Duckett.

105   Duke Ellington: Duckett.

105   The Miles Davis Sextet: Duckett.

105   "Duke signified on Davis": Ralph Ellison, *Living with Music* (New York: Random House, 2002), 246.

105   "You don't see the picture-book Billie Holiday": Duckett, "Showbiz."

106   "She gets into the song": Duckett.

106   Willie Ruff: See Willie Ruff, *A Call to Assembly: The Autobiography of a Musical Storyteller* (New York: Viking Penguin, 1991).

106   "After our show": Willie Ruff, interview by the author, May 2021.

107   On May 1: Billie Holiday with William Dufty, *Lady Sings the Blues* (New York: Doubleday, 1956; repr., Harlem Moon/Broadway Books, 2006), 47.

107   She often spent her time: Holiday with Dufty, 117.

107   Nina Mae McKinney: Anita Gates, "Nina Mae McKinney, Who Defied the Barri-ers of Race to Find Stardom," *New York Times,* Jan. 31, 2019.

107   "to prove something": Holiday with Dufty, *Lady Sings the Blues,* 117.

107   she eloped with Monroe: "[Billie Holiday] Eloped to Elkton," *New York Amsterdam Star-News,* Aug. 30, 1941, 20.

108   "Giving her age as 25": "[Billie Holiday] Eloped."

108   Returning home to discover: John Chilton, *Billie's Blues: The Billie Holiday Story 1933–1959* (New York: Da Capo Press, 1975), 78–79.

108   Her next extended engagement: Truman Capote, *Portraits and Observations* (New York: Random House, 2013), 385–86.

108   It was drugs: Julia Blackburn, *With Billie: A New Look at the Unforgettable Lady Day* (New York: Vintage Books, 2006), 106.

108   When Monroe was found guilty: Blackburn, 106.

108   Looking back on their short-lived union: Holiday with Dufty, *Lady Sings the Blues*, 119.

108   Orson Welles: Holiday with Dufty, 106.

109   "[So Eddie and I] went back": John Simmons, interview by Patricia Willard, Jazz Oral History Project, Institute of Jazz Studies, Rutgers University Libraries, Archives and Special Collections.

109   Simmons remembered: Simmons interview by Willard.

109   Born in Haskell, Oklahoma: Simmons interview by Willard.

109   As they spoke, Billie paid Simmons: Simmons interview by Willard.

109   Years later, Simmons: Simmons interview by Willard.

110   Simmons was surprised: Simmons interview by Willard.

110   As it happened, Simmons: Sue Simmons, interview by the author, 2021.

110   Her solution to his reluctance: John Simmons interview by Willard.

110   When she joined him: Simmons interview by Willard.

111   "Come to find out": Simmons interview by Willard.

111   "So, no sooner [did I]": Simmons interview by Willard.

111   "But before I left home": Simmons interview by Willard.

111   "A white boy from Dallas": Simmons interview by Willard.

111   Once Billie developed a heroin habit: Simmons interview by Willard.

111   So, on the day he left, he packed: Simmons interview by Willard.

112   "She had never thought": Simmons interview by Willard.

112   "He was violent with my mother": Sue Simmons interview by author.

112   Not long after her affair: Stuart Nicholson, "Lady Day Marries," *Billie Holiday* (Boston: Northeastern University Press, 1995), 142.

112   "Billie Holiday . . . caused commotion": "Lady Day Marries," *Down Beat,* June 1, 1945, 5.

113   During this time, Billie lived: Christopher Lehmann-Haupt, "Elizabeth Hardwick, 91, Author and Critic," *New York Times,* Nov. 5, 2007.

113   her first Town Hall concert: Blackburn, *With Billie,* 160–61.

113   "That hotel was the mess of the world": Unpublished document, Owen Dodson papers, Stuart A. Rose Manuscript, Archives, and Rare Book Library, Emory University.

113   "Billie was an artist": Unpublished Dodson.

113   Devastated, Billie hurried to New York: Chilton, *Billie's Blues,* 100.

114   "She was late for her mother's funeral": Elizabeth Hardwick, *Sleepless Nights* (New York: Random House, 1979), 41.

114   Owen Dodson was given: Owen Dodson papers, Stuart A. Rose Manuscript, Archives, and Rare Book Library, Emory University.

114   After completing her tour: Chilton, *Billie's Blues,* 100.

114   "Her white gown glittered": *The Autobiography of Malcolm X: As Told to Alex Haley* (New York: Ballantine Books, 1964; repr., 2015), 215.

114   "Lady Day sang": *Autobiography of Malcolm X.*

114   "I've got two strikes against me": Michael Levin, "Don't Blame Show Biz!," in *DownBeat: The Great Jazz Interviews: A 75th Anniversary Anthology,* eds. Frank Alkyer and Ed Enright (New York: Hal Leonard Books, 2009), 27.

115   Guy continued to be: Terry Teachout, *Pops: A Life of Louis Armstrong* (New York: Houghton Mifflin, 2009), 253.

115   The origin of the film: Teachout, 253.

115   "And let me tell you": Document is contained in the archives at the Louis Armstrong House Museum, Queens, New York.

115   Biberman later remembered: John Szwed, *Billie Holiday: The Musician and the Myth* (New York: Penguin Books, 2015), 61.

116   "That's what made me a communist": Frank Harriott, "The Hard Life of Billie Holiday," *PM,* Sept. 2, 1945.

116   "Now when I'm in the South": Harriott.

116   Abel Meeropol: Nancy Kovaleff Baker, "Abel Meeropol (a.k.a. Lewis Allan): Political Commentator and Social Conscience," *American Music* 20 (Spring 2002): 62.

117   That same year, the FBI: For targets of the FBI associated with Café Society, see David W. Stowe, "The Politics of Café Society," *Journal of American History* 84, no. 4 (Mar. 1998).

117   Two years later: Lee Josephson, interview by the author, May 2020.

117   Meanwhile, since his involvement: Josephson.

117   "Hoover disliked both of them": Josephson.

117   "She had a record in the FBI": William Dufty, interview by Joel Lobenthal, Aug. 22, 1994.

117   "The alleged activities of Josephson": "Key Witness Balks at Hearing as Red," *New York Times,* Mar. 6, 1947.

118   "cited for contempt of the House": "Key Witness Balks."

118   On March 22, J. Parnell Thomas: "Concept Citation Set for Josephson," *New York Times,* Mar. 23, 1947.

118   On April 22, almost the entire House: "Josephson and Dennis Are Cited by House on Contempt Charges," *New York Times,* Apr. 23, 1947.

118   "a bold and contemptuous challenge": "Josephson and Dennis."

118   On May 5, he posted: "Deny Congress Contempt," *New York Times,* May 6, 1947.

118   "Under the nasty pressure": Billie Holiday, "I'm Cured for Good Now," *Ebony,* July 1949.

119   The pursuit of Billie: "Billie Holiday Fled Phila. Raid," *Philadelphia Inquirer,* May 20, 1947, 3.

119   "I suppose," Billie later wrote: Billie Holiday, "How I Blew a Million Dollars," *Our World,* Mar. 1953, 31.

119   a two-week engagement at Club 18: Chilton, *Billie's Blues,* 114.

120   John S. Wilson reviewed: John S. Wilson, "Billie Holiday Sings with Old Magic in 'All-Star Jazz Show' at Town Hall," *New York Times,* Sept. 15, 1958.

120   Five days later, on the eighteenth: "Daytime TV," *Detroit Free Press,* Sept. 15, 1958, 14.

120   The following night: "Gay Hits Gay Haven Opener," *Detroit Free Press,* Sept. 19, 1958, 32.

120 "A lot of folks": Ziggy Johnson, "Zig and Zag with Ziggy Johnson," *Chicago Daily Defender,* Sept. 30, 1958, 19.

120 "Encyclopedia of Jazz": *New York Daily News,* Sept. 26, 1958, 14.

121 One Connecticut critic: "Have You Heard," *Record-Journal* (Meriden, Conn.), Sept. 30, 1958, 8.

121 He also wrote about an offstage moment: Leonard Feather, *From Satchmo to Miles* (New York: Stein and Day, 1972), 81.

121 In a telegram dated September 30, 1958: The telegram is in the private collection of Ken Schwartz.

CHAPTER 7: IT HAPPENED OUT WEST

124 At the end of September: Hal Schaefer, music column, *San Francisco Chronicle,* Sept. 27, 1958.

124 "We were on the plane": An interview with Mal Waldron about the release of "Left Alone" is available on YouTube.

125 A contemporaneous description: "Nightclubs: Success in a Sewer," *Time,* Aug. 3, 1959.

125 In 1956, Dave Brubeck: *Jazz at the Black Hawk* was released by Fantasy Records in 1956.

125 Cal Tjader had cut: *A Night at the Blackhawk (Live)* was released by Fantasy Records in 1959.

125 The intimate room: Tenderloin Museum, San Francisco.

125 It happened to be another performance: Gerald Clarke, *Capote: A Biography* (New York: Carroll & Graf, 1998), 304.

125 "Never before": C. H. Garrigues, "Chords and Changes," *San Francisco Examiner,* Oct. 5, 1958, 171.

126 Billie made her way to "the powder room": Herb Caen, *San Francisco Chronicle,* Oct. 3, 1958, 15.

126 While she was there: Caen.

126 When she came to: Caen.

126 In his national column on October 1: Walter Winchell, "Broadway and Elsewhere," *Terre Haute (Ind.) Tribune,* Sept. 30, 1958, 4.

126 *Jet* magazine: *Jet,* Oct. 2, 1958, 63.

126 Another story making the rounds: *Las Vegas Daily Optic,* Oct. 11, 1958, 7; and *New York Daily News,* Oct. 21, 1958, 261.

127 Apparently, Billie: Chazz Crawford, "Soundtrack with Chazz Crawford," *California Eagle,* Oct. 9, 1958.

127 Herbert Henderson: John Chilton, *Billie's Blues: The Billie Holiday Story 1933–1959* (New York: Da Capo Press, 1975), 185.

127 The source of that ordeal: "Harlem Era Ends with Demise of 'Poor' John Levy," *New York Age,* Dec. 22, 1956, 2.

128 Located in Times Square: "Of Time and the Strand Theatre," *New York Times,* Aug. 21, 1938, 126.

128 But for six weeks starting on July 16: Bill Higgins, "Hollywood Flashback: In 1948, a Hurricane Hit Bogart and Bacall in 'Key Largo,'" *Hollywood Reporter,* Sept. 13, 2017.

128 With doors opening: Higgins.

129 "As very few singers": Quoted in Donald Clarke, *Wishing on the Moon* (New York: Da Capo Press, 2000), 283.

129 Billie's salary: Higgins, "Hollywood Flashback."

129 "It was the first time I saw her": Dan Morgenstern, interview by the author, July 2020.

129 Or, as Ned Rorem later wrote: Ned Rorem, *Knowing When to Stop: A Memoir* (New York: Open Road Media, 2013).

129 It was, as James "Stump" Cross remembered: Linda Kuehl book manuscript, Institute of Jazz Studies, Rutgers University Libraries, Archives and Special Collections.

129 She had become a theater star: Hugh Leonard, "The Darling of the Gallery Girls," *Irish Times,* Dec. 7, 1996.

130 The 1930s saw Bankhead: Entry for Tallulah Bankhead, IMDb.

130 *The Little Foxes:* Brooks Atkinson, "Tallulah Bankhead Appearing in Lillian Hellman's Drama of the South, *The Little Foxes," New York Times,* Feb. 16, 1939, 16.

130 *The Skin of Our Teeth*: "Premiere Tonight for Wilder Play," *New York Times,* Nov. 18, 1942, 30.

130 She finally made a memorable picture: Bosley Crowther, *"Lifeboat,* a Film Picturization of Shipwrecked Survivors, with Tallulah Bankhead, Opens at the Astor Theatre," *New York Times,* Jan. 13, 1944, 17.

130 Tallulah was born: For information about Bankhead's youth, see Joel Lobenthal, "Lace Curtains," chap. 1 in *Tallulah!: The Life and Times of a Leading Lady* (New York: Regan Books, 2004).

130 Tallulah's father: Murray Schumach, "Tallulah Bankhead, the Vibrant and Tempestuous Stage and Screen Star, Dies Here at 65," *New York Times,* Dec. 13, 1968, 1.

130 Tallulah's grandfather: Schumach.

131 In fact, even though in 1937: "Tallulah Bankhead Is Married to Actor," *New York Times,* Sept. 1, 1937, 14.

131 "Tallulah was": Kuehl manuscript.

131 Near the end of the run: "Star Chat," *Alabama Tribune,* Aug. 27, 1948, 2.

131 The newspaper noted: "Star Chat."

132 All the while: Schumach, "Tallulah Bankhead."

132 "To Tallulah, Billie was beautiful": William Dufty, interview by Joel Lobenthal, Aug. 22, 1994.

132 "Billie wasn't impressed": Dufty interview.

132 Lobenthal believes: Joel Lobenthal, interview by the author, June 2020.

132 He was, according to *The New York Age:* "Harlem Era Ends."

132 "He was," to quote one account: John Wesley Noble and Bernard Averbuch, *Never Plead Guilty* (New York: Bantam Books, 1955), 188.

133 Here was how Billie described: Billie Holiday with William Dufty, *Lady Sings the Blues* (New York: Doubleday, 1956; repr., Harlem Moon/Broadway Books, 2006), 175.

133 The development prompted: Billy Rowe, "Billy Rowe's Notebook," *Pittsburgh Courier,* July 24, 1948, 22.

133 "Banky was about the only person": Kuehl manuscript.

133 Charles "Honi" Coles: Kuehl.

134 Tallulah was ringside: "Billie Holiday Star at Ebony," *New York Age,* Sept. 21, 1948, 26.

134 Then again, Levy: "Billie Holiday Drawing Celebs to Club Ebony Show," *New York Age,* Oct. 1, 1948, 9.

134 The opening was such an event: "Billie Holiday Drawing."

134 (She later discovered it was not): Joel Lobenthal, correspondence with the author, Mar. 2021.

134 Tallulah was so involved: *Daily Press* (Newport News, Va.), Oct. 11, 1948, 12.

134 During a four-week run: "Berg Night Spot in New Law Clash," *Los Angeles Daily News,* Jan. 7, 1949, 44.

134 A group of friends: "Nightclub Star Accused in Brawl," *Los Angeles Daily News,* Jan. 4, 1949, 3.

135 A report in the *Los Angeles Daily News:* "Nightclub Star Accused."

135 It turned out that John Levy: Julia Blackburn, *With Billie: A New Look at the Unforgettable Lady Day* (New York: Vintage Books, 2006), 206.

135 A week into the engagement: J. W. Ehrlich, *The Lost Art of Cross-Examination* (New York: Dorset Press, 1970), 136–37.

136 Billie made a mad dash: Ehrlich, 137.

136 Still, White succeeded: Ehrlich, 137.

136 One report noted: "Singer Held in Dope Raid," *San Francisco Examiner,* Jan. 23, 1949, 1.

136 Upon departing the building: "Singer Nabbed on Dope Charge," *Oakland Tribune,* Jan 23. 1949, 23.

136 "She [embraced] the mic": Noble and Averbuch, *Never Plead Guilty,* 191.

136 Two days later: Herb Coen, "It's News to Me" column, *San Francisco Chronicle,* Jan. 27, 1949.

136 With Billie in obvious jeopardy: Lobenthal, *Tallulah!,* 409.

137 She set up a three-way telephone call: John Szwed, *Billie Holiday: The Musician and the Myth* (New York: Penguin Books, 2015), 37.

137 On February 7: Sara Ramshaw, " 'He's My Man!': Lyrics of Innocence and Betrayal in *The People vs. Billie Holiday," Canadian Journal of Women and the Law* 16, no. 1 (2004): 98.

137 Two days later, Tallulah pressed her case: The letter from Tallulah Bankhead to J. Edgar Hoover is contained in the FBI file for Billie Holiday.

137 (Her father died in 1940): Lobenthal, *Tallulah!,* 323; and "Speaker Bankhead Dies in Washington," *New York Times,* Sept. 15, 1940, 1.

137 "I would have never asked": Bankhead letter to Hoover.

138 At the Sahara Hotel: Les Devor, "Vegas Vagaries" column, *Las Vegas Review-Journal,* Oct. 12, 1958, 13.

139 "The Sahara in Vegas": Ivan Paul, "Around Town," *San Francisco Examiner,* Oct. 4, 1958, 9.

139 Jimmy Lyons: Ralph J. Gleason, "The West Coast Gets Its First Big Jazz Event," *San Francisco Chronicle,* Sept. 28, 1958, 131.

139 A who's who: C. H. Garrigues, "Jazz Fete Opens Today," *San Francisco Examiner,* Oct. 3, 1958, 14.

139   For the occasion tonight: Billie Holiday was photographed at the Monterey Jazz
      Festival by Nat Farbman for *Life*.

139   The applause washed over: *At Monterey, 1958*, an album, was recorded on Octo-
      ber 5, 1958, and released by Black Hawk Records in 1986. The following scene is
      based on the recording.

141   Ralph Gleason declared: Ralph Gleason, *San Francisco Chronicle*, Oct. 7, 1958, 11.

141   A critic for the *Los Angeles Mirror*: Roger Beck, "Off the Records," *Los Angeles Mir-
      ror*, Oct. 11, 1958, 41.

141   A writer for *Down Beat*: John Tynan, "It Happened at Monterey," *Down Beat*,
      Nov. 13, 1958, 50.

142   As Miles Davis put it: Ted Gioia, *The History of Jazz* (New York: Oxford University
      Press, 2021), 216.

142   On Monday, October 6: Ken Vail, *Lady Day's Diary: The Life of Billie Holiday 1937–
      1959* (Chessington, UK: Castle Communications, 1996), 198.

142   Once again, she had been: Jerry Leichtling and Arlene Sarner, *Corky Hale Uncorked!*
      (Los Angeles: Corky Hale Publications, 2018), 46.

142   "The bandleader had just announced": Leichtling and Sarner, 46.

142   "That's the piano player?": Leichtling and Sarner, 46.

142   "For all her fame": Leichtling and Sarner, 48.

142   Many African Americans: John Przybys, "1954 Article Refers to Las Vegas as 'Mis-
      sissippi of the West,'" *Las Vegas Review-Journal*, Apr. 1, 2018.

143   "We were staying at the Sahara Hotel": Alice Vrbsky, interview by Norman Saks,
      Feb. 8, 1985.

144   "It cost me almost a thousand dollars": Holiday with Dufty, *Lady Sings the Blues*,
      185.

144   Reports later identified: Ramshaw, "'He's My Man!,'" 98.

144   "Holiday willingly underwent": Ramshaw, 99.

144   Ehrlich's plan: Ramshaw, 101.

144   Billie confirmed: Ramshaw, 101.

144   Appearing "somewhat unkempt in a beige suit": Noble and Averbuch, *Never Plead
      Guilty*, 194.

144   Asked about her condition: Ralph Gleason, "Broke, Alone, Bille Goes Back to
      Work," *Down Beat*, July 15, 1949, 3.

145   Ehrlich asked her if she had seen: This exchange, based on the official transcript,
      appears in Noble and Averbuch, *Never Plead Guilty*, 206.

145   Eventually, Ehrlich requested: Noble and Averbuch, 206.

145   "Now," Ehrlich said: Noble and Averbuch, 206.

145   "Yes, there was a phone call": Noble and Averbuch, 201.

145   On cross-examination: Noble and Averbuch, 202.

146   On multiple occasions: The cross-examination of White by Ehrlich, a portion of
      which is reproduced in the chapter entitled "The Case of Billie Holiday" in Ehrlich,
      The Lost Art of Cross-Examination, 135–47, is taken from the official trial transcript.

146   Producing the photograph: Ehrlich.

146   Startled, White attempted: Ehrlich.

146   The jury foreman: "Billie Holiday Free on Opium Charge," *Stockton (Calif.) Evening
      and Sunday Record*, June 4, 1949, 4.

147 In February 1950: "Billie Holiday Off for West Coast Tour," *Chicago World*, Feb. 4, 1950, 4.

147 One press report: "Billie Holiday Off."

147 Stump and Stumpy: Bob Goddard, "At the Night Spots," *St. Louis Globe-Democrat*, Jan. 22, 1950, 53.

147 The following month, in March: *New York Daily News*, Mar. 17, 1950, 42.

147 "The split in forces": "La 'Lady Day' Drops Levy," *New York Amsterdam News*, Aug. 5, 1950, 1.

147 Tallulah became so frightened: Mel Helmer, "My New York," *Daily Notes* (Canonsburg, Pa.), Mar. 19, 1951, 4.

148 One newspaper observed: *Daily Notes*, 4.

148 Annie Ross remembers: Annie Ross, interview by the author, Dec. 2019.

148 As for Levy: "Harlem Era Ends."

148 For some time, he had owned: "Harlem Era Ends."

148 A press account of his funeral: "Many Mourned Sportsman Here," *New York Age*, Dec. 22, 1956, 2.

148 At present, the Number 1: Carl Wilson, "The Story of Tommy Edwards, the Top 100's First Black Artist to Hit No. 1," *Billboard*, Aug. 2, 2018.

148 She had accepted two gigs: The contracts are held in a private collection.

149 Next, on the afternoon: An advertisement for the show appeared in the *Transcript-Telegram* (Holyoke, Mass.), October 18, 1958, 2.

149 For the event: "Jazz Greats, Billie Holiday and Maynard Ferguson, at UM on Oct. 19," *Transcript-Telegram* (Holyoke, Mass.), Oct. 8, 1958, 23.

149 "The details of the cancellation": Peter Munroe, "Stars Fail to Show," *Massachusetts Collegian*, Oct. 20, 1958.

149 Whatever the reason: *Record* (Hackensack, N.J.), Oct. 23, 1958, 59.

149 "Her voice wasn't the way it was": Harry Sheppard, interview by the author, Mar. 2021.

CHAPTER 8: GOODBYE TO THE CITY OF LIGHTS

152 In the 1920s: Amanda Vaill, *Everybody Was So Young: Gerald and Sara Murphy: A Lost Generation Love Story* (New York: Houghton Mifflin, 1998).

152 Hemingway called her: The widely known quote about Josephine Baker is referenced in Heather Hartley, "Even Her Feet Were Ravishing," *Tin House*, Apr. 29, 2013.

152 In the mid-1950s: Adam Clayton Powell III, interview by the author, Jan. 2021.

152 "My . . . years out of America": Hazel Scott, "What Paris Means to Me," *Negro Digest*, Nov. 1961, 61.

153 The publicity shots: *Chicago Defender*, Nov. 1, 1958, 18.

153 (Harry Sheppard remembers): Harry Sheppard, interview by the author, Mar. 2021.

153 No doubt her 1954 European tour: Leonard Feather, *The Jazz Years: Earwitness to an Era* (New York: Da Capo Press, 1987), 198–99.

154 as one publication described the bill: "Billie Holiday Asked to Quit," *Melody Maker*, Nov. 15, 1958.

154 *Melody Maker*: "Billie Holiday Asked to Quit."

154 Billie's disappointment: John Chilton, *Billie's Blues: The Billie Holiday Story 1933–1959* (New York: Da Capo Press, 1975), 189.

155 "Just a line to say hello": Leonard Feather papers, Institute of Jazz Studies, Rutgers University Libraries, Archives and Special Collections.

155 To her friend Max Jones: Ken Vail, *Lady Day's Diary: The Life of Billie Holiday 1937–1959* (Chessington, UK: Castle Communications, 1996), 199.

155 Gérard "Dave" Pochonet: Phil Schaap and Ben Young with Matt Herman, *WKCR Billie Holiday Festival Handbook* (New York: WKCR Books, 2005), 156.

156 Henry Kahn for *Melody Maker*: Harry Kahn, " 'They Call Me an Artist in Britain,' Says Billie Holiday," *Melody Maker,* Nov. 22, 1958.

156 "Lady Day," he wrote: Kahn.

156 "Paris critics failed to flip over": Dorothy Kilgallen, "Voice of Broadway," national syndicated column, Dec. 9, 1958.

156 In the end, he would pay her: Flo Kennedy, *Color Me Flo: My Hard Life and Good Times* (Englewood Cliffs, N.J.: Prentice-Hall, 1976), 48.

156 Clearly, her new representation, George Treadwell: Leslie Gourse, *Sassy: The Life of Sarah Vaugha*n (New York: Da Capo Press, 1994), 92.

157 A journalist later described: Charles L. Sanders, "Lady Didn't Always Sing the Blues," *Ebony,* Jan. 1973, 113.

157 The Mars Club was founded: Kilgallen, "Voice of Broadway," Feb. 26, 1958; and Marc Smirnoff, ed., *The Oxford American Book of Great Music Writing* (Fayetteville: University of Arkansas Press, 2012), 324.

157 On the program: Tom Reney, "Billie Sings 'Travelin' Light,' " nepr.net, Apr. 7, 2016.

158 It was near the beginning: The paragraph is based on Yolande Bavan, interview by the author, May 2020.

159 "I was visiting Paris": Bavan interview.

159 When Waldron returned to his table: Bavan interview.

159 A journalist later recorded: Sanders, "Lady Didn't Always Sing," 113.

160 The following night: Section is based on Bavan interview.

161 As a gray, wintry evening: Sanders, "Lady Didn't Always Sing," 113.

161 a majestic apartment building: Karen Chilton, *Hazel Scott: The Pioneering Journey of a Jazz Pianist from Café Society to Hollywood to HUAC* (Ann Arbor: University of Michigan Press, 2010), 173.

161 Billie and Hazel Scott: Chilton, *Hazel Scott,* 37–38.

161 Born in Trinidad: Chilton, *Hazel Scott,* 1.

161 Juilliard School: Chilton, *Hazel Scott,* 22–23.

162 married Adam Clayton Powell, Jr.: Chilton, *Hazel Scott,* 90–99.

162 A son, Adam III: Chilton, *Hazel Scott,* 130.

162 In 1950, *The Hazel Scott Show:* Chilton, *Hazel Scott,* 141.

162 "Mudslinging and unverified charges": Lorissa Rinehart, "She Was Once the Biggest Star in Jazz. Here's Why You've Never Heard of Her," Portside, Feb. 22, 2023, https://portside.org/2023-02-22/she-was-once-biggest-star-jazz-heres-why-youve-never-heard-her.

162 "My Paris," Hazel later wrote: Scott, "What Paris Means," 61.

162 One surprised guest remembered: Schaap and Young with Herman, *Festival Handbook,* 155.

163 Billie warmly greeted the other guests: Paragraph based on Clayton Powell III interview.

163 Billie felt right at home: Clayton Powell III interview.

163 insured by Lloyd's of London: Clayton Powell III interview.

163 As they ate and chatted: Schaap and Young with Herman, *Festival Handbook*, 155.

163 "In the midst of the hubbub": Schaap and Young with Herman, 155.

164 "demolished because everything was so delicious": Schaap and Young with Herman, 156.

164 "On this night": Schaap and Young with Herman, 156.

164 "If you go back," Hazel said: Clayton Powell III interview.

164 Hazel would later say: Sanders, "Lady Didn't Always Sing," 113.

165 Pinning her in a corner, Billie stood: Scott, "What Paris Means," 140.

166 Françoise Sagan: The paragraph is based on Françoise Sagan, "Billie Holiday," in *With Fondest Regards,* trans. Christine Donougher (New York: E. P. Dutton, 1985).

167 So when she joined them: Sagan, 12.

167 "She sang with eyes lowered": Sagan, 13.

167 "Anyway, darling": Sagan, 13.

167 "It was Billie Holiday": Sagan, 10.

CHAPTER 9: THE WHOLE TRUTH

170 "For a singer, who has contributed": Bob Snead, "Bob Snead's Jazz Corner," *Cleveland Call and Post,* Dec. 13, 1958, C5.

171 Dr. Eric Caminer, whose office: *Medical Directories,* 1958. Information supplied through correspondence with the New York County Medical Society.

171 When Feather offered Billie a drink: Leonard Feather, *From Satchmo to Miles* (New York: Stein and Day, 1972), 82.

171 Others in the nightlife industry: "To Test Law that Bars Billie Holiday in N.Y.," *Afro-American,* Nov. 15, 1958, 7.

171 "Last year," author Murray Kempton: George E. Pitts, "Musicians Test N.Y. Cabaret Law in Court," *Pittsburgh Courier,* June 18, 1958, A10.

172 "There's a very serious situation": "Best of Broadway," *Philadelphia Inquirer,* Dec. 17, 1958, 37.

172 *The Pittsburgh Courier:* Masco Young, "The Grapevine," *Pittsburgh Courier,* Jan. 17, 1959, 22.

172 The *New York Daily News:* Danton Walker, "Broadway," *New York Daily News,* Jan. 20, 1959.

172 During the holiday season: Yolande Bavan, interview by the author, May 2020.

173 the *Nashville Banner: Nashville Banner,* Dec. 8, 1958, 30.

173 A syndicated music column: UPI, *Traverse City (Mich.) Record-Eagle,* Jan. 26, 1959, 4.

173 The *Deseret News:* Conrad B. Harrison, "Music News," *Deseret News,* Jan. 15, 1959, 40.

173 As Dorothy Kilgallen reported: Dorothy Kilgallen, "Voice of Broadway," national syndicated column, Nov. 27, 1958.

174 She was going about her afternoon: Information about the telephone call comes

from William Dufty, "The True Story of Billie Holiday," article 4 of series, *New York Post,* July 23, 1959.

175 She had known Maely Dufty: Julia Blackburn, *With Billie: A New Look at the Unforgettable Lady Day* (New York: Vintage Books, 2006), 234, 261. Film titles are listed in entry on Freddie Bartholomew, IMDb.

175 "Maely Dufty," according to one account: Sherie M. Randolph, *Florynce "Flo" Kennedy: The Life of a Black Feminist Radical* (Chapel Hill: The University of North Carolina Press, 2015), 60.

175 their only son, Bevan: For a biography of Bevan Duffy, go to the Bay Area Rapid Transit website at bart.gov.

175 "I could tell from her voice": Dufty, "The True Story."

175 The Duftys were guests: Randolph, *Florynce "Flo" Kennedy,* 60.

176 Birdland: Randolph, 60.

176 "Flo was brilliant": Eleanor Pam, interview by the author, July 2020.

176 Judge Emily Jane Goodman: Emily Jane Goodman, interview by the author, July 2020.

176 Attorney Edward W. Hayes: Edward W. Hayes, interview by the author, July 2020.

176 Author Sandra Hochman: Sandra Hochman, interview by the author, July 2020.

176 Robin Morgan says: Robin Morgan, correspondence with the author, Mar. 2023.

176 She had come to New York: Randolph, *Florynce "Flo" Kennedy,* 38–56.

176 "They said she was being rejected": Goodman interview.

176 She also happened to be a fan: Flo Kennedy, *Color Me Flo: My Hard Life and Good Times* (Englewood Cliffs, N.J.: Prentice-Hall, 1976), 48.

177 "As we talked": Dufty, "The True Story."

177 Quickly researching the topic: Dufty, "The True Story."

177 Potential violators included: Dufty, "The True Story."

177 "what a difference a day makes": Dufty, "The True Story."

177 "She called the liquor store": Dufty, "The True Story."

178 Billie and Jack Gilford: Madeline Lee Gilford, interview by the author, July 2007.

178 Harry Anslinger: William J. Horvath, "The 1950s 'War on Narcotics': Harry Anslinger, the Federal Bureau of Narcotics, and Senator Price Daniel's Probe," 2020, Harvey M. Applebaum '59 Award, Yale University Library.

178 "With Harry Anslinger": Sonny Rollins, interviews by the author, 2020.

178 "It sounded like the jungles": Johann Hari, "The Hunting of Billie Holiday," Politico Magazine (website) Jan. 17, 2015.

178 Annie Ross says: Annie Ross, interview by the author, Dec. 2019.

178 "She flaunted her way of living": Hari, "The Hunting of Billie Holiday."

178 "It was her brazenness": David Margolick, interview by the author, June 2023.

179 On May 27, 1947: The courtroom episode, which ends with the sentence handed down by Judge Ganey, is based on the court transcript for the District Court of the United States for the Eastern District of Pennsylvania on May 27, 1947.

181 Without being allowed to go: Billie Holiday with William Dufty, *Lady Sings the Blues* (New York: Harlem Moon/Broadway Books, 2006), 151.

181 She told the officer she was born: The intake document is in Billie Holiday's prison file housed at the National Archives and Record Administration.

181   "Subject is a wholesome influence": The progress report is in Billie Holiday's prison file.

182   prison rules sheet: Holiday prison file.

182   One person with whom she corresponded: The letter from Billie Holiday to Leonard Feather is in the Leonard Feather papers, Institute of Jazz Studies, Rutgers University Libraries, Archives and Special Collections.

182   Lorraine Feather says: Lorraine Feather, interview by the author, June 2020.

182   "Joe," Billie wrote on August 5: The letter from Billie Holiday to Joe Guy is in the private collection of Ken Schwartz.

182   "Jim Crow was the rule everywhere": Billie Holiday, "I'm Cured for Good Now," *Ebony*, July 1949.

183   "The most lonely sound in the world": The line comes from the unpublished autobiography of Tony Scott.

183   "a scholarly, bespectacled little man": Mel Heimer, "My New York," *Linton (Ind.) Daily Citizen*, Apr. 13, 1948, 5.

183   The *New York Daily News* declared: "Lady Day Rocks 'Em in Carnegie Hall," *New York Daily News*, Mar. 29, 1948, 73.

183   Meanwhile, *Time* observed: "Music: New Life," *Time*, Apr. 12, 1948.

183   "The police have been particularly vindictive": Holiday, "I'm Cured for Good."

183   Count Basie interacting with: John Chilton, *Billie's Blues: The Billie Holiday Story 1933–1959* (New York: Da Capo Press, 1975), 139.

184   In the wake of their deaths: Nancy Kovaleff Baker, "Abel Meeropol (a.k.a. Lewis Allan): Political Commentator and Social Conscience," *American Music* 20 (Spring 2002): 64. Michael Meeropol, "A Spy Who Turned His Family In: Revisiting David Greenglass and the Rosenberg Case," *American Communist History*, vol. 17, no. 2 (2018), 247–60.

184   Though he did not know them: Baker, 64.

184   Then, in 1955: "Gloria Agrin Josephson, 65, Lawyer, Dies," *New York Times*, June 22, 1988, 119.

185   "Mrs. McKay," McVeigh said: The following question-and-answer examination, which concludes with McVeigh's comment beginning "I am going to refer this matter," is taken from the official transcript as recorded at the Customs House and reproduced in large part in Khanya Mtshali, ed., *Billie Holiday: The Last Interview and Other Conversations* (Brooklyn: Melville House, 2018), 79–94.

185   "Agent Cozzi and I": For information about the two agents, see "Martin McVeigh, Customs Agent, Dies at Age 58," Ancestry.com, and "Mario Cozzi, 72, Dies; Led Customs Inquiries," *New York Times*, Feb. 6, 1988, 10.

190   "Billie came out of the hearing shaken": Dufty, "The True Story."

CHAPTER 10: "I'M BILLIE HOLIDAY!"

192   "This, then, is my complaint": Billie Holiday, "I'm Cured for Good Now," *Ebony*, July 1949.

192   Her feelings of fear and apprehension: Billie Holiday's telethon appearance is described in "Billie Holiday Gives Talents, Teas to Thorns' [*sic*] Emceed by Martha Raye," *Chicago Daily Defender*, Feb. 18, 1959, A18.

193   Dressed in a stunning white strapless evening gown: "Billie Holiday Gives Talents."

193   When she finished: "Billie Holiday Gives Talents."

193   "There is nothing unique about La Holiday": "Billie Holiday Gives Talents."

193   That was true: Al Monroe, "So They Say," *Chicago Daily Defender,* Feb. 23, 1959, 18.

193   Miles Davis would remember: Miles Davis with Quincy Troupe, *Miles: The Autobiography* (New York: Simon & Schuster, 2011), 235–36.

193   "She was looking real bad": Davis with Troupe, 235–36.

193   Alice Vrbsky remembered: Julia Blackburn, *With Billie: A New Look at the Unforgettable Lady Day* (New York: Vintage Books, 2006), 317.

194   She saw Dr. Caminer: The prescription is contained in the Billie Holiday collection, Stuart A. Rose Manuscript, Archives, and Rare Book Library, Emory University.

194   A date was set in early February: William Dufty, "The True Story of Billie Holiday," article 4 of series, *New York Post,* July 23, 1959.

194   Day after day: Alice Vrbsky, interview by Norman Saks, Feb. 8, 1985.

194   Finally, a new date for the hearing: Dufty, "The True Story."

194   As they proceeded down: Dufty, "The True Story."

194   At last, in a government building in Brooklyn: Dufty, "The True Story."

194   With her lawyers by her side: Dufty, "The True Story."

195   The attorneys decided: Dufty, "The True Story."

195   on Sunday, February 22: Ken Vail, *Lady Day's Diary: The Life of Billie Holiday 1937–1959* (Chessington, UK: Castle Communications, 1996), 201.

196   He was going to play his gig: Robert Sylvester, "Dream Street," *New York Daily News,* Feb. 28, 1959, 77.

196   Upon her arrival at Heathrow: Max Jones, "I'm Settling in London," *Melody Maker,* Feb. 28, 1959, 5.

196   In 1954, when she arrived in London: Max Jones, *Jazz Talking: Profiles, Interviews, and Other Riffs on Jazz Musicians* (New York: Da Capo Press, 2000), 247.

196   He had never met her before: Jones, 248.

196   "I'm trying to get": Jones, 248.

196   "The whole thing was a rush": Jones, "I'm Settling in London."

196   At a pay phone: The telephone call is based on Yolande Bavan, interview by the author, May 2020.

197   "most of my waking hours": Jones, *Jazz Talking,* 257.

197   "[An] event I cannot forget": Jones, *Jazz Talking,* 257–58.

197   But it was a conversation: The paragraph is based on Jones, "I'm Settling in London."

197   Billie confirmed a potential move: Jones, "I'm Settling in London."

198   Billie presented: Jones, "I'm Settling in London."

198   "I'm Billie Holiday!": Jones, "I'm Settling in London."

198   The Palace Theatre: Rob Baker, "Burlesque at the Chelsea Palace, and the Last Great Performance of Billie Holiday," Flashbak.com, Feb. 23, 2018.

198   John Osborne was inspired: Brooks Atkinson, "The Entertainer," *New York Times,* Feb. 23, 1958.

198   Before Max collected: Jones, *Jazz Talking,* 257.

198   "She had nobody else": Bavan interview.

199   With Bavan to keep Billie company: Jones, *Jazz Talking,* 257.

199   "Hi Alice": Vail, *Lady Day's Diary,* 201.

199 She also sent Leonard Feather: The postcard is contained in the Leonard Feather papers, Institute of Jazz Studies, Rutgers University Libraries, Archives and Special Collections.

199 But the main errand: Jones, *Jazz Talking*, 257.

199 "We had a bottle of vodka": Bavan interview.

199 Peter Knight: Jones, *Jazz Talking*, 258.

199 folk singer Josh White: Elijah Walk, *Josh White: Society Blues* (Milton Park, UK: Routledge, 2002), 191.

200 "Billie was very jumpy": Bavan interview.

200 Wearing a conservative suit and tie: A copy of the complete *Chelsea at Nine* segment featuring Billie Holiday (introduction, three songs, and outro) was made available to me from the private collection of Will Friedwald.

201 Billie could not see: Bavan interview.

202 After the taping, Max escorted Billie: Bavan interview.

203 Billie took matters into her own hands: The exchange with the receptionist is based on Blackburn, *With Billie*, 274.

203 When Billie suggested: Blackburn, 274.

203 Billie had not even recovered: Jones, "I'm Settling in London."

203 The topic was certainly in the air: Phil Schaap and Ben Young with Matt Herman, *WKCR Billie Holiday Festival Handbook* (New York: WKCR Books, 2005), 150.

204 During the session: For a list of musicians who played on the album, see Schaap and Young with Herman, 150–51.

204 Later, Ellis was brutal: Blackburn, *With Billie*, 275.

204 For the second session: Schaap and Young with Herman, *Festival Handbook*, 150–51.

204 "She was sick": The quote comes from an interview with Milt Hinton conducted by Terry Gross for an unaired television program, recorded September 6, 1984.

205 the evening of March 11: Schaap and Young with Herman, *Festival Handbook*, 151.

205 It was likely during the week: Press articles from late January report Mal Waldron playing at the Five Spot with Peck Morrison and Jimmy Wormworth.

205 "Billie came in with Harry Edison": John Handy, interview by the author, Apr. 2021.

205 On the eleventh, when Bank first saw Billie: Schaap and Young with Herman, *Festival Handbook*, 151.

206 Bank remembered Billie: The quote comes from Marc Myers, "Interview: Danny Bank on Billie," JazzWax, September 7, 2007, https://www.jazzwax.com/2007/09/billie-and-dann.html.

206 Bank mistook Alice: Meyers.

206 Somehow, she managed to record: Schaap and Young with Herman, *Festival Handbook*, 151.

206 "She may have knocked out": Marc Ellis, interview by the author, June 2020.

CHAPTER 11: THE DEATH OF THE PRESIDENT

208 Alvin Hotel: Dave Gelly, *Being Prez: The Life & Music of Lester Young* (New York: Oxford University Press, 2007), 135.

208 Down in Greenwich Village: The information and quote in the paragraph come from John Handy, interview by the author, Apr. 2021.

209   (A fashion enthusiast): Joel Dinerstein, "Lester Young and the Birth of Cool," in
       *Signifyin(g), Sanctifyin', & Slam Dunking: A Reader in African American Expressive
       Culture,* ed. Gena Dagel Caponi (Amherst: University of Massachusetts Press,
       1999). The essay is included in Joel Dinerstein, *The Origins of Cool in Postwar America*
       (Chicago: University of Chicago Press, 2017).

209   At the end of 1958: Douglas Henry Daniels, *Lester Leaps In: The Life and Times of
       Lester "Pres" Young* (Boston: Beacon Press, 2002), 353–54.

209   Dan Morgenstern saw Young: Dan Morgenstern, interview by the author, July
       2020.

209   "I ran into Lester": Willie Ruff, interview by the author, May 2021.

209   In Paris, Young opened: Gelly, *Being Prez,* 138, 139.

209   He began to drink even more: Lewis Porter, *Lester Young* (Woodbridge, CT: Twayne,
       1985), 30.

210   On February 6, at the end: François Postif, "Interview with Lester Young," in *A
       Lester Young Reader,* ed. Lewis Porter (Washington, D.C.: Smithsonian Institution
       Press, 1999), 173–91.

210   His drink of choice: Dr. Luther Cloud quoted in Gelly, *Being Prez,* 139.

210   "I remember Lester coming over": Adam Clayton Powell III, interview by the
       author, Jan. 2021.

210   On March 4, Young agreed: The information is included on the album's liner notes.
       The album, *Le Dernier Message de Lester Young,* was released posthumously.

210   Ben Benjamin recalled: Porter, *Lester Young,* 30.

211   He played his final set: Gelly, *Being Prez,* 140.

211   "It pains me to remember": Hazel Scott, "The Truth About Me," *Ebony,* Sept. 1960,
       139.

211   On the flight home: Daniels, *Lester Leaps In,* 354.

211   When he landed: Gelly, *Being Prez,* 140.

211   Finally, he lay down on the bed: Gelly, 140.

211   Swain called a doctor: Gelly, 140.

211   Lester Young died: Gelly, 140.

211   News reports identified the cause of death: Daniels, *Lester Leaps In,* 354.

212   For two decades now: Recording details are in Phil Schaap and Ben Young with
       Matt Herman, *WKCR Billie Holiday Festival Handbook* (New York: WKCR Books,
       2005).

212   "They were the epitome": David Amram, interview by the author, June 2021.

212   "From then on," Billie wrote: Billie Holiday with William Dufty, *Lady Sings
       the Blues* (New York: Doubleday, 1956; repr., Harlem Moon/Broadway Books,
       2006), 51.

212   Born in Woodville, Mississippi: Jamie Katz, "Lester Young Turns 100," *Smithsonian
       Magazine,* Aug. 24, 2009.

212   His father, Willis Handy Young: Katz.

212   Moving to Minnesota: Katz.

212   Young left the family permanently: Katz.

212   Ralph Ellison remembered: Ralph Ellison, *Shadow and Act* (New York: Random
       House, 1964), 236–37.

213   "Young was the first jazz musician": Dinerstein, "Lester Young," 250.

213   "bread," as he called it: Dinerstein, 250.

213   Favorite expressions: Katz, "Lester Young Turns 100."

213   Bassist Bill Crow: Bill Crow, interview by the author, July 2021.

214   "I always felt he was the greatest": Holiday with Dufty, *Lady Sings the Blues,* 55.

214   But members of the Blue Devils: Daniels, *Lester Leaps In,* 7.

214   Young decided Sadie also needed: Holiday with Dufty, *Lady Sings the Blues,* 55.

214   "an unregistered guest": Holiday with Dufty, 54.

214   "a big dirty old rat the size of my dog": Holiday with Dufty, 54.

214   "When I first came to New York": Postif, "Interview with Lester Young," 185.

214   "Fletcher's wife, Leora": Linda Kuehl book manuscript, Institute of Jazz Studies, Rutgers University Libraries, Archives and Special Collections.

215   "Prez and Herschel": Nat Hentoff, "Lester Young," in *A Lester Young Reader,* 56.

215   "One of the things he was fond of saying": Lester Young, Jr., oral history interview conducted by Sady Sullivan, January 31, 2008, Bedford Stuyvesant Restoration Corporation oral histories, Brooklyn Historical Society.

215   In 1943, Young starred in: Dinerstein, "Lester Young," 253.

215   Linda Kuehl wrote: From an unpublished document contained in Linda Kuehl papers, Institute of Jazz Studies, Rutgers University Libraries, Archives and Special Collections.

215   "Drafted in September": Dinerstein, "Lester Young," 259.

216   "A nightmare, man, one mad nightmare": Quoted in Allan Morrison, "You Got to Be Original," in *A Lester Young Reader,* 135.

216   Billie was at the Rendezvous: advertisement, *Philadelphia Inquirer,* Jan. 31, 1951, 25.

216   Lester and his band: Frank Brookhouser, "It's Happening Here," *Philadelphia Inquirer,* Jan. 30, 1951, 21.

217   As he told a friend: Martin Torgoff, *Bop Apocalypse: Jazz, Race, the Beats, and Drugs* (New York: Da Capo Press, 2016), 299.

217   "I had lined up Teddy Wilson": George Wein, interview by the author, Apr. 2021.

217   "[Young] shuffled onstage": The quote, originally in *Down Beat,* is reprinted in James Maycock, "Billie Holiday and Lester Young: The Intimate Friendship Between Lady Day and Prez," *Guardian,* Apr. 18, 2015.

217   from *Billboard*: *Billboard,* Mar. 23, 1959, 6.

217   *South Bend Tribune*: "Lester Young," *South Bend Tribune,* Mar. 16, 1959, 21.

218   *New York Daily News*: "Lester Young," *New York Daily News,* Mar. 16, 1959.

218   *The New York Times*: "Lester Young, 49, a Jazz Musician," *New York Times,* Mar. 16, 1959, 31.

218   The funeral was scheduled: Daniels, *Lester Leaps In,* 359.

218   "The abstinence probably lasted a few weeks": Leonard Feather, *The Jazz Years: Earwitness to an Era* (New York: Da Capo Press, 1987), 148.

218   Then, in the taxi ride: Leonard Feather, *From Satchmo to Miles* (New York: Stein and Day, 1972), 82.

218   The funeral was well attended: Daniels, *Lester Leaps In,* 359.

219   And Billie, as she sat on a pew: Billie Holiday's emotional response to the funeral service comes from Morgenstern, interview by the author.

219   "She kept saying": Morgenstern interview.

220   "The best thing that ever happened": Eric Larrabee's comment, which appeared originally in *Harper's,* is reprinted in the liner notes for the original *The Sound of Jazz,* released by Columbia Records, Feb. 1958.

220   Producer Robert Herridge: Nat Hentoff, *At the Jazz Band Ball* (Berkeley: University of California Press, 2010), 29.

220   "[Young] was waiting": Hentoff, *Jazz Band,* 130.

220   "During a sound check": Hentoff, *Jazz Band,* 129–30.

221   The show began, and when it came time: A copy of "The Sound of Jazz" is in the archival holdings of the Paley Center for Media in New York City.

CHAPTER 12: MEMORY AND DESIRE

224   As she waited for showtime: This sentence and the next are based on a brochure from the Academy of Music, Philadelphia; and Jimmie Rivers, "Jazz in Review," *Philadelphia Tribune,* Mar. 28, 1959, 14.

224   Located downtown on Broad Street: Academy of Music, Philadelphia, correspondence with the author regarding its history.

224   It was said that in 1865: Based on correspondence between the author and both the Abraham Lincoln Presidential Library and Museum and the Philadelphia Orchestra.

225   Magnolia Ballroom: "Billie Holiday Plays Magnolia Easter Sunday," *Atlanta Daily World,* Mar. 25, 1959, 3.

225   "She was really frail": Philip Yale Nicholson, interview by the author, 2020.

226   It had been fifteen years: Leonard Feather, "Requiescat in Pace," *Down Beat,* Aug. 20, 1959, 21.

226   another recalled fish stuffed with hamburger: Robert O'Meally, *Lady Day: The Many Faces of Billie Holiday* (New York: Da Capo Press, 1991), 181.

226   Annie Ross, an old friend: Unpublished document on Billie Holiday, Annie Ross papers, Institute of Jazz Studies, Rutgers University Libraries, Archives and Special Collections.

226   There was Flo Kennedy: Flo Kennedy, *Color Me Flo: My Hard Life and Good Times* (Englewood Cliffs, N.J.: Prentice-Hall, 1976), 47.

227   "skinny rather than slender": Leonard Feather, *From Satchmo to Miles* (New York: Stein and Day, 1972), 82.

227   Born in London: Peter Keepnews, "Annie Ross, Jazz Vocalist of 'Twisted' Renown, Dies at 89," *New York Times,* July 22, 2020.

228   The day after she signed: The paragraph is based on "It Cost Me a Lot," BBC, Aug. 21, 1969, transcript page 11.

228   Billie was opening: Ken Vail, *Lady Day's Diary: The Life of Billie Holiday 1937–1959* (Chessington, UK: Castle Communications, 1996), 152.

228   Annie would recall their first encounter: "It Cost Me a Lot," 11–12.

229   The women remained in touch: The paragraph is based on and quotes are taken from Annie Ross, interview by the author, Dec. 2019.

230   "probably the most successful": Keepnews, "Annie Ross."

230   a moment Ross recalls: Ross interview.

230   Annie Ross remembers: Ross interview.

230   In early 1959, he was still married: Albert Goldman, from the journalism of Law-

rence Schiller, *Ladies and Gentlemen—Lenny Bruce!!* (New York, Random House, 1971).

231   when he started seeing Annie in Chicago: Annie Ross recalls the first time she met Lenny Bruce in an unpublished document in the Annie Ross papers, Institute of Jazz Studies, Rutgers, University Libraries, Archives, and Special Collections.

231   After the Chicago gig: The paragraph is based on Goldman, *Ladies and Gentlemen,* 262.

231   On April 5, Lenny Bruce: Goldman.

231   On April 15, Dorothy Kilgallen: Dorothy Kilgallen, "Voice of Broadway," national syndicated column, Apr. 15, 1959.

232   "Lady was using a lot": Ross interview.

232   Then, taking her into the bathroom: The paragraph is based on an unpublished document about Billie Holiday written by Annie Ross, Annie Ross papers, Institute of Jazz Studies, Rutgers, University Libraries, Archives, and Special Collections; and Ross interview.

232   They were singers, after all: Ross document; Ross interview.

CHAPTER 13: FAREWELL TO STORYVILLE

236   "Now, ladies and gentlemen": The evening's performance is contained on *Billie Holiday: The Complete Storyville Broadcasts,* released by Jazz Twin Records, 2017.

237   Storyville was named for the neighborhood: Historic New Orleans Collection.

237   The namesake Boston nightclub: Richard Vacca, *The Boston Jazz Chronicles: Faces, Places, and Nightlife 1937–1962* (Boston: Troy Street, 2012), 229.

237   When Billie finished: *The Complete Storyville Broadcasts.*

238   Seven months later: Vacca, *Boston Jazz Chronicles,* 50.

238   "The sight of sixteen men": Billie Holiday with William Dufty, *Lady Sings the Blues* (New York: Doubleday, 1956; repr., Harlem Moon/Broadway Books, 2006), 80.

238   *The Boston Globe* singled out: "Symphony Hall: Louis Armstrong," *Boston Globe,* Apr. 19, 1947, 4.

238   whom the *Globe* described as: John A. Hamilton, "Time Out," *Boston Globe,* Feb. 2, 1951, 26.

239   "A new Lady Day": Nat Hentoff, "Billie Holiday, Now Remarried, Finds Happiness, a New Sense of Security," *Down Beat,* vol. 19, iss. 1 (Nov. 1, 1952), 2.

239   But during the engagement: George Wein, interview by the author, Apr. 2021.

239   Then, in August 1957: "Jazz Lovers to Throng Manning Bowl Tonight," *Daily Intern,* Aug. 23, 1957, 8.

240   "In those days," Wein recalls: Wein interview.

240   After one set, Wein went backstage: The dialogue exchange is based on Wein interview.

240   In "The Jazz Scene": "Billie Holiday Can Teach 'Em," *Boston Traveler,* Apr. 28, 1959, 10.

241   In black-and-white photographs: The photographs taken by Mel Levine would eventually be published in various outlets.

241   "My father loved her as a jazz singer": Oren Levine, interview by the author, 2020.

241   "Of course," Wein recalls: Wein interview.

242 "The Billie Holiday-Eddie Heywood contains": Ralph J. Gleason, "Commodore Releases Recall the Old Days," *San Francisco Chronicle,* May 7, 1959.

242 "One has only to compare": Gleason.

242 Even though it was two o'clock: The exchange is based on information in Leonard Feather, *From Satchmo to Miles* (New York: Stein and Day, 1972), 82.

243 Tony Scott was among the finest: Margalit Fox, "Tony Scott, Jazz Clarinetist Who Mastered Bebop, Dies at 85," *New York Times,* Mar. 31, 2007, A16.

243 On the evening she called on Tony: The evening is described in the unpublished autobiography of Tony Scott.

244 May 11 at the Flamingo Lounge: See Chapter 1: "The Last Night at the Flamingo Lounge."

245 "Billie Holiday plans to buy": Dorothy Kilgallen, "Voice of Broadway," national syndicated column, May 13, 1959.

245 A popular singer: Mark A. Ohlig, "Billie Daniels, Who Sang in Nightclubs, Dies at 73," *New York Times,* Oct. 9, 1988, 48.

245 On the business front: Kilgallen, "Voice of Broadway," May 10, 1959.

245 She had met Terkild Vinding: The information concerning the concert and after-party comes from Lone Malast, interview by the author, May 2023.

246 Since that night, Lone's father: Malast interview.

246 Sitting in her living room: Donald Clarke, *Wishing on the Moon* (New York: Da Capo Press, 2000), 431.

246 "You must go at once to a hospital": Clarke, 431.

246 On the evening of Monday, May 25: *New York Daily News,* May 24, 1959, 99.

247 She made her way to her dressing room: A description of the dressing room is contained in the unpublished autobiography of Tony Scott.

247 "[She was] seated at the makeup table": Feather, *From Satchmo,* 83.

247 "[T]here was a little old Negro lady": Robert O'Meally, *Lady Day: The Many Faces of Billie Holiday* (New York: Da Capo Press, 1991), 179.

248 "When I went to her dressing room": The quote from Tony Scott is contained in Giorgio G. Campanaro, "A Case for Billie Holiday," *Ufahamu: A Journal of African Studies* 16, no. 2 (1988): 4.

248 "She spoke with an effort": Campanaro, 41.

248 Once he overcame his shock: The exchange comes from information in the unpublished autobiography of Tony Scott.

248 "All I could do was to keep my hands on her shoulders": Campanaro, "Case for Billie Holiday," 41.

249 "Ladies and gentlemen": From information in the unpublished autobiography of Tony Scott.

249 Then he and Feather: Feather, *From Satchmo,* 83.

249 She snapped her fingers: From information in the unpublished autobiography of Tony Scott.

249 Tony Scott was watching from the wings: Scott autobiography.

CHAPTER 14: FADE OUT

252 As it happened, Billie's friends: Leonard Feather, *From Satchmo to Miles* (New York: Stein and Day, 1972), 83.

252   "The next morning": Feather, 83.

252   "As we sat in her apartment": Feather, 83.

253   After an hour, the three men gave up: Feather, 83.

253   Frankie Freedom, who had been spending time: Julia Blackburn, *With Billie: A New Look at the Unforgettable Lady Day* (New York: Vintage Books, 2006), 317.

253   Alice Vrbsky, who visited only in the evenings: Blackburn, 317.

253   Around two o'clock in the afternoon: Donald Clarke, *Wishing on the Moon* (New York: Da Capo Press, 2000), 433.

253   "She was fighting with me": William Dufty, "Billie Holiday—Did Old Addiction Cause a Hospital Runaround?," *New York Post,* June 4, 1959, 3.

253   she slipped into a coma: George Hoefer, "How Death Came Near for Lady Day," *Down Beat,* July 9, 1959, 11.

254   Frankie stayed with her: Hoefer.

254   There, as Freedom later said: Hoefer.

254   Records indicated: John Chilton, *Billie's Blues: The Billie Holiday Story 1933–1959* (New York: Da Capo Press, 1975), 193.

254   Billie was admitted: Clarke, *Wishing on the Moon,* 433.

254   Part of the problem: Dave Balch, "Horns Moan Low for Billie Holiday," *New York World-Telegram,* June 3, 1959.

254   "cardiac emergency": "Hint Lady Day Was Given Runaround at Hospital," *Baltimore Afro-American,* June 13, 1959.

254   In his reporting, William Dufty: Dufty, "Billie Holiday—Did Old Addiction," 3.

255   At first, Billie was placed: Blackburn, *With Billie,* 296.

255   She was in Room 6A12: The information in the paragraph comes from an affidavit filed by Earle Warren Zaidins in Surrogate's Court of the County of New York on June 26, 1965.

255   Looking Zaidins over, Billie shot back: Chilton, *Billie's Blues,* 194.

255   That Monday, Zaidins: Zaidins affidavit.

256   "Billie Holiday in Hospital": "Billie Holiday in Hospital," United Press International, June 3, 1959.

256   "Billie Holiday Ill": "Billie Holiday Ill Condition Critical," Associated Press, June 3, 1959.

257   In a subsequent article: Clarke, *Wishing on the Moon,* 443.

257   Maria Cooper Janis: Maria Cooper Janis, interview by the author, 2020.

257   By Saturday, it was reported: "Billie Holiday Critically Ill," *Cleveland Call and Post,* June 13, 1959, C8.

257   On Monday, however: "Billie Holiday Still Critical in N.Y. Hospital," *Chicago Daily Defender,* June 9, 1959, 2.

258   To spur on her recovery: Blackburn, *With Billie,* 306.

258   When Zaidins received a copy: Clarke, *Wishing on the Moon,* 435.

258   He also reported that MGM: Blackburn, *With Billie,* 307.

258   Bill Dufty was also involved: Dufty discussed "I Needed Heroin to Live" with Joel Lobenthal in the interview he granted him, Aug. 22, 1994.

259   "You watch, baby": Martin Torgoff, *Bop Apocalypse: Jazz, Race, the Beats, and Drugs* (New York: Da Capo Press, 2016), 316; also referenced in Nat Hentoff, "The Real Lady Day," *New York Times,* Dec. 24, 1972, 8.

259   "The motherfuckers": Annie Ross, interview by the author, Dec. 2019.

259   Figueroa: Blackburn, *With Billie*, 296.

259   Becoming suspicious: Sidney Kline, "Billie Caught with Heroin in Hospital," *New York Daily News*, June 13, 1959, 35.

259   "Mind your own damn business": Kline.

259   The nurse confiscated the foil: Kline.

259   When the powder was revealed: Kline.

259   On Friday, police descended: "Singer in Hospital, Held on New Narcotics Charges," Associated Press, June 13, 1959.

259   Meanwhile, she would remain: Blackburn, *With Billie*, 296.

260   Maely Dufty recalled: The quote is in Hentoff, "The Real Lady Day."

260   Alice Vrbsky remembered: Alice Vrbsky, interview by Norman Saks, Feb. 8, 1985.

260   Florynce Kennedy wrote: Flo Kennedy, *Color Me Flo: My Hard Life and Good Times* (Englewood Cliffs, N.J.: Prentice-Hall, 1976), 47.

260   "Certainly the [drugs] that were used": Ross interview.

260   Regardless of what led up: "Billie Holiday Held," *New York Times*, June 13, 1959.

260   Afterwards, because she was being held: Johann Hari, "The Hunting of Billie Holiday," Politico Magazine (website), Jan. 17, 2015.

261   Edward F. Carey announced: Sidney Kline, "Billie Caught with Heroin in Hospital," *New York Daily News*, June 13, 1959, 35.

261   Soon after the arrest: "Lady Day Says She'll 'Fool Them,'" *New York Amsterdam News*, June 20, 1959, 1.

261   "The persecution she was going through": Sonny Rollins, interviews by the author, 2020.

261   "My father," Mala Waldron says: Mala Waldron, interview by the author, July 2021.

261   as later described by: William Dufty, "The True Story of Billie Holiday," article 4 of series, *New York Post*, July 23, 1959.

261   Even so, on Thursday: Dufty, "The True Story."

262   It was when she refused: Dufty, "The True Story."

262   She felt well enough: Vrbsky interview.

262   Alice Vrbsky also stopped by: Vrbsky interview.

262   The police, quite literally: William Dufty, "A Muted Record: 'Just One More Chance,'" *New York Post*, June 16, 1959, 26.

263   On Saturday, with Billie's approval: "Joe Glaser Takes Over Lady's Woes," *New York Age*, June 20, 1959, 1.

263   So the lawyers prepared: Ken Vail, *Lady Day's Diary: The Life of Billie Holiday 1937–1959* (Chessington, UK: Castle Communications, 1996), 205; Dufty, "The True Story of Billie Holiday," article 5 of series, July 24, 1959.

263   "Wilkes," Kennedy later wrote: Kennedy, *Color Me Flo*, 47.

263   "It's highly unusual": Emily Jane Goodman, interview by the author, July 2020.

263   On Tuesday, June 16: "Singer Billie Holiday Police Guard Removed," Associated Press report, July 17, 1959.

264   while Wilkes countered: "Singer Billie Holiday Guard Removed," *Democrat and Chronicle* (Rochester, N.Y.), June 17, 1959, 8.

264   "If she ever becomes able to face arraignment": Dufty, "A Muted Record."

264   With this assurance in mind: Dufty, "A Muted Record."

264   Later that day, after Epstein made his ruling: "Lady Day Says She'll 'Fool Them.' "

264   Then, on Sunday, June 21: Vail, *Lady Day's Diary,* 205.

264   To get into the hospital: Johann Hari, *Chasing the Scream: The First and Last Days of the War on Drugs* (London: Bloomsbury, 2016); and Margalit Fox, "Rev. Eugene Callender, Who Saw Potential of School Dropouts, Dies at 87," *New York Times,* Nov. 10, 2023, A32.

265   "Suffering from a condition": William Dufty, " 'Ghost Writer' for Billie Holiday Describes Scene at 'Last Curtain,' " *New York Post,* June 17, 1959, 3.

265   To underscore his point: Dufty, " 'Ghost Writer.' "

265   "I had never given up hope": Vrbsky interview.

265   Despite the setback: George Wein, "Billie Holiday Apparently Through Her Critical Illness," *Boston Herald,* June 28, 1959.

266   Around this time, Joe Glaser: Wein.

266   So she was holding out for more money: The telegram is in the private collection of Ken Schwartz.

266   "Her body was defeated": George Jacobs and William Stadiem, *Mr. S: The Last Word on Frank Sinatra* (London: Pan Books, 2003), 150.

266   "I can't tell you how much": Jacobs and Stadiem.

267   Now, sensing the severity of her condition: Jacobs and Stadiem.

267   "I may have showed you how": Jacobs and Stadiem.

267   Louis McKay was staying: William Dufty, "Billie Holiday Dies After Relapse; First Lady of Blues Was 44," *New York Post,* July 17, 1959, 26.

267   On July 10, doctors ordered: Vail, *Lady Day's Diary,* 206.

268   By early Wednesday, July 15: Vail, 206.

268   "She was still rather beautiful": Kennedy, *Color Me Flo,* 47.

268   "She was beautiful": Dufty, "Billie Holiday Dies."

268   "I saw death in her face": Blackburn, *With Billie,* 321.

268   When Alice left: Blackburn, 321.

269   Around 2:40 a.m.: Dufty, "Billie Holiday Dies."

269   She continued to breathe: Death certificate of Billie Holiday.

269   "She's gone": Clarke, *Wishing on the Moon,* 444.

CHAPTER 15: ANGEL OF HARLEM

272   "Billie Holiday died": William Dufty, "Billie Holiday Dies After Relapse; First Lady of Blues Was 44," *New York Post,* July 17, 1959, 26.

272   "I can still remember": Lorraine Feather, interview by the author, June 2020.

272   Louis Armstrong: From a document in the archives at the Louis Armstrong House Museum, Queens, New York.

272   "He locked himself in [his] 72nd Street penthouse": George Jacobs and William Stadiem, *Mr. S: The Last Word on Frank Sinatra* (London: Pan Books, 2003), 151.

273   "When she last visited us": Adam Clayton Powell III, interview by the author, Jan. 2021.

273   "I was overcome": Karen Chilton, *Hazel Scott: The Pioneering Journey of a Jazz Pianist from Café Society to Hollywood to HUAC* (Ann Arbor: University of Michigan Press, 2010), 181.

273   "After Billie passed": Mala Waldron, interview by the author, July 2021.

273 "Tragedy surrounded Billie Holiday": Dexter Gordon, "A Letter," *Down Beat,* Sept. 3, 1959.

274 The AP obituary: "Singer Billie Holiday Dies," Associated Press, July 17, 1959.

275 The UPI obituary: "Singer Billie Holiday Dies," United Press International, July 17, 1959.

275 The *New York Times* obituary: "Billie Holiday Dies Here at 44; Jazz Singer Had Wide Influence," *New York Times,* July 18, 1959, 15.

276 The *New York Daily News* observed: Sidney Kline, "Billie Holiday Meets Last Cue, Dies at 44," *New York Daily News,* July 18, 1959, 179.

276 "Few others could ever sing the blues": "High Mass Today for Billie Holiday," *Baltimore Afro-American,* July 21, 1959, 1.

277 The funeral could be held: "Billie Holiday Rites Tomorrow," *New York Times,* July 20, 1959.

277 First, though, the body of Billie Holiday: "Billie Holiday Rites Tomorrow."

277 She wore one of her favorite: "3000 Attend Holiday Funeral," *Los Angeles Sentinel,* July 23, 1959, A1.

277 "[There] stretched a line of people": "High Mass Today."

277 as exemplified by one "middle-aged woman": "High Mass Today."

278 The two had been in communication: Joel Lobenthal, *Tallulah!: The Life and Times of a Leading Lady* (New York: Regan Books, 2004), 486–87.

278 Billie sent her a letter: The letter can be found on Et Als, hiltonals.com.

278 If her true feelings: Lobenthal, *Tallulah!,* 487.

278 Instead, as a gesture: Lobenthal, 487.

278 A card read: Lindsey Jenkins, "The Politics of Tallulah Bankhead," Women's History Network, Jan. 18, 2023, https://womenshistorynetwork.org/the-politics-of-tallulah-bankhead-ashley-steenson/.

279 When the hearse: "3000 at Funeral of Billie Holiday," *New York Times,* July 22, 1959.

279 "The throng at the church": "3000 at Funeral."

279 Among the forty honorary pallbearers: "3000 at Funeral."

279 and not Louis McKay: "The Last Song Is Sung," *New York Daily News,* July 22, 1959, 86.

279 "There was no eulogy": "For Billie Holiday Rites," United Press International, July 22, 1959.

280 "And the conclusion": Benny Green, *The Reluctant Art: Five Studies in the Growth of Jazz* (New York: Da Capo Press, 1991), 124.

280 In 1959, Monday: Brad Gooch, *City Poet: The Life and Times of Frank O'Hara* (New York: Alfred A. Knopf, 1993), 328.

281 "Kenneth Koch and Larry Rivers": Gooch, 328.

281 Near the end of her life: Gooch, 328.

281 On this occasion, Mal was: Gooch, 328.

281 "Man," Billie said to Koch: The quote is in Michael Magee, "Tribes of New York: Frank O'Hara, Amiri Baraka, and the Poetics of the Five Spot," *Contemporary Literature,* XLII, 4.

281 Later, Billie had taken a table: The dialogue is based on information in Gary

Giddins, "The Highs and Lows of a Great Jazz Club," *Village Voice,* Feb. 16, 1976.

281   Kenneth Koch remembered: David Kastin, *Nica's Dream: The Life and Legend of the Jazz Baroness* (New York: W. W. Norton, 2011), 145–46.

282   O'Hara had seen Billie: Gooch, *City Poet,* 327.

282   "We didn't leave": Gooch, 327.

282   Brad Gooch wrote: Gooch, 327.

282   During his lunch hour: Gooch, 328.

283   In the *Nashville Banner:* Bob Battle, "Movierama," *Nashville Banner,* Aug. 12, 1959, 48.

284   Lynn Hopper wrote: Lynn Hopper, "Album Shows Billie at Blues Best," *Indianapolis Star,* July 26, 1959, 106.

284   In his syndicated column: Henry C. Schwartz, "On the Record," *Paterson (N.J.) News,* Nov. 19, 1959, 37.

284   On July 21, 1959: The file for Eleanora McKay, aka Billie Holiday, is available in the Surrogate's Court, County of New York.

284   As Annie Ross says: Annie Ross, interview by the author, Dec. 2019.

285   "One of the first things I did": Flo Kennedy, *Color Me Flo: My Hard Life and Good Times* (Englewood Cliffs, N.J.: Prentice-Hall, 1976), 49.

285   According to Kennedy: Kennedy, 48.

285   "We did finally manage": Kennedy, 52.

285   "She didn't [talk about Billie]": Gloria Steinem, correspondence with the author, 2021.

285   The first artistic homage to Billie: *Sinatra & Company* was released by Reprise Records in 1971.

286   Mal Waldron released a tribute album: *Blues for Lady Day* was released by Freedom Records in 1972.

286   Produced by Jay Weston and Berry Gordy: Credits for the film *Lady Sings the Blues* appear in Vincent Canby, "Billie Holiday: *Lady Sings the Blues* Stars Diana Ross," *New York Times,* Oct. 19, 1972, and in the entry for the film on IMDb.

286   Consider Vincent Canby writing in *The New York Times:* Canby, "Billie Holiday."

286   In the *Chicago Tribune:* Gene Siskel, "A Nice Lady, but She's No Billie," *Chicago Tribune,* Oct. 27, 1972, 35.

287   In *Newsday,* Joseph Gelmis: Joseph Gelmis, "Black Dream Machine," *Newsday,* Oct. 18, 1972, 102.

287   In 1978, *Listening to Billie:* Alice Adams, *Listening to Billie* (New York: Alfred A. Knopf, 1978).

287   to quote *The Philadelphia Inquirer:* William J. Harding, "A Tragic Muse Pursues Eliza," *Philadelphia Inquirer,* Jan. 15, 1978, 140.

287   Then, in 1979, Elizabeth Hardwick: Elizabeth Hardwick, *Sleepless Nights* (New York: Random House, 1979).

287   "She was fat": Hardwick, 34–35.

288   "Her work took on . . . singing over and over, again and again": Hardwick, 34–35.

288   In *The Women of Brewster Place:* Gloria Naylor, *The Women of Brewster Place* (New York: The Viking Press, 1982).

288   Gloria Naylor, according to *The New York Times:* Annie Gottlieb, "Women Together," *New York Times Book Review,* Aug. 22, 1982, 11.

288   On March 10, 1981: "Louis McKay, Was Wed to Singer," *Courier-Post* (Camden, N.J.), Mar. 13, 1981, 50.

288   Six years earlier: "Louis McKay."

288   In the mid-1980s, most of the revenue: Bernice McKay v. Estate of Louis McKay, decided Nov. 9, 1984, in Superior Court of New Jersey, Law Division, Probate Part, Atlantic County.

289   In 1988, on *Rattle and Hum: Rattle and Hum* by U2 was released by Island Records in 1988.

289   "the film that jazz deserves": Howard Fishman, "The Film That Jazz Deserves," *New Yorker,* Apr. 7, 2021.

289   In 1997, Tony Bennett: *Tony Bennett on Holiday* was released by Columbia Records in 1997.

289   Chris Parker, who played drums on the album: Chris Parker, interview by the author, July 2020.

289   In 2014, Annie Ross: *To Lady with Love* was released by Red Anchor Records in 2014.

290   "one of the most unusual and . . . disturbing hooks": Glenn Kenny, "*Billie* Review: A Legend, in a Different Light," *New York Times,* Dec. 3, 2020, C6.

290   In February 2021: *The United States vs. Billie Holiday,* directed by Lee Daniels, written by Suzan-Lori Parks and Johann Hari, was released on Hulu in 2021.

290   "The most problematic aspect": Ty Burr, "Andra Day Shines Bright in *United States vs. Billie Holiday,*" *Boston Globe,* Feb. 26, 2021, G1.

290   But musician and author Lewis Porter: Lewis Porter, "*The United States vs. Billie Holiday,*" *Jazz Times,* Oct. 27, 2022.

290   In April 2021, the Dallas Symphony Orchestra: Tim Diovanni, "The Dallas Symphony Gives the Texas Premiere of a Genre-Hopping Double Concerto," *Dallas Morning News,* Apr. 10, 2021.

291   "There is no evidence": Federal Bureau of Investigation, correspondence with the author, 2021.

292   As journalist Philip Martin: Philip Martin, "Happy 100th, Lady Day," *Northwest Arkansas Democrat Gazette,* May 3, 2015.

292   George Wein: George Wein, interview by the author, Apr. 2021.

292   Sheila Jordan: Sheila Jordan, correspondence with the author, July 2021.

292   Annie Ross agrees: Ross interview.

292   Camille Thurman feels: Camille Thurman, interview by the author, July 2020.

292   Madeleine Peyroux contends: Madeleine Peyroux, interview by the author, 2023.

293   Yolande Bavan notes: Yolande Bavan, interview by the author, May 2020.

293   Bassist Chuck Israels: Chuck Israels, interview by the author, July 2020.

293   Charles McPherson believes: Charles McPherson, interview by the author, July 2021.

293   Bassist Larry Ridley: Larry Ridley, interview by the author, July 2021.

293   Loren Schoenberg concurs: Loren Schoenberg, interview by the author, 2023.

293   To Sonny Rollins: Sonny Rollins, interviews by the author, 2020.

293   And David Amram proclaims: David Amram, interview by the author, June 2021.

Index

Page numbers of illustrations appear in italics.

Illustration Credits

A Note on the Type

The text of this book was set in Garamond No. 3. It is not a true copy of any of the designs of Claude Garamond (ca. 1480–1561), but an adaptation of his types, which set the European standard for two centuries. It probably owes as much to the designs of Jean Jannon, a Protestant printer working in Sedan in the early seventeenth century, who had worked with Garamond's romans earlier, in Paris, but who was denied their use because of Catholic censorship. Jannon's matrices came into the possession of the Imprimerie nationale, where they were thought to be by Garamond himself, and were so described when the Imprimerie revived the type in 1900. This particular version is based on an adaptation by Morris Fuller Benton.